Labor Relations in the Public Sector

Fourth Edition

PUBLIC ADMINISTRATION AND PUBLIC POLICY

A Comprehensive Publication Program

EDITOR-IN-CHIEF

EVAN M. BERMAN

Huey McElveen Distinguished Professor
Louisiana State University
Public Administration Institute
Baton Rouge, Louisiana

Founding Editor

JACK RABIN

Available Electronically

Principles and Practices of Public Administration, edited by
Jack Rabin, Robert F. Munzenrider, and Sherrie M. Bartell

PublicADMINISTRATION*netBASE*

Labor Relations in the Public Sector

Fourth Edition

Richard Kearney

CRC Press
Taylor & Francis Group
Boca Raton   London   New York

CRC Press is an imprint of the
Taylor & Francis Group, an **informa** business

CRC Press
Taylor & Francis Group
6000 Broken Sound Parkway NW, Suite 300
Boca Raton, FL 33487-2742

© 2009 by Taylor & Francis Group, LLC
CRC Press is an imprint of Taylor & Francis Group, an Informa business

No claim to original U.S. Government works
Printed in the United States of America on acid-free paper
10 9 8 7 6 5 4 3 2 1

International Standard Book Number-13: 978-1-4200-6314-1 (Hardcover)

Library of Congress Cataloging-in-Publication Data
Kearney, Richard C.

Kearney, Richard C.
    Labor relations in the public sector / Richard Kearney. -- 4th ed.
       p. cm. -- (Public administration and public policy ; 150)
    Includes bibliographical references and index.
    ISBN 978-1-4200-6314-1 (alk. paper)
       1. Collective bargaining--Government employees--United States. 2.
Employee-management relations in government--United States. I. Title. II.
Series.

HD8005.6.U5K4 2009
331'.04135173--dc22
                                                   2008041365

Visit the Taylor & Francis Web site at
http://www.taylorandfrancis.com

and the CRC Press Web site at
http://www.crcpress.com

Contents

List of Case Studies

Preface

Since the completion of the third edition of this book, unions seem to have remained poised at a crossroads. Those in the private sector have suffered membership declines for more than 50 years, even under new leadership. The AFL-CIO has splintered into warring factions, with the secession of those organizations comprising the Change to Win Coalition. The unions have made little — if any — progress in stemming the powerful tide against them in the private sector. In government, union membership has been stagnant since the 1980s. Although some positive incremental changes have occurred in the state-level legal environment for collective bargaining, including the first state employee bargaining statute since 1992, conservative forces against them are in a perpetual attack mode in many states and localities. Meanwhile, spurred by the Reinventing Government and New Public Management movements, fundamental restructuring of private and public organizations and the processes they use to conduct their business has been occurring at a fast pace. Globalization of labor, manufacturing, and services profoundly challenges unions in the business sector. For their counterparts in government, continuing citizen resistance to government taxing and spending joined with efforts to marketize and outsource government have posed new challenges that provide both threats and opportunities. In any event, managing in a union environment is a reality for approximately 40 percent of public managers, with unions remaining as key political actors in the federal government and in a large proportion of state and local jurisdictions.

This fourth edition of *Labor Relations in the Public Sector* has been completely updated in terms of the scholarly and professional literature and relevant events. As in previous editions, collective bargaining and labor relations are addressed at all levels of government, with comparisons to the private and nonprofit sectors. Interest-based ("win–win") negotiations are a prominent theme in discussions of the bargaining process and contract administration. The fourth edition features several new case studies that are intended to provide students with experiential learning opportunities. The fundamental organization of the book remains the same.

The fourth edition is designed to be classroom-friendly. As before, the book is intended for use in graduate and undergraduate courses in labor relations, collective bargaining, human resource management, and problems in public administration.

David G. Carnevale of the University of Oklahoma contributed to the third edition, and many of his insights are retained in the present volume. I appreciate the comments and suggestions of professors and students who have used earlier editions of the book. Thanks also goes to Danielle Seale at North Carolina State University, who helped gather information and materials for the fourth edition. I am indebted to Kathy, Joel, Laura, Andrew, and Nicole for their love and support.

Richard C. Kearney

Chapter 1

History and Background

I. Introduction

As the industrial revolution dawned in England in the mid-18th century, the employer's authority was absolute and completely free from laws or government regulations. Employers unilaterally determined wages and the terms and conditions of employment for their workers. As a practical matter, all but the most skilled workers had to take jobs as they came, with little or no opportunity to influence compensation levels or the nature of the work. Early efforts to form trade unions were violently suppressed by laws forbidding organization as a criminal conspiracy that interfered with commerce.

It was a long, hard struggle for employees in England and Europe to gain the rights to organize and bargain collectively — and it took nearly 200 years in the United States. The transition from autocratic corporate authority to organized labor and collective bargaining was long, arduous, and sometimes bloody. Early union organizers and their supporters were often met with brutal repression by police and hired thugs (see, for example, Salmond 2004; Green 2006). Today labor rights are held in nearly all nations. Labor, in this sense, is triumphant. But unions in the United States today face new sets of problems and challenges, the outcomes of which could well determine their very existence in the next few decades.

This initial chapter discusses the history and development of unionization and collective bargaining in the private sector and in government. The roots of government unions are traced through a historical examination of the American trade union movement. The development of public sector unionization is examined, including key factors that contributed to the growth of unions in government.

A. Early American Unionism

Labor organizations have existed in the United States since the earliest days of the Republic. The environment within which they have been created and grown, however, has not always been friendly or even tolerant.

The earliest domestic roots of American unionism may be traced to the self-help organizations formed by workers in the crafts and skilled trades prior to the Revolutionary War. These organizations were, in a sense, transplants of the European guilds, which have been traced back to professional trade associations in the Middle Ages. These guilds regulated wages, working hours, product quality, and other concerns in such trades as bookbinding, weaving, and animal skinning. Probably the first guild to develop in the United States was the cordwainers (shoemakers) in 1648 in Boston (Commons 1980). This guild eventually evolved into what some historians believe to be the first American trade union — the Society of Master Cordwainers. The guilds were not true "unions" in that there was no separation of labor between worker and owner. Nonetheless, workers were united in a common cause of self-protection.

The early American labor organizations were based on handicraft technologies such as shoemaking, stone cutting, carpentry, hat finishing, and printing. Their membership was composed of skilled laborers organized along the lines of individual crafts. Today, such organizations are known as craft unions. It is not surprising that organized labor began with highly skilled, strategically situated workers, because they were the first to enjoy what is referred to today as bargaining power.

Public policy toward early labor organizations was, to put it kindly, suppressive. Unions had no legal basis for existence and were considered "criminal conspiracies in restraint of trade" under common law. This criminal conspiracy doctrine emerged from a court case involving the cordwainers, in which a judge ruled it illegal for Philadelphia shoemakers to act collectively in efforts to raise their wages. Several of the early craft unions were prosecuted for criminal conspiracy until the doctrine was ended by the Massachusetts court decision of *Commonwealth v. Hunt* (1842), which held that such organized union activities were lawful.

Some local labor organizations entered the political arena during the 1820s and 1830s through affiliating with "workingmen's parties." They pressed Congress and state legislatures for job-related concessions, such as the 10-hour day, and also for broader reforms, such as free universal education, an end to the military draft, abolition of debtors' prisons, and expansion of suffrage. Many of these organizations, which were strongest in large cities such as New York and Philadelphia, even took a short-lived step toward national organization in 1834 by forming the National Trades Union to coordinate the activities of the locals.

It was during this same time period (1820s to 1830s) that labor organizations began to penetrate public employment, as public workers in skilled occupations sought the 10-hour day won in some cities by their private counterparts. Most of this activity was concentrated in federal naval shipyards in Philadelphia, Boston, and New York. Later, when agitation for the 8-hour work day began, the first employer to grant it was the federal government, at the Charleston, South Carolina, Navy Yard in 1842. According to Spero (1948: 87), the drive for the 8-hour day "led to the crystallization of the principle of the state as a model employer maintaining the highest possible working standards in its services as an example for others to follow."

During this early period of growth and development, unions' organizational health was highly dependent on national economic conditions; unions suffered during hard times and were revived during more prosperous times. For example, there was a tremendous increase in union membership during the Civil War and immediately afterward as a consequence of industrial growth related to the war effort. The Depression of 1873, however, was accompanied by a startling decline in national union membership, from 300,000 to 50,600 within 5 years. By 1885, improved economic conditions pushed membership growth back to the 300,000 mark. The direct relationship between economic tailspins and union membership declines reversed early in the 20th century. Unions suffered during the prosperous 1920s and made their most spectacular gains during the Great Depression era of the 1930s.

Nonetheless, economic conditions continue to influence union fortunes today. For instance, when unemployment is low and consumer demand for products is high, employers tend to accommodate employee demands, perhaps even the demand for unions. Concurrently, risk-taking union advocates and organizers find it relatively easy to locate new jobs if they are fired. Thus, unionism would seem likely to flourish during favorable economic conditions but flag during periods of high unemployment and a weak economy (Reder 1988: 92–93). Of course, many other factors also influence union growth. During the past five decades, private sector unions have struggled with membership losses during good economic times and bad.

Even though labor organizations could no longer be legally prosecuted for criminal conspiracy in restraint of trade after the 1842 *Commonwealth v. Hunt* decision, this did not by any means signal a new era of tolerance and encouragement of unionism. Bitter union–management battles erupted during the 1870s. Employer "union-busting" tactics such as lockouts, espionage, blacklisting of union organizers, summary firings of "agitators," and, in order to break strikes, club-swinging "goon squads" forced some unions to go underground and operate as secret societies. One of these societies — the Molly Maguires, formed by coal miners — met employer violence with violence of its own, perpetrating acts of arson and murder in the Pennsylvania coal mines.

Many opposing union philosophies competed for the allegiance of the American working class during the late 1800s and early 1900s. Some groups sought victories through the political process whereas others advocated collective bargaining. Most organizations wanted to operate and pursue their goals within the boundaries of the capitalist system, but others spoke out in favor of the emerging European philosophies of socialism and communism.

Perhaps the strongest of the leftist groups was the Industrial Workers of the World (IWW), which rejected capitalism outright and strove to organize the working class, take control of the State, and overturn the capitalist system.

Founded in 1905 by radical socialists and syndicalists, whose penchant for a good fight took precedence over "planning, negotiating, and politiking [sic]" (Stegner 1990: 13), the "Wobblies" enjoyed their greatest strength among mining, lumbering, and agricultural workers in the western states of Idaho, Colorado, and Utah. (Their nickname reportedly was taken from a Chinese cook's pronunciation of IWW as "I wobble wobble.") The Wobblies committed numerous acts of industrial sabotage and were successful in leading several large strikes in the United States and other countries during the first World War. Many martyrs were produced along the way, including the legendary Joe Hill, who, just before his execution in 1915, cried to his fellow Wobblies, "Don't waste time mourning — organize!" However, severe repression by the federal government — including the incarceration and lynching of union leaders such as Joe Hill — and the lack of broad appeal of IWW philosophies to the American working class, led to the organization's demise shortly after the war (see Rosemount 2002; Buhle and Scholman 2005). The Wobblies' utopian vision of "one big union" for the workers of the world remains a historical curiosity to all except a handful of diehards who have recently sought to revive the IWW through leftist movements. (For current information on this unique organization, see the IWW website: www.IWW.org.)

Other labor organizations on the ideological far left have enjoyed some support in the United States, including the Farm Equipment Workers, Tobacco and Allied Workers, United Office and Professional Workers, and the Fisherman's Union. Two communist unions even managed to survive the McCarthy-era repression of the 1950s: the International Longshoremen's and Warehousemen's Union and the United Electrical, Radio, and Machine Workers. But a number of factors have conspired to mitigate socialist- and communist-oriented labor organizations in the United States. The rigid class structures of Europe have never developed in the United States to set the boundaries for class conflict, largely because of the rapid economic growth of the country, a relatively high standard of living for the working people, fairly steady economic growth with the opportunity for individual advancement, and the diverse ethnic and religious characteristics of American immigrants. From a political perspective, organized labor has been hemmed in by the absence of a labor-based political party and by actions of federal and state courts that have constricted the boundaries of union political and organizing activities (Galenson 1980: 73–79; Forbath 1991).

The real battles within the labor movement in the United States have not been fought over questions of political ideology, but over the issues of which types of workers should be organized and by whom. The ethos of business unionism, as originally professed by Samuel Gompers, has dominated the American labor movement.

Economic gains and improvements in working conditions have served as the primary objectives of trade unionism, not social and political change. Theories of the labor movement in the United States reflect the early ascendancy of business unionism, asserting that American workers have joined unions out of concern for job security (Tannenbaum 1921; Perlman 1928), as a means for democratizing the workplace (Webb and Webb 1897), as a result of expansion of the job market from increased industrialization (Commons and Associates 1936), from a crystallization of group interests arising from workers' social and economic situations (Hoxie 1928), and in response to various pay and fringe benefits incentives (Olson 1965). The Marxist philosophy that unions should form the locus of a working class consciousness and serve as the basis for restricting competition over jobs has never been widely accepted in the United States.

As already noted, the earliest organizing efforts were among the craft unions. Heavy industrialization, which began during the mid-1800s, provided a new and rapidly growing industrial labor force of unskilled and semiskilled workers who were not trade or craft oriented. Organization of this new pool of workers would have to be along "shop" lines, based on the place of work rather than on the type of work. The Knights of Labor made the first significant effort to capture this industrial segment of the work force.

Originally formed in 1869 as a craft union for custom tailors in Philadelphia, the Knights gradually began to include other crafts under its organizational umbrella. Within 10 years it had evolved into the first national labor union in the United States. The Knights dropped its status as a secret society and, under the leadership of an affable Irishman named Terence V. Powderly, began to seek both craft and industrial affiliates throughout the country. By the time of its successful 1886 strike against financier Jay Gould and the Wabash Railroad, the Knights claimed a membership of 700,000. However, the Knights' membership was somewhat unstable and divisive and a subsequent series of ill-conceived and violent strikes led to one defeat after another for the union (Phelan 2000). By the turn of the 20th century, the Knights of Labor was nearly extinct. Further organization of unskilled workers awaited the development of the Congress of Industrial Organizations in the 1930s.

The remaining craft union pieces of the complex Knights of Labor organizational mosaic were quickly gathered up by the American Federation of Labor (AFL), which was originally established in 1881 in Pittsburgh as a federation for skilled craft workers. The 25 national craft union affiliates elected Samuel Gompers, head of the Cigar Makers Union, as their first president. The ultimate pragmatist, Gompers soon made the AFL a major actor in the American economic system. Gompers was, in essence, a free marketeer who rejected philosophical, political, and social issues in favor of an almost laissez-faire environment for labor. Under his leadership the AFL grew steadily, surviving both the depression of 1893 to 1896 and a violent strike that broke the back of an AFL local at the Carnegie Steel Company in Homestead, Pennsylvania. The AFL also proved strong enough to withstand the scientific management movement of Frederick W. Taylor, court injunctions against strikes and other union actions, and years of stifling "yellow-dog contracts" (a contract in which a worker promised not to join a union while under the hire of an employer). There were, however, some dark times, particularly following World War I and during the early years of the Great Depression.

The AFL's resurgence after the Great Depression was, in the words of Sloane and Witney (1981: 75–76), "in spite of itself," as the union "almost snatched defeat from the jaws of victory." A leadership gap was part of the problem (Gompers had died), but more to blame was the union's continuing reactionary posture against mass production workers whom the Knights of Labor had first tried to organize. The AFL's unrelenting refusal to allow unskilled industrial workers into the organization eventually prompted a secessionist movement steered by John L. Lewis of the United Mine Workers. After Lewis' efforts to gain affiliation for industrial workers failed at the 1935 AFL convention in Atlantic City, he did not exit meekly. According to Sloane and Witney (1981: 77), "Lewis, never one to camouflage his emotions for the sake of good fellowship with his AFL colleagues, left Atlantic City only after landing a severe uppercut to the jaw of Carpenter Union president William L. Hutcheson...." Lewis then formed his own industrial union, which came to be known as the Congress of Industrial Organizations (CIO). There followed another, later attempt to affiliate under the AFL banner, but it culminated in the expulsion of CIO leaders and the more than 30 national unions that had joined forces with the CIO.

Lewis' independent CIO was highly successful in organizing industrial workers, such as those in the automobile and steel industries, so much so that the AFL finally recognized the error of its ways and itself began competing for unskilled workers. Not to be outdone, the CIO responded in kind by organizing craft workers. In 1955, after years of fierce inter-union conflict and competition, the AFL merged permanently with the CIO, becoming "the united house of labor."

The labor battles had been fought not over political ideology or competing grand visions of American society, but over organizing workers and the mundane bread-and-butter issues that today remain paramount: wages, benefits, working conditions, and job security. To George Meany, as well as to the other mainstream labor leaders, ideology was "baloney" (Sloane and Witney 1981: 94). Unions did become active in the political arena during the 1960s and remain so today, pressing a broad national agenda for social betterment and economic reform with varying degrees of success. However, no coherent ideology is apparent. Ironically, the year following the AFL-CIO merger marked the beginning of a long and continuous decline in union organization in private employment.

In 1956, the first year in which the total number of U.S. white-collar employees exceeded the number of blue-collar workers, one-third of the nation's nonagricultural workers were unionized. By 2007, only one in eight was a member — just 12 percent of the total work force and only 7.4 percent of private sector workers. The absolute number of private sector union members continued to rise until 1970, but

Table 1.1 Membership in Largest Private Sector Unions, 2007

Membership Count	Union
1,396,174	International Brotherhood of Teamsters
1,311,548	United Food and Commercial Workers International Union
754,978	United Steelworkers of America
704,794	International Brotherhood of Electrical Workers
669,772	Laborers' International Union of North America
653,781	International Association of Machinists and Aerospace Workers
557,099	International Union, United Automobile, Aerospace, and Agricultural Implement Workers of America
545,638	Communications Workers of America
522,416	United Brotherhood of Carpenters and Joiners of America
455,346	Union of Needletrades, Industrial, and Textile Employees
424,579	Longshore and Warehouse Union
392,584	International Union of Operating Engineers
361,362	Maritime Trades
324,043	United Association of Journeymen and Apprentices of the Plumbing and Pipe-Fitting Industry of the U.S. and Canada

Source: Self-reported figures from each organization's Internet website and U.S. Department of Labor. (Does not include public and nonprofit sector membership.)

it has since declined to 8.7 million (U.S. Bureau of Labor Statistics 2007). Table 1.1 provides membership figures for the largest private sector unions today. Table 1.2 displays union membership for all workers — public and private — by state.

B. Factors Contributing to Private Sector Union Decline

The fading fortunes of unions in the private sector have spawned a great amount of discussion and debate. Four major factors have contributed to union decline,

Table 1.2 Union Density for All Wage and Salary Workers, Public and Private, 2005

State	Union Members		Represented by Unions	
	Total (K)	Percent	Total (K)	Percent
Hawaii	139	24.7	146	25.9
New York	1,981	24.4	2,060	25.4
Alaska	62	22.2	67	23.8
New Jersey	770	20.1	825	21.6
Washington	549	19.8	583	21.0
Michigan	842	19.6	879	20.4
Illinois	931	16.4	979	17.2
Minnesota	395	16.0	416	16.8
California	2,273	15.7	2,444	16.9
Connecticut	247	15.6	263	16.5
Rhode Island	76	15.3	79	16.0
Wisconsin	386	14.9	415	16.1
Nevada*	167	14.8	191	17.0
Massachusetts	414	14.5	438	15.3
Ohio	734	14.2	801	15.5
West Virginia	101	14.2	110	15.5
Oregon	211	13.8	225	14.7
Pennsylvania	745	13.6	802	14.7
Maryland	342	13.1	386	14.8
Montana	48	12.2	52	13.1
Indiana	224	12.0	362	13.0
U.S. Average	**15,400**	**12.0**		
Maine	69	11.9	79	13.5
Iowa*	161	11.3	199	14.0

Table 1.2   Union Density for All Wage and Salary Workers, Public and Private, 2005 (Continued)

State	Union Members Total (K)	Union Members Percent	Represented by Unions Total (K)	Represented by Unions Percent
Vermont	34	11.0	39	12.9
Missouri	284	10.9	310	11.9
Delaware	43	10.8	45	11.4
District of Columbia	25	10.3	30	12.2
New Hampshire	63	10.1	70	11.3
Kentucky	172	9.8	196	11.2
Alabama*	170	8.8	194	10.0
Wyoming*	19	8.3	24	10.0
Kansas*	99	8.0	115	9.3
Nebraska*	66	7.9	79	9.5
New Mexico	62	7.8	92	11.5
Colorado	165	7.7	186	8.6
Arizona*	197	7.6	250	9.7
North Dakota*	20	6.8	24	8.0
Oklahoma*	93	6.4	112	7.7
Louisiana*	107	6.4	121	7.2
Idaho*	37	6.0	45	7.2
Tennessee*	153	6.0	174	6.8
South Dakota*	21	5.9	25	7.2
Mississippi*	60	5.6	78	7.3
Utah*	61	5.4	69	6.1
Florida*	397	5.2	497	6.5
Arkansas*	58	5.1	67	6.0
Texas*	476	4.9	576	5.9

Table 1.2   Union Density for All Wage and Salary Workers, Public and Private, 2005 (Continued)

State	Union Members		Represented by Unions	
	Total (K)	Percent	Total (K)	Percent
Georgia*	176	4.4	230	5.8
Virginia*	139	4.0	179	5.2
South Carolina*	59	3.3	74	4.2
North Carolina*	126	3.3	155	4.1

* Right-to-work states.
Source: U.S. Bureau of Labor Statistics (2006).

although their relative importance is subject to dispute (e.g., Bennett and Kaufman 2002; Freeman and Medoff 1984).

1. Structural Elements

Structural elements refers to the broad social and economic changes that have affected the composition of the work force, the general nature of employment, the shift of jobs from the heavily organized Northeast and Midwest to the predominantly nonunion South and Southwest, and the demographic characteristics of the work force. More specifically, the labor force has become increasingly female, minority, contingent, and part time, with correspondingly different needs than the mostly white male workers of the past. It is also increasingly white collar, as employment has shifted from union-dense manufacturing, mining, construction, and transportation jobs to services such as banking and finance, insurance, telecommunications, and information-based technology. Forces of globalization have pushed and pulled some traditionally union jobs to other countries (Farber and Western 2001). Historically, white-collar workers have been difficult to organize because of the prestige and professionalism associated with their jobs, special interests and needs that have not been attended to by the unions, and the generally poor image of organized labor among this group (Sloane and Witney 1981: 10–13). In a sense, unions have also been victims of their own success. Union-ratcheted salaries and wages placed firms in Pennsylvania, Illinois, Michigan, and New York at a competitive disadvantage, encouraging many of them to move to low-wage nonunion states such as Texas, Tennessee, and North Carolina and, increasingly, to developing countries. The structural explanation seems compelling on the surface, but empirical investigations have determined that it does not tell the whole story of the factors underlying union decline.

2. Unfavorable Legal and Policy Environment

As presented above, unions have, in certain ways, been victims of their own success. In addition to elevating wages, they have aligned with other organizations to advocate for labor reforms that have effectively answered many union policy proposals. Examples include workers' compensation, federal labor standards, child labor laws, unemployment compensation, and an assortment of other social programs. It can also be argued, however, that the decline of unions is at least partly attributable to restrictions on labor organizing and other activities by the Taft-Hartley, Landrum-Griffin, and other federal legislation. For example, Taft-Hartley prohibits the requirement of union membership as a condition of employment (the "closed shop," which makes union membership mandatory *before* employment) and permits "right-to-work" laws (which also bar the "union shop," which requires union membership *at the time of* employment). Taft-Hartley also restricts slowdowns, sit-down strikes, and wildcat strikes. Moreover, the National Labor Relations Board (NLRB), which administers federal labor law and investigates and decides allegations of unfair labor practices against employers and unions, has delivered a high proportion of unfavorable decisions to unions in the last three decades (Gross 1995; Forbath 1991).

The federal courts have been criticized for anti-union decisions as well. For example, the so-called MacKay Doctrine, promulgated by the U.S. Supreme Court in 1938 but not widely applied until President Ronald Reagan emboldened business by sacking 11,000 air traffic controllers in 1981, allows firms to hire permanent replacements for striking workers. These concerns have led union supporters to call for congressional actions to level a labor–management playing field that appears to be tilted against the unions. Yet Congress is heavily influenced by business interests who have frequently succeeded in rallying Republicans and conservative Democrats to defeat labor-friendly legislation. For instance, bills to ban permanent replacement of striking employees have been regularly introduced in the Congress but just as regularly have been defeated by business interests.

3. Management Opposition

Employer resistance to unions has progressed from "blackjacks to briefcases" (R. M. Smith 2003). Toting those briefcases are employees of hundreds of management consulting firms specializing in "union-busting" (Bernstein 1985; Gagala 1983: Ch. 3). Various tactics bolster employer resistance to unions. "Positive employee relations" means establishing a compensation system and working conditions that are as good as or better than those found in unionized workplaces. Other resistance techniques involve negative tactics to suppress unionization. These include hiring consultants to help contest union elections through tough, well-financed campaigns to keep the unions out; stirring worker doubts about the potential benefits of unions; delaying certification elections until a majority of employees have lost interest in joining a union; and refusing to bargain collectively or negotiate and sign a contract even if a union is established.

Some firms also engage in blatantly illegal activities to fight unions, calculating that it is cheaper to pay a small fine to the NLRB now than to meet the demands of the union later (Kleiner 2001: 528–532). Workers are threatened or intimidated, union organizers are fired, and lies and distortions are disseminated. Such employer opposition is asserted by some scholars to be the leading "cause of the slow strangulation of private sector unionism" (Freeman and Medoff 1984: 239; see also Goldfield 1987). The reasons for management intransigence are not difficult to fathom. Keeping unions out means higher profits for the firm. It also means that certain managers keep their jobs; those perceived to be responsible for losing a union election may find themselves quickly on the street (Freeman and Kleiner 1990: 363)!

4. Strategic Factors

The strategic choices made — and not made — by union leaders have contributed to union decline. Some critical choices made decades ago, including the rejection of ideological approaches to labor's relationship to government and the failure to mount a labor party to compete for a legitimate voice in government, have debilitated labor's political power and influence today. Labor's long-term reliance on the Democratic Party for political clout continues today (Francia 2006; Dark 1999). To many Democrats, however, labor is just another interest group.

From the 1970s until 1998, unions spent less money on organizing new members and participated in fewer NLRB certification elections than in earlier years (the trend was reversed in 1998 with AFL-CIO President John Sweeney's organizing initiatives). What's more, management won far more union elections than they lost. Merely to survive, unions must continually recruit new members. Organized labor has not told a compelling story of why today's workers should want to join a union, nor has it manufactured the positive public image and support necessary to nurture a receptive audience of unorganized workers.

Ultimately, the responsibility for strategic errors by unions must be laid at the feet of unimaginative, reactive, and — all too often — self-interested and corrupt union leaders. Private sector unions, like other failed or flagging organizations, have failed to adapt to a changing environment (Kearney 2003). Labor has too often poisoned its own well by betraying its members through fraud and corruption and by forming indefensible alliances with organized crime (Fraser 1998).

Can the private sector union decline be reversed, or is it an inevitable part of a postindustrial society? Where is the bottom? The hemorrhaging has been going on for more than 40 years and shows limited signs of arrest. However, unions suffered earlier periods of decline (Rachlett 1999). For instance, unions lost almost 40 percent of their membership from 1920 to 1933, then recovered strongly. Another such reversal is possible, but it presupposes more astute union leadership, more effective organizing strategies, effective coalition-building strategies with other powerful interest groups, a shift in employer and public opinion in favor of unions, and a more facilitative legal environment, among other factors (see Tillman and Cummings 1999).

Some cause for optimism arose in 1995, when former SEIU (Service Employees International Union) president John J. Sweeney was elected president of the 13-million-member AFL-CIO (Dark 1999: 178–184). Sweeney, whose SEIU membership had doubled even as most other AFL-CIO affiliates' ranks thinned, worked hard to reverse labors' declining fortunes and provoked a far-reaching reexamination of labor's role in the 21st century. Sweeney took steps to include more women and minorities in union leadership positions, dedicated millions of new dollars to organizing drives, and greatly elevated labor's profile during the presidential election of 1996 and the congressional elections of 1998.

Sweeney's actions were not sufficient to stimulate a rebirth of labor in the U.S. private sector. For every action taken to rejuvenate the unions, business interests and their Republican allies have countered with efforts to rewrite labor laws and other strategies designed to disadvantage unions, such as restrictions on using members' dues for political and lobbying expenses.

And it seems that each time the resuscitation of the sickly patient is being widely heralded, labor once again suffers an untimely relapse. Self-destructive leadership actions and decisions, including the almost predictable Teamster scandal, reinfect the union movement and send it back to its death bed. Sweeney's desire to reinvent, reinvigorate, and reposition organized labor was effectively countered by congressional Republicans and business interests. Then, in 2005, following a year of internal labor turmoil, rising dissatisfaction with Sweeney's leadership, and continuing decline in the private sector, four dissident unions seceded from the AFL-CIO. The new group, called the Change to Win Coalition, consisted of the United Food and Commercial Workers, UNITE HERE, the Teamsters, and SEIU; three other unions joined subsequently. Together the seven unions make up less than half of total AFL-CIO membership of 13 million. The rift was reminiscent of the old CIO split from the AF of L in the 1930s.

C. Unions in Government — The Early Years

As noted above, public employee organizations first became active during the early 1800s, particularly in federal shipyards. However, until 1836, even in the shipyards they experienced limited success, because their military bosses tended to be rather insensitive to the opinions of their workers. In that year a Washington, D.C., naval shipyard strike and a mass demonstration led to intervention by President Andrew Jackson, who personally granted the federal employees the 10-hour day they sought. A tradition of direct presidential involvement in federal labor problems was established that continues today.

The New York Letter Carriers formed the first federal employee organization of national significance in 1863. In 1886 the Knights of Labor chartered locals in Chicago, Omaha, and other cities. Postal clerks were organized in 1888 in New York, and the National Association of Letter Carriers was created in 1890. Rural carriers formed their own national organization in 1903.

The rise of the postal workers under the banners of their various organizations was not met with equanimity by the federal government. In 1895, Postmaster General William L. Wilson issued a departmental order prohibiting any postal employee from visiting Washington for lobbying purposes, at the risk of being fired. When intensive lobbying by postal workers and their organizations continued, much to the annoyance of the executive branch and some members of Congress, President Theodore Roosevelt retaliated in 1902 with his infamous gag rule forbidding all federal employees from seeking congressional legislation in their own behalf, directly or indirectly, individually or through their organizations (Spero 1948: 117–127). Postal employee militancy was also met with union-busting tactics that included the use of paid informers, the discipline and/or discharge of organizational leaders, and, ironically, the opening of their personal mail (Nesbitt 1976: 8).

Ever tenacious, the postal workers responded with an anti-gag rule campaign, spearheaded by a magazine, *The Harpoon*, which was edited by a railway clerk named Urban A. Walter. Finally, the postal workers, led by the AFL and the National Federation of Post Office Clerks, garnered sufficient congressional support to win passage of the Lloyd-LaFollette Act of 1912, guaranteeing federal employees the First Amendment right to organize and petition Congress for a redress of grievances. Although the Lloyd-LaFollette Act had only a small effect on federal union-busting activities (which continued), it did denote a positive direction in the development of postal and other federal labor organizations as they increasingly began to seek the full labor rights granted to private sector workers in the National Labor Relations Act (Spero 1948: 143).

Early organizational efforts outside the defense establishment and post office included "almost every civil occupation from charwoman to zoologist, from astronomer to stone cutter" (Nesbitt 1976: 56). These efforts were rebuffed by the U.S. Civil Service Commission. In 1912, however, the customs inspectors organized successfully on a national scale, and in 1917 the National Federation of Federal Employees (NFFE) was formed as an umbrella organization intended to cover all federal civilian employees except for the postal employees and workers permitted to join AFL affiliates (Nesbitt 1976). Two other significant general-purpose federal organizations followed: the American Federation of Government Employees (AFGE) in 1932 and the National Association of Government Employees (NAGE) soon thereafter. As will become evident later in our discussion, however, substantial growth in these and other federal organizations awaited implementation of President Kennedy's Executive Order 10988 of 1962.

Organizational progress in the state and local government sectors was also uneven before the 1960s. A crafts orientation was clearly prevalent during the formative years, especially in local government, as teachers, firefighters, and police organized separately. The National Teachers Association (NTA) was formed in 1857. The National Education Association (NEA) was created in 1870 through a merger of the NTA and two other teacher associations. Although these early teacher associations were set up and directed by administrators and other school authorities to advance the interests of the teaching occupation and to provide mutual aid programs, a steady accumulation of grievances eventually drove the teachers into a more aggressive posture. State laws and local ordinances forbade teachers from smoking, placed restrictions on their dress, imposed curfews, and even sought to regulate their leisure time. In Westchester County, New York, for example, teachers were ordered to bed by 10 p.m. One North Carolina town admonished its teachers "to sleep at least 8 hours a night, to eat carefully, and to take every precaution to keep in the best of health and spirits" (Spero 1948: 298–300). In 1900 the Chicago and San Antonio teachers' federations responded to such intrusive rules by affiliating with the AFL. Joined by other teacher organizations in 1916, they formed the American Federation of Teachers (AFT).

Firefighters and police began organizing during the late 1800s and the early years of the 20th century, primarily as mutual benefit societies to provide pension and insurance programs to fulfill the social needs of their members. In 1918 the AFL chartered the International Association of Fire Fighters (IAFF), which today remains the second oldest nationally affiliated state or local union (after the NEA). Police officers first applied for an AFL charter in 1897 in Cleveland. By 1919, 37 local police organizations had received certification. A relatively large number of strikes in the public safety services occurred during 1918–1919 as evidence of growing militancy by police and firefighters, particularly in the larger cities. One of those strikes — by police officers in Boston — took on serious national proportions after several days of looting and mob rule and eventual intervention by Governor Calvin Coolidge and the Massachusetts National Guard. Negative public reaction to the 1919 Boston Police Strike set back public safety unionization by some 40 years (see Chapter 8). Local police benefit associations continued to exist, but little union activity took place again in the public safety services until the 1960s.

The largest state and local union today, the American Federation of State, County, and Municipal Employees (AFSCME), was born in 1932 as the Wisconsin State Employees Association. Efforts to expand its scope of organization to other states and to extend membership to local employees were made through a 1935 affiliation with the AFGE. However, the AFGE affiliation was unworkable, and AFSCME successfully won independent status the very next year (see Kramer 1962). As in the case of the public safety organizations in local government, AFSCME's progress was uneven. By 1950 it had reached a membership total of about 68,000, but in most jurisdictions the organization was "harassed, coerced, dismissed — or entirely ignored" (Spero and Capozzola 1973: 18). Although the founder of AFSCME, Arnold Zander, eventually supported collective bargaining and use of the strike when deemed necessary, the formal goals of the organization were rather conservative, being "to stimulate the growth and extension of civil service and to improve existing merit systems" (Kramer 1962: 31). A leadership change at the 1960 national convention produced a new president with a more aggressive style (Jerry Wurf), a more militant posture by the national union and its locals across the United States, and substantial membership gains.

As the 1960s progressed, it became clear that government employers could no longer bank on a docile, passive worker, content with a secure job and a rather modest salary and pension. Federal, state, and local government employees in many jurisdictions were on the cusp of launching a new venture that few had imagined.

The next section explores the reasons for the rise of public employee unions in the United States, after first considering the converse question that is begged; that is, why public sector organization lagged behind the private sector for some 30 years.

D. Why Government Employees Did (and Did Not) Unionize

In retrospect, there seem to be three principal factors that inhibited public employee unionism and collective bargaining prior to the 1960s: the sovereignty argument, the nature of government employment, and an unfavorable legal environment. Each of them is examined below.

Ideology for its own sake has never been widely embraced in the United States. For many government employers determined to resist unions, however, the doctrine of sovereignty assumed the aura of ideology, although the aura was somewhat dimmed by its self-serving usage by those opposed to unions. Briefly, the sovereignty argument contends that in a representative democracy the people are sovereign, and their will is served by their elected representatives. If government, through these representatives' appointees or civil servants, bargains over terms and conditions of employment with a union, then sovereignty is violated through the illegal delegation of the people's sovereign power (Slater 2004).

The argument would perhaps stand if the various American governments could demonstrate their delegative virginity. However, representatives of the national, state, and local governments have for more than two centuries negotiated contracts and arrangements with private sector entities without the expressed permission of the electorate. (Examples include contracting weapons systems to private manufacturers or garbage collection to firms.) As a consequence of the daily deflowering of sovereignty throughout the country, invoking the doctrine in opposition to unions appears to be at best self-serving and at worst hypocritical. Stieber (1973: 17) sums up the counterargument well: "...the doctrine of sovereignty as applied to employment has been substantially dismembered by legal and academic critics, joined by government lawmakers and rulemakers. Governments, however supreme, make deals." Nonetheless, the sovereignty argument has been used with various degrees of success to stifle government unionization, and it continues to be a credo held by some political conservatives.

The nature of government employment also had a strong bearing on slow public sector union growth and development. A number of factors are salient here. Government work is predominantly white collar in nature, and government work forces frequently include disproportionate numbers of women and minorities. In the past, all three categories of employees were traditionally difficult to organize. Moreover, government employment, particularly at the federal level, has been characterized by strong job security, generous pensions, and merit system protections against partisan political pressure and other forms of management abuse. Merit systems offered an alternative to collective bargaining for determining wages, benefits, and working conditions, and for providing formal grievance procedures for unhappy workers wishing to file complaints.

Finally, the legal environment for public sector unionism was highly unfavorable prior to the far-reaching labor law changes instituted at all levels of government during the 1960s. Many public employees were forbidden to strike or take other job actions and, most important, statutory provisions for recognizing public employee organizations and implementing collective bargaining were very rare. When unions asserted their rights to be recognized and to bargain with employers in the courts, they were usually spurned by a hostile judiciary.

E. The Growth of Unions in Government

As mentioned, circumstances changed dramatically during the 1960s, as public employee unions and collective bargaining spread rapidly across jurisdictions at all levels throughout that decade and the next. Several important developments moved the unions into the forefront of government employment. Although the causal variables facilitating government union growth are complex, multiple, and interrelated, it is possible to identify several factors that have contributed significantly to unionization: (1) the growth of government, (2) the private sector experience, (3) changes in the public sector legal environment, and (4) the social change and turmoil that characterized the 1960s and early 1970s (Shaw and Clark 1972: 901–904).

1. The Growth of Government

During the 1960s and 1970s the number of civilian government jobs approximately doubled, with most of the growth occurring in the state and local sectors. This greatly expanded work force presented an attractive target for union organizers. By 1980, almost one of every six working people in the United States was employed at some level of government. From a base year of 1951, employment in federal government rose 24 percent to 2,866,000 workers in 1980, while state and local employment increased by about 227 percent to 13,383,000. The nation's total employment over this time period registered a gain of 89 percent.

The number of federal civilian employees has actually declined, dropping from about 2.9 million in 1980 to 1.85 million in 1998, primarily as a result of massive downsizing during the Clinton–Gore administration, then rose in the early 2000s with the wars in Afghanistan and Iraq and federalization of airport security under the Transportation Security Agency (see Figure 1.1).

Several factors help explain the enormous gains in state and local government employment that commenced in the 1950s and continue today. First, national population growth necessitated additional government workers to service the expanding number of programs intended to address people's health, education, social service, and other needs. Second, the age distribution of the population shifted. Larger proportions of the population were situated in the "less than 25" and "65 years and over" ranges, the two groups that claim the bulk of government services. Finally, federal mandates for state and locally administered programs (including social services, transportation, and environmental protection programs) contributed to the surge in state and local jobs.

Not surprisingly, government employment figures also depict a steady shift from blue-collar to white-collar jobs as well as gains in the proportion of women and minorities in government employment. More than half of public employees are women. African Americans, Latinos, and Asian-Americans make up more than 25 percent of total public employment.

Along with the growth of government came increasing bureaucratization and depersonalization of the public service, twin forces that tend to isolate and alienate the individual employee (Shaw and Clark 1972: 902; Shutt 1986). No longer is most government employment characterized by a small "family" of people

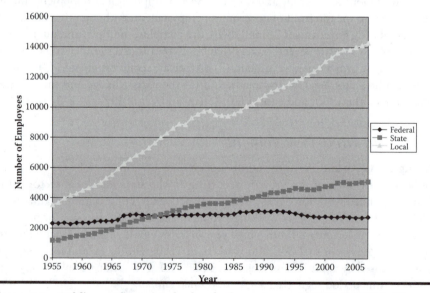

Figure 1.1 Public employment, by level of government, 1955 to 2006. (*Source:* U.S. Bureau of Labor Statistics 2007.)

who know and relate to one another in a neighborly fashion from the top of the hierarchy to the bottom. Dissatisfaction with paternalism, personalism, arbitrary management actions, and clogged communication channels within an increasingly complex organizational structure convinced many government workers of the need for intermediary organizations like unions to represent them collectively in their relationships with management.

Ballooning government employment rolls presented a very attractive organizing target for private sector unions, which were suffering from a precipitous decline in the number of blue-collar jobs in industry. Unions that heretofore had concentrated their membership drives on the private sector began courting public employees, often through their existing professional organizations. A natural community of interest among public workers such as teachers, firefighters, and police officers had found expression through professional associations and had preconditioned them to the values of organizational membership (Moskow et al. 1970: 287). Unions helped convince members of these associations that they could enjoy the same benefits of unionization as union members in the private sector.

2. The Private Sector Experience

Unions in the private sector had successfully won wage and benefit increases and improved working conditions for their members. This did not go unnoticed by public employees, who were becoming increasingly dissatisfied with government wages and conditions of employment. Even the traditional job security of government employment had become problematic in some jurisdictions.

The civil service systems entrenched in most large government jurisdictions were unable or unwilling to respond satisfactorily to public employee demands. For instance, wage and benefits adjustments typically required legislative — not collective bargaining — action. In light of these circumstances, public workers became more receptive to the notion of unionization to give them a collective voice and began demanding compensation and labor rights equal to those in the private sector.

As private sector unions moved aggressively into the relatively unplowed and fertile fields of public employment, the preexisting professional organizations rightfully felt threatened. Strong organizing efforts by emerging unions such as the AFT, for example, spurred the NEA to reconsider its own future role in public education and eventually to embrace the full panoply of union activities. In many jurisdictions, predominantly private sector unions such as the SEIU and the Teamsters began to compete directly with the professional associations. In some cases, professional and fraternal organizations had to adopt an overt union strategy in order to survive. The rivalries between these various types of organizations led to increased militancy and intensified organizing drives, which, on the whole, further enhanced government unionization (Stieber 1974: 830).

3. Changes in the Legal Environment

However widespread within a government jurisdiction, unions may be functionally impotent in the absence of a legal framework requiring public employers to
recognize and bargain with them. Two events during the early 1960s contributed
indirectly to the creation of a more favorable legal environment for enactment of
public sector labor laws. First, the U.S. Supreme Court ordered reapportionment of
the Congress and the 50 state legislatures *(Baker v. Carr* 1962; *Reynolds v. Simms*
1964) on the basis of one person, one vote. These decisions ended or at least eased
the domination of many state legislatures by rural, predominantly anti-union interests. Unions, which have always found their strongest support among people in
metropolitan areas, soon discovered more sympathetic ears in the reapportioned
legislative bodies of the states.

The second development encouraging bargaining legislation was President John
F. Kennedy's Executive Order 10988 of 1962, which guaranteed unionization and
bargaining rights for federal employees. This order might have been the turning
point in state and local unionization. Although it is impossible to ascertain a direct
cause-and-effect relationship between Executive Order 10988 and the subsequent
enactment of labor relations legislation in numerous jurisdictions, it did have a substantial spillover effect in legitimizing public employee unionization and collective
bargaining practices.

4. An Era of Social Change and Turmoil

There was a massive infusion of young people and racial minorities into the public
work force during the 1960s. Both groups were somewhat distrustful of authority
and the existing management structure. Furthermore, both groups, on the whole,
were favorably disposed to unions (Barrett 1973). Meanwhile, public life in general
was riddled with conflicts over the unpopular war in Viet Nam and rising pressure
for social change.

Police officers, for instance, became "sick and tired of being harassed, cursed,
spit on, and shot at" (Juris and Feuille 1973: 18). Especially in large urban areas,
police found themselves working in an extremely hostile environment inhabited
by militant blacks and students whose ire was often directed specifically at law
enforcement personnel. Supreme Court decisions that restricted police discretion,
such as *Miranda v. Arizona* (1966), and community demands for civilian review
boards to assess alleged police misconduct were seen as threats to the officers' professional and personal well-being. At the same time, public officials lodged increasingly adamant demands for "law and order" and improved police protection for the
community. To many police officers, these intense and often conflicting external
pressures, when examined in conjunction with perceptions of low pay and antiquated personnel practices, became unbearable. The options, as Hirschman (1970)
has pointed out, are exit (resign), voice (protest), or loyalty (suck it up). Some,

indeed, decided to look for other, less demanding lines of work; others chose to suffer through the experience while awaiting retirement. Many, however, elected to give voice to their complaints through unions.

II. Why Government Workers Join Unions — The Individual Perspective

Identifying the broad societal forces that precipitated and accompanied the growth in public sector unionization during the 1960s and 1970s provides only a partial explanation of the union phenomenon. In order to gain a more complete understanding of collective action within government employment, one must also consider the problem from a micro, or individual, perspective. What leads the individual government worker to join a union?

Extensive research shows clearly that American workers join unions because they are dissatisfied. They want higher wages and better benefits, job security, participation in decision making, and protection of their rights as workers. Job-related conditions especially conducive to unionization include hazardous, physically demanding, or repetitive tasks; little input into job-related decisions; and perceptions of arbitrary and unfair management actions and decisions (S. M. Hills 1985; Hundley 1988; Sherer 1987; Premack and Hunter 1988). Seldom have political or ideological appeals persuaded U.S. workers to organize. Rather, the principal motive has been to improve conditions of employment through collective voice and action (Friedman, Abraham, and Thomas 2006). For blue-collar workers the bread-and-butter economic issues are usually paramount. For white-collar workers psychological reasons such as job security and the desire for a stronger voice in decision making are of somewhat greater significance (Kochan 1980: 26). For almost all private sector employees job dissatisfaction "must be quite severe before a majority will support unionization as an option for improving these conditions" (Kochan 1980: 26). Recent examples include janitors, nurses and other health care providers, meat cutting and packing plant workers, and agricultural laborers.

But dissatisfaction alone is not sufficient. Workers must also believe that union representation will be instrumental in securing the desired benefits, and that the value of these benefits will exceed the costs associated with unionization. Race, gender, and life experiences also play a part in the propensity to join a union. Research indicates that women, African Americans, Latinos, the less educated, and individuals who have been previously exposed to unions are more likely to join them, for example, than are highly educated white males born of parents who are professionals (S. M. Hills 1985; Hundley 1988; Leigh and Hills 1987; DeFreitas 1993). No doubt these factors are related. For instance, historically, women, African Americans, Latinos, and the less educated have had fewer opportunities for career advancement and thus may tend to see unions as a vehicle for gaining status and pay. Individuals with these union-friendly characteristics are also more likely to have blue-collar, union parents.

Union membership is still higher among men (13 percent) than women (10.9 percent), but the gap is closing. In 2006, a higher percentage of African Americans (14.5 percent) were members of unions than whites (11.7 percent) and Latinos (9.8 percent) (U.S. Bureau of Labor Statistics 2007). Today's propensity of women and African Americans to join labor organizations reverses a long-term pattern in which these groups were least likely to join. Historically, women and minorities were systematically discriminated against by unions in both the public and private sectors. In the 1960s and early 1970s, however, the civil rights movement and the women's movement forged links with organized labor. Today, low-paid women and minority employees often have the most to gain from unions, and many public employee organizations in particular have recognized the tremendous potential for membership gains represented by unorganized minority groups, including recent immigrants.

The case of Latinos is complex and remains a work in progress for researchers. The Latino labor force is rapidly accelerating in the United States, largely because of high immigration rates from the Caribbean, Central America, and Mexico. However, the growth rate of Latino union membership, although it now exceeds that of whites, has not kept pace with the increasing penetration of the labor force. Among the factors that may be depressing unionization among Latinos are immigration status, short duration of residence in the United States, and deficient English-language skills (Milkman 2000; Briggs 2001; DeFreitas 1993: 285).

As this segment of the population continues to surge and unions fully recognize their organizing potential and reach out to Latinos, higher unionization rates are likely to follow. The success of the "Justice for Janitors" campaign in organizing large numbers of Hispanic custodial workers in Los Angeles, San Diego, and many other cities is one indication of the potential for low-skilled, low-paid immigrants to join unions (Johnston 1994). Heroic struggles by immigrant workers in New York City to overcome their "illegal" status, employer opposition, and the challenges of a new social and economic environment are chronicled in a recent book by Ness (2005).

III. Future Prospects

Unions continue to exercise important political influence in the U.S. private sector despite the steep declines in their representation of the labor force. However, powerful economic and political forces continue to deplete the ranks of organized labor in the private sector.

The picture is quite different in the public sector. Although overall membership leveled off years ago, several public employee unions have increased their membership during the past decade, including the NEA, AFT, SEIU, and AFSCME. Moreover, traditionally private sector unions have captured significant numbers of public workers. Public employee unions are now, and will remain in the future, forces to be reckoned with within U.S. politics and public administration. The final chapter in this book assesses their prospects in detail.

Chapter 2

The Unions Today

I. Introduction

This chapter explores the organizational landscape of public employee unions, including the factors that are correlated with unionization. The key term is *diversity*. For virtually every generalization about public employee unions there are noteworthy exceptions. Public sector unions vary along many dimensions and across levels of government and the nonprofit sector. They are different in terms of affiliation. Some are federated with national organizations such as the AFL-CIO. Others are local independent organizations with no national affiliation. Some unions representing government workers also organize and bargain for workers in the private and nonprofit sectors (e.g., Service Employees International Union [SEIU]). Others (e.g., the Fraternal Order of Police) essentially restrict their boundaries to public employees. There are unions with membership rolls numbering more than one million, and there are unions whose ranks are counted in double digits. The occupations of union members are also highly diverse. Clerical personnel, firefighters, nurses, social workers, welders, physicians, architects, and university professors all work under union banners. Wherever workers experience high levels of job dissatisfaction, unionization is a possibility.

II. The Federal Government

Despite the early recognition of federal employee organizing rights by Executive Order 10988, federal unions do not benefit from national policy as favorable as that which governs private sector labor relations. The scope of bargaining in federal labor relations is quite restricted; federal employees represented by bargaining units do not have to join the union, and there is a strong no-strike policy. Federal employee unions represented about 34 percent of the 3.38 million civilian work force (including postal workers) in 2006 (U.S. Bureau of Labor Statistics 2007).

Between 1964 (the first year for which such data were collected) and 1968, federal employee union membership figures climbed rapidly to about half of the total federal civilian work force. The high water mark was 1987, when 59 percent of federal employees were covered by collective bargaining agreements. But dramatic reductions in the size of federal employment, particularly through outsourcing of union-dense blue-collar and technical jobs, have driven down the number and percentage of employees represented by unions.

Federal labor relations policy, as embedded today in the Civil Service Reform Act of 1978 and subsequent agency-specific legislation and presidential executive orders (see Chapter 3), severely constrains the potential influence of federal unions on wages, benefits, and working conditions. It is important to note that federal law prohibits membership-enhancing union security provisions such as the Fair Share, which requires individuals whom the union represents in collective bargaining to either join the union or pay their "fair share" of union dues for representational expenses. This provides an ideal situation for encouraging free riders, who enjoy the benefits of union representation in collective bargaining and grievances, but who are not required to contribute out of their own paychecks for union services. Free riders pose a serious problem for federal unions, which are mandated by law to represent, equally and fairly, all members of their bargaining units, whether they belong to the union or not. Financial resources are the primary measure of a union's strength and ability to finance representational and political activities, and members' dues make up a substantial proportion of such financial assets.

Many federal employees are, indeed, free riders. For example, the largest federal union, the American Federation of Government Employees (AFGE), represented approximately 600,000 bargaining unit members in 2007, but much less than half of them were dues-paying members. All told, out of the approximately 1,139,000 federal wage system (blue-collar) and General Schedule (white-collar) employees who are represented by a collective bargaining contract, only one third actually belong to the union and pay dues.

The most notable exception to this pattern is the U.S. Postal Service. As noted in Chapter 1, postal workers were instrumental in early federal employee unionization efforts. They are the most highly organized of all federal workers today. They enjoy their own statutory framework, which was won in the aftermath of a 1970 postal strike. As a consequence, postal unions have full private sector collective bargaining rights, with the exception of union security provisions and the right to strike. Postal union membership figures are almost equal to the proportion under contract, about 90 percent. The near absence of a free-rider problem for postal unions is attributable to these superior bargaining rights and, in turn, to the unions' greater success in winning improvements in wages, benefits, and working conditions from management.

Federal employee unions represent employees in nearly every agency, from the U.S. Department of Agriculture to the U.S. Information Agency. The largest numbers of represented employees are found among civilian workers for the Armed Forces and the departments of Homeland Security, Veterans' Affairs, and Treasury. Some 90 unions represent employees in at least one federal bargaining unit; the National Treasury Employees Union (NTEU) alone represents federal workers in 31 different agencies.

It is useful to review briefly the principal federal unions and some of their distinctive characteristics. The largest federal union, the AFGE, represents 600,000 employees. It was created by the AFL-CIO in 1932 when a preexisting organization, the National Federation of Federal Employees (NFFE), withdrew from the AFL-CIO over jurisdictional and policy conflicts. AFGE membership today is heaviest in the District of Columbia area and, somewhat surprisingly, in the Southeast, where large numbers of civilians are employed in military facilities. AFGE has substantial minority and female representation both in the rank and file and in leadership positions.

Former AFGE president Kenneth Blaylock helped convince convention delegates in 1976 to approve a resolution supporting extension of the union's jurisdiction to military personnel. Although a vote of the total membership later soundly defeated the resolution, merely raising the issue was enough to generate consternation and apprehension in the defense establishment and, subsequently, in Congress.

Ostensibly, the American military would appear to offer a ripe environment for union organizers. Pay is quite low in relation to comparable work for private defense contractors and many civilian jobs (although some fringe benefits are superior) and working conditions certainly do not rank among the finest. In addition, a highly defined and rigorously enforced division exists between military "management" and "labor," represented by distinctions in uniformed dress, privileges, and other factors, creating a natural and sometimes intense adversarial relationship. Not of least importance to the unions is the huge number of potential members in the active military (more than 1.2 million).

Organization of the armed forces in several Western European nations (e.g., Germany, the Netherlands, Sweden, Belgium) shows that military unionization is feasible. However, some rather serious objections may be lodged. The strike issue is of obvious importance, as is the matter of maintaining military discipline. Other troubling questions involve allocation of less desirable job assignments, effective representation of diverse military occupations by a single large union, and the potential scope of bargaining. Joining a labor union or organizing military personnel by the AFGE or other unions is precluded by federal law and a Department of Defense directive. Civilian workers in defense establishments may belong to unions, but uniformed personnel may not.

As AFGE's major competitor, NFFE has historically assumed a much lower profile in its organizing and political tactics. The currently independent NFFE began in 1917 as an affiliate of the AFL, but withdrew in 1931 largely because of opposition to the strike and other aspects of collective bargaining as practiced by AFL affiliates in the private sector. NFFE even opposed the conservative provisions of Executive Order 10988 for some time. The timid posture of the organization led to steady declines in its membership until 1967, when new leadership was elected. NFFE, like AFGE, then purged a no-strike pledge from its constitution and assumed a more active political posture. NFFE (110,000 employees covered by collective bargaining agreements) is much smaller than AFGE and suffers even more from the free rider problem.

The second largest federal organization, with 150,000 covered under bargaining agreements, is the NTEU. The NTEU is a nonaffiliated union that began in the Internal Revenue Service in 1938 (as the National Association of Collectors of Internal Revenue) and has since expanded throughout the Treasury Department and other federal agencies. Its aggressive organizing drives have made NTEU one of the fastest growing federal unions in recent years, and it enjoys a higher percentage of dues-paying members than most other federal unions.

The National Air Traffic Controllers Association (about 20,000 members) rose from the ashes of the Professional Air Traffic Controllers Organization (PATCO), which was effectively destroyed by the actions of President Ronald Reagan. Several associations (e.g., Senior Executives Association and Federal Managers Association) represent upper level federal employees in lobbying the president and the Congress for improvements in compensation and working conditions and greater respect for the public service.

Postal employees, who officially work for a quasi-government corporation, are represented by several major organizations. The oldest, the National Association of Letter Carriers (NALC; 214,000 active duty letter carriers), was founded in 1890 and later became an affiliate of the AFL-CIO. The other, larger postal organization is the American Postal Workers Union (APWU; 360,000 members), formed in 1971 through an amalgamation of five smaller organizations that represented clerks, carriers, and crafts workers. Other postal organizations of significance today are the National Rural Letter Carriers Association and the National Postal Mail Handlers Union (see Table 2.1).

Prospects for membership growth in postal unions are rather dim. Continuing technological changes, and competition from private firms such as United Postal Service, DHL, and Federal Express, have been eliminating jobs in the postal service. With membership figures already around 90 percent, postal unions can gain little or no benefit from attempting to enlist the remaining represented (but non-union) workers.

Prospects seem equally doubtful for the other federal unions, most of which remain unable to bargain over the important issues of wages and benefits and continue to lack union security provisions that would allow them to increase their

Table 2.1   Major Postal Employee Unions, 2007

Organization	Membership
American Postal Workers Union	272,000
National Association of Letter Carriers	224,000
National Rural Letter Carriers Association	117,000
National Postal Mail Handlers Union	55,000

Source: Union websites.

membership. Far-reaching reductions in force, again during the Clinton administration (1992 to 2000), reduced the absolute number of jobs, translating directly
into membership losses and a concomitant weakening of federal union strength
and influence. To reverse these negative trends, federal unions must do a more
effective job of addressing the needs of women and minorities, who comprise a
rapidly growing proportion of the federal work force, as well as find a means to
overcome the free-rider problem.

III. Nonprofit Organizations

Churches, some schools, charities, hospitals, lobbying organizations, museums,
and even labor unions themselves are nonprofit organizations. Although there are
various legal distinctions based on state law and the federal tax code, all nonprofit
organizations exist for purposes other than generating profits. They rest uneasily in
a vast and expanding gray area of organizational society: neither government nor
business, but typically partnering or otherwise interacting with both. They range in
size from a one-woman daycare center to a massive hospital complex.

The nonprofit or "third sector" is an attractive organizational arena for unions.
Health care organizations, which account for some 60 percent of the nonprofit
sector's resources, are a particularly tempting target. The SEIU, the American
Federation of State, County, and Municipal Employees (AFSCME), the Office
and Professional Employees International Union, and many others court nonprofit
workers throughout the United States.

Print and Internet resources do not permit identification of the extent of union
membership and representation in the sector. Existing data are sketchy, although
one must assume that a significant portion of the membership of SEIU, AFSCME,
United American Nurses, and other unions with significant presence in the third
sector is composed of nonprofit workers.

IV. State and Local Government

As of January 2006, according to the U.S. Bureau of Labor Statistics, 30.2 percent of state government employees and 41.9 percent of local government employees belonged to labor organizations. When occupation is considered, the most heavily organized are the teachers, firefighters, and police officers, followed by sanitation workers, welfare workers, highway personnel, and hospital workers. Gains have been registered in sanitation, health care, and social services in recent years.

A. The Determinants of State and Local Unionization

Sophisticated econometric models have been reasonably successful in explaining private sector unionization, assisted, from a practical perspective, by a national legal setting that places all private workers and employers on an equal footing under the National Labor Relations Act and its amendments. These econometric models indicate that levels of unionization are influenced by wage and benefit levels, the rate of unemployment, urbanization, region, "right-to-work" laws, and various worker- and job-related characteristics.

Determining the correlates of state and local unionization is more problematic because of the complex legal environment (one set of laws for federal workers and 50 sets for the states, plus numerous executive orders, local ordinances, legal rulings, provisions, and practices). It is well accepted that organizational membership is closely related to the presence and scope of state bargaining legislation. Those states with the most permissive legal environment report the highest levels of union membership. Table 2.2 provides information about organized state and local employees for all 50 states and the presence or absence of collective bargaining laws.

The relationship between public employee labor relations policy and unionization, however, recalls the chicken and egg dilemma. This intriguing question of which comes first receives further discussion in Chapter 3; for now, let it suffice to note that the relationship is reciprocal: political pressure from unions helps foster favorable policy outcomes from the state and local legislative processes, and, at the same time, union organizing drives have been aided greatly by laws encouraging or mandating collective bargaining.

Economic models are not particularly helpful for understanding or explaining public sector unionization. A more useful approach is to treat unionization in government as a socioeconomic, political, and policy phenomenon. Figure 2.1 displays a suggestive comprehensive model that identifies the direct and indirect effects of the state's socioeconomic environment, the political culture, the state political system, and labor relations policy.

As shown in Table 2.2, unionization is lowest in the Sunbelt states, such as Arizona, Arkansas, Mississippi, North Carolina, South Carolina, Texas, and Virginia. Clearly, collective bargaining laws make a difference in levels of unionization. Even within a single state the salience of law can be seen. For instance,

Table 2.2   Bargaining Status, Political Ideology, and Union Density, 2006

State	State Collective Bargaining Law	Local Bargaining Rights	State Political Ideology Score[*]	State Union Density[**]
Alabama	—	Local gov't	23.1	28.9
Alaska	X	All	15.6	49.2
Arizona	—	None	13	24.6
Arkansas	—	None	24	10.3
California	X	All	2.6	52.6
Colorado	X[3]	None	8.6	22.8
Connecticut	X	All	0.9	59
Delaware	X	All	3.7	39.2
Florida	X	All	11.1	22.6
Georgia	—	MARTA/firefighters	18.5	9.6
Hawaii	X	All	0	55.1
Idaho	—	Teachers/ firefighters	21.7	15
Illinois	X	All	6.9	49.5
Indiana	—	Teachers	19.2	27.8
Iowa	X	All	15.4	30.9
Kansas	Y	All[2]	22.1	19.4
Kentucky	—	Police/firefighters	17.5	16.3
Louisiana	—	None	23.7	15.5
Maine	X	All	8.4	46.3
Maryland	X	Education/park police/local gov't	4.4	31.5
Massachusetts	X	All	−3.5	59.1
Michigan	X	All	10.9	55.8
Minnesota	X	All	8.2	52.1

Table 2.2 Bargaining Status, Political Ideology, and Union Density, 2006 (Continued)

State	State Collective Bargaining Law	Local Bargaining Rights	State Political Ideology Score[*]	State Union Density[**]
Mississippi	—	None	30.2	12.2
Missouri	X[4]	All[4]	16.5	20.3
Montana	X	All	18.9	34.8
Nebraska	X	All	20.7	25.5
Nevada	—	All	16.3	32.9
New Hampshire	X	All	7.4	44.9
New Jersey	X	All	2.4	64.4
New Mexico	X[3]	All	8.8	17
New York	X	All	15	68.8
North Carolina	—	None	19.6	10.8
North Dakota	Y[2]	Teachers/all local gov't[2]	26.9	17.3
Ohio	X	All	14.3	43.5
Oklahoma	—	All	26.7	18.7
Oregon	X	All	9.1	48.5
Pennsylvania	X	All	11.5	51
Rhode Island	X	All	2.6	65.5
South Carolina	—	None	22.2	8.2
South Dakota	X	All	25	21.1
Tennessee	—	Teachers	21.6	21.7
Texas	—	Police/firefighters	22.1	15.5
Utah	—	Teachers	24.9	18
Vermont	X	All	−8	40.7
Virginia	—	None	14.5	8.4

Table 2.2 Bargaining Status, Political Ideology, and Union Density, 2006 (Continued)

State	State Collective Bargaining Law	Local Bargaining Rights	State Political Ideology Score[*]	State Union Density[**]
Washington	X	All	9	56.3
West Virginia	Y[2]	All[2]	14.1	30
Wisconsin	X	All	14.4	53.6
Wyoming	—	Firefighters	11.7	15.6

[*] Political ideology was calculated using pooled raw data from CBS News/*New York Times* polls. Range of scores: a positive score indicates more conservative ideology; a score of zero indicates moderate ideology; a negative score indicates liberal ideology. These scores have been reformatted from the original source. (*Source*: http://mypage.iu.edu/~wright1/CorrectAppendixTable12.1.txt.)

[**] Union density refers to the percentage of state and local employees who belong to unions. In jurisdictions where employees do not have bargaining rights, the figure includes the percentage of workers represented by a union or association. (*Source*: Hirsch and Macpherson, 2007.)

[1] Local option permitted.
[2] Meet and confer.
[3] Collective bargaining granted through executive order.
[4] Collective bargaining through court decision.

Tennessee has no collective bargaining provisions for state employees, and few of them belong to employee organizations. But teachers are permitted to negotiate in the Volunteer State, which boosts the union membership to higher levels for all local government employees. State labor relations policy may be the single most critical element that determines the fortunes of unions in state and local government.

The socioeconomic environment portrayed in Figure 2.1 may be operationalized through such variables as wealth (personal or family income), level of education, unemployment rate, urbanization, and industrialization. Wealth and high

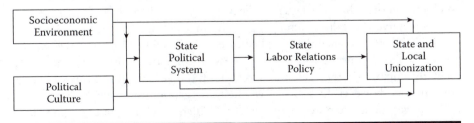

Figure 2.1 Determinants of State Labor Relations Policy.

levels of urbanization and manufacturing activity are conducive to unionization in industry, which in turn is correlated with government unionization. Bad economic times and government fiscal crises may produce retrenchment and reductions in force, which will retard unionization. High unemployment inhibits unionization because employees are concerned about layoffs and hesitate to jeopardize their jobs by joining a union. Education levels are likely to be inversely related to unionization, because a highly educated work force earns good pay, has more individualized bargaining power, has better working conditions, and generally perceives less need for unionization.

Political culture shapes unionization through historical and demographic forces. As originally formulated by Elazar (1966), a traditionalistic culture, with its characteristic of elitism, should be hostile to unions, as certainly has been the case in the South. A moralistic political culture is more conducive to unions, with its emphasis on equity and "doing good." The individualistic political culture views politics as a marketplace. Thus unions face greater obstacles in states with such a culture than in moralistic states, but through effective political action they can win bargaining rights. Political culture is related to ideology. States characterized by political liberalism are more favorable toward unions than are politically conservative states. Political ideology also helps determine public policy in the states. As shown by Berry et al. (2007), changes in citizens' "policy mood" can lead to policy change by influencing the actions of state and local officials. The expectation is that collective bargaining finds a friendlier policy environment in politically liberal states than in conservative states. Evidence for this expectation is shown in Table 2.2.

Obviously, political culture, socioeconomic environment, and political ideology have a strong regional bias. A brief look at unionization in the Sunbelt states demonstrates that conclusion. Generally speaking, the Sunbelt states (those below the Mason–Dixon Line and extending to the West Coast) do not have the characteristics that have been associated with unionization in other regions. Although Sunbelt growth has been generally accompanied by gains in urbanization and industrialization, a healthy business climate, and massive in-migration of people from other regions and countries, unions in neither government nor industry have done an effective job of attracting members and winning bargaining rights. Two special factors seem to be operating in the Sunbelt to discourage unionization: the political culture and ideology, on the one hand, and union resistance tactics by employers on the other. The latter is at least partly a product of the former.

To preserve the values comprising traditional political culture, employers in the Sunbelt have become highly sophisticated in applying union resistance tactics. Some, such as the meat packing and processing company Smithfield Foods, have regularly employed extra-legal means to fight off the unions. Most firms and many governments, however, have practiced the more gentle union suppression tactics of "positive human resource management," which involves offering competitive wages and benefits, good working conditions, and participative decision-making programs. Whatever rubric management assigns to the activity, unions tend to perceive it as at best union-averse behavior and at worst "union-busting." Often, management consulting firms are retained to direct the employer's anti-union strategies and train employers in "union-avoidance" tactics. Although these strategies and a predominantly anti-union climate are also in evidence in other portions of the United States, they are strongest in the Sunbelt.

Large gains in public sector union membership and influence do not seem likely soon in the Sunbelt, unless permissive legislation is enacted or union-friendly governors issue executive orders extending collective bargaining rights. These possibilities, in turn, presume a shift in public mood in favor of bargaining (Berry and Berry, 2007). In most of the Sunbelt, a vicious cycle seems to be present in which the traditionalistic conservative political culture, conservative political ideology, and the absence of union strength diminish the chances of new collective bargaining legislation, and in the absence of a favorable legal environment union membership gains remain arduous.

Nonetheless, there is some basis for not writing off all prospects for union growth in the region. The area continues to prosper economically and to develop characteristics similar to geographic areas with more highly unionized states. Surveys have reported a strong reservoir of potential support for unions in the region, particularly among African Americans. Moreover, population shifts and socioeconomic change have influenced political ideology, tending to make it less conservative. The problems, however, remain substantial. Unions must find a way to break through the barriers of politically conservative influences and adapt to the abiding conditions and norms of the region.

Looking again at Figure 2.1, it can be seen that the state political system is linked to the socioeconomic environment and political culture and ideology. The state political system encompasses factors such as executive–legislative relations, legislative professionalism, interparty competition, and the political and economic strength of private sector unions. For example, competitive two-party states should be more conducive to unionization because union interests are more likely to receive representation. Similarly, a strong Democratic Party presence in the three branches of state government should facilitate unionization in government; traditionally, Democrats have been more "pro-labor" than the "pro-business" Republicans.

Why, today, are government workers organized in much larger proportions (about 5:1) than workers in private sector employment? There are several major reasons. One reason is the legal environment, which, with the exception of the nonbargaining states, is more amenable to signing up members and keeping them on the rolls than the private sector legal environment under the National Labor Relations Act. Second, most public employees are protected by a blanket of civil service rules and regulations that prevent management from firing them for engaging in union activities. Third, a prime objective of unions is greater worker participation in decision making, and there is evidence that managers in government organizations are generally more willing to share authority and decision making than their counterparts in business (Freeman 1996). Part of this willingness is no doubt associated with the prevalence of highly educated professional and white-collar employees in many government organizations and the sense that both management and labor are working "for the people." Finally, government managers have much less to gain from actively opposing unions than business managers.

B. Employee Organizations in State and Local Government

Public employee organizations may be categorized according to several characteristics. The first important distinction is between associations and unions. State and local government employee associations were organized in the first half of the 20th century as mutual benefit and service-providing organizations (Stieber 1973: 8). These early organizations provided credit unions, group benefit plans for health and life insurance, and other member services; some even handled grievances. Although most associations were concerned with serving their members and, in some cases, enhancing the status of various government-related professions, they also engaged in legislative and executive branch lobbying activities in efforts to win favorable treatment for their members. Unlike these early employee associations, unions accepted collective bargaining from the beginning as the fundamental means for winning improved wages, benefits, and working conditions from government employers.

A second type of categorization involves the nature of the employer. Some of the public employee unions are primarily public, such as the Fraternal Order of Police, whereas others are mixed membership unions claiming membership in government and industry and, increasingly, in the nonprofit sector as well. Examples of mixed membership unions are the SEIU, the International Brotherhood of Teamsters (IBT), and, increasingly, AFSCME. Third, unions may be distinguished by the functional coverage of their organizing activities. Some, like AFSCME, are general-purpose organizations, which seek out members at all levels of government and in almost any occupation. Others, such as the International Association of Fire Fighters, are functionally specific, concentrating membership in a single government job category.

Most state and local government professional associations initially opposed collective bargaining and the other trappings of unions; some still do. However, as observed by Stieber (1973: 123), "Once a collective bargaining law has been enacted, associations almost invariably have adapted to it by presenting themselves for certification as employee representatives, participating in negotiations, and becoming parties to written agreements."

By the early 1970s, there was a marked convergence in goals, strategies, and tactics among many of the associations and the unions. Some of the state and local associations have maintained their independence while functioning as unions. Other associations have merged with unions; for instance, the Illinois State Employees Association merged with SEIU, as did the California State Employees Association. The Massachusetts State Employees Association joined with the National Association of Government Employees (NAGE), and the New York,

Ohio, Arizona, and Mississippi civil service employees associations affiliated with AFSCME. Nevertheless, many associations remain predominantly service-oriented lobbying organizations that do not engage in collective bargaining. Examples include the South Carolina and Virginia state employees associations.

Although there has been some debate on the relative effectiveness of independent unions versus unions affiliated with national labor organizations, it is difficult to sort out key empirical dimensions of organizational influence and power. However, the consensus seems to be that independent organizations can be as effective as or even more successful than affiliated organizations, depending on such factors as leadership, group cohesiveness, community acceptance, and the general labor environment.

Competition over members and collective bargaining recognition led to some rather severe inter-union conflicts during the late 1960s and early 1970s (Spero and Capozzola 1973: 32–37; Stieber 1973: 89–100). A stable and comprehensive legal environment in the majority of states, embodied by formal nonaggression agreements between some of the larger unions, has helped alleviate overt conflict. However, internecine union warfare broke out in 2005 when the SEIU, the Teamsters, and five other unions split off from the AFL-CIO to form the new federation called Change to Win. The battlefield is the nonprofit sector's health care providers and workers in child care and nursing home establishments. The fight between SEIU and AFSCME over child care providers in Iowa was likened by the state's human services director to "the Bloods versus the Crips" (Walters 2006: 29).

Public employee unions may be characterized by their membership and organizing targets as general purpose or functionally specific.

1. General-Purpose Unions

The paramount general-purpose organization in government is AFSCME. Membership estimates were 1.4 million in 2007 (see Table 2.2). It is the largest AFL-CIO affiliate. Although AFSCME's greatest membership gains were registered during 1962 to 1978, the union continues to grow, especially through mergers with other public sector unions. Its strongest presence is in the clerical, health care, technical, professional, and law enforcement fields. Internally, AFSCME is organized through an "international" office and its executive committee, 61 regional councils, and some 3,500 locals that report to the councils. The president (Gerald McEntee since 1981) appoints his or her own staff, which performs executive and judicial functions for the organization. The highest policy-making body is the international convention, held biennially. The locals elect their own delegates and operate under their own constitutions, with the number of delegates determined by total membership. Between conventions, policy is developed and implemented by the executive committee. Dues are apportioned among the national, local, and council (regional) organizations. Dues increases are tied to average earnings increases of full-time state and local government employees.

Table 2.2 Membership of Largest State and Local Employee Organizations, 2007

Organization	Membership
National Education Association	3.2 million
American Federation of State, County, and Municipal Employees	1.4 million
American Federation of Teachers	1.3 million
Service Employees International Union	1.8 million
Fraternal Order of Police	324,000
International Association of Fire Fighters	280,000

Source: Union websites.

As an organization, AFSCME is an indefatigable political activist. It has not hesitated to take positions on salient questions of domestic and foreign policy or to enter the electoral arena with large campaign contributions to friendly candidates and massive get-out-the-vote drives. Its principal political action committee, PEOPLE (Public Employees Organized to Promote Legislative Equality), typically ranks as one of the top campaign fundraisers in national elections. AFSCME's primary purpose in much of its political activity has been to legitimize and expand the bargaining rights of public employees (Masters, 1998: 316). Within its own ranks AFSCME usually has taken care to ensure proper representation of women and people of color, who hold a number of important national offices and a majority of the national membership.

Three other strong, general-purpose organizations operate in government, all of them mixed unions with a major presence in the private and nonprofit sectors. The fast-growing SEIU has concentrated its organizing efforts in government and the nonprofit sectors. More than half a million of its members are in government employment. SEIU is especially strong in California, where it rivals AFSCME in strength. SEIU's major organizing campaigns in the 2000s have focused on health care workers, day care providers, and long-term care workers, using the themes of quality care and consumer protection within the rapidly changing health care industries to attract new members. SEIU has also rung up victories and attained a significant presence among janitors and security guards.

The Laborers International Union (LIU) membership base in the private sector is composed predominantly of skilled and semiskilled construction workers. The LIU has had some success in organizing local government workers in streets, sanitation, and public works. The 700,000-member union claims about one third of its ranks in the public sector, in which the National Postal Mail Handlers Union is an affiliate.

The International Brotherhood of Teamsters, like the LIU, has focused efforts mostly on blue-collar employees in the public sector. They have been a strong competitor of AFSCME in some local government jurisdictions. The IBT has achieved some degree of organizing success in a wide variety of occupations, including clerks, corrections officers, custodial workers, police and firefighters, and health care workers. A relatively small but growing percentage of the Teamsters' membership of 1.4 million is in government employment. A significant proportion (about 200,000) works for the United Parcel Service.

2. Functionally Specific Organizations

A substantial amount of unionization in government has occurred along professional lines, similar in some respects to craft organization in the private sector. The major organizations in education, police and fire protection, health care, and miscellaneous government professions are examined next.

a. Education — Primary and Secondary

Public education is the largest public employer by far in state and local government — more than five million individuals work in public education. It is also the most expensive of all state and local services, consuming some $425 billion in expenditures.

Two organizations have dominated the union movement in education: the independent National Education Association (NEA) and the AFL-CIO-affiliated American Federation of Teachers (AFT). The NEA, the largest labor union in the United States, claims a national membership of about 3.2 million in 14,000 local affiliates, with its primary strength in mid-sized cities and suburbs. Eighty percent of its members are classroom teachers. The AFT, with a membership roll of about 1.3 million, is concentrated in large cities such as New York, Boston, Minneapolis, and Denver. The AFT has presented itself as an aggressive union seeking collective bargaining rights for teachers since its inception in 1919. In contrast, the NEA was born in 1857 as a professional organization open to both teachers and supervisory personnel. Even though many NEA locals function as unions today, and the national organization is officially labeled a "union" by the Bureau of Labor Statistics and the Internal Revenue Service, a large portion of the members are found in locals that do not engage in, nor seek to enter into, collective bargaining relationships.

Early in its history the NEA proclaimed that discussions on teachers' salaries with the local school board or superintendent were "unprofessional." The national organization's attitude changed, however, with the 1961 election of New York City's United Federation of Teachers (an AFT affiliate) as teacher bargaining agent for the city — a painful loss for the NEA. Soon thereafter the NEA leadership made a number of policy changes, including support for "professional negotiations" and "professional sanctions" against arbitrary or unethical school management practices. The NEA also began sponsoring state legislation for teacher bargaining.

Although there is no doubt that the NEA and AFT have become more alike in their strategies and activities, there remain important differences that have stifled recurring attempts to merge. Beginning in 1969, formal merger discussions were held and some NEA and AFT locals did join ranks (e.g., in Flint, Michigan), but the national leadership of NEA eventually backed out for three major reasons: AFL-CIO affiliation (the NEA did not desire it); the composition of bargaining units (NEA wanted to retain supervisory personnel in some locals); and, in general, more conservative NEA policy positions on a number of issues (Stem 1979: 63–64). The organizations officially decided to go their separate ways, with the NEA continuing to limit its membership to professional education personnel and the AFT electing to pursue the organization of teachers' aides, paraprofessionals, library workers, cafeteria workers, bus drivers, and noneducation employees in civil service and health care (Stem 1979: 66–67). Drawing the two organizations even farther apart was the rancorous conflict over President Carter's proposed Department of Education in 1979. The NEA supported the new department (which was subsequently created), whereas the AFT, led by late President Albert Shanker and encouraged by the AFL-CIO, fought it adamantly. During the 1980s the two organizations continued to compete for new members and to raid the others' jurisdictions for representation rights (see Cooper 1988). Nonetheless, on several occasions in the 1990s, efforts were undertaken to bring the two organizations together, to no avail.

AFT President Al Shanker died in February 1997. Shanker was a charismatic figure whose persuasive and respected voice influenced education policy debates from the White House to the schoolhouse. His arguments for higher national education standards and other reforms received much attention during the 1990s. Replacing Shanker as AFT president was Sandra Feldman.

Feldman and NEA counterpart Robert Chase helped generate a serious reconsideration of merger in 1998. An agreement negotiated by the AFT–NEA leadership would have merged the two national organizations and encouraged local union affiliates to join forces with one another, while respecting local preferences. However, at the national convention in New Orleans in 1998, NEA delegates voted down the proposal, generally for the same reasons that had halted earlier efforts. Today, a "partnership" between the NEA and AFT helps advance common goals through a joint council, though the two organizations remain fiercely independent.

b. Higher Education

Collective bargaining by college and university faculty in the United States was initiated in 1967 by the AFT at the U.S. Merchant Marine Academy. Approximately 250,000 professors are represented by faculty unions today. This amounts to about 37 percent of all faculty in higher education. Two-year colleges report the highest level of organization (63 percent), followed by four-year colleges and research universities. Among the larger universities with organized faculty are the California State University system, the State University of New York system, Rutgers University, and the University of Connecticut.

The major faculty unions are NEA, AFT, and the American Association of University Professors (AAUP). The NEA first dabbled in organizing college faculty in 1870 with the creation of a higher education unit, which was dissolved during the 1920s but recreated in 1943. After an early emphasis on teachers' colleges and community colleges, the NEA moved strongly into more comprehensive higher education institutions in the early 1970s (Ladd and Lipset 1973: 6–7). The AFT first focused its energies on organizing the nation's two-year campuses, but, following the path of the NEA, has since gained the right to represent faculty at several four-year institutions.

The AAUP, like the NEA in elementary and secondary education, existed for many years as a professional association not interested in collective bargaining or other union-like activities. The AAUP was founded in 1915 to help protect academic freedom and tenure rights and to advance faculty salaries through information gathering and other modest lobbying activities. Campus organizing successes by competing groups (the AFT and, ironically, NEA) forced AAUP to pursue collective bargaining. Since the collective bargaining strategy was officially adopted in 1972, however, AAUP has suffered losses in membership, primarily due to more effective organization and representation by its rivals, dropouts among faculty at non–collective bargaining institutions, and the negative fallout of the U.S. Supreme Court's *Yeshiva* decision (discussed below). Many AAUP chapters continue to eschew collective bargaining. Nonetheless, AAUP has demonstrated moderate success by organizing faculty at 70 colleges and universities, including the University of Connecticut, University of Alaska, University of Rhode Island, the State University of New York campuses, and the University of New Hampshire, institutions generally viewed as more prestigious than those represented by NEA or AFT.

A large majority of the organized institutions (approximately 90 percent) are publicly supported colleges and universities. The predominance of faculty organization in public institutions results from the *Yeshiva* decision of the U.S. Supreme Court in 1980. The Court ruled that faculty at private colleges are "managers" under the National Labor Relations Act and therefore are not protected for collective bargaining purposes (*NLRB v. Yeshiva* 1980). *Yeshiva* has directly resulted in the denial of bargaining rights at some 80 institutions (Metchick and Singh 2004: 54). Management responsibility, according to the Court, is found in the faculty's "absolute authority over such matters as grading, teaching methods, graduation requirements, … student discipline, … academic calendars, and course schedules." *Yeshiva* thinking has not damaged unionization in state and locally supported institutions, and the ruling does not *require* a private academic institution to forgo faculty bargaining if it determines on its own that faculty, adjunct professors, and teaching assistants are not "managers" (Metchick and Singh 2004).

A number of theorists have attempted to explain the reasons for the rather abrupt reversal of scholars' historical aversion to unionism. Faculty in American higher education long valued a tradition of high social status and professional independence, two norms in deep conflict with the egalitarian and collective values associated with those occupations most given to unionization (Ladd and Lipset 1973: 2–4). Conditions changed rapidly in academe during the late 1960s and early 1970s, however. Low salaries became less acceptable, and threats to the sacrosanct tradition of academic tenure arose through reductions in force at some financially hard-pressed institutions. In addition, many higher education institutions underwent a metamorphosis in size and mission that stimulated faculty organization. For example, former teachers' colleges were upgraded to major state universities, with a concomitant change in the administration's research-related expectations for faculty. Other institutions had grown so large, so fast, that seemingly vast and unresponsive administrative bureaucracies had suddenly appeared. Such a strong degree of administrative centralization led many faculty members to seek a unified and collective voice of their own, particularly in the context of the social turmoil of the 1960s, much of which was concentrated on or around campuses (Ladd and Lipset 1973: 4). Finally, it should be noted that almost all organized college and university faculties are in states that are characterized by a legislative environment conducive to faculty unionization and collective bargaining. Rarely do faculty organize into unions in the absence of permissive legislation.

Interest remains in faculty unionization as state legislatures cut higher education funding and push colleges and universities toward a business model of operations run by administrators acting like corporate CEOs. A related development has been a drive for unionization and collective bargaining rights for part-time faculty and graduate teaching assistants, who engage in part-time teaching and research but are paid far less than regular faculty, and who enjoy few, if any, benefits (Singh, Zinni, and MacLennan, 2006). The first graduate student association to win recognition was at the University of Wisconsin (Madison) in 1969. Since then, graduate assistants have successfully organized at more than 26 other public campuses in California, Illinois, Indiana, Michigan, New York, and other states (Aronowitz 1998). Long-suffering graduate assistants have gone out on strike on several occasions at prestigious Yale University, protesting their low pay and poor benefits.

c. Protective Services

Among the most highly organized of municipal employees are the firefighters. A large majority belong to the International Association of Fire Fighters (IAFF), although AFSCME does represent a small number and various independent organizations speak for firefighters in some jurisdictions. With its roots in early social and benefits societies for firefighters, the IAFF was founded as an AFL affiliate in 1918. It has a highly decentralized structure with a small national headquarters and staff in Washington, D.C., which functions mainly to distribute information on salary, benefits, and other job-related topics to the locals, provide technical assistance for collective bargaining, and facilitate congressional lobbying activities. The IAFF locals have a high degree of autonomy in their activities and in their bargaining relationships with local governments. About 280,000 members were reported by the IAFF in 2007, including a growing number of emergency medical personnel.

Unlike the firefighters, police officers are represented by several national organizations. Some locals are affiliated with general-purpose unions AFSCME (whose first police affiliate was chartered in 1937 in Portsmouth, Virginia), SEIU, and the Teamsters, although their membership figures are relatively low. The principal police organizations are functionally defined. The International Union of Police Associations (IUPA), which is in essence an "association of associations," is affiliated with the AFL-CIO. The IUPA serves as a coordinating body for local, independent police associations. Its membership is heaviest in the southern states, Massachusetts, and New York.

The Fraternal Order of Police (FOP) is the oldest existing police organization, founded in 1915. Its 324,000 members are concentrated in the north-central and southern states. Other national organizations include the International Brotherhood of Police Officers (IBPO), created in 1964, which also represents correctional officers, EMTs, and paramedics; the small American Federation of Police (AFP); and the National Association of Police Organizations (NAPO), which is a coalition of police unions and associations that advances members' interests through political and legal advocacy and education. Founded in 1978, NAPO reported representing 2,000 unions and associations and more than 238,000 sworn officers in 2007.

d. Health Care

The nation's burgeoning health care industry presents an enticing organizing target for the unions. Nurses, technical employees, maintenance workers, clerical workers, and employees in nursing homes, assisted living facilities, clinics, and other health care facilities face uncertainties (e.g., facility mergers, privatization) and experience dissatisfaction (e.g., low wages, tough working conditions) that make unions look attractive. "Professional" health care employees in proprietary and nonprofit institutions were excluded from collective bargaining coverage until an amendment to the National Labor Relations Act in 1974 unleashed intense organizing activity by the American Nurses Association (ANA), AFT, United Nurses of America (UNA), SEIU, and other unions.

The UNA, an AFSCME affiliate, represents 60,000 nurses. SEIU, which has been concentrating on organizing hospital, nursing home, and health maintenance organization (HMO) chains, represents about 84,000 nurses. One of the oldest nurses' organizations is the California Nurses Association, which, together with the National Nurses Organizing Committee, records an estimated 75,000 members.

The health care sector represents a ripening fruit for organizing as the nation's population continues to age, with growing numbers of people entering nursing homes, long-term care facilities, and other health care institutions. Even physicians, looking for an antidote to the perceived intrusions of HMOs, managed care organizations, and insurance companies into doctors' pay and autonomy with patients, have been actively exploring union representation. In 1999, the American Medical Association voted to form a labor union on behalf of profoundly discontented practicing physicians. A key issue, however, is the status of private and nonprofit sector physicians under the National Labor Relations Act. Are they "employees" of HMOs, for instance, and therefore employees who may engage in collective bargaining? Or, like professors in private colleges and universities, are they "supervisors," who are excluded from National Labor Relations Act coverage? Eventually, this question may have to be resolved by the U.S. Supreme Court, which issued a ruling in 2001 implying that nurses are supervisors, and therefore lack collective bargaining rights, if they direct the activities of less-skilled workers (*NLRB v. Health Care and Retirement Corporation of America* 1994).

V. Prospects for Future Growth

When union strength is measured by the proportion of potential public and private sector members who actually belong to a union, the United States trails all other industrialized or "developed" countries. Union strength in the United States has declined significantly in the private sector since its 1954 peak and has dropped slightly in government since its peak in the mid-1980s. Union membership has also declined in most other industrialized countries since 1985, but labor remains politically strong, particularly in Germany, the Netherlands, and the Scandinavian countries. The membership losses appear to be the result of various forces, including reductions in the size of heavily organized public sectors, the shift to service and information-related employment in the private sector, and the expansion of the temporary and part-time ("contingent") work forces. There are no convincing indications that the declining fortunes of unions worldwide are poised for a reversal. Indeed, many of the same negative patterns for organized labor that have been observed in the United States appear to be present across the globe.

In the U.S. federal sector, downsizing initiatives continue to shrink membership numbers and financial resources of most federal unions, especially those that represent employees in the Department of Defense. A decision by the Bush administration (2000–2008) effectively stripped collective bargaining rights from several categories of federal workers (Thompson 2007: 108). Considering the modest incentives for joining a union and paying dues, the inability to negotiate compensation levels and many working conditions, negative public opinion toward unions, and the privatization movement, the forecast is for hard times ahead. It will take new, more permissive labor laws to boost the fortunes of federal employee unions, and such legislation is not evident in the foreseeable future.

In state and local government, the picture is mixed. The importance of state collective bargaining laws in encouraging unionization is illustrated by the leaps in membership following new legislation or gubernatorial executive orders in the 1980s and 1990s. Perhaps other states with restrictive labor policy environments will enact more permissive legislation in the next few years, but several factors militate against it. As in the case of the federal sector, most states and localities are operating within a context of limited government growth, potential taxpayer revolts, and a citizenry indifferent or even hostile toward public employees. Management resistance to state and local union demands has stiffened. Reductions in force have depleted union ranks in some jurisdictions. And Sunbelt states remain highly resistant to unionization.

Still, unlike in industry, no state or local employer has yet figured out a way to "bust" or decertify a union, short of terminating a public service or contracting it out. Unions will remain powerful political and economic forces in many state and local settings during the next decade, and fully deserving of study and understanding.

Chapter 3

The Legal Environment of Public Sector Labor Relations

I. Introduction

The legal basis for government labor relations and collective bargaining is a hodge-podge of statutes, ordinances, attorney general opinions, executive orders, and court decisions. The federal government does not have a single policy governing labor–management relations for all of its workers, and to say that state and local government labor policy varies widely is to be guilty of a gross understatement. Some states continue to prohibit collective bargaining in government, while in others, virtually all civil service employees are in a bargaining unit. Most states forbid public employees to strike, but some permit strikes under certain conditions. Such extreme labor relations diversity is in stark contrast to other industrialized nations, wherein a single, national collective bargaining law prevails for all public workers.

This chapter describes the legal environment of public sector labor relations in the federal, state, local, and nonprofit sectors, and introduces the major institutions and political actors that establish the legal context, including the president, Congress, federal and state courts, state and local legislative bodies, governors, attorneys general, and the public. After a brief examination of the right to form and join unions (which is shared by virtually all public employees in the United States), the federal context of labor relations is described, including the 1978 Civil Service Reform Act. The remainder of the chapter focuses on the state and local legal environments and authorization for unionization and collective bargaining.

II. The Right to Form and Join Unions

Before 1967, public employee assertions of the right to form and join unions were frequently met by words similar to those of Justice Holmes in the case of *McAuliffe v. City of New Bedford* (1892). Holmes allowed that whereas the petitioner in the case, a former policeman who had been fired for engaging in electoral activities, "may have a constitutional right to talk politics, ... he has no constitutional right to be a policeman, ... There are few employments for hire in which the servant does not agree to suspend his constitutional right of free speech. ... The servant cannot complain as he takes the employment on the terms which are offered him."

Although *McAuliffe* did not directly address the issue of freedom of association, the case was influential because it invited "judges to analyze governmental restrictions on public employees' First Amendment rights in a curious way; that is, as if public employees were different from everyone else; as if, with respect to public employees, government is especially empowered to restrict the political and civil rights the rest of us enjoy" (Wellington and Winter 1971: 70). In other words, government could condition employment on forfeiture of the employees' right to organize, thereby restricting application of the First Amendment right of association to workers in private employment. Holmes' line of reasoning was cited as late as 1963 by the Supreme Court of Michigan in the case of *AFSCME Local 201 v. City of Muskegon* (1963), upholding the constitutionality of a regulation issued by Muskegon's chief of police that prohibited labor unions.

Denial of the right of government workers to form and join unions was buttressed by the sovereignty doctrine. A sovereign government, the argument goes, has the power to fix through law the terms and conditions of government work. This power is unilateral, and it cannot be given away or shared through negotiations with a public employee organization. But the counterpoint to the sovereignty argument is a strong one. As noted by Wellington and Winter (1971: 71–73), the right of Americans to join together freely in what constitutional framer James Madison called "factions" has long been recognized as characterizing a free society and constituting a necessary safeguard against a tyranny of the majority:

> Organizations based on mutual economic interests, such as trade associations or labor unions, are paradigms of associations, factions, or as they are usually called today — interest groups. Such groups are absolutely necessary to the survival of political democracy in the United States. They are the means by which individuals make claims upon government; thus they are important to the structure of our federal system

… . [T]he point is that unless individuals can freely band together to advocate whatever they please, we shall not have democracy.

These arguments are interesting in their own right, but what is important is how they have been applied by the federal arbiters of constitutional disputes — the courts. Since 1967, the federal courts have held that the First Amendment's freedom of association clause outweighs government sovereignty claims. The first in a long line of cases was *Keyeshian v. Board of Regents* (1967), in which the U.S. Supreme Court ruled that public employment could not be predicated on relinquishing the right of free association. Other important decisions include *Atkins v. City of Charlotte* (1969), in which a U.S. District Court invalidated a North Carolina state law, which prohibited law enforcement personnel and firefighters from joining or being members of labor organizations, because it violated the right of association and the Fourteenth Amendment's equal protection clause; and *Letter Carriers v. Blount* (1969), a case in which a federal district court found that a federal statute and oath intended to prevent postal workers from asserting the right to strike, and from joining any organization claiming the right to strike, violated the First Amendment.

The landmark case supporting the right of public employees to organize and join unions, however, is *McLaughlin v. Tilendis* (1967). In this case, one Cook County, Illinois, teacher was dismissed and another one's contract was not renewed because of their alleged association with the local chapter of the American Federation of Teachers. The Seventh Circuit of the U.S. Court of Appeals held that these actions violated the employees' right of free association and that they unjustly interfered with the employees' right to due process under the Fourteenth Amendment. The court concluded that "unless there is some illegal intent, an individual's right to form and join a union is protected by the First Amendment." He or she cannot be disciplined or dismissed for joining a union or advocating that others join.

Today, then, the constitutional right of public employees to organize and join unions is protected by the courts. The sovereignty-based "doctrine of privilege," which granted public employees few rights vis-à-vis their employer, has been discarded by the courts. It is now accepted that public employees also have the rights (1) to engage in protected political activities and (2) to receive due process through a written statement of reasons for dismissal and/or a formal hearing (*Cleveland Board of Education v. Loudermill* 1985). In public employee–employer relations generally, the U.S. Supreme Court's reasoning in *Pickering v. Board of Education* (1968) prevails: the state's interest in restricting public employees' First and Fourteenth Amendment rights must be significantly greater than its interests in limiting similar rights for members of the general public. In this respect, public employees enjoy greater constitutional protection than private sector workers.

However, the courts have held that public workers have no constitutional right to force their employers to bargain collectively, unless there is legislation that mandates bargaining *(Smith v. Arkansas State Highway Commission Employees Local 1315*

1979). In *Indianapolis Education Association v. Lewallen* (1969), the same Seventh Circuit Court ruled shortly after *McLaughlin* that "There is no constitutional duty to bargain collectively with an exclusive bargaining agent. Such duty when imposed is imposed by statute." However, nothing prevents a public employer from voluntarily engaging in collective bargaining in the absence of enabling legislation.

Private sector labor relations and collective bargaining are governed by the Railway Labor Act of 1926 and the National Labor Relations Act of 1935 (also known as the Wagner Act), as amended by the Labor Management Relations Act of 1947 (the Taft-Hartley Act) and the Labor Management Reporting and Disclosure Act of 1959 (the Landrum-Griffin Act). In the Railway Labor Act (RLA), Congress sought to establish labor–management peace in the railroad industry by requiring firms to negotiate with bargaining representatives selected by railroad employees. The RLA was extended to the airline industry in 1936. Under the National Labor Relations Act (NLRA), which provides coverage to all other private sector workers, labor policy is administered by the National Labor Relations Board, which investigates and adjudicates allegations of unfair labor practices and administers matters concerning the composition of the employee bargaining unit and selection of the union to represent the bargaining unit. Since passage of the Wagner Act, official national policy has been to encourage private sector workers to form and join unions and engage in collective bargaining with their employers. Taft-Hartley balances the Wagner Act by imposing certain restrictions on union procedures and conduct, such as prohibiting compulsory union membership. Landrum-Griffin requires unions to meet various internal operating standards, such as guaranteeing their members' rights of free association and speech, maintaining certain financial records, and accounting for expenditures.

The NLRA specifically exempts public employees. Section 2(2) of the Taft-Hartley amendment to the NLRA states that "The term 'employee' includes any person acting as an agent of an employer, directly or indirectly, but *shall not include* [emphasis added] any state or political subdivision thereof." It also excludes agricultural workers, independent contractors, supervisors, managerial employees, small businesses employees, and domestic workers.

III. Labor Relations in Federal Employment: The Legal Basis

Although employee organizations have existed in federal employment since the 1830s, it was 1960 before any union was formally recognized by a federal employer (with the exceptions of the Tennessee Valley Authority, Bonneville Power Administration, and a handful of other quasi-governmental organizations). Furthermore, no statutory basis existed for federal employee collective bargaining before passage of the Civil Service Reform Act of 1978.

The Pendleton Act of 1883 established the federal merit system and gave Congress the authority to regulate the wages, hours, and working conditions of federal workers. It did not grant a collective voice for employees. As workers began to organize extensively anyway, two presidents (Theodore Roosevelt in 1902 and William Howard Taft in 1906) felt obliged to issue executive orders to preclude employee organizations from collectively lobbying Congress for improved wages, working conditions, or other matters, upon threat of dismissal. These "gag rules" stifled federal union activity until 1912, when passage of the Lloyd-LaFollette Act guaranteed federal workers the right to petition Congress and to join labor organizations, as long as those organizations prohibited strikes against the federal government. As a result, federal employees were permitted to lobby members of Congress for pay increases and improved benefits and working conditions. Employer–employee relationships, however, continued to be determined unilaterally by management.

As private sector unions received statutory permission for collective bargaining under the 1935 National Labor Relations Act (Wagner Act) and the Railway Labor Act, public employee organizations continued to be ignored. The only mention of public unions in the 1947 Taft-Hartley Act was Section 305's prohibition of federal employee strike activity. Thereafter, federal employees attempted to gain statutory recognition for their organizations through support of the Rhodes-Johnson bill, which failed repeatedly in Congress from 1949 to 1961. This proposed legislation would have required federal agencies to meet and confer with employee representatives and established an arbitration board to resolve federal labor disputes. Finally, recognition was won indirectly in the administration of President John F. Kennedy. Kennedy, who was strongly supported by organized labor throughout his campaign, appointed a presidential task force headed by Secretary of Labor Arthur Goldberg to recommend a labor–management relations program for the federal service. The task force's recommendations later were embodied in President Kennedy's Executive Order 10988, which became the foundation of federal employee labor relations.

A. The Executive Orders

Executive Order 10988 of 1962 established for the first time the principle that federal workers have the right to form and join unions and bargain collectively. It proved to be of tremendous importance in public sector labor relations, stimulating employee organization and collective bargaining at all levels of government. Within 2 years 730,000 employees were covered by collective bargaining agreements (Blum and Helburn 1997). Although many of the provisions of Executive Order 10988 (E.O. 10988) were supplanted by subsequent executive orders and provisions of the Civil Service Reform Act of 1978, it is useful to consider the labor relations framework it established.

The order covered almost all federal workers with the exception of the uniformed military, FBI, CIA, and others whose work involved security needs. Three forms of recognition for labor organizations were provided: informal recognition was granted to any organization that could demonstrate it represented a minimum number of employees; formal recognition was gained when the organization could claim at least 10 percent of the workers in a proposed bargaining unit as members; and exclusive recognition, the only form of recognition allowed under present federal policy, was awarded to an organization that gained the support of a majority of a unit's employees. Exclusive recognition meant that the designated union had the right to meet and confer with agency management over personnel policies and practices and working conditions affecting all members of the bargaining unit represented by the union. Determination of the bargaining unit was based on the NLRA model of an identifiable "community of interest" among employees. Managers and supervisors were excluded from exclusive bargaining units.

E.O. 10988 established a code of Fair Labor Practices to regulate the interactions between unions and management. The code, essentially consistent with the provisions in the NLRA, stipulated various unfair labor practices by both unions and federal agencies and listed procedures for hearing complaints. (Examples of unfair labor practices are coercion of employees, discrimination, and "bad faith bargaining.") Certain management rights enumerated in E.O. 10988 remain important today and continue to be in effect in most federal collective bargaining contracts:

To direct employees of the agency

To hire, promote, transfer, assign, and retain employees in positions within the agency, and to suspend, demote, discharge, or take disciplinary action

To relieve employees from duties because of lack of work or for other legitimate reasons

To maintain the efficiency of government operations entrusted to them

To determine the methods, means, and personnel by which such operations are to be conducted

To take whatever actions may be necessary to carry out the mission of the agency in situations of emergency

E.O. 10988 served as the basic legal framework for federal labor relations for approximately 7 years, but dissatisfaction arose from a variety of sources, particularly the unions. From their perspective, the executive order did not go far enough. The scope of bargaining was severely restricted by the management rights' clause and by prohibitions on bargaining over wages, benefits, and union security provisions. Furthermore, although the strike was forbidden, no substitute for the strike had been provided, and final authority for implementation and administration of the executive order, including the arbitration of grievances, remained with the respective federal department and agency heads. The scales were clearly tilted in favor of management.

President Richard Nixon's Executive Order 11491 of October 1969 was intended to alleviate these and other deficiencies. The deficiencies had been officially identified by two presidential committees: one appointed by President Lyndon Johnson (whose recommendations were not acted upon by a president awash in more pressing issues, including the war in Viet Nam) and the other by a Nixon-appointed review committee headed by Secretary of Labor George P. Schultz. The Schultz Committee advised six major policy changes (Fox and Shelton 1972: 118), most of which were adopted in E.O. 11491 of 1969. A Federal Labor Relations Council (FLRC) composed of the chairman of the Civil Service Commission, the Secretary of Labor, and one or more presidential designees was named to administer and interpret the new executive order, decode major labor policy issues, and hear appeals resulting from decisions rendered by the new Assistant Secretary for Labor–Management Relations (ASLMR). The ASLMR's duties included resolving unit determination and representation disputes, supervising and certifying elections, and hearing unfair labor practice allegations and other alleged violations of labor relations procedures and standards.

E.O.11491 abolished the unwieldy formal and informal types of recognition, retaining only exclusive recognition. The nonbargaining status of supervisors remained unchanged, but the scope of bargaining, contrary to union aspirations, was restricted even further. In addition, financial disclosure and reporting requirements similar to those set forth for private unions under the Landrum-Griffin Act were imposed on federal unions.

Major changes were made in procedures for resolving bargaining impasses and grievance disputes. Binding grievance arbitration was authorized as negotiable for the first time. To resolve impasses, two new entities were created: the Federal Mediation and Conciliation Service (FMCS) to mediate labor disputes and the Federal Service Impasses Panel (FSIP) to settle impasses or recommend impasse resolution procedures to the parties involved. Thus, a third party could now overrule agency heads and resolve impasses over contract negotiations and grievances.

Nixon amended E.O.11491 with Executive Order 11616 of 1971, which, among relatively minor changes, made mandatory the use of the negotiated grievance procedure for settling contract disputes. Further amendments to E.O.11491 were issued in 1975 by President Gerald Ford. The final document in this chain of presidential directives, Executive Order 11838, marginally broadened the scope of bargaining, encouraged the consolidation of small bargaining units, defined "supervisor" more specifically, and implemented minor procedural changes.

Thus, the early legal basis of federal labor–management relations was determined incrementally through a series of executive orders, rather than through statute. Even though executive orders have the effect of law, their provisions are easier to modify or abolish than provisions written into statute. Any subsequent president, or Congress, may take action to rescind or alter an executive order, whereas legislation can be modified or abolished only through formal congressional action. Not surprisingly, insecure federal employees continued to lobby for a statutory guarantee for labor–management relations. Their demands were embodied, at least in part, in the Civil Service Reform Act of 1978.

B. The Civil Service Reform Act of 1978

Passage of the Civil Service Reform Act (CSRA) was one of the few significant legislative victories for the administration of President Jimmy Carter, despite the fact that many scholars and practitioners regard it today as a well-meaning failure at best. There is no doubt that the CSRA was the most important piece of legislation regarding federal employment since the Pendleton Act nearly 100 years earlier.

The Reform Act proceeded quickly and relatively unhindered through the congressional process. Its rapid progress may be attributed to a number of factors, the most important being the strong support of the president, the influential leadership of Civil Service Commission Chairman Allan (Scotty) Campbell, widespread support among career civil servants, and the reform-mindedness of a post-Watergate Congress. Furthermore, Title VII of the CSRA, the chapter on federal labor–management relations, was endorsed, with some reservations, by the AFL-CIO and the largest federal employee union, the American Federation of Government Employees (AFGE). Although the National Treasury Employees Union (NTEU) and the National Federation of Federal Employees opposed the measure, mainly because they felt the scope of bargaining continued to be too narrow, their resistance did not stop passage of the legislation.

Federal employee labor rights were placed into statute by Title VII of the CSRA, the Federal Service Labor–Management Relations Statute (FSLMS). The act also created the Federal Labor Relations Authority (FLRA) to administer the labor relations program and established the Office of Labor–Management Relations within the U.S. Office of Personnel Management. The Office of Labor–Management Relations provides technical advice to federal agencies on labor policies, leadership, and contract administration.

Under the CSRA, employees enjoy "the right to form, join or assist any labor organization, or to refrain from any such activity, freely and without fear of reprisal, and each employee shall be protected in the exercise of such rights," including the right to present a labor organization's views to agency heads and other officials in the executive branch, and the right to "engage in collective bargaining with respect to conditions of employment. ..." Conditions of employment are defined as "personnel policies, practices, and matters, whether established by rule, regulation, or otherwise, affecting working conditions." Excluded from the scope of negotiable issues are wages and benefits, prohibited political activities, union security arrangements, and position classification. Thus, the scope of bargaining for federal employees, in essence, remained unchanged. The severely circumscribed scope of bargaining continues to be a topic of controversy and profound union discontent. President Clinton's Executive Order 12871 of 1993 expanded the mandatory federal scope of bargaining to embrace previously permissible topics, including the numbers, types, and grades of employees and positions as well as the technology, methods, and means of performing work. Clinton's executive order was revoked by President George W. Bush in 2001.

An important provision of Title VII expanded the scope of grievance activities. Under Title VII, all federal labor agreements must include negotiated grievance procedures, with binding arbitration as the final step. Previously, grievance arbitration was optional. Other sections of Title VII recognize the right of federal workers to engage in informational picketing, authorize official or "union" time for union representation, and allow the checkoff of dues at no cost to the employee or to the union.

CSRA's Title VII covers most federal employees except for supervisory personnel, members of the armed forces, foreign service employees, and workers in the Government Accounting Office, FBI, CIA, National Security Agency, Tennessee Valley Authority (TVA), U.S. Postal Service, and certain other exemptions, as described in the section below. Employees of the TVA, a government corporation, bargain collectively under the 1935 "Employment Relationship Policy," created as part of the New Deal legislation of Franklin D. Roosevelt. Postal workers, as a result of a settlement with the Nixon administration following a 1970 postal strike involving 200,000 employees, gained bargaining rights through the Postal Reorganization Act of 1970, which removed them from the authority of the executive orders and granted full NLRA collective bargaining rights with the exception of the right to strike and union security provisions. Armed forces personnel are prohibited from collective bargaining and engaging in other union activities such as strikes and picketing by a Secretary of Defense directive of October 5, 1977. GAO, FBI, CIA, and NSA personnel have no legal authority for collective bargaining.

C. Recent Exceptions from CSRA Coverage

As noted, President Clinton's Executive Order 12871 modestly expanded the scope of bargaining under Title VII. Most importantly, it directed federal agencies to develop "partnerships" with the unions representing their workers. Through collaboration and cooperation, labor–management partnerships resulted in improvements in customer services, technology, the quality of work life, and the overall quality of labor–management relations over the span of about 7 years (Masters 2001; Thompson 2007).

Upon assuming office in January 2001, the decidedly anti-union President Bush immediately rescinded Clinton's executive order and dissolved the existing partnerships. He also set about revoking the bargaining rights of certain employees in the Department of Justice and elsewhere. Following the terrorist attacks of September 11, 2001, the Bush administration sought and won congressional approval of a new department, the Department of Homeland Security (DHS). Twenty-two existing agencies with some 175,000 employees, including FEMA, the Coast Guard, immigration and customs enforcement, border and transportation security, and other entities, were consolidated in the new department.

After a vicious battle with the unions and congressional Democrats, Bush won authority to waive collective bargaining rights for designated DHS employees on the grounds of national security (Masters and Albright 2003). Transportation

Security Administration (TSA) baggage screeners were the first to be designated. For other DHS employees, the scope of bargaining was narrowed and management authority was expanded. DHS managerial discretion over pay, discipline, and other personnel matters was enlarged. Collective bargaining disputes would no longer be addressed by the FLRA, but instead by a new DHS labor relations board. The new DHS human resource management system also restricted Merit Systems Protection Board (MSPB) review authority for adverse actions against employees and created a new pay banding system to replace the longstanding general schedule pay system.

Federal unions, led by NTEU and AFGE, filed suit against the new rules on grounds that the Bush administration had exceeded the authority granted to it by congressional legislation establishing DHS. A federal district court ruled in favor of the unions in 2005 (*NTEU v. Michael Chertoff*). The district court decision was basically upheld by the U.S. Court of Appeals for the D.C. Circuit in 2006, but many important questions remained unanswered and the rules were permitted to go forward. Finally, in October 2007, collaboration between the Office of Personnel Management and MSPB led to implementation of the new rules for nonunion personnel in DHS. Decisions concerning the 50,000 DHS employees covered by collective bargaining agreements await the next round of bargaining (Barr 2007).

Similar murkiness has occluded the implications of 2003 congressional approval of a new human resource management system for the Department of Defense (DoD). DoD's new National Security Personnel System was approved and final regulations were issued in 2005. Like the contested DHS changes, the DoD human resource management system reduced the scope of bargaining, established a new agency-specific labor relations board, expedited disciplinary and dismissal processing, and implemented a pay banding scheme (Thompson 2007: 111). Upon appeal by the unions, a federal district court enjoined implementation of the DoD rules in 2006. Congress restored bargaining rights and other personnel provisions for DoD workers in late 2007 (Barr 2007).

D. The FLRA

The FLRA is a three-member bipartisan entity charged with integrating all labor relations administrative functions previously divided among the FLRC, the ASLMR, the FSIP, the FMCS, and executive agencies. The terms run for 5 years, staggered by 2-year intervals.

The FLRA is intended to serve as the final authority in federal labor relations matters, but judicial review of most authority rulings by the U.S. Court of Appeals is permitted. Specific functions of the FLRA are very similar to those of the private sector National Labor Relations Board (NLRB). They include: (1) determining bargaining units, (2) supervising and conducting union elections, (3) resolving allegations of unfair labor practices (this constitutes the bulk of its activities), (4) resolving exceptions to arbitrators' awards, and (5) deciding issues concerning what is negotiable between labor and management. The FLRA is served by a General

Counsel — appointed by the president to investigate unfair labor practice allegations and to serve as prosecutor in such cases — and a number of administrative law judges. The FSIP and FMCS remain ongoing organizations within the FLRA, continuing their original executive-order functions of resolving federal impasses. The FMCS has also broadened its mission to include preventive mediation and alternative dispute resolution.

In its primary role as the principal adjudicatory body for federal labor–management relations, the poorly regarded FLRA has come under heavy criticism from the courts, the unions, and management. It has frustrated all parties "for its inconsistencies and the illogic of its decisions," which "encourages unions and agencies to seek judicial resolution" (Rosenbloom 1989). The FLRA provides four alternative dispute resolution paths, creating needless confusion and redundancy and often ultimately resulting in court review. The length of dispute resolution is measured in years rather than months — not exactly a morale booster for either employees or management.

The CSRA altered little in the basic federal labor relations framework, essentially placing into code what had been originally created through executive orders. The CSRA has been subjected to much criticism from many different quarters. Title VII has received special opprobrium from the unions. To all interested parties, parts of the legislation are ambiguous. According to the union perspective, the FLRA is biased and ponderously slow. Union security restrictions depress membership and free-rider problems abound. The narrow scope of nonpostal bargaining, particularly the exclusion of wages and benefits from negotiations, left little for the unions to bring to the bargaining table. Left with filing grievances as one of the few tactics available to them, unions were pressured by dissatisfied members. Taken together, the weaknesses of Title VII promoted "fierce disagreement and hostile litigation" (Tobias 1998: 263) and marginalized human resource managers. Then, President George W. Bush, with the support of a Republican majority in both houses of Congress, heaped further indignities on the federal unions by exempting DoD and DHS from even the weak collective bargaining requirements of CSRA.

IV. The Legal Basis of Labor Relations in State and Local Government

The legal framework for federal employee unionization and collective bargaining is slightly fragmented, with the great majority of workers covered under two statutes: the Civil Service Reform Act and the Postal Reorganization Act. DoD and DHS employees' status remains uncertain. But the legal basis for state and local government labor relations is a Byzantine web of myriad statutes, ordinances, court decisions, executive orders, attorney general opinions, and other policy articulations. If ever the state and local governments have served as political laboratories, it is in public sector labor relations. The advantages of diversity are many. But there are important disadvantages of legal fragmentation for governments and their workers, too.

Since the mid-1970s there has been recurring public debate on national labor legislation for state and local government employees, which would force a substantial amount of standardization in the legal environment of labor relations. Occasionally it appears that national legislation stands a reasonably good chance of passage. After briefly considering the pros and cons of a national law for state and local collective bargaining and the possibilities of adoption of the idea in the future, we examine in detail the diffusion and general characteristics of state and local collective bargaining policies today.

A. Federal Legislation for State and Local Government

A number of bills have been introduced in Congress with the intent of federally regulating state and local government labor relations. Three basic approaches have been represented in the proposed legislation. One seeks to amend the National Labor Relations Act to cover some, or all, state and local government employees. The reasoning behind this approach is that the public employees should have labor rights identical to those enjoyed by private sector workers. Accordingly, jurisdiction of the NLRB would be extended to cover nonfederal public employee collective bargaining, thereby preempting existing state and local government policies.

Another approach to federal legislation would create a new federal labor authority to cover state and local government bargaining: in other words, an NLRB or FLRA for state and local employees. The act would be administered by a National Public Employment Relations Commission, much like the NLRB. This proposal receives strong union support and would supersede all existing state and local bargaining laws and any other inconsistent statutes.

The third approach to a federal statute envisions a state–federal partnership, with the federal government setting minimum standards for labor relations and collective bargaining and ensuring conformity through the federal power of the purse, much as federal highway requirements and the mandatory 21-year legal drinking age were implemented. This "minimum standards" approach avoids complete federal preemption of labor relations while permitting a measure of continued state and local experimentation. States already conforming to the federal standards would have authority to administer their own programs without federal interference.

Proponents of the various bills have argued that federal legislation would decrease the incidence of strikes by (1) making union recognition mandatory, thereby eliminating the need for recognition strikes, and (2) stipulating impasse procedures designed to preclude the strike. Proponents further contend that federal legislation would provide equal treatment for all state and local government employees in the United States. Labor relations uniformity would, as an added benefit, enable a common national approach to training all labor relations participants, thereby enhancing the overall quality of labor–management relations.

Opponents of the proposals fail to see the alleged advantages of uniformity. "In the case of public employee unionism," argued Wellington and Winter (1971: 53, 54), "uniformity is most undesirable and diversity in rules and structure virtually a necessity." Regulation by the states "provides a more flexible approach than national legislation." State officials are likely to be more sensitive to problems of local government than federal officials, and legislation that proves inappropriate can be modified more easily at the state level than at the national. Other critics (see Nigro 1976) contend that any form of federal regulation would violate the autonomy of state and local governments and, furthermore, that there is no "one best way" to regulate public employee unionization and collective bargaining. None of the proposals has managed to make the transition from policy agenda to statute. A congressional bill that would have extended collective bargaining rights to public safety employees in state and local government passed the House but prospects for Senate passage were deflated when the prime sponsor, Senate Edward Kennedy, was diagnosed with cancer.

Because public employees do not hold a constitutional right to engage in collective bargaining, employers are not required to grant such a right unless specified by state law or local ordinance. Although the U.S. Supreme Court's view on congressional authority has vacillated during the past three decades, a federal collective bargaining act would conceivably be ruled unconstitutional on Eleventh or Fourteenth Amendment grounds (T. Clark Jr. and Powers 2003).

Although national bargaining legislation remains high on the wish list of the unions and will be debated in the future, congressional action is uncertain. Organized labor's political influence in Congress is weak; a presidential veto might be forthcoming, and the record now shows that the decentralized approach to state and local labor relations has functioned reasonably well. Other national laws may be enacted that influence labor relations at the margins (see Table 3.1), but an all-embracing policy change stands a slight chance at present.

B. State and Local Government Policies

Today more than 110 separate statutes govern public sector labor relations, augmented by numerous local ordinances, court decisions, attorney general opinions, and executive orders. These policies exhibit considerable divergence. State legislation, for instance, ranges from a single comprehensive statute providing coverage for all public employees in Iowa, to coverage of only firefighters in Wyoming, to the total prohibition of collective bargaining in North Carolina. In other states, public employees bargain under the authority of an attorney general's opinion (North Dakota), executive order (Colorado), or civil service regulations (Michigan state employees).

The earliest legislation regulating state and local government employer–employee relationships sought to abolish strikes by public workers. Shortly after World War II, eight states enacted no-strike laws with stiff penalties for violators. In other states, beginning in 1951, laws were passed that established the right of public

Table 3.1   Major Federal Laws Affecting Public Sector Labor Relations

Legislation	Subject Matter
Civil Rights Act of 1964	Prohibited employer discrimination on the basis of race, color, gender, religion, or national origin
Equal Employment Opportunity Act of 1972	Extended Civil Rights Act of 1964 requirements to public employers and extended the enforcement powers of Equal Employment Opportunity Commission
Age Discrimination in Employment Act (1967)	Prohibited discrimination by the employer against employees aged 40 to 70 years
Occupational Safety and Health Act (1970)	Prescribed health- and safety-related working conditions
Employee Retirement Income Security Act (1974)	Addressed pensions, health care, disability, and accident plans
Urban Mass Transportation Act (1964)	Required that interests of employees, including collective bargaining rights, be protected when ownership transit system change
Social Security Act of 1935	Stipulated personnel policies for state and local workers paid in whole or in part with federal grant dollars
Fair Labor Standards Act (as amended)	Applied federal wage and hour laws to state and local governments
Americans with Disabilities Act (1990)	Caused changes in personnel policies for mentally and physically disabled workers
Civil Rights Act of 1991	Reversed and altered 12 U.S. Supreme Court decisions that had narrowed civil rights protections
Family and Medical Leave Act (1993)	Ensured that leave is available to employees for authorized medical reasons and for compelling family reasons

workers to join employee organizations and provided a limited degree of support for developing bilateral relations between some government jurisdictions and their workers. In addition, several local governments passed ordinances or issued executive orders regulating collective bargaining. As Schneider (1988: 197) observed,

"The stand that any form of bargaining in the public sector was impossible was crumbling in the face of experience and political expediency." Finally, in 1959, Wisconsin broke out of the state legislative limbo with a law establishing collective bargaining rights for local government employees. Today, legislation or other policies imposing a duty to bargain or meet and confer with at least one group of public workers are in effect in 43 states.

Most of the bargaining laws were enacted over a period of about 10 years, from the mid-1960s through the mid-1970s. A variety of important decisions had to be faced by the state lawmakers, including (1) whether each jurisdiction within the state should be permitted to establish its own labor relations policy or all should conform to a single policy applied uniformly; (2) whether one comprehensive law should apply to both levels of government and all occupational functions or separate policies be established for state and local government and for each functional category; (3) who should administer the policy; and (4) what labor relations principles and procedures should be adopted. Legislative outcomes were hammered out in fierce battles fought between public employee unions, public employers, and numerous interest groups. Since the mid-1970s, most legislative activity has focused on refining existing policy rather than enacting new legislation. Only four states have passed major collective bargaining laws since the 1970s — Ohio, Illinois, New Mexico, and Washington — although others have implemented collective bargaining through executive orders, court decisions, and local ordnances. Table 3.2 shows the legal framework for collective bargaining in 2007.

The large percentage of states with labor relations policies reflects a realization of the need to develop a formal framework to direct bilateral relationships between public workers and their employers. Clearly, many variations in policies exist, but the trend has been to extend comprehensive coverage to all state and local government workers. Thirty-one states and the District of Columbia currently provide bargaining coverage by statute for all major employee groups, with either a single comprehensive public employee relations policy or separate policies for different functions. Thirteen states regulate employer–employee negotiations in one to four occupational categories, and seven states do not have public policies permitting bargaining for any group (see Table 3.2).

As noted in Chapter 2, bargaining laws are both a product of public employee unionization and a stimulant of unionization. This reciprocal relationship has been both observed and validated in the scholarly literature (Waters et al. 1994; Farber 1987). Specifically, politically influential public sector unions have spurred enactment of bargaining legislation in the states, and newly passed collective bargaining laws have been associated with the growth of union membership. This relationship is evident in Washington in its recent enactment of collective bargaining for state employees.

Bargaining laws are the single most important factor in determining the nature and temperament of public employer–employee relationships in state and local government. The states with comprehensive bargaining laws tend to share certain traits and experiences. Generally, they are industrialized, urbanized, relatively affluent

Table 3.2 State Bargaining Status, 2007

(X: Collective Bargaining Provisions; Y: Meet and Confer Provisions)					
State	State	Local	Police	Firefighters	K-12 Teachers
Alabama	—	Y	—	Y	—
Alaska	X	X	X	X	X
Arizona	—	—	—	—	—
Arkansas	—	—	—	—	—
California	Y	Y[1]	Y[1]	Y[1]	X
Colorado	X[3]	—	—	—	—
Connecticut	X	X	X	X	X
Delaware	X	X[1]	X	X	X
Florida	X	X[1]	X	X	X
Georgia	—	—	—	X	—
Hawaii	X	X	X	X	X
Idaho	—	—	—	X	X
Illinois	X	X	X	X	X
Indiana	—	—	—	—	X
Iowa	X	X	X	X	X
Kansas	Y	Y[1]	Y[1]	Y[1]	X
Kentucky	—	—	X	X	—
Louisiana	—	—	—	—	—
Maine	X	X	X	X	X
Maryland	X	X[2]	—	—	X
Massachusetts	X	X	X	X	X
Michigan	X	X	X	X	X
Minnesota	X	X	X	X	X

Table 3.2   State Bargaining Status, 2007 (Continued)

(X: Collective Bargaining Provisions; Y: Meet and Confer Provisions)					
State	*State*	*Local*	*Police*	*Firefighters*	*K-12 Teachers*
Mississippi	—	—	—	—	—
Missouri	X[4]	X	X	X	X
Montana	X	X	X	X	X
Nebraska	X	X	X	X	Y
Nevada	—	X	X	X	X
New Hampshire	X	X	X	X	X
New Jersey	X	X	X	X	X
New Mexico	X[3]	X	X	X	X
New York	X	X	X	X	X
North Carolina	—	—	—	—	—
North Dakota	Y[2]	Y[2]	Y[2]	Y[2]	X
Ohio	X	X	X	X	X
Oklahoma	—	X	X	X	X
Oregon	X	X[1]	X	X	X
Pennsylvania	X	X	X	X	X
Rhode Island	X	X	X	X	X
South Carolina	—	—	—	—	—
South Dakota	X	X	X	X	X
Tennessee	—	—	—	—	X
Texas	—	—	X[1]	X[1]	—
Utah	—	—	—	—	X
Vermont	X	X	X	X	X
Virginia	—	—	—	—	—

Table 3.2   State Bargaining Status, 2007 (Continued)

(X: Collective Bargaining Provisions; Y: Meet and Confer Provisions)					
State	*State*	*Local*	*Police*	*Firefighters*	*K-12 Teachers*
Washington	X	X	X	X	X
West Virginia	Y[2]	Y[2]	Y[2]	Y[2]	Y[2]
Wisconsin	X	X	X	X	X
Wyoming	—	—	—	X	—

[1] Local opinion permitted.
[2] Meet and confer established by attorney general opinion.
[3] Collective bargaining established through executive order
[4] Court ordered collective bargaining
Source: Compiled from various sources including Lund and Maranto 1996.

states of the Frostbelt. Many of them have traditionally been policy innovators. Strong private sector unionization (indicating pro-union sentiment) is associated with comprehensive public sector bargaining policy, and so is the alignment of the political stars — most of the comprehensive statutes were enacted by liberal Democratic majorities in the state legislatures and signed by a Democratic governor (see Hundley 1988: 302–303; Saltzman 1985). In Ohio, comprehensive bargaining bills passed the legislature in two consecutive sessions, only to be vetoed by Republican Governor James Rhodes. The third time was the charm, when newly elected Democratic Governor Richard Celeste signed the bill in 1983. It took 14 years of legislative struggle and a new Democratic governor for Washington state employees to win full collective bargaining rights in 2002.

C. States without Collective Bargaining Policies

Six of the eight states that do not formally permit collective bargaining are situated in the South: Arkansas, Louisiana, Mississippi, North Carolina, South Carolina, and Virginia (see Figure 3.1). The other two (Arizona and Colorado) are in the West. North Carolina and Virginia are formally on the legislative record as hostile to collective bargaining — both have passed laws that prohibit it. Nonetheless, "informal bargaining" occurs regularly in some North Carolina school districts and local governments (Rhodes and Brown 1992) and strikes have occurred in Virginia.

Arizona and Arkansas have established some semblance of labor relations policy through attorney general opinions. Dues checkoff is allowed in both states and a scope of bargaining is denoted. However, no policies providing for bargaining have been adopted for any group of employees in either state. This would appear to be

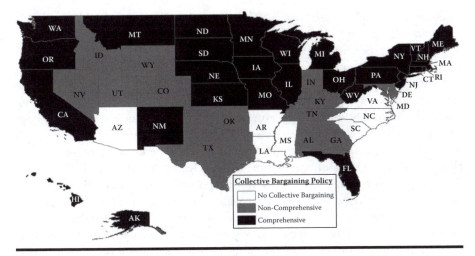

Figure 3.1   Collective bargaining policy in the states.

reason enough to categorically distinguish these two states from West Virginia, where attorney general opinions permit the right to join a union and provide for exclusive representation, impasse procedures, and meet and confer procedures with respect to wages, hours, and working conditions.

As mentioned at the beginning of this chapter, public employees in these and all other states enjoy the right to form and join unions. They also have the right to petition their employers as individuals or through an organization, but there is no concomitant obligation on the part of the government employer to meet with the organization, engage in collective bargaining, or even withhold organizational dues from paychecks. However, if the public employer voluntarily elects to conduct negotiations with a union in the absence of enabling legislation, the courts generally have upheld the bargaining relationship, with at least one exception. In the case of *Virginia v. Arlington County Board of Education* (1977), the Virginia Supreme Court unanimously ruled that public employers in that state had no authority to recognize a union or negotiate and enter into a binding agreement without express statutory authority. (At the time of the decision, about 30,000 local government workers were under collective bargaining contracts, which immediately became void.)

When a service changes from private ownership to public ownership, an interesting problem arises in those states that deny negotiating rights for public employees. Just such a situation developed in several instances involving local government takeovers of private transit systems. Prior to the transfer of ownership, of course, collective bargaining agreements are administered under the authority of the NLRA. Upon change in ownership, however, private sector policies no longer apply. The new transit authority must retain the existing contractual arrangements with the union under Article 13(c) of the Urban Mass Transportation Act of 1964, which states that "workers and unions will lose no rights as the result of public takeovers financed by federal funds." The implications for the new public owner are quite clear, but possibly disturbing.

Without a preexisting legal framework to guide labor relations, the city, county, or special-purpose government may find itself in the midst of a dilemma. One rather imaginative solution is the "Memphis Formula," which was developed in that city prior to the passage of Tennessee's 1971 bargaining law for transit employees. Under the Memphis Formula, government owners of a transit system contract out transit activities to a management services firm, which bargains collectively with the union. The management firm thus serves as the bargaining agent for the local government under the authority of the NLRA (Oestreich and Whaley 2001).

Of course, ownership can change in the opposite direction as well, with functions formerly operated by government being contracted out to a private or non-profit organization. In this event, private sector law (the NLRA) normally applies. However, there is a note of irony with respect to transit systems. As stated above, the Urban Mass Transportation Act of 1964 requires, among other things, that existing labor rights be preserved when transit operations change ownership. Early on, most ownership changes involved public takeovers of private systems. Today, the trend is to privatize transit through contracting out. Local governments and transit managers argue that the requirement to protect labor rights, including collective bargaining, impedes contracting out because union contracts, which exist in 95 percent of transit systems, are not acceptable to potential private transit contractors (Luger and Goldstein 1989). The legalities surrounding transit ownership and labor rights remain far from settled.

In most of the states that do not permit negotiations with government workers, antipathy toward unions, unionization, and collective bargaining remain strong. For many policy makers in these states, the sovereignty argument still holds water. In upholding the ban on public sector bargaining in North Carolina, for example, a U.S. District Court reasoned that:

> To the extent that public employees gain power through recognition and collective bargaining, other interest groups with a right to a voice in the running of the government may be left out of vital political decisions. ... All citizens have the right to associate in groups to advocate their special interests to the government. It is something entirely different to grant any one interest group special status and access to the decision making process. (*Atkins v. City of Charlotte* 1969)

Pressure has been building in North Carolina to invalidate the 1959 state law that prohibits public workers from collective bargaining. In 2006, Local 150 of the United Electrical, Radio, and Machine Workers of America filed a complaint with the International Labor Organization (ILO) contending that the state's prohibition of collective bargaining violates international labor law's basic principles of freedom of association. The complaint was upheld by the ILO and filed with the federal government and the State of North Carolina (to no apparent effect). Unrest among municipal sanitation workers in Raleigh led to meetings with the mayor, and their tales of low pay, tough working conditions, and arbitrary management actions gained them widespread sympathy in the capital city. Aggressive lobbying by the State Employees Association of North Carolina (SEANC) nearly won a vote on a bargaining bill in the state house of representatives in 2007; and in 2008, SEANC formerly affiliated with SEIV.

Other states, such as South Carolina, have had to confront few real "problems" with organized public employees. Any sort of legal basis for unionization or collective bargaining is unlikely to be established in the absence of strong organized pressure by public employees. In South Carolina there has been a longstanding and widely shared aversion toward unions in the private as well as the public sector. Unions are still associated in some minds with communism, socialism, and other "foreign doctrines." Many in the South still hold a basic suspicion of the purposes of unions and a fear that they exist in the public sector only to extort money from the public through winning unwarranted wage and benefit increases. In the case of some southern states, racial prejudice also has played a role in anti-union feelings. A high percentage of minorities are found in many public services, especially the sanitation, health care, and custodial functions. The Memphis sanitation strike of 1968 and the 1969 Charleston, South Carolina, hospital workers' strike convinced some people that public unions were serving as vehicles for increasing black militancy.

Today, in the group of states that do not formally permit negotiations with public workers, the policy of no labor relations appears to be a calculated choice of state decision makers interested in providing a "good business climate" by holding down public employee compensation. In Arizona and other nonbargaining states, however, a considerable amount of bargaining does transpire, but without the statutory regulation provided by a labor relations law. Labor relations policies in these states may be established by local ordinance or on an ad hoc basis by mayors, city managers, department heads, and school boards.

Indeed, it is safe to assume that some form of bilateral decision making between public employers and workers takes place somewhere within each of the seven states discussed in this section. In Louisiana, for instance, teachers bargain with school boards in several districts, even though such activities are not protected by state legislation. The Louisiana courts have ruled that collective bargaining in public education is not inconsistent with law or public policy and is therefore permitted (Dilts et al. 1993). Even in a few South Carolina school districts, representatives of the National Education Association (NEA)-affiliated South Carolina Education Association assemble at the same table with school board representatives and the district superintendent to "sit and talk" about teacher wages, benefits, and working conditions. In these states the unions have had the power to force bargaining because bargaining makes more sense than other alternatives for resolving disagreements with public employees. Public employee unions can play an important representational role even in the absence of collective bargaining. They can lobby the legislature or city council, represent members in grievance proceedings, file equal opportunity complaints, and otherwise attempt to influence policies and procedures.

D. States with Noncomprehensive Policies

Within the states that have policies permitting some form of bilateral relations for one or more employee groups, firefighters and teachers are the most common beneficiaries. Police, municipal employees, and state workers operate less frequently under a labor relations policy. This is not surprising when one considers the history of teacher and firefighter organizational activity and the strength of their national labor organizations. What is somewhat unexpected is the relatively low incidence of collective bargaining policies for police officers. Perhaps this is a legacy of the persistent ill will that followed the infamous 1919 Boston police strike (see Chapter 8) and a function of the comparatively weak and divided national police organizations.

Most of the policies in this category were enacted through statute, and a large majority requires collective bargaining rather than meet and confer activities. In principle, the two approaches are quite distinct. Meet and confer is an activity peculiar to the public sector. It implicitly rejects the legitimacy of transferring private sector bargaining rights to public employees in that it formally denies bilateral (equal) decision-making responsibility for the two parties. Under meet and confer policies the employer retains final decision-making authority — there is no obligation to negotiate and sign a written agreement. Furthermore, meet and confer laws typically are less comprehensive in their treatment of labor relations issues, such as determining and representing bargaining units, establishing an administrative framework, and settling disputes and unfair labor practices. Although a meet and confer approach is sometimes favored by management, unions argue that the arrangement more closely approximates "collective begging" than collective bargaining. Actually, true meet and confer activities rarely take place. In reality, employers have adopted a modified approach to bilateral relations that more closely approximates collective bargaining than meet and confer. In practice, it often is not an easy matter to distinguish between the two anyway.

Nearly half of the comprehensive bargaining states achieved across-the-board coverage in an incremental fashion, authorizing negotiations first for one or two occupational categories and then later for others. California is such a case, as are Maine and Washington. It is plausible that other states presently offering noncomprehensive coverage will eventually enact legislation for additional occupational categories. However, the struggle is likely to be a difficult one for unions, as illustrated by setbacks suffered by public workers in Indiana and Kentucky. In 1980, Indiana's original comprehensive state and local government bargaining law was declared unconstitutional on the basis of a technicality (Klingner and Smith 1981). Efforts to enact a new statute in the late 1980s foundered because of gubernatorial vetoes. The election of pro-labor Democrat Governor Evan Bayh stirred hopes for passage of a bargaining bill in 1992, but the bill did not pass the senate. Governor

Bayh did issue an executive order that lasted for 16 years, granting state workers the right to collective bargaining. Then, on his second day in office in 2005, Governor Mitch Daniels rescinded it.

In a case study of Kentucky, Wanamaker (1977) offered some perspective on the Herculean tasks involved in winning bargaining legislation. Police and fire-fighters lobbied strongly for 4 years before the Kentucky General Assembly authorized collective bargaining statutes for the two groups, and even then the legislation was restricted in scope to counties with a population of more than 300,000. Only one county fit that description: Jefferson County (which contains Louisville). (Lexington's population has since also exceeded 300,000.) Teachers' hopes for a bargaining statute that same year (1972) were dashed when the governor vetoed a bill that had passed both houses of the legislature.

The next year, Kentucky teachers decided that their best strategy was to join a coalition of several other public employee unions to seek passage of a comprehensive bill permitting bargaining for all Kentucky public employees. The coalition was composed of virtually every important employee organization in the state: AFSCME (American Federation of State, County, and Municipal Employees), AFL-CIO, Associated Professional Fire Fighters of Kentucky, the Fraternal Order of Police, Kentucky Nurses Association, and local chapters of the AAUP (American Association of University Professors), NEA, and AFT (American Federation of Teachers). However, groups opposing bargaining legislation carried more clout in the general assembly. Business interests, school administrators, the Chamber of Commerce, the Farm Bureau, and the Municipal League managed to kill the bill in legislative committee.

Frustrated by their notable lack of success with the legislature, the teachers next tried the executive branch, asking the new governor to extend them bargaining rights through an executive order. The strategy was declared illegal by the attorney general. Today, although teachers do conduct negotiations with school boards in a few of the larger jurisdictions in Kentucky, they still have no statutory right to bargain.

E. States with Comprehensive Collective Bargaining

Of the states that provide for collective bargaining for all major groups of state and local government workers, only three are in the Sunbelt: California, Florida, and Hawaii. Florida truly is an anomaly because it is the only southern state with a comprehensive labor relations policy. As one might suspect, the circumstances surrounding the Florida case are unique.

The judicial role in public sector labor relations in the South typically has consisted of responding to requests from government employers for injunctions to halt job actions. And, as discussed previously, early court decisions regarding the legality or constitutionality of collective bargaining frequently were anathema to negotiating rights for public employees. In Florida, however, the state supreme court in effect initiated and implemented a comprehensive bargaining policy (see B. Miller and Canak 1991).

In the case of *Dade County Classroom Teachers Association v. Ryan* (1968), the Florida Supreme Court enforced a provision in the 1968 Revised Constitution that afforded that state's government workers the same right to engage in collective bargaining as Florida's private sector employees. The court held that, except for the right to strike, it was incumbent on the state legislature to enact appropriate legislation to set regulations and standards implementing this constitutional provision. Nonetheless, collective bargaining legislation failed to pass during the 1969 through 1971 legislative sessions. The following year, the chief justice of the Florida Supreme Court notified the legislature that failure to implement the constitutional requirement for bargaining legislation for public employees would force the court to issue its own guidelines in lieu of legislation, under the same authority it had used to redraw school boundaries when public schools had failed to desegregate in that state. When legislation still was not forthcoming, the court appointed a seven-person commission to study the issue in preparation for issuing court-mandated guidelines for collective bargaining. The commission reported the guidelines in 1974. Shortly thereafter, with a legal gun held to its collective head, the legislature finally enacted the Public Employee Relations Act of 1974.

Collective bargaining also came in through the courthouse door in Missouri, although the case is less dramatic than Florida's. In May 2007 the state supreme court overturned 60 years of a policy prohibiting collective bargaining by public employees. In response to litigation from the Missouri National Education Association, the court interpreted language from the 1935 Missouri constitution in ruling that state and local workers "should have the right to bargain collectively through representatives of their own choosing." According to the court, "'employees' plainly means employees. There is no adjective; there are no words that limit 'employees' to private sector employees" (Lieb 2007: 2).

In most of the other states with comprehensive labor relations policies a more predictable approach was employed. Staudohar (1973) provided an interesting description of the events preceding passage of the Hawaii Public Employee Relations Act of 1970, one of the nation's most comprehensive state collective bargaining statutes. Hawaii has had a history of strong organized labor since World War II. As early as 1950, public workers were granted the right to organize and present proposals and grievances to their employers. Even in this labor-friendly environment, however, public employees had to work hard for passage of collective bargaining legislation. A bill that would have granted limited bargaining rights failed in 1965. But in 1967, a meet and confer statute requiring discussion on working conditions, personnel policies, and other matters affecting public employees was enacted, and the new 1968 state constitution mandated a public employee collective bargaining law. The struggle then turned to questions of how bargaining was to be structured.

A total of eight bargaining bills were considered during the next 2 years, each bill differing substantially in major provisions and each supported by separate interest groups and employee organizations. Major points of contention were: (1) bargaining over wages as opposed to using a prevailing wage rate tied to private sector pay, (2) union security provisions, (3) appropriate bargaining units, and (4) the right to strike. The issue of appropriate bargaining units was especially salient in Hawaii. It is a small state that has only four counties. The county governments provide many traditional municipal government services such as police and fire protection, public works, and sanitation, whereas the state handles typical county functions such as welfare services and property taxation. In the 1970 act, it was decided to establish statewide bargaining units in order to provide uniformity in personnel practices.

The right to strike also presented a sensitive issue in a four-county state where education, for example, is governed by a single jurisdiction and a teachers' strike can cripple the education system of the entire state. After concluding that prohibitions of the strike in other states had been ineffective, and at times even dysfunctional, the legislature granted a limited right to strike. Before striking, Hawaii unions must first exhaust mandatory dispute settlement procedures, wait through a cooling-off period, and give a 10-day notice of the intent to strike to the employer and the public employee relations board. In addition, no strike may threaten the public health or safety, which effectively prohibits police and firefighter strikes. Interestingly, a strike was called to spur desired legislative action on the very day the legislature was scheduled to vote on the collective bargaining bill.

The first states to enact comprehensive bargaining legislation tended to be strong two-party states with active and powerful organized labor groups and a strong manufacturing sector. These early innovators, such as Michigan, Rhode Island, New York, Massachusetts, Delaware, and Connecticut, patterned their legislation on the National Labor Relations Act. Most of the subsequent public sector labor relations statutes also were guided by NLRA principles on employee labor rights, scope of bargaining, unit determination and recognition, unfair labor practices, and other bargaining topics.

The major provisions of typical comprehensive labor–management relations legislation found in the comprehensive bargaining states are briefly examined below. (Each of these concepts receives extensive discussion in subsequent chapters.)

1. Employee Rights

Generally, the NLRA (Section 7) rights apply to public workers: "Employees shall have the right to self-organization, to form, join, or assist labor organizations, to bargain collectively through representatives of their own choosing, and to engage in other concerted activities for the purpose of collective bargaining or mutual aid and protection, and shall also have the right to refrain from any or all of such activities." In the comprehensive bargaining states, all nonsupervisory workers typically are guaranteed recognition and bargaining rights upon request.

2. Employer Rights

The great majority of the state statutes provide a management rights clause excluding certain matters from the scope of negotiations. Typical management rights include the right to determine the nature of work to be performed and how it is to be performed; the tools and equipment necessary to do the work; retention of traditional personnel management functions, including recruitment, hiring, promotion, and dismissal; and the right to determine the mission of the agency and the efficiency and effectiveness of government operations. Some states (e.g., New Hampshire) stipulate that existing merit system provisions are excluded from collective bargaining, whereas others (e.g., Washington) provide that negotiated agreements supersede all existing policies or regulations.

3. Administrative Agency

All comprehensive statutes identify some form of administrative machinery to administer public sector labor relations. The administrative agency may be an existing entity such as the state department of labor or the civil service commission, or, as is now the norm, a new agency called a public employee relations board (PERB) or something similar may be established especially to implement labor relations policies. Regardless of which strategy is employed, it is important to establish an administrative agency to resolve recognition claims by employee organizations, certify bargaining representatives, hear complaints of unfair labor practices, resolve disputes between the parties, and otherwise provide authoritative interpretations of existing policies. A major advantage of the PERB is its neutral posture, which is necessary if the agency is to develop the confidence and respect of both parties, which is required for its effective functioning. PERBs normally are composed of three to five members appointed by the governor for staggered terms of office.

4. Unit Determination

The PERB or other administrative agency determines the appropriate bargaining unit of employees. A bargaining unit consists of one or more workers represented by a single union under one contract. These workers select a bargaining agent (union) to represent them as a unit. The most commonly used criteria for unit determinations are "community of interest" among the employees, the history of employee representation, the effects on the efficiency of agency operations, the exclusion of supervisory employees, and the avoidance of unnecessary fragmentation of units. The number of recognized bargaining units varies widely from state to state. New York, for example, has hundreds of local government bargaining units, whereas Hawaii has only a handful. In practice, unions often determine the bargaining unit's boundaries by way of their organizing activities and the initial "showing of interest" through petition signatures.

5. Recognition Procedures

Once the bargaining unit is determined, employee organizations compete over the right to represent that unit's members in collective negotiations. All comprehensive statutes, such as the NLRA, provide for exclusive recognition, wherein a single union has the authority to speak on behalf of all employees in the bargaining unit. Exclusive recognition generally is obtained through an expression of support by a majority of workers via a secret ballot. [In almost all other countries recognition is achieved through signatures of a prescribed percentage of employees; this is permitted in some states as well (e.g., Ohio).] After exclusive recognition is authorized by the administrative agency, management must deal only with that labor organization in bargaining matters, and the union must effectively and fairly represent all individuals in the unit, whether they are dues-paying members or not. Most statutes also establish procedures for decertifying a previously recognized organization.

6. Scope of Bargaining

Collective bargaining items may be mandatory, permissive, or illegal depending on provisions of the bargaining policy. In the absence of specific language, administrative agencies or the courts resolve ambiguities in the scope of bargaining.

Although state scope of bargaining provisions vary greatly, most comprehensive policies follow the NLRA in mandating a broad scope of negotiations over wages, hours, and other terms and conditions of employment. As noted above, most states exclude certain management rights or civil service provisions from negotiations. The norm is to treat all topics as negotiable unless specifically excluded by statute or administratively interpreted to fall within the realm of agency "mission." As a general rule, management prefers a narrow scope of bargaining, whereas unions seek a broad scope. Because the vital interests of both parties are at stake, battles over the scope of bargaining tend to break out frequently.

7. Impasse Resolution Procedures

In the private sector, impasses may ultimately (and legally) be resolved by a strike. In public employment, however, strikes are either prohibited or severely restricted. Thus, the need for other procedures to resolve impasses is quite clear. With only one or two exceptions, state labor–management relations policies address the need to resolve impasses resulting from grievances or contract negotiations. Each state with a comprehensive labor relations statute provides for one or more forms of dispute resolution that are either invoked by the administrative agency or left for the parties to adopt voluntarily. The three primary dispute settlement devices are mediation, fact finding, and arbitration. Most states that permit strikes make them subject to compliance with pre-strike impasse procedures.

8. Union Security

Five options exist for securing the institutional viability of a union as exclusive representative of a bargaining unit:

- *Closed shop.* Under this arrangement, the prospective employee must become a union member prior to initial employment and maintain membership as a condition of continuing employment. This "union hiring hall" approach is illegal in both public and private sectors under the Taft-Hartley amendments but continues to exist de facto in a few settings.
- *Union shop.* All ongoing and new employees must, as a condition of employment, join the union within a specified time period (usually 30 days) and maintain their membership through the duration of the contract. Unlike the closed shop, there is no pre-employment membership requirement. This arrangement is provided for in only five states, and it applies to a limited number of employee functions.
- *Agency shop/fair share.* Under this provision employees are not required to join the union, but they still must pay the employee organization a sum of money equivalent to union dues (agency shop) or a portion of union dues to defray union expenses incurred during contract negotiations and administration of the agreement (fair share).
- *Dues checkoff.* Most comprehensive public employee relations laws permit an arrangement in which the employer automatically deducts union dues from paychecks of employees and remits the funds to the employee organization. The dues checkoff normally is found in conjunction with one of the other union security provisions.
- *Maintenance of membership.* All union members must maintain their organizational affiliation as a condition of employment. Nonmembers need not join. Three states — Alaska, California, and Wisconsin — specifically provide for this arrangement, although in practice it is prevalent throughout the comprehensive bargaining states.

Union security policies are desirable for the unions because they help increase or maintain membership in the organization and ensure a high rate of dues payments. A financially sound union is a more secure union and a more powerful organization politically. Furthermore, union security provisions obviate the problem of "free riders," who enjoy the benefits of exclusive union representation in contract negotiations, grievance procedures, and other activities without paying organizational dues. It also may be argued that union security is beneficial for the public employer, which gains labor peace from a stable union with a steady membership and income.

A powerful argument against the union shop and closed shop is that they violate an individual employee's right to freedom of association and speech under the First

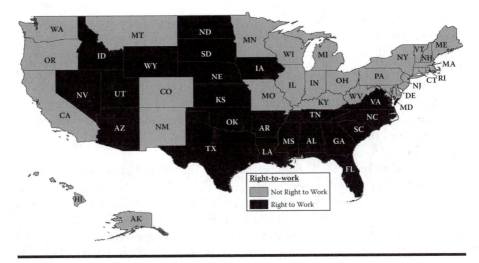

Figure 3.2   Right-to-work states, 2007.

Amendment by compelling the individual to join a union. Twenty-three "right-to-work" states prohibit union security arrangements requiring union membership or financial contributions as conditions of employment (i.e., union and agency shops and fair share). Eleven right-to-work states are in the old Confederacy; the remainder are scattered about the United States west of the Mississippi River (see Figure 3.2). None of the right-to-work states has a history of strong organized labor, and none is a traditional industrialized state. Unions are adamantly opposed to right-to-work laws and have fought to have the authorizing provision removed from Section 14(b) of the Taft-Hartley amendments for many years.

The empirical evidence is not clear on whether right-to-work laws hinder union growth and effectiveness through depressing the number of dues-paying members. Preexisting anti-union sentiment may inspire adoption of right-to-work laws and lower workers' interest in unions. Alternatively, right-to-work policies may independently depress future unionization. A careful review of the scholarly research, however, indicates that right-to-work laws do depress union membership by 3 to 8 percent in the long run and boost free riding by 6 to 10 percent (Moore 1998). However, other research shows that right-to-work states have significantly higher average wage rates than non-right-to-work states (Reed 2003).

The reasoning behind a ban on stronger types of union security is that unions are private voluntary organizations in which membership should be by conscious free choice of the worker. An individual made to join a union or pay dues may be forced to support an organization, ideology, or political program he or she does not condone. Thus, union security provisions may appear to violate an employee's First Amendment rights of free speech and association. It is also argued that union security measures conflict with the merit principle, because all public employees should be hired on the basis of their job qualifications, not membership in an organization.

The federal courts have upheld the right of individual states to bar union security provisions through right-to-work laws (*Davenport v. Washington State Education Association* 2007). The federal courts have also addressed the First Amendment rights of free speech and association that are raised when a union uses dues for purposes not related to collective bargaining, such as campaign support for a political candidate or legislative lobbying. If an employee objects to supporting these activities financially, does this not constitute a violation of free speech? The courts have examined the procedural safeguards that a union must establish for nonunion members to receive a rebate of nonchargeable fees.

In a triad of cases, the U.S. Supreme Court upheld and protected private sector employees' First Amendment rights under the Railway Labor Act (see Mitchell 1978). In *Railway Employee Department, IAM v. Hanson* (1956), the Court found that a union security agreement was constitutional as long as dues collection did not serve as a "cover for forcing ideological conformity ... in contravention of the First Amendment." In *International Association of Machinists v. Street* (1961), the Court held that unions cannot utilize dues to support political causes if an employee objects. And in *Brotherhood of Railway Clerks v. Allen* (1963), the Supreme Court suggested that unions adopt a voluntary plan to enable dissenters to avoid having a portion of their dues used for political expenditures. The principles developed in these three cases were applied to the public sector in *Abood v. Detroit Board of Education* (1977) and *Communications Workers of America v. Beck* (1998).

It is not a simple matter to draw a bright line distinguishing between the acceptable and unacceptable use of service fees. This problem was first addressed in the private sector case of *Ellis v. Railway Clerks* (1984), in which the Supreme Court decided that "the test must be whether the challenged expenditures are necessarily or reasonably incurred for the purpose of performing the duties of an exclusive representative of the employees in dealing with the employer on labor–management issues." The Court specifically approved national conventions, social activities, and publications as "necessarily or reasonably incurred" while prohibiting a portion of the service fee for activities not directly related to contract negotiation or administration or to grievance handling. In *Ellis*, the Court also found "inadequate" the union's scheme for rebating the portion of the service fee not spent on allowable items. By collecting an amount equal to full dues, then refunding a portion later, the union was in effect borrowing from nonmembers and not providing them with a viable mechanism for challenging the size or proportion of the rebate (see Darko and Knapp 1985).

In *Chicago Teachers Union v. Hudson* (1986), the Supreme Court specified a procedure for drawing a line between acceptable and unacceptable use of a service fee. The Chicago Teachers Union had negotiated a contract with the Board of Education requiring nonmembers to pay a service fee of 95 percent of members' dues. The Court ruled that the union was required to give nonmembers "an adequate explanation of the basis for the fee, a reasonably prompt opportunity to challenge the amount of the fee before an impartial decision maker, and an escrow for the amounts reasonably in dispute while challenges are pending." The non-union employee was "entitled to have his objection addressed in an expeditious, fair, and objective manner." In the 1991 case of *Lehnert v. Ferris Faculty Association*, the Supreme Court provided further instruction by devising a three-part test to determine the share of dues that may be deducted for a nonmember's agency fee. Under *Lehnert*, expenses are chargeable to nonmembers if they are (1) germane to collective bargaining activities, (2) justified by the government interest in labor peace and avoiding free riders, and (3) not significantly burdensome to free speech. Permissible expenditures include national and state union convention expenses and strike preparation costs. Disallowed are lobbying, electoral, and other political activity costs.

The *Ellis* and *Hudson* decisions cast doubt on the constitutionality of agency fee practices in a number of state and local jurisdictions. At least two states, Minnesota and New Jersey, have acted to keep the service fee issue out of the federal courts by statutorily providing for a maximum service fee percentage of 85 percent of full union dues (Volz and Costa 1989). Although this approach holds promise for balancing the unions' free rider problem against the First Amendment rights of nonmember workers, more litigation has followed in the state courts. Generally, the *Lehnert* principles have been applied by state courts, but there are inconsistencies. Expenses found to be chargeable to union dues in Indiana, for example, are not chargeable in Wisconsin (Lund and Maranto 1996: 35–45). The facts of the individual situation determine which union expenses are payable with nonmembers' dues. Several states have explicitly identified chargeable expenses (e.g., California and New Jersey).

9. Unfair Labor Practices

Following the model of the NLRA, most bargaining statutes specify unfair labor practices (ULPs) that must not be committed by public employers or unions. These ULPs are intended to protect the rights of the parties under the law.

Prohibited practices by public employers include:

Interfering with, restraining, or coercing public employees in the exercise of their rights granted under statute

Dominating, interfering with, or assisting in the formation or administration of an employee organization

Encouraging or discouraging membership in any labor organization through discrimination in hiring, tenure, or other terms or conditions of employment

Questioning employees about their union sentiments

Discharging or discriminating against an employee because he or she has filed charges or given testimony under the labor relations statute, or because he or she has formed or joined an employee organization

Refusing to meet and bargain in good faith with the recognized employee organization

Denying rights of exclusive representation to the duly designated bargaining agent

Refusing or avoiding statutory impasse procedures

Instituting a lockout

Dealing directly with employees rather than with their bargaining representatives on matters within the scope of bargaining

Violating the terms of a collective bargaining contract

Unfair labor practices by an employee organization may include:

Interfering with, restraining, or coercing public employees in the exercise of their rights granted under statute

Interfering with, restraining, or coercing a public employer with respect to protecting the exercise of employee rights under statute or selecting a bargaining representative

Refusing to meet and bargain collectively with a public employer in good faith

Refusing or avoiding statutory impasse procedures

Engaging in or instigating a strike

Hindering or interfering with an employee's work performance or productivity

Upon written notice from an employer or union plaintiff, the administrative agency determines whether an unfair labor practice has occurred. The accused party has a certain period of time in which to respond (normally seven days). If the alleged ULP is found to have taken place, the administrative agency generally has authority to issue a cease-and-desist order against the accused and to reinstate any unjustly dismissed employees, with back pay.

F. The Initiative and Referendum

As illustrated above, state legislation is not the sole means of regulating labor relations in the public sector. Court decisions, attorney general opinions, and executive orders have played significant roles in establishing labor relations policies in a number of states. And in some states, most notably California, an additional vehicle for public policy making has been utilized to govern labor relations — the public referendum.

Twenty-four states permit citizen initiatives to amend the state constitution and adopt statutory law. Most states also allow local initiatives and referenda. Under California's version of home rule, a local government can amend its city charter through action by the legislative body (council), a charter commission, or citizen initiative petition. Normally, charter amendments or ordinances are enacted by council. However, the initiative petition plays an important part in California local governance. The local initiative was used by police and firefighters to set wages, establish retirement systems, and enact rules governing working hours as early as

1907 (Crouch 1978: 191). A state initiative created the Civil Service System for California local government workers, and the process also has been utilized to establish prevailing wage principles and parity formulas.

California's state initiative procedure requires supporters to obtain the signatures of at least 5 percent of the total votes cast for all gubernatorial candidates in the last general election for a statewide initiative. Proposition 13, which severely limited state taxation and expenditures, was perhaps the most famous, or infamous (depending on one's perspective), statewide measure ever passed. Any number of local initiatives are decided each year throughout the state.

That California's use of the initiative has been so popular is a function of the state's political system. California has long been known for its weak political parties. Because interest aggregation and articulation must occur if democracy is to be a reality, other entities — namely, interest groups — have assumed direction and some degree of control over politics of the state. California politics is interest group politics, and nowhere else have interest groups enjoyed more successful application of the initiative procedure as a means of influencing and determining public policy. Needless to say, organized labor is one of the most powerful interest groups.

The California State Employees Association and California Teachers Association have used the state initiative process to achieve goals denied them at the bargaining table, including police and firefighter pay parity. However, increasing voter discontent with large salary gains by police and firefighters culminated in a rebellion of sorts in San Francisco, in 1975, when the city government refused to honor the wage and parity amendments. Police and firefighters went on strike, but voters used the initiative procedure against them by approving strong anti-union charter amendments. Since then, anti-union initiatives have also been passed in Oakland, Santa Barbara, San Diego, and other California cities.

Through the initiative process, state employee organizations have suffered both dramatic defeats and stunning victories. Recent union victories include defeating "paycheck protection" initiatives that would have required unions to obtain permission from their members each year before spending their dues for political purposes.

The tremendous expense of conducting initiative campaigns has dampened the interest of public employees in this method of policy change. (In California, it costs more than $1 million just to place an initiative on the ballot.) However, employee organizations participate aggressively when their interests appear to be threatened.

G. Labor Relations in Nonprofit Organizations

As a general rule, nonprofit organizations occupy an uncertain legal terrain (see Chapter 2). The NLRA is the governing law for some nonprofit organizations in the United States. In other cases state law prevails. As observed in Chapter 2, the rapid growth of the nonprofit sector along with a friendly environment for labor and its causes have heightened union interest in organizing nonprofit agencies.

Nonprofit management tends to be at a serious disadvantage when unionization occurs. The board of directors and CEO may find themselves in unfamiliar territory and with little or no knowledge of the NLRA or state labor provisions. Even if they were inclined to fight unionization, they rarely have sufficient funds to hire a union-busting firm.

From a practical perspective, nonprofits differ fundamentally from firms and public government organizations in their missions, assumptions, and operating procedures. For example, a nonprofit that operates a number of assisted-care homes for the aged and disabled under a state contract may find itself in a dispute with one or more unions demanding a substantial wage increase. If the nonprofit cannot or refuses to pay, the assisted-care workers may legally walk out the door, abandoning their patients. What is the role of the state government in such a situation? Legally, it probably has insufficient authority to intervene, unless, as in California, the workers are employed by and paid through an agency of state government (see Mareschal 2006). Morally and politically, it must act to protect the lives and well-being of citizens who do not have the resources to take care of themselves. Such crises have induced governors to take direct action to hike employee pay through unilaterally amending the operating contract with the nonprofit.

V. Summary and Conclusions

This chapter has described the legal basis of labor relations in federal, state, and local governments in the United States, including the right to form and join unions, and the various statutes, ordinances, executive orders, attorney general and court decisions, and public referenda that have established labor relations policies for public employees.

The "political laboratory" of labor relations policies in the states was examined by classifying state policies into three groups: those with no statutory bargaining rights, those with partial coverage, and those with comprehensive policies mandating bargaining. Major provisions of typical collective bargaining legislation were outlined, including employee and employer rights, administrative agency, unit determination, recognition, scope of bargaining, impasse resolution procedures, union security, and unfair labor practices.

Unlike in the private sector, there is no single, coherent legal framework for public sector labor relations. In the federal sector, the Civil Service Reform Act regulates labor–management relations through an increasingly inadequate framework that has not withstood the test of time. Federal unions struggle to justify their existence in the absence of union security arrangements and of a broad scope of negotiable topics. The prohibition of bargaining over wages and benefits is particularly burdensome to the federal unions. The Reform Act itself is in dire need of reform.

It has been only for about four decades that public employees in the United States have enjoyed the legally protected right to form and join employee organizations.

Many state and local government employees still do not have statutory collective bargaining rights. Regional variations in labor relations policies and union membership persist, with Sunbelt states likely to continue denying bargaining rights to public workers. With a few possible exceptions, the legal environment will probably be altered only at the margins, barring the emergence of a new pro-labor majority coalition in the respective state legislative bodies or a profound change of course by Congress and the president.

The legal environment for public sector labor relations is important and deserving of careful attention by scholars and practitioners. It is strongly associated with levels of unionization, the extent and nature of collective bargaining, and the general character of employer–employee relations. The legal environment of public sector labor relations underrides and shapes everything that follows in this book, and it largely determines who wins and loses on the labor–management playing field.

Chapter 4

Fundamentals of the Bargaining Process

I. Introduction

Collective bargaining and other forms of management–union relations in government are replete with formal and informal procedures, official and unofficial participants, and — perhaps above all else — politics. This chapter examines the multidimensional bargaining process in the public sector and attempts to shed some light on the mysteries of labor–management negotiations. At the outset, it is important to understand the ways in which collective bargaining differs between government and the private sector. Next, the basic elements of the bargaining process are considered in some detail. The chapter concludes with a look at the internal and external politics of public sector collective bargaining.

II. Public–Private Sector Differences

Perhaps because of the sovereignty doctrine or, in some cases, the shock of early union successes in government, the differences in collective bargaining between the public and private sectors are often overstated. Upon close inspection, one sees that the same sorts of people and occupations are involved in government and corporate jobs and frequently the work is identical. The day-to-day activities of the printer, the classroom teacher, the vehicle operator, the maintenance person, and the information technology specialist are indistinguishable regardless of public or private ownership of their place of employment. Most would dispute the claim that the duties of county hospital personnel are somehow less "essential" than those performed in private hospitals. Moreover, the principles and processes of collective bargaining exhibit many more sectoral similarities than differences.

Nonetheless, important distinctions can be drawn between government and business concerning the environment, actors, and processes of collective bargaining.

A. The Environment

Chapter 3 established that the environment of collective bargaining in government differs from that of business in the legal framework, particularly with regard to statutory and regulatory policy. Three additional environmental factors distinguish collective bargaining in the two sectors: (1) financial setting and incentives, (2) the nature of work, and (3) the role of politics.

1. Financial Setting and Incentives

Private sector financial policy is driven by the profit motive. A corporate entity cannot remain a going concern unless assets and net income exceed liabilities and net expenses over the long haul. In simple terms, a corporation that falters must fold its tent and move its operations to a more favorable location (most recently to Asia or Latin America), declare Chapter 13 bankruptcy, or negotiate a takeover by a more successful firm. Private sector organizations adjust financial policy in response to the demands of the marketplace. For example, increased labor costs may be passed on to consumers through boosting product prices; they may be offset through introducing productivity improvements; or they may be absorbed internally through lower profits.

As the mortgage debt conflagration showed in 2008, general-purpose governments may confront serious fiscal crises and revenue–expenditure imbalances, but they cannot "go out of business." Municipalities may file bankruptcy under Chapter 9 of the federal code, but they cannot lock their doors, lay off all employees, and cease the provision of public services, as Bridgeport, Connecticut's experience with Chapter 9 demonstrated in 1991 (C. Lewis 1994 and Vallejo, California in 2008). The uninterrupted provision of law enforcement, fire protection, potable water, sewer services, and (especially during July and August) trash collection is critical to the health and well-being of the citizenry. And although consolidation of a financially troubled government with a fiscally healthy counterpart is a possible (though unlikely) alternative, Bridgeport did not have the option of picking up and moving to China is not an option.

Furthermore, there is no profit motive in government. Higher service-provision costs must be passed on to consumers through a fee or tax increase or ameliorated through productivity gains. Because there are no "profits" to reduce, and a balanced budget is usually mandated by law, governments sometimes must respond to a fiscal imbalance with hiring freezes or reductions in force, or hope for a bailout from a higher level of government. On the whole, public sector choices are rather constrained.

2. The Nature of Work

Similarly, the nature of government services differs from services provided by the private sector. In general, government services are labor intensive. They also tend to be monopolistic; typically there is no convenient alternative supplier of police and fire protection, water, sewage, or garbage pickup. This is not to say that no alternatives exist: one may sink one's own well, install a septic tank, and take the trash to the nearest sanitary landfill in the trunk of the family vehicle; volunteer fire departments are responsible for protecting the great preponderance of property in the United States; private schools educate hundreds of thousands of children; and private security firms can perform the police and military functions, to some extent, as demonstrated by the U.S. Defense Department contractors in the Iraq War. Indeed, one is hard pressed to imagine a single government function that could not, in theory (if not in practice), be performed by a nongovernmental entity. However, the point is that alternative services are not immediately available in most cases. The implications of an employee strike in services essential to the health and safety of a community are obvious and are not to be taken lightly.

3. The Role of Politics

Finally, public sector labor relations are deeply and inherently suffused in politics. The activities of all labor unions (organizing workers, lobbying elected and appointed officials, influencing public opinion, and representing workers in collective bargaining and grievance procedures) are political in nature. But the level of politicization is much higher in the public sector.

The primary distinction between the politics of public and private sector unions and bargaining rests in the basic contexts of the two systems: the public arena (and public policy) versus the marketplace (and corporate policy). Private sector firms are responsive to the citizenry primarily through adjusting to and influencing consumer demand for their products. In the public sector, government service providers must be responsive not only to their immediate "customers," or service recipients, but also to elected officials, civil servants, the voting public, and other levels of government. Collective bargaining assumes a multi-participant character, with its outcomes highly dependent on the political interplay among unions, elected officials, interest groups, and taxpayers. In addition, the access points of labor organizations to the government employer are much more numerous than those of private sector unions. For example, in government, public employees may help elect their own employers through voting and campaign support. As pointed out by Stieber (1973: 20), "In both public and private sectors, organized employees use power to affect the distribution of resources and the management of men [sic] and materials. In the private sector they do this primarily as employees. In the public sector they exert influence as employees, as pressure groups, and as voting citizens."

The principal reason for the high level of involvement by government employees in politics is that legislative bodies have the authority to appropriate funds, enact laws that permit and regulate collective bargaining, and even supersede agreements between labor and management. Therefore, both labor and management engage not only with one another but also with whatever political entities and individuals can help them realize their objectives. This is not to say that private sector bargaining is apolitical and that private meetings do not occur, or that broader constituencies are completely insignificant. But private dealings with external parties away from the table is generally considered bad faith bargaining in the private sphere.

B. The Parties

The principal actors in private sector labor relations have well-defined roles. The union team entails the union leadership, bargaining representatives, and rank and file; the management team includes designated labor relations specialists and negotiators. Both parties are likely to have legal counsel at the table or readily available. Teams may vary on occasion as specialists are brought in to address special topics such as pension or health care benefits.

Management authority is securely situated at the top of the organizational hierarchy. Major corporations delegate responsibility for contract negotiations to specified individuals within various divisions or geographic locations. Management is rewarded according to that division's or management's contributions to corporate profits; profits depend in large measure on minimizing labor costs. Typically, division heads are assisted in collective bargaining and contract administration by a human resource director or industrial relations specialist, whose future with the company depends on his or her success in negotiating and administering the contract. There are strong career and financial incentives to "deliver" for corporate executives. Of course, union negotiators who don't deliver for their membership face the same grim possibility as does management's negotiator: losing the job.

Management's labor relations roles in public sector collective bargaining are less clearly defined. Separate staff functions for labor relations are found predominantly in the largest local governments and in states with comprehensive bargaining laws and many years of bargaining experience. In other jurisdictions, the responsibility for labor relations is not clearly fixed. This is unsatisfactory for at least two reasons: (1) because no individuals are held directly accountable for promoting and protecting management's interests, and (2) if labor relations is not treated as a distinct function, it is likely to be a secondary duty of the management negotiators and not receive the careful attention it deserves (Shaw and Clark 1972: 867–886). Faced with a well-prepared opponent, disorganized or indifferent participants pay high costs.

Blurred management responsibility for labor relations fosters motivation problems. Motivation suffers when a poorly trained, part-time negotiator fails to see how this temporary job assignment will further his or her career. Unclear management responsibility also invites the union to exploit any fragmentation or inconsistency in management's position. Although projecting team solidarity on both sides of the table is a time-honored tradition, certain differences usually exist, and the apparent team solidarity is usually an illusion. A good negotiator detects this and can use it to advantage.

Negotiations are not a war game or an exercise in sheer cunning. No amount of style can substitute for preparation and teamwork. It is imperative that both sides come to the table focused, organized, and prepared to work hard to reach a settlement. It is one thing to fail to successfully negotiate an acceptable contract because of intractable issues or the determination of the other party not to make concessions. It is quite another for negotiations to break down because of a lack of clear lines of authority, carelessness, or failure to prepare.

Weak or unfocused management responsibility for labor relations is compounded by the diffuse nature of management authority in government. Even those with only a vague familiarity with federal and state constitutions seem to believe intuitively in the separation of powers and checks and balances among institutions of government. Power is divided both between levels of government (federal/state/local) and within individual governments (executive/legislative/judicial), and all relationships are characterized by elaborate provisions for checks and balances.

In this context, labor relations responsibility is ambiguous. With respect to municipal government labor relations, for example, the federal government regulates some working conditions, the state legislature may establish benefits packages, and the city council may set salaries. A coherent chain of command may be lacking and may be compounded by the election cycle. Such diffusion of management authority poses serious problems during the early stages of a collective bargaining relationship, and it encourages unions to circumvent formally designated management representatives through "end runs" to more sympathetic individuals. At the very least, the process becomes extremely political.

A final nettlesome problem in government concerns how merit system provisions mesh or clash with collective bargaining processes and agreements. Central personnel office staff may participate in or closely observe the negotiations process to discern how any agreement will affect provisions of the merit system.

C. The Process

Finally, public and private sector labor relations differences exist in the process of collective bargaining. Some of them are obvious. For example, the diffusion of management authority results in multiple decision points in government labor relations. And, as previously noted, the bargaining process is highly politicized in government and subject to influence by citizens and interest groups. Additionally, some of the formal elements and steps in collective bargaining differ, such as the legal absence of the strike option in most government jurisdictions and the corresponding reliance on other impasse resolution procedures. The next section discusses the elements of the collective bargaining process in government, pointing out the distinctions between the public and private sectors where appropriate.

III. Electing a Union and Getting a Contract: The Elements of Collective Bargaining

Although recognizing that informal, meet and confer arrangements are not uncommon in government, especially where negotiations are not sanctioned (see Brown and Rhodes 1991), this section limits discussion to conventional collective bargaining relationships. "Collective bargaining" refers to the continuous process in which representatives of the employer (government) and employees (the union) meet jointly to establish the terms and conditions of employment for workers in a bargaining unit. The discussion proceeds sequentially from bargaining unit determination to contract ratification (see Figure 4.1). Strikes, impasse resolution procedures, and contract administration receive extensive treatment in subsequent chapters.

A. Bargaining Unit Determination

Unit determination refers to the identification of a specific group of employees for the purposes of collective bargaining; this group of employees composes

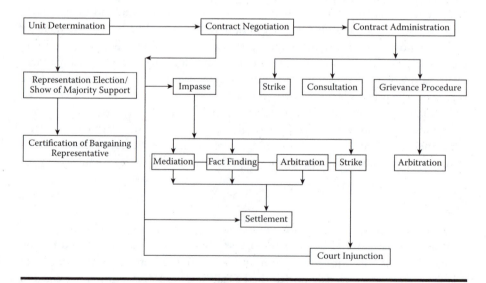

Figure 4.1   The collective bargaining process.

the bargaining unit. The appropriate bargaining unit may be (1) specified by a state PERB (public employee relations board) or other administrative agency, in accordance with statute; (2) arrived at through adjudication on a case-by-case basis; or (3) accepted as defined by a union seeking recognition as the bargaining agent with a show of majority support from members of the tentative bargaining unit. Support for the union is documented by a majority of eligible employees signing cards or petitions for union recognition as bargaining agent.

In federal employment, unit determination is the responsibility of the Federal Labor Relations Authority (FLRA). In the private sector and nonprofit sector, unit determination depends on the type of organization and its functions. The National Labor Relations Board (NLRB) determines units in the nonpublic sector.

During the early (pre-statutory) years of collective bargaining in state and local governments, the makeup of the bargaining unit frequently was decided by the union's preferences and the exercise of political power; management simply concurred out of weakness or ignorance. In most cases today, however, the process is set forth in statute or in the administrative procedures of a state public employee labor relations board. Unit determination and certification usually require multiple steps: petition for a certification election, proper showing of employee interest in the election, a hearing to establish the petition's validity, determination of the unit by an administrative entity, and final certification (see Figure 4.2). A proper showing of interest typically requires signed cards or a petition demonstrating that at least 30 percent of the workers in the proposed unit desire collective bargaining representation. The hearing is used to gather information on the validity of the show of interest and the timeliness of the petition. A petition is timely only if (1) there has not been an election within the past 12 months, (2) an existing certification is not in effect, and (3) a valid collective bargaining contract is not in effect (R. S. Rubin 1979: 123).

Statutory and administrative agency criteria for unit determination decisions vary greatly but usually take into account these factors: (1) community of interest, (2) bargaining history, (3) extent of prior union organization, (4) efficiency of agency operations, (5) avoidance of fragmentation of bargaining units, and (6) exclusion of supervisory and confidential employees. The parameters of the unit may depend in part on the union's membership structure. The AFSCME, for example, may desire a citywide non-uniformed bargaining unit, whereas the International Association

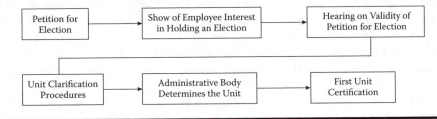

Figure 4.2 Steps for determining the bargaining unit.

of Fire Fighters is likely to want uniformed firefighters only. The union's bottom line is that it wants a unit that will support it in the representation election and that will be strong enough to negotiate a favorable contract.

1. Community of Interest

Usually the most salient criterion in determining the bargaining unit, *community of interest* refers to job factors held in common among employees. These employees are engaged in similar work or are treated in a like fashion by management. The wishes of employees are also taken into account. Workers with clear conflicts of interest are not usually placed within the same unit (e.g., teachers and principals).

2. Bargaining History

Bargaining history refers to previous relationships between labor and management within the jurisdiction, including patterns of negotiation and recognition that may reflect traditions or appropriateness of unit determination.

3. The Extent of Prior Union Organization

The *extent of prior union organization* within the bargaining unit refers to previous union efforts to force representation elections and current union membership structure.

4. Efficiency of Agency Operations

The *efficiency of agency operations* becomes a factor if a proposed unit would disrupt standard personnel policy and practice.

5. Fragmentation of Bargaining Units

Fragmentation of bargaining units, which is most often found in the absence of legislative guidelines or administrative regulations, is related to unit size and the occupational characteristics of unit members. The conventional wisdom is that a large number of small bargaining units creates serious administrative problems for management. Such problems include multiple, time-consuming negotiations; constant problems in administering the labor agreements; end runs to elected officials or other third-party "friends"; leapfrogging (where each union fights to position its wage increase and other bargaining gains at a level higher than any other union's); and disruptive jurisdictional battles and rivalries between competing organizations (Spero and Capozzola 1973: 142–145).

Additional disadvantages of a large number of small bargaining units are the difficulty of maintaining uniformity and equity in wages, benefits, and working conditions for all workers in the jurisdiction, a greater potential for conflicts and job actions, and problems estimating total labor costs in the jurisdiction's budget. In general, fragmentation means inefficiency and complexity. In a state government with 50 bargaining units, management might have to go to the table half a hundred times with assorted unions. Significant administrative support is required on behalf of both parties. And administering numerous contracts with multiple unions can be a nightmare for management and a headache for union leaders (who find that what they have negotiated is compared by their members with the performance of every other bargaining agent).

The bargaining unit is, in effect, the election district in which employees vote for a union (or for no union) to represent them. Objective criteria for unit determination notwithstanding, unions have a pragmatic interest in organizing units for which they can win elections against both competing unions and the employer. An analogy is found in activities to reconfigure, or redistrict, legislative districts following each census. Although the principles of good government and fair representation may be espoused to justify a change in boundaries, gerrymandering districts to favor one candidate or party over another is common practice.

Because of these widely recognized problems with bargaining unit proliferation, there is a tendency to consolidate existing units. In New York City, for example, 400 units were collapsed into fewer than 100 over a 10-year period; in the federal government, the Civil Service Reform Act encouraged a 32 percent drop in the number of bargaining units from 1975 to 1981. At the state level, problems with unit fragmentation have also led to a trend toward statewide units.

Thus, the boundaries of bargaining units are not etched in stone. They may be amended through unit clarification procedures such as accretion, which permits assimilation of employees filling newly created positions, and consolidation, which combines two or more existing units into a single entity. A consolidation might involve combining police and firefighters into a single unit within a public safety department. But strong professional identification by members of each group leads to vigorous opposition to consolidation. Many police and firefighters' unions have negotiated a ban on consolidation into the contract.

Despite arguments in favor of large units, numerous small bargaining units offer certain advantages. First, it is simpler to identify the bargaining interests of a small unit. Diverse membership interests within a broad unit can create negotiating problems and tensions that the union may find difficult to manage. The union may have trouble placating each faction in the bargaining unit. Second, a small group of craft or other specialized workers might have its interests ignored within a larger unit and thus can make a case for separate recognition. This is closely related to the community-of-interest principle, which posits that employees with similar work and job interests should be located within the same unit. Third, there is evidence that in some cases small, occupationally based units reflect the needs and objectives of their members better than units organized along departmental or agency lines (Perry and Angle 1981). Finally, from the perspective of the public employer, small bargaining units can be dealt with effectively in some cases through a strategy of divide and conquer. Small units tend to be weak in political power and thus easier for the employer to dominate.

6. Exclusion of Supervisory and Confidential Employees

The sixth criterion usually taken into account in unit determination decisions is the *exclusion of supervisory and confidential employees*. In the private sector, Taft-Hartley excludes supervisors from membership in a bargaining unit. Recent rulings by the NLRB have expanded the definition of "supervisor," thereby reducing the number of private sector workers eligible for union representation.

Supervisors in the federal government are likewise prohibited from being represented in a bargaining unit. Eleven states, like the federal government and the National Labor Relations Act (NLRA), deny all bargaining rights to supervisors. Six states exclude only certain classes of "bona fide" supervisors. Eighteen states permit supervisory bargaining by creating separate units for supervisors. The most prevalent approach, used by 22 states, is to provide for mixed units of supervisors and rank-and-file employees. Forces such as downsizing and decentralization of authority have pushed local government supervisors in the direction of collective bargaining to protect their jobs and to secure pay raises commensurate with those won by their unionized subordinates (Piskulich 1995).

The conventional operating assumption is that supervisors are part of management and therefore should not be permitted to bargain in league with their subordinates. Moreover, supervisors included in subordinates' bargaining units face significant role conflicts, may be less loyal to management, and may be less effective in dealing with disciplinary problems and grievances. However, evidence concerning these assumptions is mixed, and the question of supervisors' bargaining rights remains very much unresolved.

In the private sector, it once was simple to distinguish supervisors from nonsupervisory employees, with the exception of some skilled trades such as printing and construction. More recently, greater decision-making responsibility for workers in manufacturing and particularly in the service sector has complicated the situation.

In government, the laws, job titles, and other position characteristics are highly variable, and "sprawling bureaucracies make empty shells of many impressive titles" (Spero and Capozzola 1973: 145). Furthermore, public sector managers frequently hold close working relationships with and perform many of the same duties as the rank and file, particularly in such functions as police and fire protection, nursing, and teaching. As team approaches to work have continued to expand, role ambivalence among public sector supervisors has grown.

The principle that legitimate, bona fide supervisors should not be placed with their subordinates in bargaining units is seldom disputed. The bona fide supervisor is the primary management agent in contract administration, and, to further the goals of the organization, he or she should be committed to the management point of view. The key determination that must be made is who is a bona fide supervisor and who is a supervisor only in title. Some collective bargaining statutes and administrative procedures spell out what constitutes a bona fide supervisor and exclude those individuals from bargaining units composed primarily of subordinates. Less-than-bona-fide supervisors are placed within units of rank-and-file employees. Several states have adopted this approach, including Wisconsin, Connecticut, Nevada, and Oregon, which apply an NLRA-type operational test to the definition of supervisor and then exclude only bona fide supervisors from bargaining law coverage. Typically, bona fide supervisors have the authority to hire, fire, promote, and discipline or are involved in policy formulation, collective bargaining, or contract administration activities.

That supervisory identification is not always a cut-and-dried affair is illustrated by the complexities of higher education institutions. The management line is drawn at the level of the department head in some universities and at the dean's office in others. Recall from Chapter 3 that the U.S. Supreme Court ruled that faculty at Yeshiva University held certain managerial duties, including involvement with hiring and retention decisions, and therefore had to be excluded from faculty bargaining units (*National Labor Relations Board v. Yeshiva University* 1980).

When managers join a union and win collective bargaining rights, they may encounter some interesting role conflicts. As managers, they tend to have a natural antipathy to unions, and they will fight tooth and nail to defend management rights. But as union members themselves, managers are aligned against their own appointed and elected bosses. In a sense, these "supervisors have discovered how to have it both ways: managerial authority with union benefits" (Piskulich 1995: 281).

B. The Representation Election or Show of Majority Support

When de facto bargaining arrangements exist within a legal vacuum, a union has already been selected to represent workers and no new election need be held if a collective bargaining statute is enacted. In most instances, however, there must be a formal determination of which union, if any, shall represent the unit in collective bargaining. This may be accomplished through a representation election or by the employer's voluntary recognition of a unit representative. The latter normally occurs only where a single employee organization seeks recognition and is able to demonstrate to the satisfaction of the employer that it enjoys the support of a majority of the employees in the unit.

If more than one union is involved or majority support has not been demonstrated to the employer's satisfaction, a representation election is normally held. The election may be requested by the employer or, under some state laws, by a union. If the union asks for an election, it usually must present evidence (a "showing of interest") indicating a show of support of at least 30 percent of the bargaining unit. This showing of interest or support is typically done by employees signing "authorization cards" designating a union to represent them or by signing a petition for the same purpose. For years, private sector unions have made it a legislative priority in Congress to enact a bill amending the NLRA to grant bargaining rights upon presentation of signed authorization cards by a majority of the unit. Unions believe that the current requirement for a secret ballot election disadvantages them. In comprehensive bargaining states, the show of support is validated by the state labor relations agency.

Once it is decided that a representation election will be conducted, a number of procedural issues must be resolved, including who will pay for the election and who will administer it. Typically, the PERB or other state labor board will do both. Next, the agency must determine who is eligible to vote (typically, those employees working within the unit on election day), when the election is to be held (usually within 30 days), the type of election (public or secret ballot), and what vote percentage is required for certification (usually the majority of votes cast).

As a general rule, the secret ballot is preferred. Use of the secret ballot, a long-standing tradition within the American democratic experience, helps protect voting employees from undue pre-election pressures from management or the union and, after the election, from retributive measures taken by a sore loser. A union election for representation rights looks much like any election for public office. For example, there are voting booths, voter lists, and rules against campaigning near the polling sites.

Before voting day the employer posts notices of the forthcoming election and takes other steps to ensure a large turnout of eligible voters. Each of the principal parties usually is permitted to post observers at the polls and at the site where election results are compiled. The ballot itself includes the names of all organizations demonstrating a show of support along with a choice of "no representative." In the event that none of the choices receives majority approval, a runoff election is held between the top two. Voting matters, particularly when turnout is low. In Florida's first election for a statewide administrative clerical unit of nearly 30,000 employees, AFSCME certified the unit with only about 5,000 votes.

During the period preceding the election, management sometimes attempts to influence the results through various activities. Employer-induced election delays can help management's cause. Public concern with future compensation increases or costly benefits package can also boost the employer's chances. Union suppression tactics may even continue after a union election victory, through formal objections, court action, and other activities. As noted in Chapter 1, employers in the private sector often use illegal tactics such as threats and reprisals to suppress unions, and often they get away with it. Such behavior is less common in government, but not unknown. Because these are all considered unfair labor practices, charges can be filed by the injured party with the appropriate labor board for redress.

If an employee organization wins majority support, and various challenges to the election are resolved short of a change in outcome, the union is certified as bargaining representative. Obviously, if "no representative" is victorious, the unit remains unrepresented and no collective bargaining will occur. If a union wins the vote, an "election bar" typically prohibits new elections for 1 year, to give the union sufficient time to negotiate a contract and otherwise "prove itself."

C. Certification of the Bargaining Representative

Certification by the state or local labor relations agency (or FLRA in federal employment and NLRB in the private sector) normally stands for at least 1 year from election day. The status of unit representation thereafter may be challenged by a rival organization or by dissidents within the certified union through petition for a decertification election. Election procedures similar to those outlined above then come into effect to determine if the union will be decertified as bargaining representative — a fairly common outcome in the private sector since the early 1980s, but still rare in the public sector. The process works in the same way as certification, only in reverse, with a showing of interest of 30 percent to decertify the union and a subsequent vote.

Workers may decertify unions for a variety of reasons, including nonresponsiveness to member needs and demands, anti-union campaigns by the employer, and the union's failure to win and maintain favorable wages, benefits, and working conditions. If the union loses, it ceases to function as bargaining representative. A second election may then be held to select a new representative; otherwise, the collective bargaining status of the unit is dissolved.

The employer grants exclusive recognition to the successful employee organization. Exclusive recognition provides significant benefits to the employer, the employees, and the union. The employer is assured that the union, and only that union, will represent all employees in the bargaining unit whether they are members of the union or not. Management will have only one organization to deal with, simplifying administration, saving time, and eliminating costly inter-union struggles.

The union is guaranteed that management will deal with it alone concerning any issue within the scope of bargaining, both at the bargaining table and during administration of the contract. Exclusive recognition also benefits employees because a negotiated contract applies to all members of the bargaining unit even if they are not dues-paying union members. The organization has a duty to fairly represent all employees without any form of discrimination or favoritism (see *Vaca v. Sipes* 1967). The duty of fair representation can be a double-edged sword for a union, however. If a union fails to adequately represent a member of the bargaining unit, it may be sued for lost earnings or other damages (*Bowen v. U.S. Postal Service* 1983).

D. Negotiating the Contract

After union recognition we move into the heart of labor relations — negotiation of the contract between union and management representatives. Bargaining is a way to change the terms and conditions of a relationship and to make decisions between competing alternatives. What happens at the bargaining table determines the substance, tone, context, and commitments in labor relations during the next 1 to 3 years. The satisfaction of employees with their wages, benefits, and working conditions is directly influenced by the outcome, as is the financial solvency of the jurisdiction. At issue as well is the nature of the relationship between the parties. Poor relations between some unions and employers have little to do with present-day issues, but rather reflect bitter memories of unresolved prior conflicts. Resentments and vengeance can blur the primary objectives of the bargaining process, which are to provide both parties with an agreement they can live with, achieve good working relations with representatives of the other party, and protect the interests of the jurisdiction's citizens.

The Participants

1. The Union

Management and union representatives are the primary participants in contract negotiations. Unless an impasse necessitates the intervention of a third-party neutral or other individual(s), labor and management representatives, sometimes assisted by a professional negotiator, hammer out the terms of the labor agreement on their own. Later, of course, the contract must be ratified by the union rank and file and by elected public officials, but the contract wheeling and dealing is the responsibility of the individuals sitting across the table from one another. The primary union figure — not only during contract negotiations but throughout virtually the entire process of labor–management relations — is the union leader, or president of the local. Although the union leader has many responsibilities, it is primarily what he (the vast majority are men, so the masculine form is used) carries to the membership from the bargaining table that determines his tenure in the position. Victor Gotbaum (1972: 77), former president of District Council 37 of the American Federation of Teachers, describes it this way: "It is one thing to show workers new horizons. It is more important, however, to obtain a wage that feeds and clothes their families. ... If his wages do not keep up with the cost of living, hell will have no fury like the worker scorned."

The job of the union leader is a demanding one, requiring strong political, managerial, interpersonal, and oratorical skills. Union leaders have been found to exhibit high activity and energy levels, strong goal direction, idealism, and a desire to change things for the better (Sayles and Strauss 1967: 58–60). Successful union leaders must be sharp negotiators and effective public relations people as well. They are faced constantly with the need to prove themselves to their membership, who may include militant extremists, avowed dissidents, loyal supporters, and the apathetic. "The script," according to Spero and Capozzola (1973: 115), "calls for a mixture of reason, explosive talk, threats, fear, justice, optimism, and pessimism."

Union leaders must be careful not to appear too friendly with management or they risk dissension that may produce a strong opposing faction within the union and ultimately result in membership rejection of a negotiated contract. Obtaining ratification of agreements is probably the most difficult problem union leaders confront. The membership may spurn the proposed contract because of dislike or distrust of the leader, overblown expectations for a settlement, disenchantment because of more substantial gains won by other organizations, or for any number of other reasons. Thus, it is critical that union leaders keep their fingers on the pulse of the organization and be highly persuasive in communicating with the membership.

A time-tested means of "rallying the troops" for a leader whose status and position are challenged is to create a crisis and an "us versus them" situational perception — not a difficult task given a highly adversarial and emotional bargaining context. Overt enmity between the late union leader Mike Quill, president of the Transport Workers' Union (TWU), and his nemesis, Mayor John Lindsey, was evident during the 1966 New York City transit strike. Quill took great delight in humiliating "Lindesley," publicly calling him a "pipsqueak" and an "ungrateful sourpuss" (Horton 1973: 80–81). Quill carried his disdain for the mayor and other opponents to new theatrical heights. During the strike (Raskin 1972: 129–130), "The TWU chief was near death from heart disease; he had to swallow great gobs of pills in his moments of privacy; but none of them dulled his appetite for melodrama. He went before the television camera to tear up no-strike injunctions like confetti. When a judge ordered him carted off to jail, he said, "Let the judge drop dead in his black robes."

Although such drama may help unite the rank and file behind the union leader and draw clear lines of battle with management, it can severely inhibit agreement making and compromise when carried too far; settlement may come only after a protracted and painful strike. As management–union relations have matured, such histrionics have yielded to cool professionalism and quiet political deal making. In many settings, bargaining responsibility is turned over to union staff, with the leader active only behind the curtain.

Perhaps more so than most organizations, unions are victims of the "Iron Law of Oligarchy." As originally described by Michels (1949), the Iron Law of Oligarchy refers to control of an organization by a small, self-perpetuating, self-interested elite. The membership, except during times of extraordinary provocation, remains apathetic. Even when new leaders emerge, they soon revert to oligarchic tactics in order to thwart opposition and ensure their own survival. This pattern does indeed appear to be applicable to most large labor organizations where a leader emerges, consolidates power, and, along with a small but loyal staff, controls the organization's activities with an iron fist. Contract rejections by union membership may reflect dissatisfaction with this situation and the perception (sometimes accurate) that the leadership is cutting "backdoor deals" with management while maintaining an elaborate public charade.

Occasionally, disenchanted internal opponents arise to challenge the union and to displace the leadership. For some unions, such as New York City's Transit Workers Union, rank-and-file revolt has been a fact of daily life. The TWU represents bus and subway workers — a diverse, volatile, and chronically dissatisfied lot. Since the 1940s, various factions have attempted to unseat the ruling oligarchy. One called "Hell on Wheels/New Directions" successfully attacked the entrenched union bureaucracy through election of its own supporters to leadership positions in 2001.

The roles and behavior of rank-and-file union members received some early scholarly attention. Child et al. (1973) suggested a four-celled typology of member attachment to the union, based on the congruence between union policies and member expectations. "Cardholders," the most typical members, are committed to the organization as long as they benefit from its policies. "Troublemakers" are highly involved in union affairs, but their notion of what union policies should be is not congruent with that of the ruling elite. The "stalwarts" also are very active in the organization, but they are loyal to the leadership and personally identify with union objectives. Finally, "alienated members" may be ideologically opposed to unions themselves or, in some cases, are defeated former troublemakers who have withdrawn from active union involvement.

Recently, researchers have been interested in identifying the correlates of employee commitment to the union. The level of commitment is important because it helps determine union effectiveness in organizing, bargaining, retaining membership, and taking political action (Gallagher and Clark 1989). Four dimensions of union commitment have been identified (Gordon et al. 1980): (1) union loyalty — member pride in the union; (2) responsibility to the union — the extent to which the member fulfills the obligations and duties of membership; (3) willingness to do special work on behalf of the union; and (4) belief in the concept of unionism.

Interesting differences characterize male and female members. Women tend to believe there is more to be gained from union membership and express greater loyalty to the organization than men, but women appear to feel less responsibility to the union and are not as willing to work for it. This divergence could be due to the fact that women typically have greater family commitments that limit their ability to participate and because men still dominate the top leadership positions (Gallagher and Clark 1989: 57). Little difference has been found in participation rates of African Americans versus whites (Hoyman and Stallworth 1987). Hispanic participation has not been reported in the published literature.

Union commitment is positively related to commitment to the employer: the quality of one relationship apparently feeds the other (Gallagher and Clark 1989: 58–60). However, union commitment is bolstered by a poor relationship between the member and his or her immediate supervisor, particularly when the supervisor and/or the employer is believed to have broken their "psychological contract" with the worker by failing to maintain jobs or benefits, for example. Members also appreciate democratic processes (Jarley et al. 1990), an effective grievance procedure

(Clark 1989), a certain level of personal trust in the union leader (Hoell 2004), and, of course, a union that produces the bread and butter — good pay and benefits (Fiorito et al. 1988). This perceived positive impact of the union on compensation, benefits, working conditions, and factors known as "union instrumentality" may be the strongest correlate of union commitment (Turnely et al. 2004).

Are union members more satisfied with their jobs than nonmembers? Research findings are somewhat contradictory (Freeman 1978; Kochan and Baderschneider 1981). During an organizing campaign, the union may attempt to garner support by pointing out negative aspects of the job. Once certified, however, it is in the union's best interest to increase worker satisfaction through collective bargaining and to proudly herald the many benefits won for members of the bargaining unit. In other words, happy members keep the union in business (Gordon and Denisi 1995).

2. Management

The initial problem that must be confronted by a jurisdiction becoming involved in union–management relations is developing a satisfactory operational definition of "management."

a. Diffusion of Authority — In government, as we have already observed, there are myriad complications in identifying and designating management for the purposes of collective bargaining. Power and managerial authority are divided among the three branches of government. For instance, personnel authority is situated within the executive branch, whereas budget authority resides with the legislative body. Both are critical to negotiating outcomes, yet the two functions are rarely coordinated. In addition, budgetary and personnel authority are themselves frequently fragmented among various agencies and departments. Further management identification problems are created by overlapping functional responsibilities and jurisdictions among the approximately 88,000 governmental entities in the United States; state and county welfare agencies provide one common example.

Jurisdictional confusion in management authority is compounded by the intergovernmental nature of government revenues. It is highly unusual for a public jurisdiction to raise all its funds from its own sources. The vast majority of governmental entities draw revenues from a variety of sources, including other governments. The federal grant-in-aid is the prototypical example, in which billions of federal dollars are transferred to state and local governments for various functions. The transfer of dollars is almost always accompanied by "strings" on how those funds may be spent. When the strings apply to personnel-related expenditures, as they often do, management authority in a very real sense is located one level of government removed from collective bargaining activities, thereby obscuring who is authorized to make certain personnel-related decisions at the bargaining table.

b. Multilateral Bargaining — The diffusion of public management authority has been the focus of a considerable body of research, much of it concentrated on a principal outcome of diffusion — multilateral bargaining. Multilateral bargaining is characterized by a plethora of direct and indirect participants, official and unofficial, all of whom seek to influence the outcome of negotiations. According to Kochan (1973), multilateral bargaining develops from four factors: (1) goal diversity among management officials, (2) dispersion of management power, (3) open management conflicts, and (4) union political influence and access to management officials.

Based on his analysis of negotiations in city governments, Kochan demonstrated the variety of professional goals and personal agendas brought by management officials into the bargaining process. Elected officials are most concerned about their constituencies and prospects for reelection, whereas department heads, city managers, budget directors, and human resource directors are driven by different considerations. Overt evidence of goal diversity is displayed, for example, when a city council refuses to ratify a proposed contract that has gained union and management bargaining team approval. As a rule, high goal diversity translates into high levels of management conflict during negotiations, producing multilateral bargaining.

c. Management Conflict — From a broad perspective, the dispersion of management power and authority results from the legal separation of powers in American government and the principle of checks and balances. Conflict between and within branches of government is an inherent part of politics, as is conflict between levels of government. The greater the dispersion of authority, and the more it is fueled by individual political and personal agendas, the greater the conflict within the ranks of management.

Open conflicts are especially inimical to effective management negotiations. Such conflicts often develop and fester when unresolved personal and professional frictions and controversies spill over into the collective bargaining process. Kochan (1973: 25) provides the following example from a dispute over police and firefighter salary parity:

> Clear and open disagreement among management officials existed on what the city's position should be on this issue. The city personnel director, who was acting as chief negotiator, vigorously opposed it. The mayor did not take a position at the outset of the dispute but ended up arguing in support of it. The city council was rather evenly divided on the issue. Finally, there were two civil service types of bodies involved in the dispute and one opposed parity and one supported it.

A predictable result of this open conflict was an impasse over the parity issue. Hearings were conducted by one civil service commission, the council passed various resolutions in response to the impasse, and the second civil service body sought court action. A 3-day strike prompted a final settlement.

Kochan (1975) developed a model of management conflict and multilateral bargaining through an analysis of city government. According to the model, goal incompatibility among management officials and the extent to which decision-making authority is dispersed determine the level of internal management conflict, which in turn determines the extent of multilateral bargaining. Union negotiating and political tactics such as end-runs can expand the scope of conflict and multilateral bargaining. That management conflicts will exist during the bargaining process is a given. The important policy question is how to resolve them so that management effectiveness is not diminished.

The initial response of most jurisdictions to unionization and collective bargaining is to superimpose the new bargaining responsibility over the existing organizational structure (Burton 1972). Thus, management attempts to utilize existing expertise and personnel while maintaining prevailing authority relationships. However, the time-consuming nature of bargaining and the typical dearth of labor relations expertise among existing staff intensify the dispersion of management authority, heighten conflict, and create an altogether unstable and unfavorable situation for management.

More effective coordination, preparation, and conduct of negotiations usually requires transferring bargaining authority to the executive branch. Eventually, ongoing organization for collective bargaining is centralized within the executive branch as well (especially in larger jurisdictions and with big, comprehensive bargaining units) with the emergence of a labor relations office or agency. Full-time specialists may be appointed as chief management negotiators. The ideal situation, according to labor relations experts, is to specify clearly in statute or administrative regulations exactly where management responsibility for collective bargaining is located. Several states have done this, including New York, Connecticut, and Hawaii. Nonetheless, bargaining remains inescapably multilateral. Internal management cohesiveness may improve, but multiple external actors, such as legislative bodies and interest groups, remain actively involved.

There is no conventional model of management representation for collective bargaining in government. The actors and their roles vary greatly among jurisdictions and levels of government. The following discussion examines the principal actors in the drama of collective bargaining and the roles that they play in a "typical" labor relations situation in each level of government.

Federal government: In federal employment, collective bargaining is essentially an individual agency's responsibility subject to the provisions of the Civil Service Reform Act and the oversight of the FLRA. (Excepted agencies have their own arrangements, as discussed in Chapter 2.) The negotiating team normally is composed of full-time labor relations specialists appointed by agency heads. The Congress has no direct involvement in collective bargaining.

Overall, the federal system is highly decentralized, with around 4,000 bargaining units and a wide variety of bargaining participants. Employer and agency-wide bargaining takes place in the U.S. Postal Service, TVA, and the small number of other agencies that permit bargaining over compensation issues.

State government: During the early history of collective bargaining in state government, management negotiating responsibility was frequently added to the duties of existing bodies, such as the state civil service commission or department of labor, or handed over temporarily to individuals on a part-time basis. Such arrangements became untenable as bargaining activities expanded. Eventually, most states centralized negotiating responsibility within the executive branch under the ultimate authority of the governor.

Composition of the bargaining teams varies among states, but a general operating principle is to include a chief negotiator with direct responsibility to the governor, a budget or finance officer, a personnel officer, and representatives from the relevant state agencies. In Wisconsin, where bargaining units are statewide by occupation, the team is composed of a labor relations specialist from the Office of State Employment Relations (OSER), who serves as chief negotiator, representatives from the two largest agencies participating in the negotiations, an individual representing the interests of all other affected agencies, and additional labor relations specialists. Primary responsibility resides with the OSER members.

As a rule, it is important to include agency representation in negotiations. Agency management must live with the contract on a day-to-day basis and thus has a very high and direct stake in the bargaining outcomes. Agency management should be involved throughout the bargaining process, including the formulation of management positions and the evaluation of the potential impact of union demands on agency budget and personnel. Generally speaking, the larger the bargaining unit conducting negotiations, the greater the extent of agency head involvement.

The role of the state legislature in collective bargaining activities usually is quite limited. Nonetheless, the legislative body has the legal and budgetary responsibility to ensure that negotiated agreements are in tune with the public interest and fiscal limitations. Unacceptable bargaining outcomes may lead (in theory more than practice) to legislative override and renewed negotiations. From the management perspective, bargaining proceeds best when the executive and legislative branches are unified on major negotiating issues and resistant to union efforts to win favorable settlements through the end-run. Legislative–executive cooperation is attained through early, regular, and meaningful communications between legislative leaders and staff and the bargaining team on key issues being negotiated, when and how they are resolved, and remaining sources of contention. If the legislative body feels blind-sided with the terms of a negotiated contract, it may reject it outright, sending the whole process back to the table. Similarly, a governor may veto a bargaining settlement that the legislature supports.

Approximately 35 states have state labor relations agencies that act as quasi-judicial bodies with administrative and oversight authority for labor relations. The agencies consist of from three to seven members (usually three) appointed by the governor. There may be labor and management representatives and one or more "neutrals," or all may be neutral members. Connecticut's State Board of Labor Relations consists of three members and two alternates appointed by the governor for 4-year terms; Ohio's three-member board is appointed by the governor for terms of 6 years. Because the state agency is charged with protecting the rights of both labor and management, it is critical that the appointees be acceptable, credible, and legitimate in the eyes of both parties.

In at least nine of the comprehensive bargaining states the agencies were created solely for the purpose of administering and overseeing labor relations. Some states, however, have placed labor relations administrative responsibility within existing entities, such as the state department of labor, the state personnel office, or the civil service commission. Other states have lodged administrative responsibility in existing functional entities, such as the state board of education. The opinion of most labor relations professionals is that the optimum situation is centralization in an entity created expressly for public sector labor relations. This type of arrangement encourages professionalism, centralizes executive financial controls, promotes consistent compensation and human resource management policies statewide, and, in general, helps stabilize union–management relations.

Although combining public and private sector labor relations functions within an existing agency also offers certain advantages, including reduced administrative costs and the use of existing experienced personnel, public–private sector differences in labor relations are substantial enough to require staff personnel with distinctive backgrounds and training. However, none of the possible organizational arrangements is inherently superior. As Helsby and Tener (1979: 34) explain, "the single most important ingredient appears to be the caliber of the persons selected for and employed by the agencies ... the ideal is to combine good law with top quality appointments."

Local government: As might be expected, local government has the widest variety of management participants in collective bargaining. There are, of course, tens of thousands of municipal, county, town, school district, and other local governments within the United States, and each has its own set of labor relations policies and actors. Some of the actors have expertise in labor relations, but the majority, especially those employed in small to medium-sized governments, can hardly be considered labor relations professionals.

Management representation in local government is following a similar path as that of state government. Not unusually, aborted attempts by mayors or council members to negotiate for the city or county has led directly to centralized management responsibility within the executive branch. However, the structure of municipal or county government influences union–management interactions and the locus of management authority. In "strong mayor–council" forms of government, the mayor is the center of gravity in management authority. In "weak mayor" cities, the council may play a significant or even dominant role in labor relations. In the council–manager form of government, primary executive branch authority for labor relations typically resides in the city manager's office.

Although it is difficult to pinpoint any specific union advantages or disadvantages that are related to city government structure, it would be logical to conclude that the council–manager form results in some loss of leverage for the unions, primarily because the council tends to remove itself from the bargaining process. Moreover, it may be argued that city managers view themselves as management representatives and therefore are basically disposed to oppose union demands and protect management authority. Furthermore, the city management profession tends to attract individuals who are politically and socially moderate to conservative.

In some council–manager cities the manager takes on the role of chief management negotiator; in others the assistant manager is appointed to that job. Often, both are team members. In large to medium-sized cities (>100,000 population), professional negotiators, consultants, city attorneys, and labor relations staff frequently act as management negotiators regardless of government form. In small to midsized cities (<100,000), a part-time bargaining team approach has yielded gradually to delegating bargaining responsibility to the city attorney or a labor relations professional. The most common approach appears to be city manager/assistant manager, city attorney, personnel director, and department head in council–manager cities. In mayor–council forms of government a chief administrative officer or other representative of the municipal labor relations office (large city) or mayor's office (small to midsized city) typically is joined on the management team by an attorney, personnel director, department head, and, in some cases, the budget director (Hebdon 2000; Chandler and Judge 1993).

The logic behind the presence of the legal and personnel officers is obvious — they will have to administer the city payroll and benefits, position classification plans, personnel procedures, and the final labor contract, all of which are affected by the outcomes of negotiations. A legal officer or attorney may prove valuable in assessing important questions of law in the proposed contract. Labor lawyers and other labor relations professionals are increasingly serving as chief city negotiators and team members in mayor–council cities. They are particularly likely to sit on negotiating teams in cities with an extensive union presence and history of high levels of strikes and other job actions (Hebdon 2000; Gely and Chandler 1993).

The role of the department head is more nebulous. Department chiefs rarely are directly involved in negotiations, largely because they want to avoid a potentially adversarial relationship with department personnel. The department heads usually participate only insofar as they furnish information to the regular management team, make relevant recommendations, and, in general, serve as observers and advisors. The specialized knowledge and direct interest of department heads in bargaining outcomes argue strongly for some form of participation, even if they merely dispatch their personnel director to serve as liaison with the bargaining team.

Mayors and members of council rarely sit on the bargaining team or become directly involved in the negotiation process. A deadlock, however, may force their intervention as mediators. And they will eventually have to approve or disapprove the agreement that is submitted to them in their formal capacity as elected officials. Where management conflict is at a high level and the local government is highly politicized, however, the mayor and/or individual council members may fall victim either to the "hero syndrome," by attempting to arrange a settlement personally, or to an end-run by a union seeking to circumvent the bargaining team. Such direct involvement, however, may have a political price in the next election. It is usually a no-win situation for elected officials. If they take a hard-line stance against the unions, they risk sacrificing union votes in the next election. If they side with the union, conservative taxpayers will cast their votes for another candidate.

Both management and the unions must always designate a chief negotiator. The duties of the chief negotiator are to present one side's views and, in general, serve as leader and chief spokesperson. The chief negotiator leads the discussion during caucuses and serves as the main link with other local government (or union) officials. The most valuable attributes of the chief negotiator are courage, personal integrity, patience, stamina, intelligence, and intimate familiarity with the issues, motives, and pressures in the negotiations. Practice and painstaking preparation are also demanded. Table 4.1 is an interesting exercise for those who think they might want to be a chief negotiator.

Administration of local government labor relations varies among and within states. For example, in public schools the chief administrative agency may be the state board of education. Alternatively, the labor administration function may be provided by the superintendents of the individual school districts or, where schools are established by municipal, town, or county governments, by a central labor relations agency. In large cities there is usually some form of central labor relations office, although often it is exclusively devoted to management interests. The most prominent example of an independent agency is New York City's Office of Collective Bargaining (OCB), which was created jointly by the city and municipal unions. It is comprised of two management representatives appointed by the mayor, two labor representatives appointed by the unions, and three "impartial" members elected by unanimous vote of the city and labor representatives. OCB also includes a Board of Certification and a Board of Collective Bargaining. The former has the task of determining bargaining units and certifying unions; the latter makes scope of bargaining determinations, issues advisory opinions on city bargaining law, handles grievance arbitration, and helps resolve disputes arising during negotiations.

State administrative agencies in some cases exercise administrative oversight over labor relations in local governments. Iowa's Public Employee Relations Board, for instance, oversees allegations of prohibited practices, enforces the duty to bargain in good faith, aids in dispute settlement, and determines the appropriate bargaining unit. Thus, although local administrative machinery may exist, those states that have established statewide agencies often enjoy overall responsibility for local government labor relations.

Table 4.1 Do You Have What It Takes to Be a Chief Negotiator?

Can you spend an entire day asking questions and only asking questions?	The ability or inability to answer questions will affect expectations over time. The harder the question is to answer, the lower the expectation of success by the responder becomes. The seller of a concept has to know they must have the answers to convince the customer of its value. Learn to ask hard questions and be persistent about seeking acceptable answers.
How good are you at silence?	If the ball is in the other guy's court, don't be too quick to get it back. If you're owed an answer, learn to wait for it. Many people have difficulty dealing with silence and thus may reveal much in filling what is to them an unacceptable vacuum. Also, wait past an answer to see what else may be forthcoming.
Is patience a virtue or an issue for you?	The passage of time also can impact expectations. Waiting for a right moment to press an issue, make an argument, propose a solution, or counter an offer is a practiced skill, not a gift of birth.
Can you follow a plan?	If it's your plan to relate a group of issues to each other, package a proposal, or take a hard line on some issues and a soft response on others, develop a plan and implement it.
How easily do your buttons get pushed?	Learn your hot buttons. Work on internalizing the expression, "It ain't about you!" If you feel that familiar tingle in your gut or warm in the face (or however you get when you're getting upset), get out of the room and get control of yourself. Conversely, if you have a reason to demonstrate an emotion (usually outrage at the other person's sheer audacity in making such silly demands), make sure it is carefully planned and staged. If you're really ticked off, stay away from the table until you get over it. Remember, "It ain't about you."
Can you spend a month setting up a deal?	I'm not talking so much about patience here as systematically laying the groundwork piece by piece to make a deal attractive at a point in time. Lots of issues get put on the table at the same time. The ones you put there should each be a part of an orchestrated effort to advance a number of potential deals. You can't be taught this. You have to set it up based on your sense of timing, readiness, etc.

Table 4.1 Do You Have What It Takes to Be a Chief Negotiator? (Continued)

Can you let someone else do your talking for you?	There are issues and times when it's better for you not to do the talking on an issue until you're ready. That's not to say the matter isn't discussed, but you've made a conscious decision to have a team member take the issue to a certain point before you weigh in. This works well in a number of situations but the one most cited is "good cop–bad cop."
Can you let a member of your team make a mistake without correcting it?	There's always time to fix an error. Interrupting a team member you've charged with carrying an issue may demonstrate lack of confidence to the other side of the table. There's no commitment until you, as chief, make one so don't be eager to react. There may be things to learn in your counterpart's reaction or lack thereof.
Can you suffer a fool?	You will have virtually no control over who sits on the other side of the table. A good negotiator develops a behavior or two to use when confronted with a variety of difficult-to-stomach advocates for the other guy. If you are lucky (and be sure to get religious and say prayers of thanksgiving if it happens), you'll get a counterpart chief negotiator that's a decent person to deal with. My favorite behavior when stuck with a fool or apparent mad dog is to look at the person I know is more rational while the tirade from the idiot proceeds. If you never understood the idea of "coping behavior," sitting first seat at a bargaining table will bring it home to you.
Do you need to be visibly in control?	Management owns the cookie jar. The decision to dispense cookies puts the jar holder in charge in a very real way. The need to appear in control often signals a lack of confidence in your role. There's no deal unless you sign it and unless you are willing to pay for it.

Source: Adapted with permission from Robert J. Girson (2008). www.fedsmith. com/article/1267. (Accessed Dec. 6, 2007.)

c. The Public

The role of the general citizenry in collective bargaining is highly variable and controversial. Public participation in the negotiations process can range from an active and formal role at the bargaining table to simple citizen access to the terms of the negotiated agreement. Public involvement represents, of course, a major point of departure from private sector collective bargaining, where there is no meaningful third-party role for the general public.

Public access to collective bargaining may be either direct or indirect. Direct access provides a formal and legal means of citizen involvement through, for example, formal comments on bargaining proposals, public hearings on negotiations, trilateral bargaining with citizens participating in bargaining sessions, citizen observation of open negotiating sessions, or voter referenda on contract settlements or other labor relations issues. Indirect access includes citizen or interest group participation in hearings on the budget, use of court injunctions, lobbying elected officials, and opening up informal lines of communication to legislators and other elected officials.

The trend has been toward formal, or direct, access with the call for more accountability and transparency in government. Public disclosure and open meetings laws open up government policy making to some extent in all states and localities. However, most such laws exempt collective bargaining activities, thus permitting negotiations to be carried out behind closed doors. Also, tides of public resentment of government in general and "underworked and overpaid" public employees in particular has led to demands for increased citizen oversight of public sector collective bargaining. After all, the taxpayer must pay the final costs of the negotiated settlement. Where the perception exists that elected officials have not effectively represented the public's interest in negotiations, movements for direct citizen involvement may ensue.

Several states have institutionalized a public role in collective bargaining through "sunshine laws." Eighteen states require some sort of bargaining in the sunshine (i.e., in public). Florida's collective bargaining law is the strongest, mandating that all negotiations be held in public. Kansas law provides that teacher bargaining be open. California's statutes for state employees and public schools require initial bargaining proposals to be presented at a public hearing and new proposals to be made public within 48 hours. Furthermore, a reasonable period of time must be allowed for the public to become informed and express opinions on all proposals before a new round of negotiations begins. Tennessee requires open meetings for teacher negotiations, as does the Texas police and firefighter bargaining law. In Montana, Maine, Florida, and Oregon, students in higher education institutions have the right to attend negotiations. In Idaho, the state teachers' law mandates that minutes of negotiating sessions be made public and that contracts be ratified in open meetings. Sunshine bargaining is optional (both parties must agree to it) in Iowa, Massachusetts, Nevada, and New Jersey.

Much debate has raged on the pros and cons of bargaining in the sunshine. Advocates of sunshine laws contend that public deliberation on important public policy issues promotes citizen understanding and confidence in government and makes government more responsive to voter concerns. It deters misappropriation of public funds and conflicts of interest and helps the public become a constructive partner in reaching hard decisions on difficult problems. It is also believed to help moderate union demands by subjecting them to formal public and media scrutiny.

Public management, union leaders, elected officials, and professional labor negotiators are all quick to point out the disadvantages of bargaining in the sunshine. Open negotiations are time consuming, and may promote rancorous conflict and stalemates, thus destroying productive working relationships. The presence of the media may encourage "bargaining through the press" and grandstanding instead of constructive bargaining over the issues (Cassidy 1979: 12). The process may "… take on the aspects of a poorly produced drama where emotions upstage good judgment and egos, not issues, get the best lines" (Sherman 1979: 274). Skeptics assert that sunshine bargaining suffers from inexpert and uninformed reporting in the media and very little citizen interest.

Although the alleged advantages and disadvantages of bargaining in the sunshine have not yet been systematically assessed across the states, it has become apparent particularly from the Florida experience (where substantial majorities of labor and management representatives have supported it) that many of the criticisms have been exaggerated (see West and Feiock 1989). For instance, despite delays caused by the presence of the media and other representatives of the public, the content of the vast majority of agreements has not been affected. Moreover, the more stringent requirements of some of the laws may be circumvented through creative actions. In one state requiring that school board meetings be open, for example, mediators have avoided open meetings by carrying out delicate negotiations with a few of the board members at a time or by meeting with the board in executive session.

It is clearly consistent with democratic processes for citizens to have a formal third-party role in public sector collective bargaining. Examined judiciously, collective bargaining as it is presently conducted in most jurisdictions may or may not be conducive to the best interests of the public. Appointed officials typically control the negotiations; final agreements are usually rubber-stamped by elected representatives. Public participation is sparse and indirect, coming perhaps only in the guise of after-the-fact judgments on the performance of elected officials. Yet citizens have a fundamental right to hold officials accountable for how their tax dollars are being spent.

There is no simple formula for involving the public in collective bargaining. But given the high levels of citizen discontent and distrust in government that have generally prevailed since the mid-1970s, benefit of the doubt might be given to inclusive, sunshine-style experiments. Exclusion of the public builds neither confidence nor trust, and it perpetuates ignorance.

IV. Summary and Conclusions

Collective bargaining shares common structures and processes in the public and private sectors, but it also differs in many important respects, including the environment of labor relations, the major actors and their motivations, and the process itself.

Unit determination raises a number of important issues in public sector bargaining, including criteria with which to determine the unit, the size of the unit, fragmentation of bargaining units, the inclusion or exclusion of supervisors, and the possibilities of multi-employer bargaining. Once the unit is determined, a representation election is held to select the organization that will represent the unit in collective bargaining, or the employer may voluntarily recognize the union upon a showing of majority support. The victor is certified as exclusive representative of the bargaining unit.

The next step is negotiation of the contract. The union leader and designated management representatives play the starring roles. It is difficult, however, to identify "management" in the public sector because of the large number of interested parties who participate directly or indirectly in multilateral bargaining. This is reflected in the wide compositional variety of management bargaining teams within and among the three levels of government. Public concern with some of the less edifying aspects of bargaining has led to increased interest in sunshine bargaining and the institutionalization of a public voice in collective bargaining.

The collective bargaining process in government is highly politicized, with politics pervading behavior at the bargaining table and suffusing the labor relations environment. Collective bargaining has been compared to a Byzantine play, complete with actors, roles, and script. The ending of the play, however, is not predetermined. It depends on the bargaining power of the parties, how they play the game, and whether the bargaining is primarily about getting to "yes" or just getting the best of the other side. Bargaining outcomes also depend on the effectiveness of public employee unions as interest groups engaged in lobbying, electoral activities, and public opinion making.

Case Study 4.1: Whose Union Is It?*

Simon looked down at the stack of petitions on his desk. Union members were reacting with signatures to rumors that they had heard regarding the layoff of 500 workers. They were calling for the ouster of the current union president and all union stewards. A membership survey (see Table 4.2) that had been conducted by union leaders to determine the bargaining path for the union had produced results that were not followed by the union. The largest majority of respondents had indicated that Scenario 4 was acceptable, yet the union was negotiating for Scenario 5.

Simon, a union steward for 15 years, was not accustomed to feeling uneasy with the posture of the union he represented. But this one made him wonder.

---

* Adapted from Trella (1996).

Table 4.2   Union Survey

Please indicate which scenarios are acceptable or not acceptable to you regarding a 40-hour work week. Please mark each scenario.
Scenario 1 — The contract provides for no general wage increase for five years, skips the payment of one annual increment, makes no guarantee to avoid layoffs, and institutes a 40-hour work week phased in with pay.
– Acceptable   – Not Acceptable
Scenario 2 — The contract provides for three 2% general wage increases in January of the last three years of a five-year period, skips the payment of one annual increment and delays the payment of the other annual increments for five months, makes no guarantee to avoid layoffs, and institutes a 40-hour work week phased in with pay.
– Acceptable   – Not Acceptable
Scenario 3 — The contract provides for general wage increases that keep pace with inflation, pays annual increment on time, makes no guarantee to avoid layoffs, and does not institute a 40-hour work week.
– Acceptable   – Not Acceptable
Scenario 4 — The contract provides for no general wage increases, pays annual increment and lump sum payments on time, makes a guarantee of no layoffs for general and special transportation fund employees, and institutes a 40-hour work week with pay.
– Acceptable   – Not Acceptable
Scenario 5 — The contract provides for general wage increases that exceed inflation, pays annual increments on time, institutes a 40-hour work week with pay, and results in 500 P4 employees being laid off.
– Acceptable   – Not Acceptable
Demographics

Cleaning Up the State Budget Crisis

The latest budgetary crisis in state government had caused the governor once again to request concessions from all state employee unions. The concessions took the form of an increase in the length of the work week (from 37½ to 40 hours) with a corresponding increase in pay. The increased work week was meant to calm state residents, who saw state workers as underworked and overpaid and who wanted massive layoffs to reduce their state income taxes. Because the budget supporting the state workers' salaries was not to increase, the extension to 40 hours per week would result in layoffs in every union.

Workers in the union who had been with the state for more than 10 years had a nice pension built up, paid medical benefits upon retirement, and job security. They were not anxious to work an extra 2½ hours a week, even with the additional pay. Ernie Banks, with the Department of Transportation (DOT) for 19 years, made it his business to know how his share of the pie would be affected. And he did not like what he saw.

> "Simon, Ernie here, just wondering about the union's stand regarding the 40-hour work week proposal. We're not going to work longer hours, are we?"
>
> "Well, Ernie, you know I'm always out to protect our interests. What do you think about it?"
>
> "Don't like it. I'm getting ready to start thinking about retirement. The last thing I need to do is work longer hours. You keep on protecting our rights, okay, buddy?"

Simon swallowed hard as he hung up the phone. The "good" days in state government were over. Every year now it was how much will you give up. Three years with no increases and now an addition of 2½ hours per week. But the message was not getting to the older union members. They wanted to hold on to an era gone by, when unions got much of what they bargained for.

Ernie knew the leaders in the union. He called the president and negotiators by their first names. And he let each of them know that he expected his union to protect his rights earned through 19 years of state service.

Union Represents Many Faces

Brenda McGuire worked as an entry-level engineer at DOT. She got the position right out of college, and although the wages were lower than those in the private sector, she opted for the job security of working for the state. After 2 years, she felt fairly comfortable performing her duties and understood how the public sector functioned. She was happy to have a steady job.

Jason Steel, Brenda's coworker, stopped her on the way to a meeting.

> "Did you hear about the layoffs?"
>
> Brenda bristled, "No, what have you heard?"
>
> "The older union members are selling us out. The union won't agree to reduce wage increases to compensate for the addition of the 40-hour work week, so the governor is going to order layoffs. Anyone with under three years of service has no seniority."

Brenda thought of her daughter who had just started preschool. That would have to stop with no job. "Well, what can we do?"

"There's a meeting right after work to discuss the options for the younger members of our union. Seems there are a lot of us who don't believe the union represents us. We're pretty certain that we younger members represent the majority. There's talk that they may try to get rid of Evans and all of the union officials. Maybe you should attend."

[*DOT Commissioner's Office*]

"There's a message here from three of the field supervisors. They're wondering why the union has agreed to layoffs. Each of them has field staff with under three years experience with the department. They are concerned that they will not meet their deadlines if they lose staff. All would like a return call from you."

Commissioner Smith wasn't certain how to proceed. He had major projects with funding that were going to suffer serious delays if the layoffs went through. That would reflect badly on his executive management objectives and he would lose the bonus he'd been working toward. He also had people who had worked in the department for more than 20 years who had little sympathy for the "youngsters" who could lose their jobs. He needed their experience to make the projects go.

Smith called Simon, the union steward, to request a meeting.

[*Simon's Office — Phones Ringing*]

"That makes 210 against and 33 for. The callers are not appreciating the stance of the union on this one. Saying we don't care about young families, only the retirement age workers. Is this really worth it? Heard rumors that they may call for your resignation," said Samantha Edwards, Simon's longtime assistant.

Simon sat down heavily. There did not seem to be a way out. Another phone rang.

"Commissioner's on the phone ... wants to come over for a meeting to discuss the options."
"Oh, great."

[*After-Work Meeting of Union Members*]

"I say we get rid of Simon. He is so out of touch with the majority of this bargaining unit. Who does he think he's representing?"

"I need my job. I don't really want to work more hours, but I need the job. We do what we have to do."

"Can we oust Simon? Will that help our cause? Do we have legal recourse if we see no hope of our views being represented?"

Simon knew the contract inside and out. He had special coverage under the contract that made him the last to go if layoffs ever went that deep in the agency. They called it superseniority. He also knew that "incompetence, inefficiency, neglect of duty, or misconduct" were grounds for dismissal.

The contract survey that the union members had filled out had shown that the majority of members opted for Scenario 4, which did not include layoffs. Although this information had not been publicly acknowledged, it had somehow found its way back to the membership. In fact, the union had decided to opt for Scenario 5 because they thought they would end up in a better bargaining position by asking for as much as possible and then, perhaps later, conceding on some points. The union's plan, however, had backfired. Now they faced a membership who sought retribution for not having their wishes followed.

[*Simon's Office*]

"Commissioner Smith is here."

Simon got up to present his plan.

Discussion Questions

1. What are the main issues in this case study?
2. If you were union steward Simon, how would you proceed?
3. Are layoffs preferable to givebacks in this situation?
4. Would the ouster of the union president help the younger union members?
5. What are the possible outcomes of this situation?

Chapter 5

The Process and Politics of Public Sector Collective Bargaining

I. Introduction

Collective bargaining in the private sector is about economics. In government, politics is added to the equation within an environment composed of a rich variety of interests with clashing views and values. The outputs of the bargaining process in government — decisions rendered concerning staffing levels, compensation, the allocation of tax dollars — are produced in this often chaotic milieu. And the direct participants are clearly political players, locked in a political contest with high stakes.

II. Internal Process and Politics

Collective bargaining is both a relationship and a process. It involves both formal and informal relationships that continue over time between labor and management with the purpose of jointly determining wages and other terms and conditions of employment. The process embraces activities that include identifying proposals, preparing for bargaining, negotiating an agreement specifying the terms and conditions of employment for a fixed period of time, and administering the agreement on a day-to-day basis. (Contract administration is discussed at length in Chapter 10.) The formal collective bargaining process prevailing in most jurisdictions is discussed below.

A. *Identifying Proposals*

Both sides in the bargaining process anxiously anticipate the receipt of proposals that either alter the existing agreement or identify key issues for the first time in a new collective bargaining relationship. Initial agreements can be particularly difficult because they represent the first attempt by the parties to significantly change the process used to solve problems and determine the terms and conditions of employment. Today, most contract bargaining involves parties who have already negotiated one or more formal agreements.

As proposals are being readied on both sides, decisions must be made as to how to package them and sort out the more important from the less important. A "bargaining book" or spreadsheet can cross-reference contract clauses and provide the history and meaning of contract terminology and clauses. Negotiators must bring their teams together to help them make these strategic determinations and to talk about readiness and strategy. There are a lot of "what if" scenarios to ponder. A division of labor is made in terms of the contract sections and language. Certain team members may be assigned to watch interpersonal dynamics, body language, and facial expressions on the other side of the table. The customary principle is to have a single spokesperson for each team.

How are subjects for negotiation identified? The union will have a standing list of issues, many of them arising from difficulties with the existing contract. Some issues may be a reexamination of compromises made during past negotiations that are no longer satisfactory because certain situations have changed. Other union demands may resurrect objectives not realized in past contracts but that are still important to the labor organization. The union holds membership meetings in which the rank and file can raise new issues or provide guidance that limits the chief negotiator's discretion on key matters that might have to be brought back to the membership for discussion. Some unions do a special mailing or survey to solicit input from members. Invariably, certain individual members will insist that a pet problem or concern become part of the bargaining proposals, usually to no avail. In successor agreements, there is typically a series of complaints emerging from grievances that the labor organization lost because present contract language did not support its position before an arbitrator. If the local union is affiliated with a national union, it is possible that matters may be advanced that were identified as priorities during the past national meeting. The challenge is to pare down the membership's "wish list" into a package of realistic proposals.

Management brings proposals to the table, too. This may seem obvious, but for years the union was the only moving party at the table. Management's posture was to react to what the union wanted. That has changed. Management understands that there is more to negotiating an agreement than getting the state legislature or city council to pay the bill. Contracts cover nearly all human resource management functions, issues, and operational matters that deeply influence how the organization's work gets done every day. Managers have ideas, too, about how to change the organization to make it run better, but union cooperation may be required. Effective managers are not indifferent to how people feel about their work. Managers do their homework by examining grievance files, the scope and cost of benefits, wage surveys, and practices in other departments or agencies. When management and the union both come to the table ready, the negotiations process proceeds more efficaciously.

B. Preparation for Bargaining

Preparation is the most critical component of bargaining success. The best prepared party, the one that has "done its homework," is usually the one that emerges from negotiations with the balance of its objectives secured. It is an axiom that "Table time is show time, but preparation time is dough time."

Preparation usually entails the steps sketched out below:

1. Establish a bargaining committee and a negotiating team, including a chief spokesperson.
2. Analyze the experience under the previous contract (if any). This process often starts soon after the current agreement was signed. Department heads and supervisors are asked to determine problem areas from management's perspective and offer advice on the next contract. Both parties study the grievance records under the old contract, including arbitration awards, and consider the motives, strategies, views, and likely demands of their counterparts on the opposite team. The union committee solicits and screens issues arising from the membership (see above).
3. Analyze wage and benefits data, particularly comparable information from similar jurisdictions and occupational groups. Conduct a wage and benefits survey if necessary. Respond to the other party's requests for data. The union reviews the employer's budget and other financial data.
4. Analyze recent legal developments and relevant agreements in other jurisdictions for personnel, law, and policy changes.
5. Prioritize demands and prepare justifications for them.
6. Arrange pre-negotiation conferences to establish the rules of the game and determine schedules. Include preliminary discussions on acceptable data, facts, and definitions to be used during negotiations.
7. Make formal presentations of written proposals and demands.
8. Set the bargaining agenda, including which issues will be considered first. Attempt to resolve simple, noncontroversial matters first to create a cooperative atmosphere. Consider dividing controversial issues into those that are

primarily economic in their implications and those that are not, and decide whether to take up issues as a package or break them down into smaller decision units.

9. Arrange negotiating sessions. These normally should be held during regular working hours for short (1- to 3-hour) periods of time. They should be held at a "neutral" location at the workplace or elsewhere. Provide for separate, private caucus rooms. Minutes of each meeting should be maintained by a neutral secretary and kept by each party as well.

10. Conduct negotiations. Hold caucuses to exchange reactions of members of the bargaining team, reconsider tactics and strategy, and check with superiors for guidance and direction.

11. Draft and sign a written agreement.

12. Have union membership and the legislative branch ratify the written agreement.

The reality of the bargaining process is not nearly as orderly and straightforward as these steps imply. The process is highly dynamic, changing in response to the role behavior and personalities of the participants, the actual and perceived bargaining power of the parties, and any number of other tangible and intangible factors that may impinge on negotiations.

Not surprisingly, unions and management increasingly rely on information-based technology. Such technology helps them develop and respond to proposals, keep historical records and personnel data, analyze the costs of alternative wage and benefit proposals, and compare contracts and data across other jurisdictions. Spreadsheets, database management software, and other decision support systems are utilized to examine and display data. Perhaps some employee organizations of the future will be known as "cyber unions," which knit together information technology to redefine, reinvent, and reinvigorate themselves (Shostak 2002a).

C. The Duty to Bargain

All state bargaining laws include the duty of the parties to bargain or meet and confer in good faith. In most of these states the duty to bargain closely approximates that defined for the private sector by the National Labor Relations Act (NLRA). It applies only to mandatory subjects within the scope of bargaining. Permissive subjects may be discussed at the discretion of the parties. Prohibited topics, such as those listed in a management rights clause, may not be enforceable even if they find their way into a written agreement. The NLRA (Section 8) describes the duty to bargain as: "The mutual obligation of the employer and the representative of the employees to meet at reasonable times and confer in good faith with respect to wages, hours, and other terms and conditions of employment ... but such obligation does not compel either party to agree to a proposal or require the making of a concession."

In essence, the obligation to bargain in good faith, as interpreted by the courts, requires active participation in negotiations with a sincere effort to reach an agreement. It is a cooperative state of mind that is evidenced in specific standards of behavior. In the public sector, those states that provide for collective bargaining (rather than meet and confer) have adopted statutory standards that closely approximate the NLRA's (see Table 5.1).

Once a term or condition is legally embodied in a signed ratified contract, neither party is obligated to reopen discussion on that term or condition during the life of the contract. Such discussions may ensue, however, if mutually agreed upon.

D. The Script

In the traditional model of collective bargaining, the processes and activities are sometimes compared to those of a poker game, complete with bluffs, deceptions, and the luck of the draw. The bargaining process is highly variable across juris-

Table 5.1   Standards for Bargaining in Good Faith

1.	Time limits for commencement of negotiations. Parties must furnish notice of the intent to modify or terminate an existing agreement, usually within at least 60 days.
2.	Obligation to provide information. The public employer is required to provide relevant information on any matter within the mandatory scope of bargaining that the employee organization requests.
3.	Prohibitions against bypassing the bargaining representatives. In an effort to avoid the end-run, some jurisdictions prohibit communications between the union representatives and any other official not a designated management bargaining representative.
4.	Requirement that the employer make no unilateral changes in existing wages, hours, and working conditions while negotiations are under way. Unilateral implementation usually is permitted for nonmandatory bargaining subjects.
5.	Prohibition against work stoppages during negotiations.
6	Formal procedures to resolve impasses.
7.	Duty to reduce the bargaining agreement to writing and to execute it.
8.	Prohibition against bad faith bargaining, which exists when one or both of the parties simply go through the motions without any real intention of reaching agreement. Indications of bad faith bargaining include dilatory tactics, failure to offer proposals or counterproposals, or refusal to make concessions on any issue.
9.	Requirement that both parties sign the written, negotiated agreement.

dictions, but certain common strategies and informal patterns of behavior are recognizable everywhere.

For example, the chief negotiator is normally the only bargaining team member to speak at the table. He or she seeks to keep the other team members under control and restrained from speaking out of turn (unless it is part of the script). Team members strive to keep a "poker face" — uttering a squeal of delight upon hearing a generous counteroffer is not recommended. Disagreements among team members are carefully concealed to prevent the opposing team from driving a wedge between them and weakening their overall position. Usually one person on each side acts as a recording secretary, keeping detailed notes of the proceedings. Recording devices are normally forbidden. They can cause problems later if, for example, heated words are exchanged and individuals say things they later regret.

As noted above, one member of the team may be assigned responsibility for observing members of the opposing team, scanning their faces for telling expressions, eye contact, or blinking; listening for voice tone and volume, involuntary sighs, laughs, or other nonverbal language; and observing body language for gestures or other indications of true feelings and reactions. All can convey important messages (Lincoln 2000).

During the initial presentation of demands and proposals, there may be some grandstanding as each side tries to sniff out the resistance points of the other and the strength of feelings on separate issues. During this stage, union leaders in particular sometimes make demands "that exhibit a greater use of imagination than that shown by Fellini or Hitchcock" (Sloane and Witney 1981: 190). A Long Island, New York police association once demanded "85 concessions, including a gymnasium and swimming pool; 17 paid holidays, including Valentine's Day and Halloween; and free abortions." This strategy, sometimes called "blue-skying," is intended to (1) appease influential members of the union by formalizing their pet demands, (2) allow ample room for later concessions, and (3) raise new issues that may become important in future contract negotiations. As one would expect, management usually takes the full plate of demands with a grain of salt, rejecting some items outright and ignoring others. Serious demands must be justified with documentation, appropriate data, and compelling arguments.

A classic illustration of "the script" in the traditional bargaining model involves negotiations between the New York City Transit Authority and President Mike Quill of the Transport Workers Union (Spero and Capozzola 1973: 108):

> Along about May or June every other year, Quill ... would summon members of the press to announce the demands of the TWU for justice, the 30-hour week and various other possible — and impossible — goals to be enshrined in the forthcoming contract with the Transit Authority. "Or else," Quill would thunder, "the trains won't run!" After the rejection of the union's demands by the Transit Authority and possibly the breaking off of a meeting or two, quiet would descend upon New York

for the balance of the summer. In the fall a series of meetings, usually stormy, would take place, building up to a peak in early December, when someone, usually the TWU leader, would break off negotiations. Quill would warn that there would be no transportation for Christmas shoppers unless talks became serious. The Transit Authority would announce that there was no money to meet the union's "exorbitant" demands. Just in the nick of time a third party would step in, at the request of the Mayor, to mediate the dispute. Shoppers would be saved, the negotiations would begin to build up to a New Year's climax. Both parties would be summoned to city hall; the mediators would move from the union to the Mayor to the union, building suspense as they went. Finally, a settlement would be announced — usually in time for late television and radio news broadcasts and the morning papers, and Quill would declare that the embattled transit workers had been victorious.

After initial meetings have permitted each party to size up the other and estimate its "true" bargaining position, serious negotiations begin over the substantive issues. The negotiating atmosphere from that point on depends on a number of factors, including the past history of the bargaining relationship and outcomes, the basic attitude of the employer toward unions, macroeconomic and employer financial factors, the political environment, and motivations of management and union representatives. As a general rule, however, as illustrated by the above example from New York City, as the deadline approaches for completing negotiations, the talks take on increasing intensity. The expectations of the parties in "the game" are that if one side moves toward the other on one or more issues, the second party will reciprocate. Informal discussions away from the bargaining table in a hallway or restroom may be used to explore possible avenues toward compromise. All-night bargaining may become necessary. There is nothing like the tedium and discomfort of round-the-clock bargaining to separate the insignificant issues from the truly important. Negotiations continue until an agreement is attained or all movement toward a settlement stops and the two parties declare an impasse. For a settlement to be reached both sides must avoid rigid or unrealistic positions and try to remain flexible, while keeping in mind the reciprocal nature of the bargaining relationship (see Tables 5.2 and 5.3).

E. Concession Bargaining

Flexibility is usually in short supply when government fiscal problems produce crisis or concession bargaining. Unions, which often have contributed significantly to fiscal problems through predictable activities designed to drive up wages, expand benefits, and maintain jobs, are asked to make givebacks to the employing jurisdiction.

Concession bargaining has always occurred in the private sector during the down cycles of capitalism. The first major experience with it in the public sector

Table 5.2   Twenty Bargaining Homilies

1.	Know the law and contract provisions.
2.	Be sure that you have set clear objectives on every bargaining item and that you understand on what grounds the objectives were established.
3.	Do not hurry; practice patience.
4.	When in doubt, caucus.
5.	Be well prepared with firm data to support clearly identified objectives.
6.	Always strive to keep some flexibility in your position — don't get yourself out on a limb.
7.	Do not concern yourself only with what the other party says and does — find out *why*. Remember that economic motivation is not the only explanation for the other party's conduct and actions.
8.	Respect the importance of face-saving for the other party.
9.	Constantly be alert to the true intentions of the other party — with respect not only to goals, but also to priorities.
10.	Be a good listener.
11.	Build a reputation for being fair but firm.
12.	Learn to control your emotions — don't panic. Use emotions as a tool, not an obstacle.
13.	Be sure as you make each bargaining move that you know its relationship to all other moves.
14.	Measure each move against your objectives.
15.	Pay close attention to the wording of every clause negotiated; words and phrases are often the source of grievances.
16.	Remember that collective bargaining is by its very nature part of a comprehensive process.
17.	There is no such thing as having all the pie.
18.	Learn to understand people and their personalities — it may pay off during negotiations.
19.	Consider the impact of present negotiations on future negotiations.
20.	Shake hands all around the room when the agreement is signed.

Source: The author, with the contributions of John Dodd (1996).

Table 5.3 Negotiating Your First Contract: Tips and Tricks for Management

1.	Don't forget your basic logistical requirements. You will need computers, a printer, memory sticks, an overhead projector, tape, paper, scissors, a copy machine, three-hole punch, etc. Plan ahead.
2.	Remember bargaining discipline. Know who will speak for your side. Know and understand the rules for a caucus before sitting down at the table.
3.	Go for a small agreement early. Agree that the weather is … nice, crummy, cloudy, cold, or whatever. The important thing is to obtain a mindset of agreement. This may sound trivial, but it is important because it works!
4.	Once you are bargaining, go for another small agreement early. Select something that neither side cares about. Your goal, once again, is to obtain a mindset toward agreement.
5.	Find out as much as you can about the union's agenda. Find out as much as possible about potential schisms in the union's bargaining team.
6.	Foster poor discipline on the union team by talking directly to members other than their principal spokesperson.
7.	Listen to what they say. Explore alternatives. They may want less than you think they do and less than you were willing to give. Go first with your initial proposal(s), but don't go first with your last best offer!
8.	Use interest-based techniques. The union doesn't care a fig about your position.
9.	Be respectful and courteous. Never talk down to the union.
10.	Be patient. Negotiating labor agreements is a frustrating endeavor. Often it is the most patient team that gets the best contract.
11.	Don't believe everything said, but don't call anyone a liar.
12.	Movement is the most important thing. If the parties keep moving toward the goal (a contract) you will eventually get there. *Do not allow yourself to get stuck on anything.* This can lead to impasse and a general mindset of futility.
13.	Ask the union to explain their proposals. Sometimes they want something that you will be happy to give them, but they didn't ask for it in the right way. Properly done, management can end up writing (for better or worse) almost all the language that ends up in the contract.
14.	Remember the old school crossing instructions: Stop, Look, and Listen!

Source: The author, with the contributions of John Dodd (1996).

came in 1975, as a consequence of New York City's fiscal collapse (see Maier 1987). Concession bargaining has been more commonplace during economic recessions since then, whenever state and local fiscal crises erupt and "doomsday budgets" threaten to shred services to the bare minimum. New York City, confronted with various budget gaps, has been known to turn off street lights, lay off thousands of city employees, and close libraries, clinics, and even the Central Park Zoo. Maine and Rhode Island have instituted rolling 1-day shutdowns of state government, during which "nonessential" employees stay home without pay. Workers have forfeited one or more years of pension benefits to save jobs. Public employees in nearly all jurisdictions have begun copaying health care insurance premiums for themselves and their families and increasing their deductions for prescription drugs and medical procedures.

Concession bargaining implies changes in the script. Instead of asking for more, unions must fight to avoid giving back what they have already gotten. Management takes the bargaining initiative, seeking wage and benefit givebacks and changes in work rules. If the union refuses to bend, layoffs are one likely alternative.

Concession bargaining poses serious problems for the union. Members react to layoffs and other management concessionary threats with "insecurity, frustration, and strong suspicion" (Craft et al. 1985: 169). Frustration mounts as hard-fought gains from past contract negotiations come at risk. Union leaders tend to lose their credibility and control over the rank and file. Combined with low levels of public support, these patterns portend a loss of union power and influence. Future relations with management are more likely to be confrontational and adversarial. Frustrated unions, weakened at the bargaining table, are likely to seek to win objectives outside the bargaining process, through grievances, the courts, and the political arena.

Ironically, a financially weak government employer may flex its muscles and become stronger at the bargaining table. Retrenchment presumes reducing, or at least holding the line on, personnel expenditures, which means reductions in force, wage freezes, and similar actions. If the unions are uncooperative, the public employer can act unilaterally in several important ways besides layoffs. For instance, most of the state bargaining laws provide that the financial agreements in labor contracts depend on legislative appropriation of funds, which might not be forthcoming in a fiscal emergency. Also, the U.S. Supreme Court and lower courts have recognized that a state may break a bargaining contract in certain cases of financial emergency (Befort 1985: 1243–1251). In a worst-case scenario, local governments can seek bankruptcy protection under Chapter 9 of the Federal Bankruptcy Code and, presumably, break union contracts.

In general, fiscal crises tend to stiffen the backs of public employers and tip the balance of power in their favor. Fortified by support from unhappy taxpayers, public management in fiscally stressed states and localities can successfully limit, and in some cases recover, previous union bargaining gains.

III. External Politics

In public sector collective bargaining the intensely political nature of the enterprise frequently spills over from the bargaining table into the broader environment of labor–management relations and vice versa. Public employee unions are influential and active interest groups whether contract negotiations are taking place or not. As interest groups, they participate in lobbying, campaigning, and other activities typical of organized interests seeking to mold public policy to the benefit of their members. Government unions enjoy a special place in the public sector decision-making process in those jurisdictions where they have gained collective bargaining rights.

Public officials are legally required to recognize and bargain with unions in most jurisdictions, an advantage rarely available to other interest groups. In addition, most labor–management decisions are made in private and beyond the immediate influence of other interest groups that also stake claim to a piece of the public pie. Although public employee unions do enjoy distinct access points not available to other groups, it should be recognized that government employees are vulnerable to counteracting political pressures. They may, for instance, have their jobs taken away from them for participating in an illegal strike; or the union may suffer the wrath of the voters in an anti-union referendum. Other interest groups cannot be slapped down so resoundingly when they offend the general public. To lessen their vulnerability and to manipulate levers of power and influence beyond the bargaining table, public employee organizations engage in a variety of political activities. This discussion on external politics considers the major political activities of public employees and their unions, specifically lobbying, electoral activities, and efforts to influence public opinion.

A. *Lobbying*

Union lobbying activities assume a variety of forms, including writing letters and emails to elected officials; introducing, preparing, or sponsoring bills; making presentations on proposed legislation at hearings and meetings; providing information to elected officials; and cultivating an ongoing atmosphere of trust and cooperation with elected officials. Lobbying activities may be specific (aimed at a specific objective such as legislative approval of a wage increase) or diffuse (promoting goodwill toward unions among legislators). Before collective bargaining was institutionalized in government, lobbying constituted the preeminent means of political influence for public employee organizations.

Lobbying efforts are usually directed at members of legislative bodies, because of the legislative role in structuring the legal environment and approving the financial provisions of any negotiated agreement. However, executive branch officials also are targets. Most lobbying activities are concentrated at the same level of government; that is, the teacher union focuses on members of the school board, the firefighters lobby the city council, and state employees devote their attention to state representatives. However, local government organizations often attempt to influence legislative decisions at the state level when state law controls local terms and conditions of employment or when a more general piece of legislation is of indirect interest to the union. An example of a specific, state-controlled policy would be a statewide benefits package for teachers or, in the case of firefighters, statewide fire safety standards. General legislation of interest could involve tax increases or taxation and expenditure limitations.

Union interest and active involvement in the legislative process is appropriate and legitimate. Public employee organizations are registered to lobby in most states. Some unions retain full-time professional lobbyists in their state capital and in Washington, D.C. Others employ their own members, particularly when lobbying efforts are aimed at the local level. It is when lobbying takes on the look of an end-run that certain activities are questioned. There are instances in which concern by elected officials for their personal political futures has compromised the process of collective bargaining. The end-run occurs when employee representatives discuss demands with officials who are not part of the bargaining team. If successful, the end-run can result in a union winning from the legislative body what it has been denied at the bargaining table. The tactic is inimical and chilling to collective bargaining. It makes future negotiations more problematic and undercuts management authority. In several states, the end-run is treated as an unfair labor practice.

As is the case with most interest groups, it is difficult to measure the direct effects of public employee union lobbying. At a national level, unions in both government and industry have not been particularly effective over the past three decades. The limited impact of union lobbying activities may be due to a number of factors, including declining private union membership and leveling off of public union membership, hostility on the part of employers and the public, statutory restrictions on union political activities, anti-union bias in the media, ineffective and unimaginative leadership, and the decline of political liberalism. To these might be added the conflicting philosophies among union leaders and members, divided partisan political loyalties of members, the divisiveness of narrow occupational interests, increased competition from other interest groups, and the growing dominance of business interests.

B. Electoral Activities

Electoral activities are designed to help elect candidates for public office who are believed to be sympathetic to the union. The relationship clearly is intended to be reciprocal: "We'll help you win the election if you will support the union." Many union electoral tactics are commonly employed, often through political action committees (PACs) (Asher et al. 2001). Because federal law prohibits direct contributions of union dues to candidates for political office, PACs are used to raise and disburse "voluntary" contributions to candidates. In 2006, union PACs contributed approximately $60 million to congressional candidates (Federal Election Commission 2007).

Unions commonly endorse candidates for state, local, or national office. This of course implies that the candidate will be the recipient of the "union vote," which is usually understood to include each member's voting age family. If the candidate wins, the union presumably enjoys access and favorable consideration. If, however, the endorsee loses, the union "later finds itself dealing with the victor, who may have a long memory" (Spero and Capozzola 1973: 91). Instead of officially putting the employee organization out on a limb, union officials will sometimes proffer an informal endorsement through public statements supporting the candidate's record.

Accompanying the official or tacit endorsement of a candidate are contributions in money, human resources, or both. This may represent the most effective labor tactic in American electoral politics, because it is directly related to voter turnout for union-supported candidates. As a member of the firefighters' union in Hartford, Connecticut, once said, "councilmen are interested in two things, the vote and money. We supply both" (Gerhart 1973: 26–27). In recent years, the National Education Association has supplied enough money to political candidates to rank in the top five of all political action committees. PAC contributions from the American Federation of State, County, and Municipal Employees (AFSCME), the Service Employees International Union (SEIU), the National Association of Letter Carriers, and other large unions have grown tremendously. Human resource contributions may include door-to-door canvassing of prospective voters, distributing campaign literature, stuffing envelopes, operating telephone banks, and developing and maintaining email lists, web posts, and blogs. Such direct aid in some instances produces very tangible returns in future wage and benefits packages and increased agency and departmental expenditures (Gely and Chandler 1995; Hammer and Wazeter 1993; O'Brien 1996).

In rare instances, unions sponsor their own candidate for public office. This can create a serious conflict of interest when the victor is a union member, because he or she must try to balance what is good for the public in the jurisdiction with what is good for the union. However, the strategy may be useful to promulgate the union voice and perspectives even when the candidate stands little chance of victory.

Although union electoral activities can help a favored candidate win office and perhaps ensure a sympathetic ear in the legislative body, and research shows that unions help mobilize general voter turnout (Leighley and Nagler 2007), no union or any other interest group can guarantee delivery of all or even most of the votes. This is especially true at the national level, where the political views of union leaders often differ markedly from those of the rank and file.

Some unions, such as huge District Council 37 of AFSCME in New York, are potent political forces that can mobilize strong support for union-supported candidates or issues. But union leaders must work hard to politicize, educate, and activate the members. Most count on a dedicated core of union activists for campaign activities. District 37 sponsors "campaign courses" and other educational opportunities to entice members into politics and to hone their political skills. The union also aggressively encourages its members to register and vote on election day.

How successful are unions in organizing the vote? Empirical research indicates that union members are more likely to register and vote than nonmembers (Freeman and Medoff 1984: 192–193). Union households made up 25 percent of the national electorate in the 2006 congressional elections. Apparently, however, union family members are no more likely to vote than nonmembers (Delaney et al. 1988). Do members vote in accordance with the wishes of the union? More often than not, they do, but support varies by jurisdiction and by election. Unions must compete with larger socioeconomic and political issues for the voting allegiance of their members. For instance, New York unions supported Republicans George Pataki (2002) and Rudy Giuliani (2006) for governor. One study found that members who attend union political meetings, read the union newsletter, and otherwise participate actively in their organization are more likely to support the union-endorsed candidate than the less active rank and file (Juravich and Shergold 1988).

Historically, the union vote has strongly favored liberal and Democratic candidates, although some erosion in this pattern was noted beginning with the 1968 presidential election (Masters and Delaney 1987: 343). From the mid-1990s into 2008 the congressional strength of the Republican Party encouraged legislative attacks on laws and policies that benefit unions and their members. The Democratic Party continues to be the only friendly political port in a storm, despite regular assertions by union leaders that Democratic candidates who are not in the camp of organized labor will not receive union campaign support or votes. It is important to recognize that unions negotiate and play a game of give and take with individual candidates and office holders more so than with the political party (Dark 2003: 458). A union displeased with one candidate may quietly defect to another or strongly endorse a candidate from a different political party. A third-party movement is frequently a topic of discussion among frustrated unionists, but the political reality has been that votes for third-party candidates increase the likelihood of Republican electoral victories (Delaney et al. 1999).

The most important question, of course, is whether the union vote makes any difference in public policy; in other words, does the union vote elect national, state, and local officials who support and help win union political objectives? The answer depends on the time, place, issue, and union, but generally the unions have fought a defensive battle since 1980. It also depends on whether the glass appears to be half empty or half full. Unions have counted only precious few legislative victories (e.g., occasional hikes in the minimum wage, defeat of school choice), but labor rights have not yet been seriously diluted, either. And unions have been a major — if usually losing — force in issue advocacy for immigration reforms, trade agreements, and health care reform (Francia, 2006).

C. Public Opinion

Most political activities by any interest group are intended to influence public opinion. Certainly this is true with regard to electoral activities. Some labor organizations directly undertake campaigns designed to affect public opinion on various issues of immediate or long-range concern to the union. Information may be conveyed to the public through press releases, television and radio spots, websites, blogs, informational picketing, rallies and demonstrations, and other techniques.

AFSCME has engaged in a variety of efforts to shape public opinion. It operates through its umbrella organization PEOPLE (Public Employees Organized to Promote Legislative Equality) to coordinate its national political activities and has participated in AFL-CIO's COPE (Committee on Political Equality), a related organization. Through these efforts AFSCME promotes programs as diverse as affordable health care, anti-poverty programs, civil rights, a higher minimum wage, immigration reform, pay equity, and consumer and environmental protection. AFSCME, SEIU, and other unions concentrate some of their public opinion initiatives on national "image" advertisements designed to promote the organization and the union movement in general.

Public approval ratings of unions generally declined during the 1980s and 1990s but have experienced modest gains since 2002. Recent surveys indicate public support once again exceeds 50 percent.

D. Restrictions on Public Employee Political Activity

Civil servants have been involved in political activities of one sort or another since the earliest days of the republic. In a legal and constitutional system characterized by multiple levels of management decision-making authority at three levels of government, government workers and their unions will always have strong incentives to exploit various access points. Collective bargaining, legislative politics, and elections are not mutually exclusive processes.

Given the pervasive presence of politics in government labor–management relations, a salient issue arises: should political activity by public employees be restricted? If so, how? As observed in Chapter 3, court interpretations of the First Amendment have narrowed union activities with regard to political expenses paid with dues from nonmembers who are in the bargaining unit; this weakens union speech. Similarly, constraints on union political action groups (PACS) limit union monetary contributions and campaign activities. Another limitation on political activity is through statute. The first statutory prohibitions were included in the Pendleton Act of 1883. In 1939 the Hatch Act restricted federal employee activities; it was extended to state and local government workers paid with federal dollars in 1940. Thereafter, most states and many local governments enacted their own "little Hatch Acts" to apply to non-federally funded employees. The laws taken together are highly diverse. Some prohibit all electoral activities except voting; others permit public employees to run for office. Most restrict partisan political activities, reflecting their origins in the reform struggle against the spoils system. All constrain union members' political activities in one or more ways.

The trend is in the direction of easing the Hatch Act-like restrictions through legislative actions and court decisions. Although the constitutionality of the Hatch Act has been upheld by the U.S. Supreme Court (*United States Civil Service Commission v. Letter Carriers* 1973), it has been ignored, on the whole, by both public workers and their employers, with a few exceptions.

Unions would like to abolish virtually all restraints on political activities by public employees. Federal employee unions lobbied successfully for Congress to pass and President Clinton to sign an overhaul of the federal Hatch Act in 1993. The amendment permits most federal employees to engage in political activities that were previously prohibited, including distributing partisan campaign literature, working for partisan candidates and campaigns, soliciting votes, and holding office in political parties. Pressure on similar laws at state and local levels continues. It is increasingly difficult to justify denying public workers those fundamental constitutional rights enjoyed by their counterparts in the private sector.

IV. From Traditional to Interest-Based Bargaining

As the union and management representatives come to the table, bringing issues important to them with respect to the current contract and the agreement that is about to be negotiated, they are intent on improving or eliminating old vocabulary and creating new language for the future. A reshaping of both a document and a relationship unfolds.

The union usually submits and explains its proposals first. An opening statement sounds the theme for this round of negotiations and reminds management how dedicated, hard working, and long suffering these employees have been. Management follows the union by making its own statement, usually indicating the employer's deep concern for the agency it represents and pointing out its regard for its loyal dedicated workers. Management is clear about its willingness to find ways to help solve problems and then customarily reminds the union of various limitations that make it difficult to accommodate all of the union's demands, particularly those of a financial nature. There are countless possible responses from the union to management's statement, but the most common may be that it is not a problem of ability to pay, but rather willingness to pay, for the union's demands. The opening statements, and responses, are meant to apprise each side as to what the other wants or does not want. In a sense, during this initial session, each party is reminding the other that it has equal standing in the process and that it must be treated with respect. Much of what is said is expected, but it is not unusual to hear things quite unanticipated. This introductory period also signals the tone the negotiations might take, and teams begin the bonding process as the real bargaining is soon to commence. Both sides pledge to work in good faith.

This is all part of the opening dance ritualistically performed by the parties. Nonetheless, serious messages get delivered and sophisticated negotiators glean important information or suppositions about what to expect in future meetings. The parties watch nonverbal communication quite closely at this time, searching for clues to attitudes on the other side that may be predictive of what is to follow and identifying individuals who may represent problems in the bargaining. When the initial exchange is completed, the parties are ready for serious negotiations.

A. Traditional Negotiations*

Traditional negotiations fit the stereotype most people have about collective bargaining. That image represents what Fisher and Ury (1981) characterized as the "hard" approach to bargaining and what Walton and McKersie (1965) referred to as distributive (zero-sum) bargaining. It features: (1) looking at participants as adversaries and wanting to win at all cost, (2) low trust of the other side, (3) trying to force the other party to make concessions through sheer use of power, (4) using threats, and (5) seeing issues in dualistic terms (e.g., "right or wrong," "sensible or irrational"). In terms of collective negotiations, the hard bargaining approach frames the issues using two contested perspectives.

"Positional" is the word often associated with traditional bargaining. Having a position means having a specific idea on how any differences or problems should be resolved. Many people believe that there is a "right" answer to any question or problem. At the bargaining table, the attachment to a single "correct" concept or solution makes getting settlements very difficult. The dynamics are such that one side publicly digs into its position and rejects or denigrates the ideas of the other. As negotiators become identified more and more with a singular view of the world, they are less able to listen to contrary arguments. A mere difference of opinion can quickly turn into a personal matter. Threats or statements such as "under no circumstances will we ever…" might be made. Obviously, such behavior does not help the parties to reach a settlement and it has a deleterious impact on the relationship between the parties. For example, a management that refuses to negotiate in good faith, demanding that the union accept its nonnegotiable positions on all the issues (this behavior is known as "Boulwarism") leaves the union few choices: concede or go to arbitration (or strike). A prisoner's dilemma is created (Leventoglu and Tarar 2005). However, the parties have to work together once the contract is settled. A party can win the bargaining battle but lose the war.

Fisher and Ury (1981) also described a "soft" approach to bargaining, which is the opposite of the traditional forceful method but also dysfunctional in the long

---

* David G. Carnevale made important contributions to the following discussion in an earlier edition of the book. His assistance and insights are greatly appreciated.

run. In the soft strategy, negotiators want to see people as friends or colleagues. They make concessions to show their good faith in wanting to reach an agreement and have a tendency to yield to pressure. They perceive conflict in general as an uncomfortable and unseemly sort of fighting that is to be avoided. Soft strategists do what they can to dodge trouble and are overly willing to make compromises and accommodations to demonstrate their willingness to be collaborative. They forget that they have representational responsibilities for one side or the other and that it takes two serious strategies to fashion an agreement that works for both parties.

Avoiding conflict can lead to more problems in the future than confronting it directly when it first needs to be engaged. Collective bargaining is a process that fully recognizes that conflicts in the workplace are natural and that the parties need to resolve their differences peacefully and productively. Soft bargaining undermines the process and does damage to the public, public institutions, and public employees. It does not advance either major objective of collective bargaining: to achieve a workable contract and to maintain a productive relationship between the parties. In this regard the soft approach is "lose–lose." Avoiding conflict may be wise on some occasions. However, as an overall philosophy of bargaining, it courts disaster.

Traditional or distributive bargaining is adversarial and conflict oriented by nature. As in a game of poker, neither side reveals its hand to the other. It involves deception and bluffing and a number of other games that negotiators play. The desired image is to be tough and clever. For example, during negotiations between the California State Employees Association (CSEA/SEIU) and its own staff (union staffs are often unionized and bargain with the leaders of the union), the management team proposed installing time clocks and maintained an apparent seriousness about the issue throughout the negotiations. No manager actually wanted time clocks, but the issue was included in the package so that it could be conceded near the end of bargaining when things were most intense. This was a way of giving the union a win (no time clocks) in exchange for something management really wanted. During the same negotiations, the management chief negotiator would deliberately leave on the table at the end of the day some of the notes that are routinely passed between team members. The notes were full of false information. As expected, the union read the notes and spent time developing defenses against management strategies that were in fact nonexistent. It is no wonder that trust levels are low in negotiations in which one or both sides are intent on manipulating the other. The world's leading experts in negotiation drama might be the North Koreans, who have been known to shorten the table legs on the American negotiators' side and provide them with low chairs.

It is difficult under such circumstances to tell what is real and what is an illusion. Rumors are commonplace during negotiations, and they are often personal and negative in terms of individuals and organizations on both sides. It is also common for people to treat colleagues suspiciously if they are on the "wrong side" or appear to be insufficiently loyal to the side they are supposed to support. Information frequently gets distorted, sometimes intentionally. All of these gamesmanship dynamics make it difficult to come to mutual terms in solving problems. Fundamentally, traditional bargaining is adversarial, contentious, and emotionally draining. It does ultimately produce a settlement, but the costs may be destructive to the relationship.

The traditional approach to bargaining is about power, not collaborating for mutual gain. The behavioral characteristics associated with the traditional approach are competition (win–lose, zero-sum assumptions), aggression, resistance, hostility, and even bullying (Barrett 1995). It is replete with contentious tactics, including gamesmanship, "guilt tripping," irrevocable comments (if–then messages), and threats (J. Z. Rubin et al. 1993). The traditional approach attempts to wear down, seduce, manipulate, threaten, and dominate. Personal attacks are not unusual and sarcasm has a central place in the discourse. For example, during 2004 negotiations between the Police Benevolent Association and New York City's extraordinarily wealthy Mayor Michael Bloomberg, the union did not hold back from personal attacks. The chief negotiator spoke emotionally at a rally and on camera, yelling "We are not asking to be rich like you, Mr. Mayor. All we are asking for is to make our lives better for our families" (Steinhamer 2004). The New York City teachers' union claimed that the mayor did not want a settlement — just a scapegoat to blame for his failure to improve public education (Greenhouse 2004). Bloomberg's successor, Rudy Giuliani, turned the tables on striking transit workers in 2007, accusing them of crippling the transportation system and delaying emergency services, thus placing the lives of citizens at risk.

The underlying idea is that "I cannot get what I want unless you don't get what you want." This is zero-sum thinking. Every concession is seen as a loss. The problem with these tactics is that much of what is being done appears personal and threatening. It raises emotions, and any perceived attack generates reciprocal behavior. A spiral of conflict spins as sides form, positions harden even more, communication is impaired, hostility escalates, and threats become issues, until the top of the spiral is reached where people want revenge more than a fair and workable contract.

The style and approach of traditional bargaining is rough on the problems and tough on the people (Fisher and Ury 1981). Traditional talks gone awry damage the ongoing working relationship between the parties, disrupt teamwork, lower productivity, and spawn an "us versus them" work climate that is destructive to the creation of high-performance organizations.

Contemporary public administration theory and practice are marching in an entirely different direction from the assumptions, values, and practices of traditional bargaining. The major leadership and management models in government and business today rely a great deal on collaboration and participative decision making at all levels of organizations (Kearney and Hays 1994). A number of teamwork, reinvention, reengineering, quality, benchmarking, learning, and other innovations depend on trust and the use of genuine participative dialogue to improve performance. How organizations negotiate labor agreements, and the outcomes, both real and intangible, matter greatly in delivering high-quality public services.

B. *Interest-Based Bargaining (IBB)*

Interest-based bargaining is also known as win–win bargaining, integrative bargaining, and principled negotiations. The IBB method is intended to change the operating assumptions of persons who have learned to negotiate in traditional ways using traditional tactics (comparison of the two approaches is presented in Table 5.4). It is worth pointing out that win–win may overstate what is possible in many negotiating settings. The term makes it sound as if differences can be resolved without costs, but "win–win" ought to be used with care because it is important to keep people's expectations realistic. Level of expectations in any form of bargaining is an important factor in how the talks will go. Obviously, parties that expect to get a lot, or perhaps everything they desire, are usually in for a comeuppance.

"Winning" means being able to get an agreement that both parties can live with. Such an agreement satisfies the interests of both parties and encourages smooth administration once the pact is consummated. The idea that each side can go to the bargaining table and have all its desires met without making some concessions or having to engage in give and take is unrealistic and can make the negotiations extremely difficult. That is why mediators are cautious about the win–win phrase. What negotiators and mediators focus on instead is helping the parties to understand that the real spirit of the win–win philosophy means being assertive about one's needs and, at the same time, being willing to actively listen to what the other party wants. The idea is that agreements are produced more efficiently and equitably if the interests of both sides are taken into account. Another underlying aspect of the win–win philosophy is that there are many ways to solve problems if people will work together. Interest-based negotiation is not a "soft" approach, in which people have to like each other and bend over backwards to make concessions. It is, instead, a method to get a tough job done in a way that settles the immediate problems and sets conditions for improved future working relationships. It is meant to be efficient and fair to both sides.

Table 5.4 Comparison of Traditional and Interest-Based Bargaining Principles

Traditional	Interest-Based
Issues	Issues
Positions	Interests
Arguments	Options
Power and forced compromise	Standards and problem solving
Short-term gain	Long-term relationship
Win–lose outcome	Win–win outcome

The principles of IBB are

1. Negotiate on the merits of a proposal; don't reject it out of hand because someone from the other side suggested it.
2. Separate the people from the problem, which means "don't shoot the messenger" and don't blame someone from the other side for doing his or her job.
3. Be hard on the problem and professional with the people; avoid assigning blame and recognize the value of face saving.
4. Determine the interests of the other side instead of just reacting to their positions; understanding the overall interests helps to open up more options for solving the problems.
5. Avoid fighting issue by issue, position by position from an adversarial posture; consider using a facilitator to help generate dialogue and to mediate when called for.
6. Invent options for mutual gain; brainstorm to identify a range of possible options that reconcile differences and advance shared interests.
7. Have someone chart the ideas that are brainstormed by the groups in the room and then post the charts on the walls so that there is one set of data that is public and available to all; type up the charts each evening and give them to the parties the next morning so everyone is working from the same set of notes.
8. Establish criteria upon which a proposal may be judged on the merits and have the parties make the determination about whether any idea satisfies the interests and criteria of both parties; these become likely candidates for inclusion in the contract (Fisher and Ury 1981).
9. Develop a BATNA (Best Alternative To a Negotiated Agreement) that you could live with.

An example would be helpful. In one state, the parties knew from the outset that they would have a good deal of difficulty in getting a contract, so they asked for two labor facilitators (mediators) to help them with this new process called interest-based bargaining. Before the mediators would agree to facilitate an entire agreement, they put the workers and management through IBB training. The parties were told to pick a real problem, one that was a problem in the relationship that would certainly find its way to the bargaining table and that they had not been able to resolve. They chose a problem involving welders. After some very basic training in IBB, the parties were broken into groups and about 40 people went into brainstorming on how to fix the problem. This is a well-tested technique for inventing options for mutual gain. The groups came up with more than 60 ideas, which were written on the board. The criteria then were established — the solution had to be affordable, it should be legal, it should not lead to any layoffs, it should be ethical, etc. About a dozen of the ideas fit the criteria. Two or three ideas were especially good and were used to settle the issue. In this particular case, an entire labor agreement was negotiated using the IBB method in slightly more than 1 week.*

It would be nice to think that negotiators move smoothly and enthusiastically to IBB and away from the more pathological aspects of traditional bargaining, but it is not that easy. Individuals have different perceptions of the world. Some are open to changing their cosmology and others simply are not. Some negotiators begin the IBB process but revert to traditional tactics. The actual negotiations experience frequently involves some traditional methods and some IBB techniques. Compromise and give-and-take strategies tend to prevail in any negotiation. Things may proceed smoothly for a while, but eventually someone or something pushes the parties back to where they started — suspicious, confrontational, and adversarial. It is normal. Even the closest friendship contains some conflict. People forced to address difficult issues do not behave consistently with models. They say and do what they feel is right at the time. It is a challenge for a facilitator to allow venting and regression while gently prodding folks back to the IBB method. Bargaining is real-time and actions and reactions naturally occur. It does the facilitator no good to disallow a discussion because it fits the wrong model or is not timely. It is a sure way to get the facilitator replaced. The process has a way of working itself out in its own way and in its own time. Solid advice for facilitators and mediators is "try not to step on the conversation."

There are times and places where traditional bargaining is called for because of the comfort zone of the parties, the nature of issues in dispute, intense constituent pressures from the union's side, or the high level of strain being exerted downward from upper management in the public agency. Some traditionalists like the model they use because it is predictable and they know how to play the game. The idea of a new process like IBB is viewed as risky. The union side has many of the same fears. There are those on both sides who stereotype the other ("unions are destructive and anti-American" or "managers don't care about employees and cannot be trusted").

Some negotiating situations are doomed from the start. You cannot bargain successfully with a 2-year-old, a madman, or a fool (Schelling 1960). If one party is irrational, any agreement (other than to cease negotiations) is extremely unlikely. Perceived fairness and legitimacy of the bargaining process encourages the interpersonal trust that enables win–win solutions (Leach and Sabatier 2005).

Another barrier to implementing IBB is intraorganizational conflict. Friction, disagreement, or just plain personal animosity may surface within the union team or among union members not part of the team. Similarly, elected and appointed officials may be working counterproductively behind the scenes. Interpersonal and professional conflicts may play a role as well. Many a negotiator has had to keep one eye looking across the table and the other on the behavior of people ostensibly on his side. Bargaining teams from both sides rarely have the internal solidarity they seek to project.

---

* David Carnevale contributed this discussion on IBB.

Other confounding factors can interfere with getting a good agreement. Negotiation is a dispute-resolution mechanism, which means that it is inherently about conflict. There are honest differences of opinions about issues. This helps to explain why some negotiations can be so contentious. There is rarely agreement among a group of people on what it is the organization should be doing or where it should be headed. This manifests itself in bargaining strategy. People may come to terms with where they would like to go, but have differences on how to get there. So, we have disputes on ends and means. People have different values and ideologies and do not let go of them easily. There are personality conflicts. The same "facts" may be viewed in very different ways. People's perceptions in every aspect of life tend to be self-serving and distorted. We tend to attribute bad motives to people who disappoint us but are quick to blame situational factors beyond our control for our own failings. People don't communicate very effectively. Memories are short and information gets confused. Perhaps it is more accurate to say that people are better at being assertive about their own needs than listening to the other party express its needs.

Traditional and interest-based bargaining should be appreciated as methods and techniques that are conducted in the thicket of human personalities and emotions that exist at every workplace. Some situations are favorable for IBB, and some are not.

If these factors were not enough, there are a few more that make any successful conclusion to bargaining problematic. First, there is the pressure of time. Bargaining may start slowly, but there is normally a deadline that has to be met if the contract is to be placed before the jurisdiction's legislative body for ratification. Late-night bargaining against the clock is not uncommon. There is the problem of union ratification. Each member of the bargaining unit gets to vote on whether they accept the agreement or wish to send their negotiators back to the table. "Soft" negotiators may push their chairs back from the table with the assumptions that bargaining is essentially a friendly process; but the deals they make will have trouble being ratified because of the perception that they are too weak or "sellouts." In other words, a dominator-dominated relationship confounds a win–win solution. Another problem, "unresolved prior conflict," means there will be no new agreement until some past issue is resurrected and rectified. Experienced negotiators characterize this as "sin bagging." Issue after issue may come and go and the parties avoid dealing with them. Then, one day, an incident breaks the proverbial camel's back and all of the past problems come flooding out at once. This is another example of where problem avoidance today may cause the price of peace to be higher tomorrow.

The prevalence of integrative (win–win) or distributive (traditional) strategy depends to a great extent on the distance between the union's objectives and those of the employer. A cooperative approach tends to prevail if the two sides are not far apart to begin with. Coercive tactics tend to be used when a large gap separates bargaining objectives. The gap between the positions of the parties is referred to as the "bargaining zone" (Walton and McKersie 1965). The bargaining zone spans the distance between the resistance points of each party; that is, the point beyond which a strike or impasse will result. Each side tries to determine the resistance point of the other. A negative zone exists if there is a gap between the farthest point of compromise acceptable to each party. For instance, if the union will accept no less than a $2.00 per hour wage increase and management is unwilling to agree to a penny more than $1.50, a negative zone exists and impasse is likely. A positive zone is characterized by overlapping resistance points: the union wants no less than $1.75 and management has already decided to grant up to $2.00. Here, settlement is a foregone conclusion.

The resistance points of the respective parties depend to a large degree on their bargaining power. Power, as defined by Robert Dahl (1957: 203), is the extent to which A can get B to do (or not do) something that B otherwise would not (or would) do. In the words of Chamberlain and Kuhn (1965: 162–190), power "is the ability to secure an agreement on one's terms." Power is a product of the resources available to each party with which to influence bargaining outcomes. The resources that may be used include money, votes, political party support, budgetary expertise, negotiating skills, information, access to the media and elected officials, and job actions. In government, power resources are predominantly political. In the private sector they are primarily economic.

Collective bargaining is about dealing with differences and constructing a relationship. If it is treated purely as a game or a contest of wills, IBB techniques will be inappropriate. Getting good settlements that the parties can live with is a formidable task given the nature of the processes used, the mindsets of the parties, the maturity of the relationship, the psychological nature of human beings, and the complexity and difficulty of the issues.

Table 5.5 summarizes the differences in attitude and behavior among soft, hard, and principled bargaining approaches.

After negotiations are finished and signatures made, certain post-negotiation rituals are performed. Handshakes and congratulations are exchanged around the room. Joint media releases are issued. Printed copies of the contract are distributed. Union leadership and top management publicly recognize the achievements of the bargaining teams. A deep sense of satisfaction is experienced by all (Oestreich and Whaley 2001: Appendix A1).

V. Bargaining in the Future

Collective bargaining still follows the traditional model, although IBB is spreading to a growing number of jurisdictions. IBB promotes the kind of work climate consistent with teamwork. It has the potential to make collective bargaining a strategic asset in organizations because it pushes to the surface numerous problems management may not know exist. In other words, the bargaining process gives management and employees at all levels an opportunity to talk about mutual problems

Table 5.5 Contrasting Bargaining Approaches

Soft Bargaining	Hard Bargaining	Principled Negotiations
Participants are friends.	Participants are adversaries.	Participants are problem solvers.
The goal is agreement.	The goal is victory.	The goal is a wise outcome reached efficiently and amicably.
Make concessions to cultivate the relationship.	Demand concessions as a condition of the relationship.	Separate the people from the problem.
Be soft on the people and on the problem.	Be hard on the people and on the problem.	Be soft on the people, but hard on the problem.
Trust others.	Distrust others.	Trust, but verify.
Change your position easily.	Dig into your position.	Focus on interests, not positions.
Make offers.	Make threats.	Explore interests.
Disclose your bottom line.	Mislead as to your bottom line.	Avoid having a bottom line; have a BATNA instead.
Accept one-sided losses to reach agreement.	Demand one-sided gains as the price of agreement.	Invent options for mutual gain.
Search for the single answer: the one *they* will accept.	Search for the single answer: the one *you* will accept.	Develop multiple options; decide on one later.
Insist on agreement.	Insist on your position.	Insist on using objective criteria.
Try to avoid a contest of will.	Try to win a contest of will.	Try to reach a result based on standards independent of will.
Yield to pressure.	Apply pressure.	Reason and be open to reasons; yield to principle, not pressure.

that can be rectified. Organizational learning and performance are enhanced. In a broad sense, IBB is part of the trend toward greater employee involvement and participation (Kearney and Hays 1994). It is a type of empowerment and sharing of responsibility. IBB also comports with the growing interest in alternative dispute resolution (ADR), which is being used throughout government and the private sector to help resolve disputes involving family, labor relations, civil relations, commercial interactions, custody disputes, and many others. IBB is similar in process to many organizational development third-party peacemaking and teambuilding interventions. And, as public and nonprofit administrators know, the handling of conflict through negotiations is an important part of the day-to-day operation of every public service organization. Negotiations expertise is an important skill at work and in life.

VI. Summary and Conclusions

The bargaining process commences with each party communicating its proposals to the other. Many political and psychological considerations are relevant in determining which proposals to make and how to portray them. As in the courtroom, preparation is a critical component of the process. Both parties typically are bound by law and practice to bargain in good faith.

Government fiscal constraints in some jurisdictions have produced a trend toward concession bargaining, in which unions are pressed to make financial or work rule givebacks to their employer. Although traditional, zero-sum bargaining remains the norm, a great deal of attention is being given to interest-based, win–win negotiations. The latter approach differs substantially in its assumptions, processes, and potential outcomes. However, it involves significant changes in thought and behavior and naturally provokes resistance from parties who want to cling to a more conventional approach.

Case Study 5.1: Sanitation Workers and the City of Belview — Contract Negotiation

Instructions

Two negotiating teams should be formed, each consisting of three to six individuals. The teams should be named before the day of the exercise and given sufficient time to organize themselves and prepare for the negotiations. A leader and a recorder should be elected by each team. The job of the recorder is to record proposals, counterproposals, agreements, and other useful information in a "negotiations ledger." A laptop computer may be useful.

The teams should negotiate an agreement, record their final settlement in writing, and calculate the financial costs of the settlement. The length of the negotiations should be 1 to 3 hours. If one or more items goes to arbitration (see below), the instructor or a designated individual should serve as the arbitrator.

Background

The Belview Sanitation Department (BSD) has 75 employees. Seventy are members of the bargaining unit, which is represented by the Sanitation Workers of America (SWA). The BSD collects household and business trash and recyclables twice per week throughout the city limits. It utilizes 20 garbage trucks and five vehicles for collecting recycled aluminum cans, paper, glass, and plastics. Three employees work on each garbage truck and two on each recycle vehicle. The rolling stock is getting a bit old: the garbage trucks average about 8 years and the other vehicles around 5 years. The technology is somewhat outdated as well. Some nearby jurisdictions, for example, use one- or two-person garbage trucks that collect household trash in large, green "Herbie Curbies." This technology requires residents to push their Herbie Curbies out to the street once per week and then return them to the rear of the house.

During the past two decades the BSD employees have received competitive pay raises and their benefits package compares favorably with those of neighboring jurisdictions. There was an illegal strike to gain union recognition about 20 years ago, but recently relations between the union and management have been good. Because of a recent state supreme court ruling, however, strikes by public employees are now legal, although none has yet occurred. Deadlocked negotiations have gone, instead, to binding arbitration.

The present 2-year contract expires in 3 days. Negotiations have gone nowhere for the past month, but now the parties are prepared to engage in a marathon bargaining session to settle the remaining issues.

Interests of the Parties

Wages. The union is asking for an increase of $1.25 per hour for the first year of a new contract and $1.00 for the second year. Management, preferring a 3-year contract, has countered with an offer of $.50 for 2 years and $1.00 for the third year. The average hourly rate for sanitation workers is $15.00 per hour, slightly below the regional average of $15.75.

Health care benefits. The City of Belview currently pays the full cost of medical insurance for its sanitation workers, currently valued at $300 per month. Approximately 75 percent of the employees have dependents also covered under the city health insurance program. Under the existing contract, the city pays 50 percent of the total cost of $400 for dependent coverage, which is $200 per month. The union is asking for full (100 percent) coverage of dependents. Management has received notice from the PPO (Preferred Provider Organizations) that the cost of each policy will increase by $50 next year. Management wants employees to copay 25 percent of their personal health care insurance but is willing to continue paying 50 percent of dependent coverage.

Sick leave. The present contract includes 7 paid sick days. The BSD workers claim that the nature of their work causes them to be ill and injured more frequently than other city employees, and they are asking for 10 paid sick days. Other city employees also have 7 days.

Assignment

1. Negotiate and record your agreement on pay and benefits. If no agreement has been reached on one or more issues when time expires, the dispute(s) will have to be submitted to conventional arbitration. Each party must develop a written defense of its positions and perceived interests.
2. Each party should calculate the costs of the economic items, including the wage increase (at 2,080 hours per year), health insurance benefits, and sick leave.
3. Reflect on the bargaining approach employed by each team. Was it hard, soft, principled or a blend?

Chapter 6

Financial Impacts of Unions and Collective Bargaining

I. Introduction

Most state and local governments intermittently suffer through the throes of fiscal crisis. The fiscal problems that can assault governments are legion: inflation, recessions, increased service demands and costs, shifts in population and tax base, declining intergovernmental aid, expensive court orders or settlements, citizen resistance to tax increases, infrastructure deterioration, burdensome federal mandates — the list is almost endless. Symptoms of fiscal stress run the gamut from the near bankruptcy of New York City, Detroit, and Cleveland in the late 1970s and San Diego, California in 2006, to the actual bankruptcy filing of Vallejo, California in 2008.

Financial adversity has become a chronic affliction for some state and local governments, particularly those that have been net losers in the globalization of markets and labor. The major social, economic, and political forces contributing to government fiscal stress have shown little sign of abatement, even in comparatively prosperous economic times. Meanwhile, state and local government employment and payroll costs have risen steadily. States employ more than 5.3 million workers and local governments approximately 14.6 million. Total payroll costs exceed $61 billion (www. census.gov/govs/apea/05stus.txt; accessed February 5, 2008).

The conventional wisdom is that unions, through collective bargaining and various political activities, contribute to state and local fiscal difficulties by inflating payrolls and operating budgets. It is often asserted that the primary impact of public employee unions has been to drive up the cost of wages and benefits. Because 40 to 70 percent of the typical local government and school district operating budget is allocated to employee compensation, strong union influence in setting pay and benefits could, indeed, press financially troubled jurisdictions up against the fiscal wall by achieving monetary gains that the local government could not afford. State government payroll costs represent a smaller percentage of the operating budget, but they are also influenced by union pressures for wage and benefit increases. Because government remains a highly labor-intensive enterprise, if unions drive up pay and benefits, then they also establish an upward bias on state and local expenditures. In the private sector, a firm may recapture compensation increases through higher prices or improved productivity, or absorb them through reduced profits. In government, a wage increase may translate into a tax or fee hike, making choices more constricted, more difficult to make, and more visible to the relevant public.

This chapter assesses the financial impacts of public employee unions. There are two major types of impacts: on the budgetary process and outcomes and on employee wages and benefits. After a description and appraisal of union influences in budgeting, the empirical literature is examined to identify the dollars and cents wage and benefits effects of unionization. Various factors that influence wage and benefits outcomes are discussed, including parity arrangements, prevailing pay rules, seniority rules, and comparable worth criteria. The consequences of public sector wage and benefits decisions for government decision makers are considered, along with possible citizen reactions to these decisions. A brief description and analysis of gainsharing and productivity bargaining is followed by a look at the financial impacts of federal employee unions and collective bargaining.

The chapter provides no simple, quantitative answer to the question of what are the specific financial impacts of unions and collective bargaining in government. The nature, size, and significance of the union effects on budgeting, pay, and benefits are variable, complex, and multifaceted. The major conclusions are (1) that whereas unions have exercised an upward influence on budgeting and compensation outcomes, the overall effects have been moderate and not as substantial as the monetary impacts of unions in the private sector, and (2) that the magnitude of the impact varies greatly over time, function, and jurisdiction.

II. Budget Making and Unions

The annual (or in some states, biennial) operating budget determines who gets what monies for which purposes. To the extent that budgetary allocations go to public employee compensation, there is that much less money for other expenditure items. For public employees, however, the operating budget determines the size of their raises, the scope and cost of health insurance, retirement and other benefits, and, in tough economic times, which of them will retain their jobs. Not surprisingly, unions are active participants in the budget-setting process, through collective bargaining and political activities intended to influence the decisions of elected and appointed officials in the executive and legislative branches.

A. The Budgetary Process

In the absence of unions, employee compensation is determined almost unilaterally by elected officials and public sector management. In the case of a council–manager style of government, where mayoral power is typically weak, department heads make expenditure recommendations to the city manager, who formulates a budget for consideration by the council. In this highly simplified model, compensation decisions are implemented after the council ratifies the budget.

Public employees have no formal role in determining wages and benefits under this model. Their chief collective influence over compensation levels is limited to statements at budget hearings and informal lobbying of the manager and council as one of a plethora of interest groups in the local political arena. Indirectly, public employees may exercise some collective impact on wages and benefits through electoral support of "friendly" candidates. Acting as individuals, workers may attempt to convince superiors to recommend them for higher pay. Once compensation decisions are rendered, however, public workers must usually accept their pay allocations without recourse.

The situation is not dissimilar for nonrepresented state employees, who do exercise at least a modest collective voice through their state employees association, which testifies and introduces data before legislative budget committees. Individual state employees are largely, however, at the mercy of legislative and gubernatorial decisions and the pay distributions of supervisors.

With unions and collective bargaining, the role of public employees in budget making and compensation determination is greatly enhanced. A formal collective voice is provided through which public employees press their demands during budget making. A model of union representation in a council–manager government may be depicted as follows:

When unions are involved, public employees enjoy direct formal access to budget making as well as informal channels of influence such as lobbying and campaign and election activities. At the state level, unions negotiate their terms and conditions of employment with a management team representing the executive branch; the legislature typically honors the results by incorporating them into the budget.

The procedural implications of this bilateral (or, one might say, multilateral) arrangement for budgeting can substantially impact the budget timetable. Public employee unions can seriously constrict the ability of budget makers to rationalize, control, and manage the budget. In the absence of collective bargaining, allocations for wage and benefit increases normally are settled well in advance of legislative ratification, guided by department head and budget staff recommendations and anticipated revenues. Under collective bargaining, however, wage and benefit allotments cannot be finalized until contracts are signed between the jurisdiction and its various employee organizations. Uncertainty occurs when bargaining is extended near or past the legal deadline for having a budget in place. When this happens, the government may have to enact a continuation budget, seek new revenue sources, or take other measures to provide for an undetermined increase in compensation. Unions have been known to take advantage of the situation by deliberately drawing out negotiations beyond the budget finalization date in an effort to maximize contract gains.

Most state and local government jurisdictions try to complete all collective bargaining contracts as soon as possible and especially before the budget goes to the legislative body. But reconciling the budget and bargaining schedules is a regular problem. Some jurisdictions have attempted to resolve the problem of coordinating bargaining and budgeting through legislation. For example, collective bargaining must begin a specified period of time before budget making in New Hampshire and Massachusetts. Hawaii and Iowa tie the bargaining schedule to the fiscal year, and quite a few bargaining jurisdictions declare an impasse automatically if no agreement has been signed by a specified time. Various formal and informal venues for legislative consultation and participation are also provided in some states, including Minnesota (legislative hearings), Connecticut (formal consultation), and California (legislators may even speak at bargaining sessions) (Allshouse 1985). Still, late contract settlements are not unusual even in those jurisdictions that attempt to eliminate them through statute.

Even when jurisdictions are in the early years of a multi-year contract, the budget schedule can become derailed because of fiscal shortfalls. This occurred in numerous jurisdictions during the recession of 2008 as unions were asked to give back negotiated wage increases to avoid layoffs or furloughs. In some instances, statewide contracts were reopened, with high-stakes budget negotiations needed to produce a new agreement.

What kinds of problems do late settlements create? Clearly there is a certain loss of efficiency. Continuation of bargaining past the final budget date makes the budget process less predictable and controllable for management and may necessitate shifting other allocations or enacting supplementary appropriations, or new revenue measures, to finance late settlements. Layoffs or service cutbacks are also a possibility.

Budget makers may anticipate a late settlement and decide to earmark or "hide" dollars in unrelated budget lines or contingency accounts to pay for delayed wage and benefit settlements or to keep in reserve for other financial emergencies. Such hiding behavior is rather common and generally considered to be part of the bargaining game by both parties. Although hiding tactics are successful to varying degrees as a means of coping with late settlements, their usefulness in holding down union compensation gains remains a matter of speculation; unions are certainly not oblivious to the possibility that management has tucked away some resources. Moreover, public sector managers should consider the possible repercussions of concealing funds in case unions, the media, or citizens discover their actions.

The unions play their own budget games. They may attempt to bring supervisors into their support group by implicitly tying together a pay hike for bargaining unit members with a salary increase for supervisors. Union spokespersons seek out the relevant media, soliciting reports establishing the credibility and importance of government programs and how important new dollars are for service maintenance and improvements. Alliances with client groups help turn up the burner on the legislative body during budget deliberations.

Late contract settlements may or may not cause problems with respect to the financial situation of the government, depending on the finally agreed upon amount of compensation. In some instances a late settlement can help make a moderate pay increase more acceptable to public employees by allowing negotiations to run far beyond the contract expiration date as a way of reducing rank-and-file expectations. As workers yearn more and more for their lump-sum retroactive checks and increases in weekly paychecks, they become more "realistic" in their expectations (Juris and Feuille 1973: 68). In other cases, late contract settlement may result in a cutback of services within a particular service function. In jurisdictions, for example, that distribute to their agencies a lump-sum appropriation, late, unanticipated salary increases must be absorbed in the agency's own predetermined budget.

Clearly, integration of bargaining and budgeting would make the budgeting process more convenient, more controllable, and less stressful for management. The quandary lies in finding an effective means to achieve coordination. Statutory requirements that bargaining be concluded prior to a budget completion date apparently have not had the intended outcome; the budget finalization date comes and goes while negotiations run on with no significant legal consequences. However, non-statutory steps can help link state budgeting with collective bargaining. For instance, negotiations can begin early in the fiscal year; certain benefits such as pensions can be provided uniformly, thereby simplifying bargaining; and, in general, revenue and expenditure data can be transmitted to management and labor negotiators and analysts in a timely fashion. The widespread infusion of technology into budgeting has helped to speed up the flow of financial information to all parties, aiding budget preparation and analysis in numerous ways.

State and local bargaining and budget making are likely to remain askew where collective bargaining prevails, with mandatory budget adoption dates serving only as benchmarks. In such a context, budgeting can be frustrating for all concerned parties, including the interest and clientele groups seeking government largess for their special programs and concerns. State and local discretionary funds are already highly constricted because of tax and expenditure limitations, federal mandates, and citizen opposition to taxing and spending. With more and more special interests fighting over a shrinking government budget pie, the level of conflict climbs. The additional uncertainty introduced by a tardy collective bargaining settlement elevates the intensity of the budget battle even more.

B. Budgetary Outcomes

Because personnel costs constitute a large proportion of the operating budget for state and local governments, an increase in wages and benefits will likely result in higher budget outlays. How will the growth in the compensation bill be funded? In the absence of sufficient new revenues from economic growth or state or federal grants-in-aid, the local jurisdiction must weigh various options, including hiking the property tax rate or user fees, reducing other expenditures, reducing or contracting out services, seeking productivity gains from ongoing operations, freezing vacant positions, or using reserve funds (Kearney 2005: 30–31). Of course, compensation costs rise whether unions are in the picture or not, with "catch-up" or cost-of-living adjustments and seniority and merit pay increases. Nonetheless, unions are often blamed by public officials and the media for financial difficulties.

Empirical research indicates that unions are, indeed, associated with larger budget outlays in cities, although the impact appears to be moderate when other budget-expanding and budget-restricting factors are taken into account. Specifically, collective bargaining is linked to higher personnel expenditures (as a proportion of the operating budget), but the strength of the relationship varies by city size and the functional area examined, and it is tempered by declines in employment levels. The union effect apparently once was relatively lower in larger cities (100,000+ population), suggesting that large cities may cope with union-driven compensation increases by cutting back on employment and service levels (Benecki 1978; Kearney 1979). More recent studies (G. Lewis and Stein 1989; Valletta 1989; Zax 1988; O'Brien 1994) have found municipal unionization and collective bargaining associated with higher expenditures, but with city size less important. The important point is that municipal unions influence the budgetary process to their advantage by driving up personnel outlays through collective bargaining and political activities.

However, in some cases there appears to be a tradeoff between pay and positions — an "employment effect." Collective bargaining clearly affects compensation levels, as discussed in detail later in this chapter. Its effects on total city expenditures, however, are less certain (Valletta 1989: 438–439; O'Brien 1994), probably because wage increases are sometimes accompanied by employment reductions in the bargaining units or in nonbargaining departments.

Do unions protect pay levels at the expense of jobs? Sometimes. Under union contracts, reductions in force are applied with reverse seniority — "last hired, first fired." Junior rank and file constitute a relatively noninfluential minority of total union membership. The more numerous senior members of the bargaining unit are not usually personally vulnerable to layoffs, and they may choose to protect their pocketbooks instead of other employees' positions (see Freeman and Medoff 1984).

The negative relationship identified between unionization and employment (Clark and Ferguson 1983; Stein 1990: 491; O'Brien 1994; Trejo 1991) also indicates that some union-related factor or set of factors is at work to hold down job levels. Perhaps unions prompt a cutback in the quality and quantity of services. Or management may be able to institute productivity and technological improvements to maintain service levels with a reduced number of workers. And there is always the possibility that bureaucratic fat is being sliced off instead of muscle. Indeed, unions may force city officials to become more efficiency minded.

There are countercurrents, however, and union political activities can push overall city employment levels higher (see Zax 1989; Freeman and Valletta 1988; Valletta 1989). Union campaign contributions and endorsements of political candidates have been found to significantly affect the demand for services, and employment, of police and firefighters (Chandler and Gely 1995).

Conflicting findings on the union impact on budget outcomes and employment levels are a result of the variable time periods and employee functions examined, the quality of available data, and the researcher's methodological approach. Most likely other salient yet unmeasured factors remain unaccounted for in the empirical research, such as the average age of the bargaining unit, the quality of union leadership, and the sense of solidarity among union members.

III. Unions, Wages, and Benefits

One of the most popular research topics for the community of labor relations scholars has been the impacts of unions on wage and non-wage compensation. It is also one of the most important topics for research because it represents a fundamental measure of union power and organizational success or failure.

A great many factors influence government wage and benefit levels, including social, economic, and political forces and conditions; decision-making rules and processes; and circumstances peculiar to particular jurisdictions and settings. Before one can isolate the effects of unions and collective bargaining on compensation, these other factors must be satisfactorily taken into account.

A. Socioeconomic Factors

The socioeconomic forces that establish boundaries within which public sector compensation determinations are made are many, diverse, and interrelated. Economists refer to them as labor market factors or, more specifically, labor supply and demand factors.

Five variables that help measure the supply, or availability, of labor are cost of living, labor concentration, labor force composition, opportunity wage and employer demand for workers.

1. Cost of living represents how much one must spend to acquire the necessities and wants of life, as well as how rapidly prices are rising. High and rising cost of living is associated with higher public employee wage and benefit levels, but, in some cases, it is also associated with a shrinking labor force, as workers move to jobs located in areas with lower costs of living. Cost of living also varies according to geography. In general, wages are higher in New England, the mid-Atlantic, Great Lakes, and Pacific states, about average in most of the Midwest, and lowest in the South and Southwest. Within regions, cost of living tends to be dearest in metropolitan areas and least in small and rural communities. Unions, of course, often base wage and benefit demands on measures of cost of living, such as those compiled by the U.S. Department of Commerce (e.g., the Consumer Price Index).

2. Labor concentration, or "labor density," refers to the number of potential workers within a labor market. Wages and benefits normally are greater in government jurisdictions with high levels of population and population density. Several explanations exist for this phenomenon, including the availability of a well-trained and educated labor force in heavily populated areas, a higher tax base from which to extract resources for employee compensation, a high urban cost of living, and the simple expectation that highly populated cities and states will remunerate their workers more generously than rural jurisdictions.

3. The composition of the labor force is a third labor supply variable. These "human capital" variables account for differences in compensation that occur as the result of variations in education, experience, race and ethnicity, and gender of the work force. Because of vestiges of racial, ethnic, and gender discrimination, white males still enjoy pay advantages over their African American, Latino, or female counterparts that cannot be attributed to different backgrounds in education and job experience. Although equal opportunity and affirmative action laws and policies have assuaged these disparities, equal pay for equal work is not yet a reality across all U.S. governments.

4. The opportunity wage is a fourth labor supply influence on wages and benefits. Briefly, the opportunity wage is that which would be available to the same individual for work in a similar occupation for another government, private, or nonprofit sector employer. Raiding nearby municipalities for highly qualified or otherwise desirable workers is a common phenomenon in many metropolitan areas, and many state governments compete in the job market with private firms, nonprofits, other states, and the federal government. Thus, there are pressures on the employer to keep wages and benefits at levels high enough to discourage employee turnover for more generous economic rewards elsewhere, and at the same time to attract well-qualified job seekers.

5. Three factors related to employer demand for labor are fiscal capacity, monopsony, and unemployment. Fiscal capacity is positively associated with wage and benefit levels. Generally speaking, wealthier state and local governments

with high tax bases and relatively low expenditures enjoy revenue advantages that may accrue to the benefit of public employees. Related factors are the amount of funds obtained through federal grants-in-aid and other intergovernmental transfers and tax effort. For example, a relatively poor state may pay quite competitive wages and benefits if it receives large amounts of federal aid and taxes its citizens heavily.

Monopsony is, in effect, a monopoly in the labor market that is exercised by a single employer. Thus, an employer demands a large enough quantity of a particular type of labor so that the wages within an occupation are pushed downward. For example, a geographically isolated city with a single school district exercises a monopsony over public school teachers who have no alternative education employment available to them (except, of course, in the private sector, where wages in most cases are lower for teachers). Teachers, like nurses and university professors, may be disadvantaged in the labor market when there is a scarcity of alternative places of employment within reasonable commuting distance (Merrifield 1999).

Alternatively, where two or more school districts or hospitals compete within the same urban area for the services of teachers or nurses, the degree of competition may be positively related to employee compensation. Several studies have found that these relationships do indeed exist in the case of public education (see Delaney 1988; Merrifield 1999). However, the relevance of the monopsony argument to the public sector appears to be rather limited when other occupations such as law enforcement and fire protection are considered.

Finally, unemployment rates are inversely related to compensation. High levels of unemployment exert downward pressure on wages. Jurisdictions in low employment areas may be forced to pay a wage premium to attract qualified employees.

B. Political Factors

Political factors also have an impact on government compensation outcomes. Although numerous political variables influence pay and benefits, three of them deserve to be singled out: the legal environment, the nature of government management, and government structure.

The legal environment of public sector labor relations affects compensation in a variety of ways. Bargaining laws reflect union power and influence in the political arena, which spills over into wage and benefit decisions. One would expect, for example, that public employees benefit from more favorable compensation outcomes in a state with a comprehensive bargaining law, such as Iowa, than in a state like South Carolina, which does not legally sanction collective negotiations. Arbitration laws also may influence compensation outcomes. A study of police bargaining over a 10-year period found that the availability of interest arbitration is associated with higher police salaries (Feuille and Delaney 1986; see also Chapter 9). Recent research also has identified a positive relationship between the availability of arbitration and earnings of other local government employees, including teachers (Zigarelli 1996). Many other elements in the legal and policy environment can also affect compensation levels, including a legal or de facto right to strike (Zigarelli 1996), taxation and expenditure limitations, the threat or reality of outsourcing, and the setting of certain employee benefits statewide (teacher pensions, for instance).

How management organizes itself for wage and benefit decisions is relevant to compensation outcomes. As noted above, in nonunion settings such decisions may be rendered unilaterally — by a city manager or state legislature, for instance. But multilateral negotiations frequently take place where collective bargaining exists. One would expect that unilateral determination would tend to hold down wages and benefits, while the involvement of multiple actors, which often reflects internal management conflict and political forces, would play out to the represented employees' advantage.

The structure of government itself may affect public employee compensation outcomes. "Reformed" political institutions such as a council–manager government, nonpartisan elections, and at-large or mixed constituencies may tend to minimize the access of public workers to the decision-making arena. Public employees should have stronger influence on wage and benefit decisions where they find it relatively easy to apply political pressure to elected officials. Thus, mayor–council systems, partisan elections, and single-member electoral districts should be associated with more favorable compensation outcomes. Empirical research on the structure of government variable reports mixed findings, however (Ehrenberg 1972; Gerhart 1976; G. Lewis and Stein 1989; Chandler and Gely 1995).

C. Politics and Decision Rules in the Compensation Decision Process

As noted above, in nonunion jurisdictions the role of the public worker in compensation decisions is normally limited to informal individual or group requests for a satisfactory increase in monetary awards. But where public employee unions enter the scene by way of formal or informal bilateral negotiations, the compensation determination process assumes an important new political dimension.

The politics of compensation involve union activities in election campaigns, including member support of and financial contributions to candidates and political action committees. Politicians may trade favorable pay and benefits for union political support (Chandler and Gely 1995; O'Brien 1994; Hammer and Wazeter 1993). Lobbying elected and appointed officials; collecting, analyzing, and disseminating pertinent information on pay and benefits; and influencing citizen opinion through public relations are common tactics. Unions may apply raw political power through real or threatened job actions, warnings of electoral defeats, and other intimidating behavior.

Unions usually prefer to have pay increases awarded across the board or in equal percentages (e.g., a 5 percent hike for everybody). This limits management discretion and is perceived to be fair by most parties. But this decision rule does nothing to encourage or reward special effort or outstanding performance, and that disturbs management. Merit pay or pay for performance ties remuneration to achievement and maximizes management discretion to reward high performance and productivity. It may take the form of incentive pay or group performance bonuses. In principle, it makes a great deal of sense and it has been widely adopted in some form throughout government at all levels. But in practice, merit pay is plagued by a multitude of problems (see Perry 2003; Kellough and Selden 1997). Unions generally, and often successfully, oppose it.

Despite the intuitive appeal of merit pay, public sector compensation decisions are often based on formal and informal decision rules that tend to substitute for power politics. Unions and management each strive to gain acceptance of decision rules that work to their own advantage, but several rules have been widely adopted by both parties: the prevailing rate, pay parity, cost-of-living adjustments, comparable worth, and ability to pay.

The *prevailing pay rate* for labor is important both symbolically and substantively. Symbolically, it represents a fair day's pay for a fair day's work. Substantively, it keeps workers reasonably satisfied and helps preclude attrition of the work force to higher paying area employers. The prevailing rate is determined from secondary sources such as the U.S. Bureau of Labor Statistics' Area Wage Surveys or other appropriate data from national, state, business, or labor organizations, or it may be calculated independently through salary and benefits surveys by individual jurisdictions. All states and the great majority of local governments with populations of 10,000 or above conduct such surveys either regularly or intermittently. Some are mandated by law; others are done informally.

Typically, data comparing a jurisdiction's salaries and benefits with those of neighboring public and private organizations are sought for "benchmark" jobs such as key entry-level positions. Through mail, telephone, or Internet surveys, wage data are obtained from other relevant employers. Benchmark positions must be closely comparable in job descriptions and knowledge, skills, and abilities required, as well as in hours worked. Examples include beginning school teachers, administrative assistants, police sergeants, and social service caseworkers. It is also important to collect data on benefits. Variability in benefits sometimes makes meaningful comparison problematic, but the dollar value of major benefits such as pensions and medical care should be taken into account.

At first blush, establishing the prevailing rate through surveys appears to be rather objective and straightforward. However, politics is inherently involved. For example, which employers should be surveyed? What should be the scope of the investigation? Survey outcomes are related to characteristics of responding employers, including population and geographic size, fiscal capacity and status, prevailing labor climate, and cost of living. Thus, how the sample is drawn helps determine results. Moreover, interpretation of survey results is subject to dispute. Should data from extreme or "outlying" respondents be tossed out? Are benchmark positions truly comparable? Should respondents be classified by population size or some other characteristic? Should both union and nonunion employers be surveyed?

Because so much judgment and discretion is involved, employee organizations often seek to determine the prevailing rate independently, through their own surveys or with the help of national union staff. Data collected by unions and public employers may be shared, but each tends to look suspiciously at survey results provided by the other.

Parity is a second decision rule widely used by management and labor, particularly in many local government jurisdictions. The parity rule is an old one. As early as 1898 a parity provision for police and firefighters was in effect in New York City (the police were still fighting against it in 2007), about 65 years before collective bargaining began its great period of growth in urban areas. Parity may be set at 100 percent, where two occupational groups always receive the same levels of pay and benefits, or it may be set at a certain percentage of the pay of a key occupation. (For example, police officers in Hawaii receive a 5 percent pay advantage over firefighters.) After one bargaining unit negotiates a raise, a comparable increase will automatically be granted to the other unit. Parity provisions usually apply to the police and fire functions, with police setting the pay standard. However, parity also may exist between craft workers in the public sector and their private sector counterparts.

Parity rules may be embodied in collective bargaining contracts, state or local legislation, or city charters, or they may be implemented informally. Sometimes, as in New York City, parity rules become the subject of intense rivalry between police and firefighters. Firefighters, who often seek to achieve or maintain parity with police, claim that they work longer hours and perform more dangerous work, they must spend more time away from home and family, and their job requires a substantial amount of technical training and expertise. Police respond that their job is more dangerous, involves more intensive work, and requires greater use of interpersonal skills. Furthermore, police claim that they need higher entry-level pay to attract recruits into the demanding and hazardous field of law enforcement.

Police unions sometimes attempt to break parity arrangements, and they have been struck down by the courts in several jurisdictions, including some in Maine, Connecticut, and New York, on the grounds that they effectively withdraw bargaining rights from a union that is not a party to the arrangement.

Another decision rule is *cost of living*, which, of course, usually is rising. Cost-of-living arguments resonate with voters and public officials, who understand the pain of salaries that are stagnant in value. Unions want to incorporate its effects in salaries so that members do not lose ground in purchasing power. During periods of price inflation, unions seek to negotiate escalator clauses so that future wage increases track cost-of-living increases. Slowdowns in inflation may provoke elimination of public sector escalator clauses.

Comparable worth rose to prominence in the public sector in the 1980s largely because of public employee unions. As a compensation decision rule, it means equal pay for work of comparable value. Equal pay for equal work is a widely accepted legal principle, but comparable worth is a contentious issue that challenges conventional market-based wage-setting practices.

Fifty years ago, the vast majority of working women were employed in only a handful of occupations. Few alternatives were available beyond teaching, nursing, and clerical work. In these "female ghettos," women earned less than 60 percent of the median pay of males. Today, there are essentially no occupational barriers that large numbers of women have not broken down, yet as a group they still earn only about 78 percent of what men do. Frustration with this wage gap has mounted. Supporters of comparable worth argue that the wage differential is primarily caused by continuing (if voluntary) job segregation and wage discrimination. Comparable worth seeks to address these sources of gender-based pay inequities.

Opponents counter that comparable worth takes wages beyond the law of labor supply and demand and would wreak devastating results on national, not to mention organizational, pay policies. They further contend that wage discrimination is a myth. Women are paid less because many of them are part-time and temporary workers, they tend to leave the labor force to give birth and raise children, and they choose to segregate themselves in lower paying jobs.

In the absence of congressional action, the arguments for and against comparable worth have been addressed in courtrooms and state and local legislative bodies across the country. The bell for the first round of the comparable worth fight was sounded in San Jose, California, in 1981. AFSCME Local 101 tried to force the city to implement comparable worth adjustments to close a pay gap identified by a salary study. An agreement between union leaders and city officials was quickly reached that hiked the pay of about 20 percent of the city's employees (Flammang 1986).

Two important court cases also arose from the West Coast: *County of Washington v. Gunther* (1981) and *AFSCME v. State of Washington* (1983). In the first, female jail "matrons" (guards) sued Washington County, Oregon, under Title VII of the Civil Rights Act of 1964 because they were paid 30 percent less than male guards for substantially equal work. A lower court ruled against the matrons, but a federal court of appeals reversed the decision and was later narrowly upheld by the U.S. Supreme Court, which sent the case back for reconsideration without accepting the concept of comparable worth (Legler 1985).

In the second case, AFSCME spearheaded a class action suit against the State of Washington for failing to act on several comparable worth studies the state had commissioned. The studies had discovered a 20 percent gender-based wage gap for comparable positions. The union position prevailed in the U.S. District Court but was later overturned on appeal. Nonetheless, the state of Washington settled with the union and the 15,500 female workers it represented and fully implemented comparable worth within 10 years.

AFSCME President Gerald McEntee recognized the potential benefits of the comparable worth issue for the union, observing that "the ruling in Tacoma (Washington) is going to reach into every one of the 50 state governments, every one of the 3,041 counties, and each and all of the townships and cities and school districts. In fact, it is going to affect every one of the nearly 83,000 public jurisdictions in this land ..." (quoted in Legler 1985: 241–242). McEntee may have overstated his case, but other public employee unions joined AFSCME in latching onto comparable worth during the 1980s and thereafter, recognizing it as an excellent tool for organizing the female labor force in government. Today, unions continue to pursue comparable worth through legal actions, the collective bargaining process, and state legislation. Pay equity arrangements have been negotiated in Connecticut, Iowa, Massachusetts, and other states. Comparable worth laws have been passed in Minnesota, Montana, New York, Iowa, Oregon, Washington, Wisconsin, and elsewhere. More than 20 states have comparable worth policies in place today.

Unions must tread a fine line between accommodating the comparable worth demands of female members while avoiding the alienation of males, who may fear that pay adjustments will be extracted from their own earnings (see Riccucci 1990). The public work force is approaching 50 percent female, yet pay inequities persist, so the issue will remain salient.

Obviously, comparable worth policies drive up the price of women's labor. As a practical matter, men's wages will not be reduced to make up the difference. Thus, the total wage bill of comparable worth jurisdictions grows rather substantially. The impact of full implementation of comparable worth appears to average a 17 percent gain for women; men's wages remain approximately the same. Total payroll is estimated to have increased from one to four percent in comparable worth states (Gardner and Daniel 1998).

The basic comparable worth methodology is point factor analysis. Critical job factors, which typically include knowledge, skills, and abilities, are identified for male- and female-dominated positions and assigned numerical scores on the basis of their relative importance to the organization. The factor scores are summed for each position. Jobs with equal or nearly equal scores receive equal pay. For example, an administrative secretary's wages might be brought up to the level of a transportation department crew leader or a state grain inspector, or the pay of a nurse might be raised to equal that of a truck repair foreman.

When faced with employee demands for compensation increases, whether based on comparable worth or other factors, public employers often invoke the *principle of ability to pay*. In a sense, it is more of a negotiating tactic than a decision rule, but its omnipresence certainly demands discussion. Usually, the ability to pay principle is argued in the negative. In making an "inability to pay" argument, government is claiming that it is unable to grant its workers more than a certain amount in wages and benefits because of revenue shortfalls, expenditure demands, or other contingencies. Ostensibly, inability to pay is a valid argument. Nevertheless, public employee unions often translate inability to pay as unwillingness to pay. Certainly, the issue is subject to debate. For example, when is a government unable to pay? When it defaults on outstanding debts? When it fails to meet its payroll? Or before such crises arise?

Surely, if a state or local government is prohibited by law from running an operating deficit, a union-proposed wage settlement that would force the budget into the red could be successfully countered by an inability-to-pay argument. But government employers raise the inability to pay flag so frequently that unions no longer salute, and instead demand exquisite details on revenues, expenditures, and debts and to search assiduously for money hidden in the budget. Management may seek to bolster its own case with figures on cash flow, debt and debt service levels, inadequately funded retire pension and health care benefits, pending or actual court decisions that present future liabilities, legally mandated budget expenditures, and various comparisons with wage and benefit levels and tax burdens in other jurisdictions.

Unions carefully examine management's data and financial projections and calculate their own. Often, assistance is available from national unions, many of which maintain a budget analysis staff. Most have the capability to conduct econometric analyses. The National Education Association, for example, has a budget analysis software package for local school districts. And, in general, information technology and resources have greatly simplified such analysis. A thorough union review of data will also examine the proposed budget, including expenditure forecasts and economic assumptions, past budgets, external audit reports, budget reviews and financial statements, minutes of council or legislative meetings, news reports, bond prospectuses, promotional literature, independent fiscal data from citizen's groups, "inside" information from secretaries in key offices, a search for contingency funds or other hidden monies, and personnel reports on unfilled positions (Leibig and Kahn 1987: 194–204; Toulmin 1988: 622–623).

D. Monetary Impacts of Unions: Approaching the Research Question

Unionization (the extent, or density, of employee organizational membership) and collective bargaining (formalized labor–management decision making within a collective framework) drive salaries and wages upward. Even in the absence of collective bargaining, unions may influence compensation policies. Unions in a neighboring jurisdiction may affect compensation levels in nonunion settings through a "threat effect," as employers seek to discourage employee organizing by paying competitive wages and benefits.

Some four decades ago, unions and collective bargaining in government were unknown quantities that aroused reactions running the gamut from blind, ideological devotion to fearful, virulent criticism. The most influential and thought-provoking attack on public sector unions and collective bargaining was set out in a controversial Brookings Institution study in 1971. According to *The Unions and the Cities*, union activity and collective bargaining distort the democratic political process:

> The distortion results from unions obtaining too much power, relative to other interest groups, in decisions affecting the level of taxes and the allocation of tax dollars. The distortion therefore may result

in a redistribution of income by government whereby union members are subsidized at the expense of other interest groups. (Wellington and Winter 1971: 167)

Public employee unions "leave competing groups in the political process at a permanent and substantial disadvantage" (Wellington and Winter 1971: 30, 31), for several major reasons: (1) some municipal services are essential, so prolonged interruption resulting from a strike directly threatens public health and safety; (2) the demand for public services is relatively inelastic and insensitive to changes in price because government services lack close substitutes and competitive service providers rarely exist; and (3) the disruption of government services inconveniences voters who may punish political leaders in the next election. Implicitly, "rent-seeking" elected officials solicit and reward union political support. Thus, the authors argue, unions in government inherently have greater power than those in the private sector. A product of this power advantage, one would logically assume, is higher compensation for unionized government employees as compared with their union counterparts in private employment or nonunionized colleagues in other governmental units.

Have public sector unions achieved wage and benefits gains that outstrip their union counterparts in the private sector and nonunion workers in other governmental jurisdictions? Wellington and Winter furnished no quantitative data to support their assertions, but these claims have occupied the time of other researchers.

IV. Are Public Sector Workers Paid More Than Private Sector Workers?

Until the rise of unions in government in the 1960s and 1970s, public employees were consistently underpaid relative to similar workers in the private sector. Since then, several studies have attempted to compare wage and benefit levels in public and private sector employment. It is generally agreed that public employees improved their pay position relative to private sector workers in most occupational categories from the late 1960s through the mid-1970s (Field and Keller 1976; Reder 1975; Orr 1976).

Have public employees continued to close or even reverse the pay gap? Which sector pays the highest today? The findings are mixed on these questions. The answers depend on government function, the level and size of government, time period, methodology, and, apparently, the political values or ideology of the researcher.

The first study to directly address relative public–private sector pay (S. P. Smith 1976) determined that federal workers made substantially more (10 to 20 percent) than similar private sector workers, but state and local employees enjoyed only a very slight (1 to 2 percent) advantage. Subsequent research has tended to support these findings (Linneman and Wachter 1990), although state and local earnings growth lagged the private sector during the 1980s, according to one researcher (see Krueger 1988). Two studies using 1991 data found that public sector employees earned a "significant wage premium" that exceeded private sector pay by 5.4 percent and total pay and benefits by 10.3 percent (Choudhury 1994). The public sector compensation advantage rose to 25 percent when the shorter government work week was taken into account, leading Cox and Brunelli (1992) to call for cutting state and local jobs, reducing payroll, and contracting out government services to save money.

Research results are contradictory when federal employees are singled out. Perloff and Wachter (1984) and Krueger (1988) found that postal employees were much better paid than similar private sector workers. On the other hand, there are longstanding shortages in some federal position classifications due to inferior pay and benefits; engineers, doctors, and other health care personnel are three examples. U.S. Bureau of Labor Statistics' wage comparability studies consistently find that private sector workers are paid substantially more than most federal employees for similar work. Independent studies by the U.S. Governmental Accountability Office, the Merit Systems Protection Board, the Federal Pay Agent, and consulting firms have arrived at the same conclusion and point to an alarmingly high turnover rate for federal workers leaving for higher pay and better opportunities elsewhere. Even the apparent pay advantage of the much-maligned postal worker can at least be partly explained by the fact that the large number of female and minority employees in the postal service are not systematically discriminated against in their pay, as they are in much of the private sector.

These studies, however, are suffused with methodological difficulties and swamped by the magnitude of the task. For example, the aggregate data used in many of the studies, including those cited above, do not account for important information, including occupational categories, position levels, units of government, or geographical differences.

Two studies attempt to overcome some of the major methodological pitfalls in comparing public and private sector earnings. Belman and Heywood (1995) compared public and private sector earnings in seven states, statistically controlling for occupation and individual worker characteristics (e.g., age, experience). Results indicated that lower level government employees earned more than their private sector counterparts, but mid- to upper level employees in government were paid less than those in the private sector. For the seven states examined, six underpaid local government employees and three underpaid state government workers compared to similar workers in the private sector. An important finding is that state and local employment consists disproportionately of occupations that garner high earnings. Some of these relatively highly paid jobs are not directly comparable to jobs found in the private sector (e.g., firefighter, police officer). Moreover, government has a more highly educated work force and a much greater proportion of managerial and professional employees than the private sector (Belman and Heywood 2004; Belman and Heywood 1995: 196).

The second study, by a Bureau of Labor Statistics economist (M. L. Miller 1996), confirmed several of the findings in the Belman and Heywood research: state and local employers paid more than private industry at the low end of the pay scale and private firms paid better than state and local government for higher level jobs, particularly those involving administrative and professional responsibilities. But highly paid administrative and professional employees comprise 30 percent of local and 40 percent of the state labor force, compared to only 10 percent of private employment. This distribution artificially pushes the average earnings of government employees above that of private sector employees unless occupation is taken into account.

As observed by M. L. Miller (1996: 21), the comparability question should be framed as follows: "If two persons are doing the same job, at the same level of duties and responsibilities, with one person performing that job in state or local government service and the other in private industry, are they also paid alike?" Using Bureau of Labor Statistics data for 1993, Miller was able to directly address this research question. His findings? That "contrary to comparisons based on overall averages or broad occupational groups, private industry paid better for virtually all professional and administrative occupational job levels and for the majority of technical and clerical jobs levels. For blue-collar workers, the situation was mixed" (Miller 1996: 22). Premiums for private sector professional and administrative positions exceeded 10 percent of salary; for technical and clerical jobs, a private sector pay advantage was found in 60 percent of the jobs examined.

The related issue of pay compression is troubling for public employers. The relatively high-paid positions at lower levels of government organizations are typically easy to recruit for, but the relatively low-paid positions at upper and upper-middle levels of agencies and departments do not compare favorably to positions with similar responsibilities in business. The result is difficulty in recruiting and retaining mid- to top-level government officials.

The paycheck represents only a portion of the total compensation picture; benefits are increasingly important. The evidence with respect to the dollar value of benefits favors government workers, but not as much as commonly believed. With regard to specific benefits, state and local pension plans generally provide more generous payouts than the average private sector plan, but they are more likely to require employees to copay contributions. State and local workers can also expect to retire with fewer years of service and to experience more growth in their monthly retirement check (from cost-of-living adjustments) than private employees. Moreover, the financial risk for funding future pension payments is assumed by most government employers in defined benefit plans, which promise retirees monthly checks with the specific amount based on years of service and salary level. Firms, on the other hand, typically pass along risk to future retirees under defined contribution plans, which determine the amount of pensions based on investment choices made by the employee. Poor choices translate into low pensions. Public–private differences exist for other benefits as well. Health care insurance for public employees and their dependents is much more widely available and often more generous than insurance provided (or not provided) by firms. Vision and dental care benefits are comparable. Public workers typically enjoy more annual sick and vacation leave than their private sector counterparts (Kearney 2003).

Generous — but sometimes underfunded — pension and retiree health care plans have become a topic of great concern since accounting standards adopted by the Governmental Accounting Standards Board (GASB) required public report- ing of accrued benefits. Some state and local governments have revealed shocking levels of unfunded liabilities. New Jersey, for example, as a result of significant underpayment into its pension plan in the 1990s, along with exceedingly generous (free) health care coverage for retirees, will need approximately $58 billion to pay the benefits promised to current and future retirees (Walsh 2007). Some fiscally responsible state and local governments are in relatively good shape, but many are now faced with the need to step up retiree funding, reduce benefits, or both.

V. Comparing the Relative Effects of Unions in the Public and Private Sectors

What is the compensation impact of unions in the public and private sectors, respectively? In which sector are unions most effective in driving up wages and benefits? The empirical evidence is fairly conclusive that private sector unions are more successful than those in the public sector. The most comprehensive examina- tion of unions and wages in business is H. G. Lewis' *Union Relative Wage Effects: A Survey* (1986). According to Lewis, the wage effects of unions were 10 to 15 percent from the late 1950s to the late 1970s. Most recent research indicates that this dif- ferential prevailed into the mid-1990s but has declined somewhat since (Hirsch and Schumacher 2001). However, measurement error is more likely with declining unionization in the private sector (Hirsch 2004), so any specific comparison is subject to dispute. The relative wages of unionized workers in business tend to rise during periods of recession and fall during inflationary times, and in general, they vary greatly across time, occupation, and the state of the economy.

Direct comparisons with union wage effects in government indicate that private sector wage gains run about 10 percent higher, when controlling for occupation in the time period from 1960 to the late 1990s (Blanchflower and Bryson 2004; Shapiro 1978; Moore and Raisian 1987; Ashraf 1997). Thus, it appears that, in gen- eral, private sector workers have gained more in pay from unionization than their counterparts in public employment.

Unions in both sectors appear to change the distribution of earnings as well. As noted above, unions have been associated with salary compression, reflected in a reduction in the spread between the average pay of the lowest and highest ranking employees in an organization. To the union member, salary compression may be interpreted as less salary inequity through collective bargaining — a good thing. Unions are also associated with a lessening of inequality in earnings among women and men (Card 2001; Flaherty and Caniglia 1992). In principle, unions seek greater egalitarianism in pay structures throughout the economy. For those laboring in very low-paying jobs, unions desire a "living wage." This typically takes the form of a push for a hike in the minimum wage to a level that is conducive to self-support. Unions were influential in boosting state minimum wages above the national level during 2005–2007 and in finally convincing Congress to pass a staggered minimum wage increase in 2007. Minimum and living wage campaigns have a desirable secondary effect for unions in government, because if private sector pay is increased, this reduces the impetus for privatization of public services (Swope 1998).

VI. The Effects of Public Employee Unions on Compensation: Methodological Problems

Like all research in the social sciences, where laboratory-like conditions cannot usually be approximated, the research concerning union effects on public employee compensation suffers from certain methodological shortcomings. Seven specific problems have plagued researchers in this area of investigation.

Measurement error and unexplained variance. Almost without exception, multiple regression analyses intended to isolate the relative influence of unionization on wages and benefits have been unable to account for much more than half of the total variation in compensation for the occupational group under consideration. Poor specification and measurement of independent variables appear to be the culprit. The result is that union impacts could be overstated.

Operationalization of "union." Some studies have employed measures of unionization that are simply inadequate. For example, many ignore the potential role of nonaffiliated employee organizations or employee groups that do not call themselves unions even though they represent their members in wage and benefit negotiations. The most appropriate measures of "union" are (a) whether there is a contract and (b) the percentage of employees belonging to a union. Compounding the union measurement problem is that the Bureau of Labor Statistics no longer collects useful state and local membership data. Union membership must now be estimated through the Current Population Survey.

Unit of analysis. Most pay studies routinely aggregate data across states and localities to make broad nationwide conclusions about union effects. State- and city-level results may be confounded by variability in union representation and legal environment. For example, some state or local agencies may engage in bargaining whereas others may not, and some, as a matter of policy, may consistently pay higher salaries to their employees than local firms pay their own (Belman and Heywood 1995). Aggregation of data across governments obscures internal differences in bargaining outcomes. Generally, the study of individual functional areas (e.g., police, sanitation, social welfare) is recommended, controlling for legal environment (see Ichniowski et al. 1989).

Threat effects. Employers may raise pay and benefits of nonunion workers to forestall threatened unionization or to prevent morale problems that could result in losing valued employees. Thus, in jurisdictions that experience high levels of organizational membership and collective bargaining, bargaining tends to set market-wide pay and benefit levels, driving up payroll costs for all employers.

Cross-sectional research designs. The vast majority of compensation studies limit the scope of investigation to a narrow time range, usually a single year. Time-series research designs that attempt to capture the changing union influence over a longer period of time is preferred. This shortcoming primarily is a function of the lack of adequate longitudinal data on public employee unionization, a problem that has worsened, as noted above.

Neglect of benefits as a dependent variable. The dollar value of benefits should be included as part of a total compensation package if researchers are to depict the full impact of public employee unions. Although wage increases are the most visible aspect of bargaining settlements, benefits can be the most burdensome in the long term, as shown by the unfolding story of underfunded retiree benefits, described above. Indeed, benefits may represent the most significant long-term union influence of all.

There is evidence of a tradeoff between pay and benefits when unions participate in determining the compensation package. Unions tend to favor benefits increases over pay hikes for several reasons. First, unions reflect the desires of the "median member," who is older, typically more established in a life pattern, and concerned with health care protection, a pension, and similar benefits (Freeman and Medoff 1984). Second, there is a public choice argument for increased public employee benefits. From a political perspective, maximizing benefits over salaries makes sense. Pay hikes are highly visible to taxpayers and easy for them to oppose. Improvements in benefits, while perhaps even more expensive in the long run, provide union members with highly valued rewards that have low taxpayer visibility (Peng 2004; Belman and Heywood 1991: 112–113). Finally, most public workers, whether union or not, enjoy certain tax advantages from taking compensation increases in the form of employer-provided benefits. In sum, if benefits are not captured in the research design, union-associated impacts will likely be significantly understated.

The values and political ideology of researchers. Economic and social science research should be objective and free of investigator bias, but unfortunately sometimes it is not. For instance, there are at least three possible values or perspectives that researchers may associate with the public employee pay issue. First is equity — public and private sector employees should be paid equally for equal work, whether unions are in the picture or not. The second value is efficiency — the public sector should pay no more than is necessary to attract and retain an adequate supply of workers and should consider privatizing all possible activities. The third value is government as the model employer — public organizations should be the standard bearers for how to remunerate and treat workers fully and fairly. Thus, government should pay high salaries and benefits and have the best feasible working conditions. How a researcher feels about these values or perspectives may influence his or her assumptions, methodology, findings, and conclusions.

VII. The Effects of Public Employee Unions on Compensation: A Review of the Findings

Taken together, the 50 or more published scholarly studies on unions and public employee pay indicate that unions have exerted a slight to moderate influence, depending on methodology employed, the state or local function examined, and time period observed. Since the early 1990s, such compensation impact studies have been scarce, as the careful reader will note below.

A. Salary and Wages

Most research on the effects of union activity on public employee salaries and benefits uses a traditional economic, or market, approach. Public sector labor supply and demand equations are specified in order to "solve" the wage and/or benefits rate of public workers while statistically controlling for various nonunion influences. Multiple regression analysis is the statistical technique that best lends itself to this approach. Through multiple regression procedures the influence of input and decision process variables (such as socioeconomic characteristics of the labor market and government structure, respectively) are held constant, permitting the isolation of any specific union-related impacts on compensation.

Teachers. Most of the early studies of public employee union influence were concerned with the occupational category that continues to receive the bulk of scholarly attention — K–12 classroom teachers. It is understandable that public education has dominated scholarly interest in this field of research. About one half of all state and local government employees work in public education, and a majority of these workers are classroom teachers. Their sheer numbers, magnified by aggressive political and organizing activities and parental concern, ensure that teachers are frequently in the public eye. The intense public interest in the quality of education also fosters many newspaper columns, blogs, and media sound bites.

Results of the union and teacher compensation studies have been, at best, inconsistent. Overall, teacher salaries barely kept pace with the cost of living in the 1990s and rose less than wages for other full-time employees. Generally speaking, those who have aggregated their data at the state level have not found a significant association between unionization and teachers' salaries. Those who have examined data at the more appropriate level of school districts have uncovered statistically significant associations between unionization and teacher pay. The mean wage effect of teacher unions, calculated by averaging available research findings, was approximately 5 percent during the 1960s and 7 percent in the 1970s–1990s. These findings for the 1980s indicate a union advantage of from 1.0 to 28.8 percent of base pay (e.g., Delaney 1988; Freeman and Valletta 1988). Most of the research finds that the greatest salary advantage accrues to senior teachers. Unfortunately, none of the studies attempts to account for nonsalary aspects of teachers' earnings and their relationship to unionization.

College and university faculty. Early faculty studies matched unionized institutions with nonunion institutions with similar characteristics and found relatively modest salary and benefits advantages for unions during the late 1960s to mid-1970s (Birnbaum 1974; Morgan and Kearney 1977). In percentage terms, the salary advantage for organized faculty ranged from 11 percent in 1970–1971 (Freeman 1978), to only 2 percent in 1977 (Barbezat 1989). Apparently, however, the union-related advantage for faculty leveled off in later years (Marshall 1979; Guthrie-Morse et al. 1981), and unions may even have been a net detriment to faculty salaries since the 1980s in doctoral and research institutions (Hu and Leslie 1982; Kesselring 1991; Ashraf 1997). However, collective bargaining appears to be more favorable for community college faculty, at an advantage of 8 percent (Ashraf 1998). Research does indicate that senior tenured faculty benefit more from unionization than do junior faculty (mostly from across-the-board raises instead of merit-based pay raises) (Barbezat 1989). Also, unionized faculty tend to enjoy superior benefits in comparison to their nonunion colleagues (Guthrie-Morse et al. 1981).

Police officers. According to the published research, organized police have experienced a salary advantage of from 4 to 8 percent, which peaked around 1977 and has declined since (e.g., Ehrenberg and Goldstein 1975; Feuille and Delaney 1986; Hall and Vanderporten 1977; Kearney and Morgan 1980a,b; Chandler and Gely 1995; Trejo 1991). One study suggests that police unions temporarily force up salaries, but the threat effect pulls pay to the same level in nonunion police departments functioning within the same state legal environment (Ichniowski et al. 1989). Unionized police do appear to hold an advantage with regard to benefits. A national study of cities of 25,000 and above for the 1981 to 1984 period found a "very large and strongly positive association" between police bargaining and retirement and insurance benefits (Feuille et al. 1985b; see also Hunter and Rankin 1988). Presumably, the union advantage persists today.

Firefighters. Although no recent studies are available, early research on firefighter unionization identified a wage advantage of 2 to 18 percent, averaging about 8 percent (Ashenfelter 1971; Ehrenberg 1972; Smith and Lyons 1980; Trejo 1991).

Other municipal employees. An assortment of research efforts has investigated the compensation effects of other local government workers, including sanitation: 0 to 17 percent (Hoover and Peoples, 2003; Karper and Meckstroth 1976; Edwards and Edwards 1982; Chandler 1995); hospital employees: 8 to 12 percent (Feldman and Scheffler 1982); and secretaries: 14 percent (Gomez-Mejia and Balkin 1984). Inclusive studies of city and county workers across various functions find that bargaining increases monthly payroll by 8.5 percent (Zax 1989) and hourly compensation by 5.6 percent (Zax 1988). "Common function" employees such as blue-collar and clerical workers experience an average positive impact from unions of 8 to 10 percent (Freund 1974; Ehrenberg and Goldstein 1975; Belman et al. 1997).

State employees. State government has not received much attention from scholars, except for higher education. One study (Kearney and Morgan 1980b) of various categories of state employees across the United States found that unions captured a combined salary and benefit gain of approximately 4 percent for their members. More recent research using 1991 data indicates that unionized state employees enjoy a wage premium of about 7 percent over nonunion workers (Belman et al. 1997; Kearney 2003).

In conclusion, unions are associated with higher wages and benefits in state and local government, but the magnitude of the impact varies widely over time, function, and study methodology. The best estimate of an overall union effect is probably 5 to 6 percent, which is well below the 10 to 15 percent union compensation advantage associated with the private sector.

B. Benefits

Benefits deserve more careful examination in union impact research. They typically make up 20 to 40 percent of the total compensation package in government, averaging 31 percent in 2005 (compared to an average of 24 percent of the total compensation package for private sector workers; U.S. Bureau of Labor Statistics 2006). The quantity and quality of benefits vary considerably across states, localities, and employee function. The most costly are defined benefit pension systems and health care insurance. Unfortunately, benefits information is very difficult to collect, standardize, and operationalize. In addition, research is complicated by lags between the time benefits increases are won and when their effects become measurable. The sheer variety of potential benefits also defies precise measurement and comparison (see Kearney 2003). They include:

1. Insurance (medical, mental health, dental, hearing, vision, disability, life, malpractice, workers' compensation, unemployment compensation)
2. Leave (sick, vacation, holiday, education, military, jury duty, voting, family, maternity, paternity, union business, funeral, personal)
3. Retirement (pensions, social security, optional and supplemental retirement plans)
4. Survivor's benefits
5. Severance pay
6. Employee development (tuition reimbursement, book allowances, time off for education and training)
7. Employee assistance programs, wellness programs
8. Dependent and elder care

9. Longevity pay
10. Premium pay (emergency overtime, call-in and call-back pay, police court time, compensatory time, shift differentials, standby time, holidays, hazardous duty)
11. Miscellaneous (meals, parking fees, moving expense, uniform allowance, auto allowance, legal services, retirement counseling)

As noted, retirement (pensions) and health care benefits are potentially the most significant from a public employer's cost standpoint. This is particularly true for police and firefighters whose pensions typically commence after only 20 years on the job and who may experience extended job-related health care problems. Recent research (Kerney 2003) finds that state employee unionization pushes up the cost of retirement and retiree dependent health care at a statistically significant level.

Retirement payments typically amount to 50 to 100 percent of the employee's final salary figures, with annual adjustments for cost-of-living changes. The burden on government revenues can become substantial. A growing number of states and localities are considering moving from these expensive defined benefit plans (where, for example, the government funds the full cost of pensions, which are based on years of work experience and age) to defined contribution plans (in which the pension recipient has a proportion of his or her salary deducted and invested in retirement plan choices along with a contribution by the employer).

The debate over public employee pension funds includes how the funds are invested. Traditionally, investment decisions concerning pension funds were handled by the employer and its investment advisors. But the unions argue that the trillions of dollars in public employee pension fund assets represent deferred compensation and therefore should be controlled by public workers or their representatives, not by management. In addition, the unions prefer investment policies that favor in-state firms and firms with pro-union policies. And, in some cases, they want pension fund assets to be invested to advance certain social and political objectives.

A benefit undergoing rapid reconfiguration today is employee health care. Spiraling health care costs have damaged employers' budgets and employee pocketbooks. The average cost of state health care plans has been growing annually in double digits. Health care plans have become a major flashpoint in collective bargaining as employers, in cost-cutting moves, have adopted managed care plans, HMOs, and other arrangements that require larger financial contributions from employees but sometimes permit fewer health care options.

C. Evaluating the Union Effect on Wages and Benefits

A review of the literature concludes that unions boost wages and benefits in government. The impact varies along dimensions of time, space, methodology, and function in response to numerous and highly variable social, economic, and political factors. The union compensation impact, which averages 5 to 6 percent for salaries and perhaps a bit more for the dollar cost of benefits, is far less than the impact attributed to private sector unions. Nonetheless, the effects may be felt more strongly in states and localities, which are much more labor intensive than most private enterprises. Considering, for example, that if 50 to 75 percent of a school district's revenues are dedicated to teacher pay, a 6 or 8 percent salary increase exacts a substantial toll on the school budget. Firms, especially large ones, can usually enhance efficiencies or pass along salary and benefit hikes to the consumers of their goods and services. Governments have fewer options for funding the price of a new labor agreement.

Clearly, public sector constraints do help limit union-inspired employee compensation gains. These constraints are powerful, even though they differ in nature from the private sector market constraints of competition, profits, and product prices. In government, political and economic forces help contain union demands. Budgets must be adopted, taxes must be levied, bonds issued, and user fees imposed within a context of participatory democracy.

Citizens' groups, particularly those with an anti-tax bent, pay attention to wage and benefit settlements and look over the shoulders of responsible elected officials. Citizen oversight behavior helps stiffen the backbone of public officials during contract negotiations and reduces the scope of union demands. A patently equitable compensation settlement may proceed relatively unmolested, with little media or public attention. Citizen review is tacit in such instances. But when bargaining outcomes appear to be excessive, the media and general public may respond with outrage. A bond issue or tax proposal may go down to defeat at the polling places, or an aroused electorate may defeat incumbent politicians running for reelection.

VIII. Responding to Public Sector Compensation Cost Increases

Where compensation increases are allowed to stand by the legislative body, money must be set aside to pay the bill. Within a context of limited competition or substitutability for government services and general fiscal austerity, public managers have a variety of options available to them:

1. Raise taxes: Local property taxes usually can be increased without a referendum. State or local sales or income tax hikes normally must receive voter or legislative approval. Elected officials, of course, rarely favor the course of a tax increase and usually exhaust all other remedies first. Some state laws preclude tax increases when statutory taxing or spending limits have been reached.
2. Increase other revenues: User fees or charges may be raised in order to cover compensation awards within a particular government function. For example, water rates, trash collection fees, recreation charges, or sewer charges can be hiked. This option may be subject to state law or local ordinance, and, like a tax increase, it can be highly visible and subject to vehement citizen resistance.

3. Borrow the necessary funds: Bonds or short-term notes may be issued and sold, with the proceeds diverted to worker payrolls. A second option is to borrow from employee pension funds. Restrictive legislation, however, may prohibit borrowing.

4. Cut back elsewhere in government spending: This may take the form of an across-the-board reduction in all departmental appropriations or more selective reductions.

5. Divert capital expenditure allocations to personnel costs: Capital construction or purchasing projects may be postponed or eliminated so that wage and benefit settlements can be honored.

6. Divert intergovernmental revenues: State and local jurisdictions may be able to channel grant-in-aid funds to meet personnel costs.

7. Mandate a hiring freeze: Unfilled positions may remain unfunded, with further savings realized through attrition.

8. Impose layoffs: Reductions in force (RIFs) may be implemented across the board or by department, agency, or program.

9. Offer a "golden handshake": Provide incentives for early retirement.

10. Adopt a temporary attrition policy: Vacated positions will not be filled until the budget is in better shape.

11. Reduce the quantity or quality of services: For instance, trash can be collected once per week rather than twice weekly (quantity), or curbside pickup can replace backdoor trash collection (quality).

12. Cut working hours and reduce wages proportionately: Compensatory time off may be substituted for overtime, for example, or mandatory furloughs can be imposed.

13. Adopt labor-saving technology: Technology is available in functions such as trash collection (one-person trucks) and human resource management and budgeting (labor-saving software), for instance.

14. Contract out (outsource) services to other jurisdictions or to private firms: Water, engineering, fire protection, and sanitation are good candidates for this strategy.

15. Consolidate existing functions: Some financially pressed local governments have consolidated police and fire functions into a public safety department. Other alternatives exist as well.

16. Refuse to fund negotiated payroll increases, making the argument of inability to pay: Collective bargaining laws in at least 11 states offer this final option to public employers. For example, the Iowa law provides that "No collective bargaining agreement or arbitrator's decision shall be valid or enforceable if its implementation would be inconsistent with any statutory limitation on the public employer's funds, spending, or budget or would substantially impair or limit the performance of any statutory duty by the public employer." The efficacy of this strategy may be questioned, however, because courts generally

have affirmed the obligation of public employers to implement agreed-upon compensation increases.

17. Declare bankruptcy: When a state or local government is insolvent, it can, in theory, file for protection under Chapter 9 of Title II of the Federal Bankruptcy Code. The only general-purpose government of note to attempt to take this option since the Great Depression was Vallejo, California in 2008 but other local governments were considering it.

18. Engage in productivity bargaining and/or a gainsharing program to reap financial savings.

IX. Productivity Bargaining (Gainsharing)

Productivity bargaining involves the "negotiation and implementation of formal collective bargaining agreements which stipulate changes in work rules and practices with the objective of achieving increased productivity and reciprocal worker gains" (Newland 1972: 807). Thus, in what has come to be popularly known as "gainsharing," employee rewards are linked to increases in productivity through the bargaining process. Collective bargaining is not a prerequisite for productivity enhancements. Dollar savings may be captured through productivity improvements or changes in work procedures agreed to by a labor-management committee or through unilateral management action.

In the United States, productivity bargaining has been experimented with in a variety of industrial concerns, including meat-packing, steel, railroads, and longshoring. In government, the experience has been limited to a relatively small number of jurisdictions, primarily municipalities. One of the most popular approaches is the Scanlon Plan (Collins 1998).

Some jurisdictions have had success with "buyouts." Buyouts involve a payment of money (for bonuses) or other financial inducements by management to the union in return for union acceptance of changes in work rules that hinder productivity. The parties' agreement is formalized in the collective bargaining contract. Work rules that might be changed include work scheduling, minimum number of employees on a crew, or any previous understandings or agreements that tend to obstruct the introduction of labor-saving technologies.

Gainsharing refers to a financial incentive system in which a financial bonus is offered for measurable increases in productivity attributable to extra efforts by employees. Here, management and the union work together in identifying barriers to productivity and implementing changes that enhance productivity. The monetary savings that ensue are shared.

Gain sharing has been adopted in various forms in state and local government. Examples include the following:

Wisconsin: State employees helped create a cost-savings commission to discover means of reducing costs, with savings to be distributed through employee salaries.

Detroit, Michigan: A productivity bonus was granted to sanitation workers based on savings from attrition and reductions in overtime pay.

Michigan: State prison guards agreed to hold down their health care costs in return for a salary increase.

New York City: Sanitation workers agreed to use one-person trucks and run longer collection routes in exchange for a 17 percent raise over 4½ years.

New Rochelle, New York: Developed with local AFSCME Council 66, a gain-sharing program in which productivity gains were used to help fund wage increases. The sanitation department reduced crew size from four employees per truck to three through attrition.

Indianapolis, Indiana: In collaboration with AFSCME Council 62, gainsharing programs were implemented in the public works department.

Productivity or gainsharing savings may be paid out to workers on a one-time basis as a cash bonus, used to augment their salaries, or deferred into a shared savings plan for retirement. Most productivity provisions require a defined split of savings (e.g., 50 percent) between management and labor. Some of the productivity bargaining experiences have achieved a measure of success in cost savings and/or quality of service improvements. Most productivity or gainsharing experiments, however, have been relatively short-lived, lasting through a single collective bargaining contract. And there have been several reports of embarrassing failure for productivity bargaining, especially from management's perspective, where the agreement had unintended negative consequences.

To succeed, productivity and gainsharing programs require strong employer and union leadership and consistent oversight, widespread employee involvement, accurate measurement of service outputs, and win–win expectations (Holzer 1988; Matzer 1988: 185–186). Where such conditions do not exist, productivity improvement programs can collapse. In Detroit, for instance, problems arose in determining who was to receive productivity bonuses besides the sanitation workers on the trucks. Dispatchers, clerical employees, and supervisors also wanted a piece of the action. In other jurisdictions, lack of commitment by key participants and difficulty in negotiating the terms of the productivity bargaining agreement and in sustaining the productivity efforts led to a loss of interest. Additional problems include the natural resistance of management and union bureaucracies to change, difficulties in developing accurate and meaningful standards for measuring tradeoffs between service efficiency (quantity) and effectiveness (quality), failure to link productivity bargaining/gainsharing with overall program goals, mistrust between the parties, and interference by elected officials.

Ironically, a serious obstacle to meaningful productivity gains is cost. It often takes money to save money. For example, substantial productivity gains may ensue from technology enhancements and improved data collection, both of which require additional expenditures. Adding, rather than reducing, staff may enhance productivity (e.g., hiring a trained court administrator to handle case scheduling and other administrative duties, thereby freeing judges to concentrate on interpreting and applying the law, or hiring a consultant to identify potential cost savings). Productivity, especially in government, becomes a popular buzzword when money is tight and retrenchment is under way, so there is less money for productivity enhancements such as capital or human resource investments or financial incentives.

Productivity bargaining/gainsharing deserves further attention and experimentation. The popularity of interest-based negotiations helps promote such agreements. Almost everyone desires and benefits from improved government performance. Productivity bargaining/gainsharing offers an alternative to tax increases and directly involves employees who are most knowledgeable about service provision problems, permitting them to become a part of the solution.

X. Monetary Impacts of Federal Employee Unions

The environment surrounding unions and pay determination in federal employment is quite different from the situation prevalent in state and local government. Most relationships between unions and federal agencies are well structured, and compensation determination is generally unilateral.

The federal government, in theory, could pursue one of several possible strategies in setting wages and benefits for its employees. As a conservative approach, it could seek to award its workers as little as possible, assuming that government employment is either a privilege or not difficult work and, above all, that the taxpayer should be protected from the unnecessary burden of high federal employee wages and benefits. A far different strategy would be to assume the role of model employer, awarding above average salaries and benefits to its workers as a model for other employers. A middle-of-the-road approach, the one long accepted in federal employment, is to apply the principle of the prevailing wage.

Unlike in state and local government, the prevailing wage principle has a long formalized role in federal compensation determination. The principle was first established through statute by Congress for federal Navy yard workers during the Civil War. It was extended to employees of the U.S. Government Printing Office in 1924 by the Kiess Act, to TVA workers by the Tennessee Valley Authority Act of 1933, and to other federal employees by the Classification Acts of 1923 and 1949. However, the principle of the prevailing wage was not explicitly applied to nonindustrial (classified) employees until passage of the Salary Reform Act of 1962, which established that civil service salaries should be comparable to those of similar workers in the private sector. The Federal Pay Comparability Act of 1970 reaffirmed that principle and delegated authority to the executive branch to make periodic adjustments to the pay of Federal Schedule, Foreign Service, and other federal employees in order to establish comparability with private sector workers. These acts were major steps in coordinating federal pay setting.

Procedures for determining the prevailing, or comparable, wage vary by agency and by type of employee. They are established through collective bargaining in the Tennessee Valley Authority, by conference in the Government Printing Office, by the U.S. Bureau of Labor Statistics and the President's Pay Agent for white-collar (General Schedule, or GS) workers, and by wage boards for blue-collar employees. There are separate pay systems for blue-collar (wage board) workers, GS employees, the Foreign Service, Veterans Health Administration, Senior Executive Service, Postal Service, administrative law judges, air traffic controllers, and senior-level scientific and professional positions.

The three largest categories of employees for purposes of pay are the federal wage system, the classified civil service, and the collective bargaining system.

A. *Federal Wage System*

Blue-collar workers in federal civilian service are covered by the federal wage system (FWS). Specifically excluded are agencies exempt from the general classification and pay laws, including the TVA, National Security Agency, and the CIA. Although the FWS retains final authority for pay determination, federal unions have substantial rights of participation. The FWS is administered by the Office of Personnel Management (OPM). The organizational structure consists of a National Wage Policy Committee of 11 members, equally divided between management of federal agencies and union representatives; the director of OPM serves as the odd member of the committee, receiving policy recommendations regarding the FWS. The OPM coordinates wages regionally through designating a "lead agency" within local wage areas. This agency, typically the largest federal employer in the area, administers local wage surveys and sets pay schedules for all agencies within its geographical area, working with the Bureau of Labor Statistics where feasible. Based on the survey results, wages may be adjusted several times during the fiscal year. FWS wage rates and increases are based on position classification. There are 15 grades, each with five steps. Employees move up a step and receive a 4 percent increase as they meet time and performance standards.

Union participation is achieved in local wage areas through an Agency Wage Committee consisting of two union members, two management members, and a chairperson appointed by the lead agency. The Agency Wage Committee advises the lead agency on pay determination procedures. Further union participation occurs through Local Wage Survey Committees, which conduct pay scale surveys on private industrial job categories in more than 100 localities in the United States.

The right to participate in wage setting through the prevailing pay principle is an important one for federal unions that are precluded from formal bargaining over wages and benefits. Determination of the prevailing rate of pay for any particular occupation is a rather inexact undertaking that is greatly influenced by the techniques used to gather and present wage data, the characteristics of the firms selected for comparability purposes, and the individuals collecting the data. Strong union participation potentially can serve as a powerful substitute for formal collective bargaining over wages. However, blue-collar wage increases have been severely restricted by Congress during the past three decades, causing federal pay to slip well below comparable pay in private employment.

B. Classified Civil Service

More than one million classified federal employees are covered under the GS wage system. These white-collar workers are placed in a series of pay grades (GS-1 to GS-15), each with a salary range and ten salary steps. Under the Federal Pay Comparability Act of 1970, the Federal (or President's) Pay Agent, consisting of the Secretary of Labor and the directors of OPM and the Office of Management and Budget, made a GS pay increase recommendation to the president each year based on a Bureau of Labor Statistics survey of comparable private sector wages. This recommendation took effect unless the president put forward an alternative and justified it "because of national emergency or economic conditions affecting the general welfare." Congress then had 30 days to overturn the presidential proposal by joint resolution; otherwise, it was implemented automatically.

At first the system worked well enough to keep GS and private sector pay comparable. However, not a single president accepted the Pay Agent's recommendation, and Congress overrode the president's pay alternative only twice — in 1984, changing the increase from Reagan's 3.5 percent to 4 percent, and in 1990, from Bush's 3.5 percent to 4.1 percent — so that by 1990 the cumulative underpayment of GS workers amounted to approximately 300 percent (President's Pay Agent 1990). The pay disparity was most pronounced for federal employees living in large metropolitan areas with high costs of living. For example, it was 39 percent in San Francisco.

Recruitment and retention problems associated with this sizeable pay inequity were documented extensively by OPM, the Merit Systems Protection Board, and various federal agencies. Larger influential agencies began appealing to Congress for special pay systems for their employees, raising the distinct possibility of the return to a Balkanized federal pay structure.

Belated congressional recognition of this unfortunate problem resulted in the Federal Employees Pay Comparability Act of 1990 (FEPCA). Beginning in 1992, GS employees were to receive pay increases matching the average annual salary gains in the private sector in each major geographical area. Starting in 1994 and continuing for 9 years, extra pay increases were to be awarded to GS employees in high-cost-of-living metropolitan areas until their pay reached 95 percent of local wage levels. However, because federal wages everywhere continued to fall further behind wages in business, the President's Pay Agent now divides the nation into 32 locality pay areas. The Bureau of Labor Statistics surveys employers on 25 occupations in each geographic area. All of this activity has been to little avail, because the Pay Agent's recommendations have been consistently rejected; the federal pay disparity remains substantial. The implications for attracting and retaining qualified GS system employees are obvious.

C. Collective Bargaining System

Several groups of federal workers set their wages through collective bargaining patterned on the private sector NLRA model. The largest are the Bonneville Power Administration, the Tennessee Valley Authority, and the Postal Service.

Collective bargaining in the TVA developed shortly after Congress established the authority in 1933. Because of flexible enabling legislation, the TVA operates virtually autonomously in the area of labor relations, subject only to merit and efficiency requirements for employee hiring and promotion and a ban on political considerations in personnel actions. As a consequence of a progressive management attitude toward labor and the presence of strong craft unions in the public utility industry, the prevailing rate principle was applied very early in setting wages, and by 1940 a formal contract was signed between the TVA and a craft union. Today, wages and benefits are the subject of bargaining for both blue- and white-collar TVA workers.

Due to generous calculation of the prevailing wage, compensation levels at TVA exceed those generally prevailing in the region. However, economic downturns and a redefinition of agency mission have recently prompted hard bargaining by management, resulting in union pay concessions and a significant reduction in force.

Collective bargaining arrived in the Postal Service with passage of the Postal Reorganization Act of 1970, which abolished the 181-year-old Post Office Department and created the Postal Service as an independent entity within the executive branch. For the first time, postal unions were allowed to negotiate wages and benefits. The various postal unions always have been successful lobbyists, using strong organizations and nationwide memberships to encourage Congress to award high postal employee pay and benefits. But the strongest evidence of success followed the postal strike of 1970. As a price for setting the strike, postal unions offered their support for the Postal Reorganization Act. They received substantial pay increases, full bargaining rights over future pay determinations, and a formal comparative wage policy.

Wage and benefit gains for Postal Service employees have been consistently higher under collective bargaining than under previous arrangements. As noted earlier, postal workers also appear to be paid substantially more than comparable private sector employees.

Air traffic controllers have flown a stormier route. Several years after the morbid death of their union predecessor, the Professional Air Traffic Controllers Organization (PATCO), air traffic controllers organized a new union called the National Air Traffic Controllers Association (NATCA). In August 1998, NATCA signed a contract with the Federal Aviation Administration (FAA) that won its

14,300 members $200 million in salary increases and a staffing reorganization that significantly reduced the ratio of supervisors to controllers (Walters 1999). Air traffic controllers received the right to bargain over pay in an amendment to the FAA's 1996 appropriation bill that exempted the agency from Civil Service Reform Act restrictions on bargaining over wages and benefits.

Thus, union participation in federal wage setting varies from direct involvement for those engaging in wage and benefit bargaining, modest involvement for wage system employees, and no direct role for GS employees. Indirect union influence is brought to bear through lobbying activities. Not surprisingly, pay for collective bargaining employees measures up to private sector wages. GS and wage system employees have fallen substantially behind. As a consequence, federal employees and their unions have been looking more kindly toward the possibility of significant restructuring of the federal pay system, including greater agency discretion in setting pay and even a new performance-based pay system.

It should be noted that the federal benefits system covers all except collective bargaining employees. It generally compares favorably to private sector and state and local government plans, although benefits are not included in federal compensation surveys by the Bureau of Labor Statistics.

XI. Conclusion

The evidence is sufficiently clear to conclude that public employee unions, especially at the state and local levels, affect the budgetary and compensation determination processes. They make budgeting and pay setting highly complex and politicized. Unions have driven up total personnel costs in some jurisdictions and pushed up wages and benefits virtually everywhere. However, economic and political constraints help restrain union influence, increasingly so for the past two decades.

In many bargaining jurisdictions, the level of pay increases won in new contracts is somewhat anticlimactic. Silent understandings and cues about what the jurisdiction can afford to pay tend to give the outcome greater predictability. As a consequence, a substantial portion of negotiations today involves benefits and working conditions, topics explored in the next chapter.

Case Study 6.1: The Merit Pay Dilemma

A newly ratified state collective bargaining contract provides for a 3 percent across-the-board raise for all state employees and a 2 percent merit increase. The means for distributing the merit raises were left to agency heads' discretion. At the State Department of Corrections, agency managers met over a period of three weeks before deciding to allow unit heads to allocate the merit raise according to their own best judgments.

You are the chief warden at a medium-security prison just outside the state capital. The largest bargaining unit in your organization consists of corrections officers. All officers will receive the 3 percent across-the-board pay hike. But how should you distribute the merit increase? A number of alternatives occur to you.

Total payroll for your 60 corrections officers is $2.4 million (average salary is $40,000). The merit pool consists of $48,000. You could distribute the merit pay in percentages of base pay (perhaps in ½ percent increments up to 10 percent for the top performers), or you could allocate the merit awards in dollar amounts, such as $100 increments, and ranging from a low of $100 to a high of perhaps $3,000.

Meanwhile, the union president has appeared in your office to urge you to distribute the merit pay as 2 percent across the board with the rest of the annual pay increase. His assessment is that all the guards are fully competent and deserve merit pay. Moreover, this approach would be noncontroversial. He notes that the senior members of the bargaining unit are particularly supportive of his proposal.

The following day, three junior officers schedule an appointment in your office. They state that, in their opinion, the highest performers are the recently hired guards. They offer the observation that the senior guards are by far the highest paid, whereas the less senior officers lag far behind in salary. A true "merit" award based on performance appraisals would be more valid and in accordance with the taxpayers' interests.

Questions

1. What is your view of the state legislature's merit award program? How could it have been better structured?
2. What issues are raised by the merit pay system that you must implement?
3. Develop a plan for distributing the merit pay funds in a manner that you will be reasonably comfortable defending.

Chapter 7

Union Impacts: *Personnel Processes and Policies*

I. Introduction

The influence of public employee unions on wages, benefits, and budgets receives more than its fair share of media and scholarly attention. Impacts on personnel procedures and policies represent something of a hidden dimension of public sector unions. The average citizen has little interest in or understanding of public personnel administration (or human resource management, HRM), particularly the shadowy realm of civil service systems. Yet, the nexus between unions and human resource processes and policies is very important in shaping the nature of government work and the quantity, quality, and cost of services rendered to citizens.

Personnel matters are becoming more salient on the union–management agenda for three reasons. First, union–management relations have matured in most state and local settings. Financial relationships and understandings between the two bargaining parties tend to stabilize over time. One result is a reduction in the real-dollar, upper range of compensation settlements. Because unions, by their very nature, always want more, it is typical for them gradually to cast their bargaining nets farther and farther, expanding the scope of negotiations to include new areas. HRM rules and regulations are easily pulled into the union net.

Second, a seemingly permanent period of government retrenchment has constrained the amount of resources public employers can devote to the wages and benefits of employees. The driving philosophy behind the taxpayer rebellion of the 1970s and the recurrent antigovernment spending campaigns since then is that government spending is wasteful and should be cut back. Limitations have been imposed on state and local revenues and expenditures in most states. Discretionary funds have dramatically declined at all levels of government. One important result is that public employees rarely have an opportunity to enlarge their slice of the budgetary pie. When economic indicators turn downward in recessions, wage freezes, givebacks, layoffs, and related actions become commonplace. To maintain their membership in times of economic stress, and justify their existence, unions must be able to show positive results. Thus, they increasingly tend to turn their attention to the noneconomic personnel policy and process areas traditionally left to public sector management.

Finally, the composition of the American work force has been rapidly changing. If unions are to remain a vital force in government, they must address the needs of an increasingly large proportion of women, minorities, immigrants, temps, seasonal workers, and older workers. Full-time white males represent a declining proportion of new additions to the work force. Extraordinary changes in personnel practices are under way, forcing employers and unions alike to consider training and development needs for new workers; day care, maternity leave, and elder care policies; and programs for accommodating older workers; among many other needs.

This chapter explores the impacts of unions and collective bargaining on HRM processes and policies. First, merit systems are discussed in relation to collective bargaining. Four specific policies that threaten to undermine merit systems are examined: union security arrangements, the seniority criterion, affirmative action, and the New Public Management movement. Effects of unions on specific personnel processes are addressed, including hiring, promotions, retention, training, grievances, discipline, position classification, workload and staffing, and emerging policy areas.

II. Merit Systems

Merit systems are a product of the civil service reform movement that swept the United States during the late 19th and early 20th centuries. The purpose of the reform movement was twofold: to ensure the political neutrality of civil servants by removing them from partisan political pressure and spoils politics, and to ensure that the selection, promotion, and retention of public employees were carried out objectively in accordance with the principle of merit. The Pendleton Act of 1883 was intended to address both of these objectives at the national government level. A fundamental provision of the Pendleton Act was to create a bipartisan Civil Service Commission charged with the duties of keeping political patronage out of public personnel administration and overseeing a merit system designed to implement the merit principle.

It is important that distinctions be made among the merit principle, the merit system, and the civil service system. The merit principle seeks to make employee competence the major criterion in decisions affecting the movement of employees into, within, and out of public organizations. Merit and fitness for the job are to replace spoils, patronage, favoritism, and other subjective criteria in all personnel decisions.

A merit system is a legally established set of procedures created to implement the merit principle in the recruitment, selection, promotion, retention, and compensation of employees. The merit system is an administrative apparatus directed by a nonpartisan or bipartisan board or commission or a central personnel office with the purpose of implementing the principle of merit in government personnel decisions. In the federal sector, the U.S. Office of Personnel Management and the Merit Systems Protection Board implement personnel processes in accordance with the merit principle. In state and local governments, the responsibility is vested with an independent civil service commission or a central personnel agency in the executive branch.

Although state and local governments have their own merit systems, all state and local employees paid in full or in part by federal grant-in-aid funds in welfare, employment security, health, vocational rehabilitation, homeland security, and other programs have to be hired under a merit system under the terms of the Social Security Act of 1940 and subsequent federal legislation. Thus, the merit system is a standard feature of government personnel administration in the United States, so standard, in fact, that the terms "merit system" and "civil service system" are used here (and elsewhere) synonymously.

A civil service system is the personnel system for all nonmilitary employees of a government. The civil service system encompasses the merit system as well as all positions filled by patronage, policy making, and other appointments. A civil service system may or may not contain a merit system, but a merit system is always part of a civil service system.

The concept of the merit principle as the basis for government personnel decisions is nearly universally accepted. The problem lies in deciding what range of personnel functions is fundamental to maintaining the merit system and therefore should be exempt from collective bargaining. According to the federal Intergovernmental Personnel Act of 1970, the following elements are essential:

1. Recruitment, selection, and advancement of employees on the basis of relative ability, knowledge, and skills, including open consideration of qualified applicants for initial appointment
2. Equitable and adequate compensation
3. Training to ensure high-quality performance
4. Correction of inadequate performance or separation of those whose inadequate performance cannot be corrected
5. Fair treatment of all employees in all aspects of personnel administration without regard to political affiliation, race, color, national origin, sex, or religion
6. Protection of employees against partisan political coercion

Public employee unions take issue with many of these "essential" merit system components, especially pay and benefit determination, grievance procedures, training, and position classification. They espouse the view that such matters should be subject to collective bargaining. Furthermore, unions have leveled attacks at the concept of the merit system itself as being defined and controlled by management. Merit systems are criticized because they are based on the unilateral decision-making process that unions have fought from their earliest days. HRM directors, for example, are appointed by the chief executive. Although they may be "neutral" with regard to partisan politics, they are perceived to be management-dominated by the unions.

Originally created to provide a measure of job security and protection against patronage, few civil service commissions remain today. The typical arrangement is for the head of a state or local personnel system to report directly to the chief executive rather than to a commission. The purpose of such a reporting relationship is to integrate the personnel function with the executive function, but there is nearly always some tendency for governors or mayors to politicize the system (Newland 1987). Understandably, unions are concerned about unilateralism, favoritism, and other distasteful features of this arrangement.

Merit systems have come under increasing scrutiny by other critics as well. The credibility of the federal merit system has been seriously eroded because of allegations and subsequent investigations of widespread political patronage in federal recruitment and promotion policies. Abuse of the merit principle occurred during the Nixon administration in Housing and Urban Development; Office of Economic Opportunity; and Health, Education, and Welfare. Explicit evidence of blatant patronage procedures were found in the Machiavellian "Malek Manual," written by a Nixon appointee to assist other political appointees to circumvent the merit principle in departmental personnel actions (see Malek Manual 1980). Similar problems characterized the federal service during the Reagan years, when the merit system was undermined by converting positions from classified to appointive status; written tests for some positions were abandoned in favor of direct appointment; and career bureaucrats seemingly were debased at every opportunity by their political bosses (see Stahl 1990). The administration of George W. Bush was notorious for plugging unabashed (and sometimes incompetent) partisans into positions in the departments of Defense, Justice, Homeland Security, Environmental Protection Agency, and many other federal agencies (Moynihan 2005; Brook and King 2007; Thompson 2007).

It is not only the federal merit system that has been condemned. State and local merit systems have received equal criticism. Indeed, civil service and merit systems are under heavy and concerted attack globally (Kearney and Hays 1998). The most commonly cited deficiencies are the following (Ingraham 1996):

1. *Excessive and constraining rules and regulations.* Personnel systems continue to be plagued by stultifying, centralized control systems that hinder management authority and flexibility.
2. *Slow, unimaginative recruitment procedures* that inhibit the hiring of qualified people.
3. *Rigid classification systems* that impede the efficient assignment and reward of work.
4. *Isolation of public employees from elected officials.* Merit systems legitimately protect public employees from undue political interference, but they also tend to diminish political responsiveness to the chief executive. A typical response of elected officials is to seek to increase the number of political appointees.
5. *Isolation from citizens.* Agency goals to serve clients have been displaced in some instances by internal rules, regulations, and processes.

An early (and scathing) article by Savas and Ginsburg (1973, p. 600) pointed out problems with the New York City merit system that are, unfortunately, still typical of certain other large cities:

> In trying to prevent itself from doing the wrong things — nepotism, patronage, prejudice, favoritism, corruption — the civil service system has been warped and distorted to the point where it can do hardly anything at all. In an attempt to protect against past abuses, the "merit system" has been perverted and transformed into a closed and meritless seniority system.

The merit system, then, is seemingly under attack from all directions. Unions want to undermine it by seizing more influence over HRM policies and procedures at the bargaining table. Many elected and appointed officials would like to abolish it in favor of a flexible, management-driven system.

Clearly, the merit system is a downtrodden institution. Yet support for the merit principle remains even among most of the merit system's most adamant critics. If we throw out the merit system (so far, only Georgia has accomplished this), what will replace it? New patronage? Short-term employment contracts? Isn't incremental reform preferable? The union voice in this ongoing debate plays a critical role in determining which elements are truly essential to the merit system, and which are not.

A. The Interface between Collective Bargaining and the Merit System

We will consider several possible views on the interface between collective bargaining and merit systems. The first view holds that the two are irreconcilable and doomed to never-ending conflict; the second view maintains that one or the other ultimately will prevail, because the two systems cannot be mutually accommodated; the final perspective is that the merit system and collective bargaining can exist together peacefully if certain modifications are made with respect to the merit system. Most scholars, practitioners, and key stakeholders subscribe to the latter point of view. As the late AFSCME leader Jerry Wurf (1974, p. 433) once observed, "To pose an 'either–or' relationship between merit and collective bargaining is to ignore reality. Both have a legitimate place in government labor–management relationships. Both are here to stay."

The merit principle requires an administrative structure for successful implementation; in other words, a merit system. Abandonment of the merit system would result in alternatives that most HRM scholars and practitioners find unacceptable: "The alternatives … are political patronage, large-scale corruption, and less merit, fitness, and personal initiative. The alternatives are systems which demean and degrade employees, leaving them bereft of security and at the mercy of shifting winds" (Spero and Capozzola 1973: 209).

Few desire a return to the "spoils and boodle" days of public employment. Instead, collective bargaining and the merit system can be made to coexist, even as they evolve. The adjustment process plays out in state legislative and court decisions addressing the difficult task of placing collective bargaining and the merit system in their respective and appropriate places. Mutual adjustment between the two systems is ongoing, with outcomes varying from place to place (Guiler and Shafritz 2004).

B. Accommodating Collective Bargaining and the Merit System

In the absence of collective bargaining, merit systems remain largely unchallenged and unchanged. Personnel decisions are rendered unilaterally. Employee appeals or grievances may be dealt with individually by management or by a grievance board. In the presence of collective negotiations, however, some tenets of the merit system are no longer absolute. Bargaining and compromise become the order of the day as many personnel issues are resolved at the negotiating table. Generally, the range of personnel matters affected by bargaining depends on the scope of negotiations as defined through labor agreements, the courts, and state legislation. Areas not subject to bargaining are governed by merit system rules and regulations. It is through scope of bargaining determinations that the conflict between collective bargaining and the merit system is engaged and resolved.

Most state collective bargaining laws limit negotiations to "wages, hours, and working conditions." "Working conditions" may be interpreted broadly or narrowly, depending on the terms and conditions of employment covered by existing state or local legislation, personnel rules and regulations, and areas excluded from the scope of bargaining by management rights clauses. Most efforts to accommodate collective bargaining and the merit system have been aimed at excluding certain key personnel matters from the scope of negotiations, thereby keeping them within the domain of management.

As bargaining laws developed, some state legislation mandated blanket exclusions whereas other laws stipulated specific exclusions of merit-related items from negotiations. New Hampshire, Vermont, and Pennsylvania, for example, had blanket exclusions restricting collective bargaining to matters not covered under merit system rules and regulations. California, Massachusetts, Rhode Island, and Washington specifically excluded certain items from bargaining, such as recruitment, selection, or, more broadly, management rights. Other states, such as New York, Michigan, Minnesota, and Nebraska, did not attempt to accommodate collective bargaining and the merit system through statute, leaving decisions, essentially, to the courts.

At the heart of the dispute are two related issues: (1) which subjects should not be submitted to collective bargaining and thereby be reserved as management rights, and (2) which system should prevail when merit system provisions conflict with collective bargaining contract language.

Title VII of the Civil Service Reform Act (CSRA) established a three-tiered system. Core management rights, including agency decisions on the mission, organization, budget, and number of employees, are prohibited or nonnegotiable. So are certain operational matters, including contracting out, hiring, firing, and reductions in force. The second tier incorporates mandatory negotiating topics, which generally involve implementing agency decisions. Examples include decisions on how to ease the impacts on laid-off employees. The third tier of issues is nonmandatory, or permissive, with regard to collective bargaining. These issues, such as the use of technology in performing work, are negotiable at the option of management (Ban 1995: 131–132). Conflicts over negotiability, of which there have been many because the boundaries between the three tiers are blurred, are resolved by the FLRA or the federal courts on a case-by-case basis. For example, the unions successfully sued to block new "flexible" personnel rules promulgated by the Bush administration affecting 110,000 Department of Homeland Security employees and 650,000 employees in the department of defense (Thompson 2007: 111).

The trend in the states and localities has been to place more and more items on the bargaining table, except for those that are directly concerned with the quantity and quality of government services and those that involve policy questions related to the mission of the government employer. Most states exclude from the scope of bargaining, recruitment, selection, promotions, and other "management rights." The problem is that many such management rights are closely related to the "terms and conditions of employment" that are negotiable under collective bargaining statutes. For example, class size is both a teacher working condition and an element of education policy; similarly, the issue of one- versus two-officer assignments to police cruisers contains elements of both working conditions and policy.

Often, resolution resides with the courts, which typically apply a balancing test to determine what is negotiable. Would bargaining on the topic significantly abridge managerial prerogatives? Does the topic have a significant effect on the work of employees in the bargaining unit? Which effect is greater?

States differ as to how they respond when merit systems and collective bargaining provisions clash. Some states grant primacy to merit system provisions, but others (e.g., Connecticut, Massachusetts, Delaware, Illinois, Ohio) favor collective bargaining provisions in statute or contract. As an example, the Delaware statute (Labor–Management Services Administration 1972: 34) provides that

> where there is a conflict between any agreement ... in matters appropriate to collective bargaining ... and any charter, special act, ordinance, rules or regulations adopted by the municipal employer or its agents such as a personnel board or civil service commission, ... the terms of such agreement shall prevail.

To reiterate, if statutory law does not clearly assign priority to merit system or bargaining provisions, the courts will make that determination on a case-by-case basis.

Gradually, public employee unions have caused a shift in personnel decision making from the realm of management rights to the rhetoric of the bargaining table. Even in the federal sector, where neither the CSRA nor any other statute can legally be overridden through a collective bargaining agreement, certain personnel functions have been influenced by negotiated settlements.

Collective bargaining and the merit system are not incompatible, but their relationship has changed. Merit systems tend to be narrowest in coverage in the comprehensive bargaining states, where they are reduced to their "essential" elements, depending on bargaining outcomes, local values, political culture, legislation, and court decisions. This is not necessarily detrimental to efficiency, effectiveness, and equity in public employment, all of which are goals of unions as well as management.

However, merit systems continue to suffer a broad-based attack from individuals and organizations both inside and outside government for a variety of alleged shortcomings. Collective bargaining has furnished fuel for merit system detractors by complicating personnel rules and procedures and making "an already rule-bound field even more pervasively legalistic and litigious" (Newland 1984: 39). Government is characterized by less flexible personnel systems and procedures and less management authority than the private sector (Coursey and Rainey 1990), and collective bargaining tends to compound these tendencies. Bargaining has also raised new issues — union security and the seniority criterion — that threaten to undermine the merit principle itself. In states and localities with long experience with comprehensive bargaining systems, dual personnel systems have developed, and efforts to integrate them are seldom witnessed. According to one experienced observer (Douglas 1992), this may be inevitable because of a fundamental clash of values: civil service systems are based on individualism, open competition, political neutrality, and other values that inherently conflict with the collective bargaining values of collectivism, equality, and uniform treatment.

C. Unions and Threats to the Merit Principle

There are at least four possible threats to consistent implementation of the merit principle in government: union security, seniority, affirmative action/diversity, and the New Public Management.

1. Union Security

As discussed in detail in Chapter 3, there are five possible variations of union security: closed shop, union shop, agency shop/fair share, maintenance of membership, and dues checkoff. Union security provisions represent a threat to the merit principle. First, competition for jobs may be restricted if those who do not wish to join or otherwise support a union do not apply for available positions; those with less "merit" possibly gain employment. Second, under the union shop, and agency/ fair share, employees who refuse to join the union or contribute to it financially could be fired whether they are competent or not. Union security clauses, therefore, illustrate the tensions among the labor organization's need for institutional security, the individual's right of free association, and the merit system's requirement that employment be based on merit, not organizational membership.

Although there does appear to be a constitutional issue regarding the public employee's right of nonassociation in the case of the closed, union, and agency shops, the other less stringent union security provisions escape this problem. All things considered, it is doubtful that union security clauses present a serious threat to the merit principle. Most employees simply accept a requirement to join or contribute to a union as a condition of employment.

2. Seniority

Seniority involves granting preference in certain personnel actions based on an employee's length of service to the organization. In the private sector, the seniority criterion has long been applied through contract clauses to promotions, transfers, layoffs, vacation time, and other personnel matters without any measurable reduction in the efficiency and effectiveness of the work force. In the public sector, the role of seniority in personnel decisions may be fixed in a collective bargaining contract or, more commonly, it is implemented through statute or civil service rules. In both business and government, seniority offers an advantage in personnel decisions because it is objective and quantifiable. Length of service with the organization or in a particular job or department is a matter of record and some indication of achievement. In jurisdictions where promotional exams are not validated (demonstrably job related), seniority may even be a superior indication of merit.

Seniority and merit do not inherently conflict in public employment. For example, application of the seniority criterion in determining vacation time, shift assignments, work locations, days off, and similar working conditions is widely accepted and presents little threat to the principle of merit. In the case of promotions and layoffs, however, seniority and merit may be at odds. Public employee unions generally seek promotion of the senior qualified person. Unions regard seniority as a protection against favoritism in personnel decisions. Management, of course, believes that using this decision rule hampers flexibility, and prefers to have the option of discounting seniority in selected promotions decisions.

When layoffs are based on last-hired, first-fired (as they normally are whether unions are key players or not), a perverse sort of self-seeking logic can arise in unionized settings in which more senior union members opt to exchange jobs of less senior members of the bargaining unit for their own security and well-being. Thus, the majority gives up nothing, while a small minority loses their livelihood. New York City is an excellent case in point. As the 1990 to 1991 recession probed for a bottom, 150,000 junior city employees were threatened with losing their jobs, while more senior workers received a 5 percent raise under a new contract. In other settings, unions have chosen to protect jobs, foregoing pay raises. In negotiations with the governor during a severe budget shortfall in Connecticut, all but one of the 27 state bargaining units opted to defer pay increases to save jobs (only the state troopers chose wages, and they later reneged).

Ultimately, whether seniority detracts from merit considerations depends on how the criterion is applied. When seniority alone is the determining factor and other qualifications are ignored, merit suffers. For example, teacher unions have been criticized for negotiating seniority rules that leave principals little say in assigning teachers to classrooms. And when jobs are at stake, seniority rules can result in veteran teachers being reassigned to instruct in subjects in which they have little or no training or expertise while more junior, fully qualified teachers are laid off.

For promotions, strict application of seniority precludes management consideration of such relevant factors as exams and performance evaluations. The most senior individual simply receives the promotion. Usually, however, promotions are based on some combination of factors, with years of service treated as only one (or the tie-breaking) consideration. When seniority is used in this manner its influence is moderated to a point where it coincides with the principle of merit; length of service becomes the cutting point in promotion decisions in which more than one candidate meets the minimum job qualifications.

The use of seniority as a consideration in personnel decisions is longstanding, and it predates the growth of public employee unionism. It is a decision rule that management frequently applies voluntarily. It is much easier for personnel decisions to be grounded at least in part on an indisputably objective criterion that enhances employee morale than to rely entirely on relatively more esoteric considerations such as unstructured oral exams, nonvalidated written exams, or performance evaluations.

Seniority clearly weakens management authority, but that is not always a bad thing. The seniority criterion's threat to the merit principle is overshadowed by more serious concerns, such as favoritism, nonvalidated examinations, and biased performance appraisals. Unions strongly adhere to the seniority criterion in personnel decisions because of demonstrated problems associated with unchecked management discretion.

3. Affirmative Action and Diversity

Merit, it has been argued, has two different components: special consideration in hiring, promotion, and retention policies for competence, and special consideration in personnel decisions for being deserving. It is the latter aspect that throws collective bargaining and affirmative action into conflict.

Equal employment opportunity (EEO), as effectuated by the Equal Employment Opportunity Act of 1964, prohibits discrimination in employment procedures and practices on the basis of race, color, sex, religion, age, and other factors. EEO is a nearly universally accepted principle in the United States, but achieving the EEO ideal is difficult, if not impossible, because of systematic discriminatory practices. Therefore, in an effort to eliminate barriers and alleviate imbalances in the work force attributable to past discrimination, employers may take special "affirmative" actions, such as efforts to recruit, hire, and promote members of disadvantaged groups. The primary legal bases for affirmative action policies are Title VII of the 1964 Civil Rights Act, which prohibits private sector employment discrimination as a violation of the Fourteenth Amendment, and the Equal Employment Opportunity Act of 1972, which extends Title VII coverage to public employers.

Affirmative action and collective bargaining intersect in the use of the seniority criterion in personnel decisions. Problems arise when union-supported seniority rules inadvertently discriminate against women and other members of protected classes in promotions and layoffs, because members of these groups are often the last hired. Affirmative action policies intended to overcome past or present discriminatory practices sometimes directly conflict with seniority clauses in collective bargaining contracts.

Public employee unions have a mixed record with regard to affirmative action. Organized labor has actively advocated legal rights and better working conditions for disadvantaged groups as part of its social and political agenda. Equal employment opportunity, affirmative action, and other diversity efforts are important items on this agenda, and they have been strongly promoted by some public employee unions, particularly AFSCME, SEIU, NEA, and AFT, all of which, of course, have sizable minority memberships.

On the other hand, the craft-type unions in government have resisted EEO and affirmative action and management efforts to implement them (Riccucci 1990). Police and firefighter unions have been especially staunch opponents of these principles, and their membership rolls remain overwhelmingly white and male.

Many white male police and firefighters, and their unions, have fought to maintain discriminatory physical strength and agility tests and height requirements (the Americans with Disabilities Act of 1990 has helped reduce this) and have ostracized and verbally abused women and minority employees (Goode and Baldwin 2005; Sass and Troyer 1999; Riccucci 1990: Ch. 5; 1988: 44–46). They have also regularly challenged local government affirmative action plans. Of course, not all police and firefighter organizations discriminate against women and minorities, and there is growing evidence that police unions recently have been actively supporting hiring greater proportions of female and minority recruits (Sass and Troyer 1999). Thus occupational segregation in the protective services continues, but recent research indicates that the unions are not to blame

Not surprisingly, the empirical research presents mixed findings on unionization and minority and female employment. Kellough (1990) found that federal employee unions have not been an obstacle to African American, Latino, and female employment. Highly unionized federal agencies are likely to be more diverse in employee characteristics than those with weaker union presence, although Kellough suggests that this may be due to the fact that federal unions have simply organized more effectively in agencies that are already integrated."

The local government picture remains cloudy. Several studies found little or no relationship between municipal unionization and female and minority employment (e.g., Davis 1984; Riccucci 1986). However, Mladenka discovered that municipal unions have a strong and negative impact on African American job success, but only in cities with large black populations and nonreformed (i.e., mayor–council, district elections, partisan elections) systems of government, and the unions had little or no effect on black employees in administrative, professional, and protective service jobs (Mladenka 1991). Mladenka (1991: 545) suggests that unions have less influence in hiring decisions made by professional city managers in reformed governments than they do in nonreformed governments, where "they operate to retard minority employment prospects severely." (See also Sass and Troyer 1999.)

A variety of local conditions that are not related to unionization also influence minority and female employment. For instance, minorities generally fare better in cities with black or female mayors (Behr 2000; Stein 1986), with high levels of diversity on city councils, and with black personnel directors (Goode and Baldwin 2005).

An issue that has received a great deal of attention in the courts is the influence of seniority clauses on affirmative action during layoffs. In the private sector, the courts have found that seniority may be utilized as a decision rule for layoffs if (1) past hiring policies were not discriminatory, (2) individual workers laid off were not victims of prior employment discrimination, and (3) the criterion of seniority is applied in a neutral fashion with no intent to discriminate (*Watkins v. Steelworkers Local 2369* 1975; *Waters v. Wisconsin Steelworks* 1974). However, when seniority systems inhibit the promotion of women and minorities because of past discriminatory practices in hiring and transfers, they may be declared illegal (*Local 189, United Papermakers and Crown-Zellerback Corp. v. United States* 1969).

Several U.S. Supreme Court decisions have addressed the seniority/affirmative action conflict directly in local governments. In *Memphis Firefighters Local Union No. 1784 v. Stotts* (1984), a federal district court had approved two affirmative action plans for improving the percentage of African American firefighters. A subsequent fiscal crisis forced the city to lay off 40 firefighters, most of whom were black, in compliance with a seniority clause in the collective bargaining contract. The black firefighters filed suit and won in federal district and circuit courts. On review of an appeal by the firefighter union, however, the Supreme Court held that the lower courts should not have interfered with the seniority system to protect newly hired black employees. Thus, bona fide seniority systems take precedence over affirmative action when layoffs are required.

Importantly, the City of Memphis's affirmative action plan was in the form of a consent decree in which no finding or admission of intentional discrimination was made, and, of equal significance, the firefighter union was not a party to the decree (see Seaver 1985). Later Supreme Court decisions clarified *Stotts* and reduced its significance (*Wygant v. Jackson Board of Education* 1986).

The lesson for local governments is that affected unions should be made formal parties to consent agreements concerning affirmative action procedures. Affirmative action can be incorporated into negotiated contracts. For example, minority and female employment gains may be protected through negotiated alternatives to layoffs, such as job sharing, voluntary layoffs, or buyouts.

The same lesson should be applied to measures taken to accommodate disabled employees under the Americans with Disabilities Act (ADA). Under the duty of fair representation, unions must represent the interests of disabled members of the bargaining unit. Employers are advised to negotiate with the union on any job assignment, working hours, or other special dispensation for disabled employees. The U.S. Supreme Court decision in *U.S. Airways v. Barnett* (2002) indicates that the courts will support seniority provisions in collective bargaining contracts over the ADA. For instance, a management decision to accommodate a less senior maintenance worker with a disability by a transfer to a desk job that a more senior employee is qualified for would violate contractual seniority rights. Rather than bypassing the union, which invites a dispute, the employer should consult with the union to work out an acceptable accommodation for all concerned.

An increasingly conservative U.S. Supreme Court has shown little sympathy for affirmative action in higher education admissions, contracting decisions, and hiring and promotion policies. Today, affirmative action programs are being dismantled at all levels of government, except in instances where a past history of illegal discrimination has been documented and the affirmative action program designed to redress past discrimination has been "narrowly tailored" (see Goode and Baldwin 2005: 4; Riccucci 1997). The current emphasis is for employers to develop broadly construed diversity programs that embrace myriad workplace demographic concerns such as gender, color, language, disability, and religion. In any case, affirmative action and diversity programs do redistribute jobs to women and minorities, but with little or no loss of organizational efficiency (Holzer and Neumark 2000).

4. New Public Management

New Public Management (NPM), generally referred to in the United States as Reinventing Government, initially was based on a widely read book of the same name by Osborne and Gaebler (1992). It is a far-reaching approach to improving the performance, productivity, and responsiveness of government. Its key themes are debureaucratization, decentralization, downsizing, privatization, and managerialism (adopting business ideology and practices in government). In essence, NPM represents an attack on bureaucracy and "big government." Although NPM has chalked up many impressive achievements, as a broad strategy it remains riddled with inconsistencies and controversy (Kearney and Hays 1998; Ingraham 1997), from the specious promises of empowering the workers under assault to its simplistic theory of customer-driven government.

Unions, not unrealistically, tend to perceive NPM as a serious threat. At the federal level, Reinventing Government efforts were embodied in the National Performance Review (NPR) during the Clinton administration and spearheaded by Vice President Al Gore. The ambitious NPR initiatives included improving labor–management relations, which were widely recognized as excessively adversarial and litigious. A presidential executive order (E.O. 12871) established the National Productivity Council (NPC) to coordinate agency-level labor–management partnerships for implementing a variety of NPR recommendations. E.O. 12871 also required agencies to negotiate with their unions on all subjects not expressly reserved to the president or Congress, thereby expanding the mandatory scope of bargaining and eliminating one of the three tiers of negotiability established by the CSRA.

Through the NPC, the federal unions were significantly involved in developing labor–management partnerships. Sitting on the NPC were heads of the three largest federal unions (AFGE, NTEU, NFFE). NPC recommendations included streamlining dispute resolution processes and providing training in alternative dispute resolution techniques, and encouraged collective bargaining for improving recruitment and selection, position classification, and performance management processes (U.S. National Partnership Council 1994).

Despite serious efforts to construct an agreement on much-needed reform in federal HRM and labor relations practices and the signing of many agreements and notable progress in some agencies (e.g., IRS, Department of Labor, Bureau of Engraving and Printing), legislative and labor relations history, along with the anti-union policies of the Bush administration, conspired to limit success (Doeringer et al. 1996, Moynihan 2005). The restrictions of Title VII of the CSRA on union security, wage and benefit bargaining, and other areas effectively constrain the possibilities for union and management bilateral decision making. Decades of sometimes bitter adversarial relations have separated the parties into hostile camps in some agencies. Uncertainty over which topics should be addressed by partnerships and which should more appropriately be determined through collective bargaining creates confusion among labor and management officials. As one union leader reportedly described the ensuing role conflict, "It's hard to represent someone who's being screwed in the morning, and then flip the switch and be buddies with management in the afternoon, when we are still angry" (quoted in Ban 1995: 134).

In agencies where positive labor–management relations developed, the unions played a constructive role in government reform. In the IRS, for example, NTEU partnered with management to substantially reform an agency under extreme duress during congressional and public attacks in the late 1990s. However, in agencies unable to overcome their history of negative relationships, unions have stifled reform attempts. For instance, unions in the Patent and Trademark Office were unable to agree with management on much of anything, even resisting plans to move into a new office building and efforts to progress toward a "paperless office" ("Patent answers" 1999: 81). It "takes two to partner" and the G. W. Bush administration's rejection of the partnering process effectively killed it.

III. Specific Impacts of Unions on Personnel

A. Functions and Policies

1. Management Rights (Scope of Bargaining)

Union and management disagreements on which personnel functions and policies are essential to the merit principle, and should therefore be reserved for management decision making only, are closely linked to scope of bargaining disputes. Management rights are defined as outside the scope of bargaining and are prohibited from collective negotiations. Whereas unions seek to define it very broadly, management tries to keep the scope of bargaining narrow.

a. Federal Employment

In the federal sector the scope of bargaining is legally defined by Section 7106 of Title VII of the Civil Service Reform Act, which specifies management rights, and by management rights clauses incorporated into bargaining contracts negotiated for the various federal agencies, departments, and other bodies (see Table 7.1).

Even though management rights and the scope of bargaining appear to be clearly specified, their practical application is somewhat nebulous, with results varying from agency to agency. The CSRA provides for negotiations over the procedures to be used by management in exercising its prerogatives. Federal unions do have a voice in how promotions, assignments, position classifications, transfers, layoffs,

Table 7.1 Federal Management Rights under Section 7106 of the Civil Service Reform Act

7106. Management rights				
(a)	Subject to subsection (b) of this section, nothing in this chapter shall affect the authority of any management official of any agency			
	(1)	to determine the mission, budget, organization, number of employees, and internal security practices of the agency; and		
	(2)	in accordance with applicable laws		
		(A)	to hire, assign, direct, lay off, and retain employees in the agency, or to suspend, remove, reduce in grade or pay, or take other disciplinary action against such employees;	
		(B)	to assign work, to make determinations with respect to contracting out, and to determine the personnel by which agency operations shall be conducted;	
		(C)	with respect to filling positions, to make selections for appointments from	
			(i)	among properly ranked and certified candidates for promotion; or
			(ii)	any other appropriate source;
		(D)	and to take whatever actions may be necessary to carry out the agency mission during emergencies.	
(b)	Nothing in this section shall preclude any agency and any labor organization from negotiating*			
	(1)	at the election of the agency, on the numbers, types, and grades of employees or positions assigned to any organizational subdivision, work project, or tour of duty, or on the technology, methods, and means of performing work;		
	(2)	procedures which management officials of the agency will observe in exercising any authority under this section; or		
	(3)	appropriate arrangements for employees adversely affected by the exercise of any authority under this section by such management officials.		

* These "permissive" topics are made mandatory by E.O. 12871.

and other procedures are carried out. A large majority of federal contracts also call for official union representation in establishing promotions, assignments, and other procedures. This is important, because processes often determine outcomes. President Clinton's E.O. 12871 opened the door to a more expansive scope of bargaining, but as repeatedly noted, President George W. Bush rescinded it. Mr. Bush also launched attacks on bargaining rights and the scope of bargaining under the veil of "homeland security." The result, particularly in the Department of Homeland Security, was an expansion of management authority and consequent narrowing of the scope of bargaining (Thompson 2007; Brook and King 2007).

Federal unions are prohibited from bargaining over matters that are governed through federal statute, such as hours of work, sick leave, annual leave, and holidays. However, because these and related matters require implementing procedures, unions often have an influential voice.

Federal employee unions have made some inroads in these personnel areas and into the field of management rights. In the legal absence of wage and benefit bargaining and union security arrangements, they must struggle to justify their existence to current and potential members, and this offers one promising track. However, the uniform, formal management rights as stipulated in the CSRA and union contracts have erected a barrier, albeit permeable, to expanding the scope of bargaining. As a consequence, federal management has generally retained its traditional rights more successfully than state and local managers who must operate within a union environment.

2. State and Local Government

Although management rights clauses are common in state and local labor agreements, they frequently are less constrictive than the standard federal provisions. Most, however, are at least partly modeled on the federal management rights clause incorporated in Section 7106 of the CSRA.

Management rights clauses may be set out in state bargaining laws, local ordinances, and union contracts. Whatever the source, the effect is to place certain items outside the scope of bargaining. Unions ostensibly abide by legal restrictions on the subject matter of bargaining. As in the federal sector, however, decision-making procedures used to implement management policies may be negotiated. Additionally, state and local unions often insist on having a voice regarding the effects of management decisions in proscribed areas. As noted by Stanley (1972: 22), "The boundary is uncertain, the distinction fuzzy, because management really directs the work with the consent of employees." When management rights are not formally reserved through statute, ordinance, or contractual language, the presumption is that all working conditions and terms of employment are negotiable.

Even when management rights clauses exist, weak state and local managements have been known to bargain away some of their reserved rights. Municipal unions in New York City significantly eroded management rights more than four decades ago. Union gains were due in part to a muddied fiscal and political situation and certain decisions of the Board of Collective Bargaining interpreting management prerogatives. Horton (1973: 75) stated, "By 1970 the major unions for all practical purposes bargained with the City government on whatever managerial issues they wanted and refused to bargain on issues they wanted left alone." Like virginity, once sacrificed, the loss of a management right becomes a permanent condition.

In general, the strength of management is directly related to the strength of the management rights clause in a labor agreement and how successfully it is enforced. Municipal management today is insistent on placing management rights clauses in labor contracts. More than 90 percent of American cities have such a clause in at least one union contract. Most frequently listed is the right to determine missions, policies, budget, and general operations.

Notwithstanding formal management rights verbiage, unions continue to encroach. Their effect on management depends on many factors, including bargaining history, political and organizational culture, union–management relationships, and leadership style, but one thing is certain: managing in a union environment is more difficult and complicated than managing in a union-free setting.

3. Management Structure

"Management structure" refers to the organization of managerial authority for personnel issues. Personnel policy making has become more centralized in the public sector in response to union activity. This is a union impact long observed in private employment as well.

In a classic labor relations study, John F. Burton, Jr. (1972) documented the centralization of management authority in public employment that resulted from collective bargaining in 40 local government units. Before the emergence of collective bargaining, management structure was characterized by a "bewildering fragmentation of authority for personnel issues among numerous management officials," including the chief executive officer, civil service commissioners, personnel director, department head, budget director, and city attorney (Burton 1972: 127).

When collective bargaining appeared, the usual first response of local government management was to impose a bilateral system on the preexisting authority structure with little or no alteration. This is understandable, because local governments use whatever labor relations expertise exists to avoid disrupting authority relationships. However, the situation soon becomes unstable because (1) staff officials have little collective bargaining expertise, (2) labor relations are time consuming and necessitate full-time attention by officials, and (3) authority for labor relations remains fragmented in a jurisdiction with multiple centers of political power. The last problem is especially serious because it tends to promote end-runs and whipsawing. After an initial experience with collective bargaining under these conditions, most cities have responded with efforts to centralize management structure and thereby stabilize labor–management relations.

Collective bargaining has had similar impacts on management structure in higher education institutions. Faculty bargaining has resulted in the concentration of power in college and university central administrations at the expense of deans and department heads. Management has become more professionalized and specialized to confront the challenges of collective bargaining. Faculty power has coalesced in the union in most cases, with union committees displacing the power and influence of traditional faculty senates.

The tendency in government has been for the executive branch to acquire authority at the expense of the legislative body and independent civil service commissions. Then, as labor relations further develop, centralization of management authority occurs within the executive branch, with bargaining authority transferred from budget and personnel staff to full-time labor relations specialists. In a growing number of jurisdictions, certain aspects of collective bargaining and labor relations are contracted out to private specialists such as labor lawyers. These developments are both logical and advantageous to management, because the executive branch is the best place to devise negotiating strategies and coordinate management's positions on the issues. Labor relations specialists can master the vicissitudes of bargaining. Finally, there is an important advantage to having the executive branch negotiate the contracts that it ultimately will be required to administer.

From the union perspective, the centralization of management structure also may be considered a good thing. Unions, generally speaking, want to bargain with a party who can render binding decisions and deliver the goods. Fragmented management creates an unstable bargaining environment that can offer some short-run tactical advantages to a union, but in the long term both parties benefit from positive mutual adjustment and the lessening of conflict within the context of a mature, defined, collective bargaining relationship.

B. Personnel Processes

A wide spectrum of personnel processes are subject to negotiations. Many of them are included in Table 7.2.

1. Recruitment, Testing, and Selection

The recruitment, testing, and selection of employees are personnel functions that fall within the traditional purview of management. Generally speaking, they remain management prerogatives. Nonetheless, in some instances unions have penetrated these traditional areas of management rights.

Recruitment practices may be affected through union efforts to determine or at least influence job qualifications and position descriptions and any modifications to them. Experience suggests that resistance to changes in job qualifications is the most common. For example, the New York City Uniformed Firefighters Association successfully opposed a management proposal to lower the minimum

Table 7.2   Nonmonetary Subjects Typically Included in Contracts

Union rights	Discipline and discharge
Management rights	Holidays and vacations
Union security	Sick leave
Grievance procedures	Child care, elder care
Hours of work, work schedules	Leaves of absence
Alternative work arrangements (e.g., flextime, telecommuting)	Position classification
Health and safety	
Seniority	Training and education
Layoffs	Past practices
Bumping and recall procedures	Subcontracting
Labor–management committees	Privatization
Inclement weather procedures	New technology

height standard below 5 feet 6 inches for new recruits, a plan intended to enhance the enlistment of Puerto Ricans (Stanley 1972: 33). Police and firefighter unions won similar battles in other large cities where the recruitment of Puerto Ricans and other Latinos became a contentious issue in the 1960s (Juris and Feuille 1973). Affirmative action policies and validation studies of recruitment and selection criteria have voided most such height restrictions today.

Some public employee unions oppose examination policies because of the lack of demonstrated validity of the testing instruments. AFSCME has frequently gone on record against written tests because they may discriminate against poorly educated minorities and immigrants, suggesting that performance tests should be used instead.

Employee selection also attracts union attention. Unions generally seek to limit management discretion in hiring. Conventionally, according to civil service rules, agency or department heads in a state or local government had to select a new employee from one of the top three scorers on an entrance examination — thus, the "rule of three." By permitting some degree of employer discretion, the rule of three implicitly recognizes the vagaries and imperfections of testing procedures. The trend today is to extend the selection pool to 5, 10, 20, or even more applicants. In some jurisdictions, however, the rule of one prevails, despite recognized testing inadequacies. Here, agency or department heads are not allowed to exercise any discretion; they must offer the position to the individual who scores highest on the exams.

Teacher unions probably influence selection processes more than unions in any other occupational category. Analysis of a national sample of 80 collective bargaining contracts found that 84 percent of the teacher agreements included policies governing teacher selection to fill existing vacancies. Typically, these provisions establish a hiring pool consisting of "teachers who have been laid off recently; requested voluntary transfer; been involuntarily transferred; returned from leave of absence; or served as substitutes" (Goldschmidt and Stuart 1986: 354). Vacancies are filled by prioritizing these conditions and, usually, taking into account seniority of pool members as well.

Unions also have an interest in shortening employee probationary periods as an additional means of restricting management hiring discretion. A major fault of public sector management is the failure to remove unsatisfactory workers during probationary periods, when termination usually cannot be appealed or grieved. The union position is that management should have to render a quicker determination of employee suitability than in the usual 6 months, giving probationary employees even greater benefit of the doubt.

2. Promotions

Union interest in promotions policy is not tantamount to influence. Promotions policy safely remains a matter outside the sphere of union influence in most settings, with the exception of seniority preferences. Managers, of course, often submit that merit system provisions unduly hamstring them in selecting employees for promotion.

What do the unions want with respect to promotions? They want non-entry-level jobs to be filled through the promotion of employees in the bargaining unit, taking into account seniority. This objective is not necessarily out of touch with management's basic preferences. Promotion from within is a decision rule for many government department heads, agency heads, and personnel directors because it is good for employee motivation and morale and it minimizes recruitment and time costs. Seniority is often the primary criterion used in determining promotion for employees whose qualifications are relatively equal. It should be mentioned, however, that exclusive promotion from within is not congruent with the merit principle because highly qualified outsiders are not even considered for jobs. In fact, lateral entry that opens positions to persons outside the organization offers some distinct advantages. Public organizations, perhaps even more than private firms, need periodic infusions of new blood and fresh ideas. Moreover, individuals with private and nonprofit sector experience may contribute useful perspectives on how to do things differently in government.

Assuming continued government fiscal constraints, it is possible that the number of collective bargaining contracts that explicitly stipulate the procedures and criteria for promotion to nonsupervisory positions will grow. Competition for non-entry-level jobs may be restricted to current employees in some jurisdictions, and seniority may increasingly displace written, oral, and performance examinations.

Where public sector organizations are expanding, union attention to the allocation of government jobs wanes.

3. Training and Development

Despite the preaching and proselytizing of training and development specialists, the formal training of public workers for improvement on the job or preparation for a higher ranking position has never been a priority item in public sector human resource management. The conventional perception is that training is desirable if extra funds can be found, but that the training function should be the first to be cut during budget reductions. Thus, as a "stepchild" of public personnel administration, training has traditionally received minimal attention from management. Unions, too, were slow to recognize their potential role and responsibility in promoting the skills development of members.

However, gradually unions have begun to value training programs for their membership. Some sponsor their own programs, such as assisting members to study for high school equivalency tests and promotional examinations. Career development for members of protected classes aids equal employment and diversity goals and can help crack the "glass ceiling" that blocks them from upper level positions in many government organizations.

Unions have promoted three types of career development: helping workers in "dead-end" positions move into jobs with established career patterns (e.g., from data input clerk to office manager); creating new, permanent "bridge positions" and career ladders between existing jobs (e.g., various paraprofessional occupations); and upgrading workers' skills to qualify them for expected future vacancies (Figart 1989). Unions also favor tuition reimbursement and paid leave for training and development-related activities.

Training and development are perennially neglected in public employment. The training of government workers redounds to the benefit of the workers themselves, their unions, management, and the general public. Workers develop skills that can help them win promotions, and unions, management, and the people gain from more effective, productive, and satisfied government workers. All of this is widely recognized but seldom acted upon.

4. Position Classification and Staffing

In most public jurisdictions in the United States, jobs are organized into classes or groups on the basis of the responsibilities, duties, skills, and qualifications assigned to them. Positions are analyzed and evaluated on the work performed, then grouped into classes according to their similarities and differences. Class standards establish the boundaries for each group of positions. Unions are interested in classification plans because they serve as the framework for the organization's compensation structure.

The product of position classification is an ordering of individual positions within job classes. For example, the HRM division within a state social services agency might contain the positions of Personnel Analyst I, II, and III; or a municipal finance office might be assigned a class for accountants, with the positions Accountant I, II, III, and Senior Accountant. Usually position classification is a management responsibility of the state central personnel agency and the local government personnel director, assisted as necessary by private consultants. In federal employment, position classification is a duty of the Office of Personnel Management.

Public management has typically viewed classification as a management prerogative and hence not a proper subject for bargaining. The basic argument is that the classification of positions is an objective, scientific enterprise that serves as the cornerstone of the merit system. Positions are placed into classes in accordance with empirically determined job descriptions. However, the union position is that position classification is inherently subjective and arbitrary, especially when positions are classified across occupational functions. For example, should a data entry person be compared to a shipping clerk, or a senior secretary to a new assistant personnel officer? Such decisions, the unions claim, involve value judgments. Therefore, they should be subject to collective negotiations.

In federal employment, according to Title VII of the Civil Service Reform Act of 1978, agencies may negotiate "… on the numbers, types, and grades of employees or positions assigned to any organizational subdivision, work project, or tour of duty… ." In most federal contracts, unions participate in position classification. In some, for instance, unions exercise influence through joint committees on position classification standards.

Position classification is increasingly being pulled within the scope of bargaining in state and local jurisdictions. Unions accept the need for a system of position classification, but they want to have a voice in it because it affects compensation so directly. They want to participate in decisions to assign new jobs to higher pay grades and to create new jobs for promotional opportunities. They also seek higher pay and shorter time limits for employees working "out of class."

Reclassifying jobs to higher pay grades is a rather complex procedure involving a variety of personnel actors, including the department head, agency or department personnel staff, and the central personnel agency. Unions may negotiate directly for reclassification where it is permitted, or they may attempt to influence any or all of the personnel actors. The creation of new jobs is particularly sought for occupations in which employees have little opportunity for promotion after the first few years on the job. The police function serves as a good example. Police patrol officers can "top out" at maximum pay after about five years. Higher pay can be achieved only through cost-of-living adjustments, seniority pay, or promotion to a supervisory or investigative position (jobs for which a good patrol officer may not be suited). In some cases, unions have been instrumental in creating a new position, such as "Master Patrol Officer," to reward senior officers on the beat with higher pay for their experience.

The matter of properly compensating employees for out-of-title work in higher rated jobs is also of concern. Unions submit that when an employee performs duties of a higher paying job because of a vacation, illness, temporary vacancy, or other reason, that employee should be fully compensated at the appropriate rate of pay. Moreover, say the unions, after a designated period of out-of-class work, the "temporary" employee should be promoted into the job. Disagreements between the union and management on out-of-class work may be settled through grievance or merit system procedures, a partnership approach, or language in the contract. For example, a contract may stipulate that an employee will be paid at a higher rate if he or she works four or more hours at a higher rated position. Properly rewarding employees for the nature of the work they perform seems an equitable proposition for which unions often win support.

The trend is toward replacing stringent position classification systems with a more flexible approach known variously as broad banding, pay banding, or flexible banding. Existing position classes are collapsed into a broader range of position descriptions, permitting greater management flexibility in both reassigning and rewarding employees. Managers like the enhanced flexibility; unions enjoy any pay advantage but do not like the extension of management authority in assigning jobs.

In some federal partnerships, unions and management have negotiated the terms of new broad banding systems. A collaborative approach has proven to be productive in some state and local settings as well. But in others, where preemptory actions have abolished or significantly altered the traditional merit system and position classification in favor of nearly absolute management autonomy, the unions have been vehemently opposed (to little effect in Georgia and Florida, where unions are weak) (Battaglio and Condrey 2006). Staffing levels are of inherent interest to unions, who link staffing to the quality of services. A larger, more fully staffed unit labor force also translates into more members of the bargaining unit (see Chapter 6 for the tradeoffs between compensation levels and jobs).

5. Work Load and Scheduling

These closely intertwined issues refer to the amount of work required of individuals or groups of employees, the decision as to how many workers are required to perform that work, and the manner and time in which the work is to be done. In federal employment, agencies may negotiate with unions over the numbers of employees or positions assigned to work projects as well as the means of performing work. They seldom bargain over total hours of employment, which are fixed, but alternative work arrangements (e.g., telecommuting) are negotiable. In state and local government, maximum working hours may be set by law or by contract. In some locations, employee organizations have won major workload and scheduling concessions from management in overtime provisions, shift assignments, overtime compensation, weekend differentials, meal and rest periods, cleanup time, and transfers to other jobs or different locations.

Unions have campaigned and bargained for a shorter work week for more than a century. The 40-hour week remains the standard, but reductions to 37.5 and 35 hours have been won in some jurisdictions. Police and firefighter unions have won reductions in total working hours as well as shift hours. Teachers bargain over the length of the school year and the school day, the number and size of classes (McDonnell and Pascal 1979), and the contours of year-round schooling (Fuller, Mitchell, and Hartmann 2000). Teacher union efforts to shorten the length of the workday or school year face significant legal and practical limits, however, from state laws mandating a standard school year and citizen and parental opposition to altering the public school timetable.

In one interesting experiment aimed at improving a public education system in crisis, the Rochester, New York, City School District and the Rochester Teachers' Association actually negotiated a longer school year. In exchange for a more than 40 percent increase in salaries, teachers agreed to work an extra 5 days a year, take personal responsibility for a group of students, and make home visits (Doherty and Lipsky 1988: 56–57).

Teachers have made other gains in the general area of workload and scheduling and have managed to open the scope of bargaining wider than any other occupational function in the United States. Teachers have demanded and won relief from nonteaching chores, such as milk distribution; playground supervision; cafeteria, bus, and hall supervision; book distribution; and copying materials for classroom use. Duty-free lunch periods for teachers also have been established, as have limitations on work beyond the regular school day. Teachers have gained extra compensation for after-school administrative meetings, parent–teacher conferences, and other extracurricular activities. They have also won provisions limiting involuntary teacher transfers and requiring teacher assignments to be based on characteristics such as certification, seniority, and experience (Goldschmidt and Stuart 1986: 354).

Teachers have staked a claim in the field of education policy making by demanding to include class size in the scope of bargaining (Stone 2000: 53–54). This appears to be an instance where a workload factor links fairly directly to the quality of education. More students mean more work for the teacher, less time for the teacher to spend with each student individually, and higher probability of disciplinary problems. Where class size falls within the scope of bargaining, student–teacher ratios tend to be smaller. When it is excluded from negotiations, teachers seek to win salary increases for large class sizes and workloads (Woodbury 1985).

Other unions have been concerned with workload and scheduling, too. Nurses face enormous pressures in acute care departments and facilities under the best of circumstances, but when they have to work 12–16 hour shifts or double shifts because of staff shortages, the patients are at greater risk from nurse error. Along with managed care and the infusion of profit considerations, the national nurse staffing shortage has exerted a significant negative effect on the nursing profession. Unions rightfully capitalize (and organize) in such a setting, fighting for more nurses, shorter hours, and improved working conditions (Clark and Clark 2006).

Understaffing can create unacceptable and dangerous situations in other occupations as well. When the Federal Aviation Administration preemptively ended a negotiations impasse in 2006 by imposing a new contract with staffing cuts, new work rules, a 30 percent pay cut, and even a dress code, air traffic controllers retired in droves. According to their union president, the 6-day work weeks and staff shortages deeply concerned controllers, who feared that fatigue could lead to them making a deadly mistake in air traffic routing (Sniffen 2007).

Police unions may interpret work assignments as a safety issue in situations involving one- or two-officer patrol cars. Some unions assert that two officers are necessary to maximize officer safety, but police management wants flexibility in assigning officers according to time of day and geographical area. Police unions also have struggled with management over the matter of using civilian employees for administrative, clerical, and dispatcher jobs, preferring to post sworn officers instead. Management typically prefers to keep more officers on the street by placing lower paid civilians in support positions.

Unions have successfully promoted flexible work schedules. A growing percentage of the total public and private labor force is engaged in flextime, job sharing, telecommuting, or permanent part-time work. Interest in such arrangements has developed with the changing demographics of the work force, including semi-retired employees, working mothers, and family-oriented fathers. Flextime can help employees cope with difficult commutes and rush-hour traffic by permitting them to come and go to work at various times between 6:00 a.m. and 8.00 p.m. Nearly three quarters of federal employees take advantage of this type of program, as do a substantial number of state and local workers. Studies show that flextime has positive effects on morale, reduces absenteeism and tardiness, and enhances productivity (Kemp 1987: 79–81). It appears to be a win–win issue for unions and management, as are "flexiplace" and telecommuting, in which employees do their work at home or at regional work centers on personal computers.

6. Grievances

Grievance procedures, which provide a formal avenue for employees to tell their side of the story in an objective setting about problems arising on the job, are second in union interest only to wages and benefits. As in the case of compensation, this is an element of human resource management on which unions have had a significant effect. Virtually all bargaining jurisdictions have contracts with negotiated grievance procedures. Most provide for binding arbitration as a final step in cases where grievances cannot be settled at the agency or department level. (Grievance procedures receive full treatment in Chapter 10.)

7. Employee Discipline

Closely related to grievance procedures is employee discipline. Disciplinary actions by management are frequently the triggering mechanism for grievance procedures. In general, unions have sought to protect employees from unfair disciplinary actions by formalizing the process and placing the burden of proof on management. They also have fought to negotiate procedures through collective bargaining instead of traditional civil service rules. Typically, unions represent the accused employee in any disciplinary proceeding.

It may well be that the most important union influence on disciplinary actions is tacit. Union influence is registered long before formal disciplinary actions are actually taken, because supervisors are fully aware that hasty or unfair adverse actions will be contested. Employee discipline has been lodged in the scope of collective bargaining in nearly all unionized jurisdictions across the United States.

8. Dismissals and Layoffs

It is not a simple matter to dismiss a government employee, even under abnormal circumstances, once the initial probationary period has expired. Due process is a powerful value in public personnel administration, and the courts and arbitrators have consistently held that nonprobationary public employees have property rights in their jobs. Employers can no longer blithely follow the employment-at-will doctrine and dismiss an employee for good reason, bad reason, or no reason at all (Muhl 2001). The courts have become important policy makers in personnel matters. With regard to employee dismissals, the tendency has been for the courts to establish procedural safeguards so elaborate that, for all practical purposes, public employees have become tenured, with "ownership" of their jobs. In combination with merit system protections, vigorous union appeals, and sympathetic arbitrators, this has made most public employees nearly immune from being fired (see Hays 1995). Such elaborate job protections lower the turnover (quit) rate in government.

Generally, workers covered by bargaining contracts enjoy comprehensive protections against arbitrary dismissal. Employers must prove "just cause" in order for a sacking to stand, and unions effectively fight anything that smacks of wrongful discharge. Indeed, such protective actions are a major selling point to potential union members. Sometimes, however, unions may go too far in defense of their members. For example, a Hartford, Connecticut, firefighter was fired on three separate occasions from 1981 to 1991. A chronic alcoholic, he missed one out of every four workdays and was often sent home drunk. Incredibly, he frequently drove fire trucks. Once, when he had an accident, it was determined that his driver's license had been suspended for 6 months on a drunk-driving charge. Yet the union staunchly defended the miscreant and got him reinstated each time. Finally, more than a decade after his first sacking, the firefighter was permanently removed from his job (*Hartford Courant* 1992).

An interesting issue concerns employee dismissal for off-duty misconduct. The principle that has evolved in the courts and in arbitration hearings is that discharge is justified when the misconduct has a demonstrated adverse impact on the employer. Examples include the firing of a state liquor store employee for fatally injuring "a 71-year-old woman who asked him to stop beating his wife," a police officer who gave illegal drugs to a police department informer, and a high school teacher who was seen socially with one of her students (M. Hill and Dawson 1985). Once the alleged misconduct is proven, it must be demonstrated that it damaged the agency's image or "product" through adverse publicity, through another employee's refusal to work with the offender, or by causing the offender to be unable to perform his or her job. Generally, those in sensitive jobs such as law enforcement, fire protection, and teaching are held to higher standards than other government workers.

In some jurisdictions, overtly pro-union grievance arbitrators have made it nearly impossible to fire a union member, no matter how outrageous the offense. In Connecticut during the late 1990s, the State Board of Mediation and Arbitration "reinstated a cop fired for giving up an informant, a school warehouse supervisor caught embezzling thousands of dollars from his union, a parks worker who abused his boss," and a prison guard who uttered racial slurs and vulgarities into the answering machine of an African American state senator (Condon 1998: B1).

9. Reductions in Force

Reductions in force (RIFs) were limited in number and scope until the late 1980s, when the halcyon days of government growth in the United States ended in most jurisdictions and layoffs became commonplace. Procedural protections for individual employees apply only marginally when agency- or government-wide reductions in force are implemented. Unions do exert influence on which workers are to be laid off, what the "bumping" order will be, and what the priority and procedures will be for reemployment. Unions, of course, favor the criterion of seniority.

The basic union position is that less senior workers should be the first laid off and the last rehired. In general, this is not a point of contention with management, although seniority in retention and reemployment is a common topic in formal contract negotiations. In public education, some state laws require certification and teaching qualifications to take precedence in determining layoffs, but years in the classroom can be negotiated as an additional criterion.

Alternatives to layoffs are sometimes sought by a union, depending on member sentiment and management consent. Possibilities include work sharing (two full-time positions are collapsed into two half-time jobs), rotating layoffs, furloughs, and voluntary days off without pay. Traditionally, however, unions prefer seniority-based layoffs to alternative arrangements.

10. Other Human Resource Management Policies

In various jurisdictions, unions have been influential in designing and establishing human resource-related policies. Several are considered here: technological change; productivity; privatization; worker health and safety issues such as smoking, disability, and drug use; workers' compensation; and miscellaneous terms and conditions of employment.

a. Technological Change

Private sector unions have long been interested in the consequences of technological change for their membership, and historically they have opposed labor-saving innovations that reduce the number of union jobs. Union success in this area led to the practice of "featherbedding," in which idle employees were kept on the firm's payroll indefinitely.

There are limits to the application of labor-saving technology in the public sector because of the labor intensity of government services. Still, certain services are better candidates for technological innovations than others. Garbage collection is one such area, where changes have included curbside instead of backyard service, trash compactors, standardized carts, automated collection systems, and the one-person crew. Stanley (1972: 100) relates an amusing story involving early technological change in solid waste collection in Detroit: "Management proposed increasing the productivity of garbage collection trips by using a rig known as a 'motherloader' — a garbage truck towing a trailer. The employees took one look at it, changed its name, and started for home. Management soon dropped the idea because the equipment had technical, as well as labor-relations, drawbacks."

The employment and work scheduling effects of information technology have received union scrutiny and become a frequent subject for bargaining. Automation can replace humans with technology, resulting in reduced demand for various support workers. Information technology also presents new opportunities for alternative work schedules and workplaces, as noted above. All of this is of interest to unions.

Most public employee unions claim that they are not opposed to technological changes, given these conditions:

1. The changes can be shown to be beneficial to the particular service
2. Workers' jobs are adequately protected
3. Employees will share in any monetary gains from productivity improvements
4. Changes in the place, rules, and hours of work are negotiated or, at a minimum, subject to consultation with the union
5. The union receives advance notice of planned technological change

The most important condition is that employees be protected from job loss, or, where that is not entirely possible, that severance pay, natural attrition, reassignments, early retirement, or other arrangements are utilized.

b. Productivity

Maximizing outputs while minimizing inputs — productivity — is a significant concern of public managers (Kearney and Berman 1999). To improve levels of productivity, however, one must first be able to measure it; that presents problems in the public sector, where labor-intensive services, not goods or manufactured items, are the product. Government services do have identifiable output (process) and outcome (results) indicators, but in practice they are difficult to collect and interpret.

Empirical research on private sector unions has generated mixed findings. Freeman and Medoff (1984: Ch. 11) concluded that unions enhance productivity because in unionized settings, management hires higher quality workers, purchases more capital-intensive technology, expands training opportunities, and benefits from lower employee turnover. Research also suggests that improvements in product quality and quantity are more likely to be achieved through programs jointly designed and administered by unions and management, compared to settings with no union involvement (Kearney and Hays 1994). However, unions can thwart productivity improvement efforts, and their wage-setting activities may cause research and development funds to be displaced by payroll costs. Also, unionization may be associated with low turnover, but it is related to higher absenteeism as well. To summarize, little reliable evidence exists regarding the productivity effects of private sector unions.

In government, the influence of unions on the quality and quantity of services is also uncertain or variable. With regard to productivity in specific functions, unions have cooperated in adopting productivity improvement technologies in some municipal sanitation departments but not others (Lewin 1986), and they tend to enhance productivity in the public schools (Johnson and Kardos 2000; Eberts and Stone 1987) but not in public universities (Meador and Walters 1994).

Sanitation unions have found themselves with a Hobson's choice in cities where privatization is a looming threat. Private contractors tend to be freely available and more productive and less expensive than municipal sanitation departments in collecting household and industrial garbage, largely due to smaller crews, lower wages, inferior benefits, newer equipment, less absenteeism, and superior incentive systems (Hoover and Peoples 2003; Lewin 1986: 255). If municipal unions fight technological change (such as new sanitation trucks with smaller crews), management may pursue privatization. If instead unions accept technological improvements, work force reductions eventually follow, diminishing the ranks of dues-paying members. Unions have adamantly — even violently — opposed technological change and privatization in some cities (e.g., Tampa; Salt Lake City; Camden, New Jersey). In other cases, sanitation unions have addressed the issues through labor–management committees or productivity bargaining (Lewin 1986: 259–260).

For decades a debate has raged over the issue of teacher productivity in the public schools. The debate is really part of a larger dialogue over the role of teachers in education reform and in the quality of the schools. Conservative scholars and pundits have laid much of the blame for the perceived deteriorating quality of public education (K–12) on teacher unions, accusing them of protecting incompetent teachers, ignoring the education needs of children, and opposing meaningful reform efforts, such as educational choice. Teacher unions and progressives view teachers as the key element in any serious effort to reform the schools.

Several empirical studies have been conducted on the effects of teacher unions on public school productivity. Eberts and Stone (1987) found that for elementary schools, unionized school districts were 7 percent more productive for average students than nonunion districts, when productivity was measured in terms of student scores on standardized tests. However, union districts were about 7 percent less productive for students either significantly above or below average, possibly because teacher unions support standardized educational practices more than specialized instruction techniques of greater benefit to very advanced and very delayed students. Across all students, the union productivity advantage was a "modestly positive" 3 percent (Eberts and Stone 1987: 359).

Kurth (1987) weighed in to the debate with an analysis of SAT scores. He determined that several factors were related to student test performance, including exposure to the written word, parental involvement, an urban environment, and education spending. Teachers' unions were found to have a highly negative impact on student performance. Kurth concluded that unions significantly impair teacher productivity and student educational achievement.

Kurth's findings were vigorously attacked by Nelson, F. H. and Gould (1988), who argued that Kurth's mathematical model was misspecified ("theoretically shallow, oddly constructed") and his variables poorly defined, leading to an erroneous conclusion. Reexamining the data, Nelson and Gould found that collective bargaining was associated with significantly higher SAT scores. This provoked Kurth (1987) into a vitriolic retort in which he called his critics' comments "misleading and full of distortions." However, Kirth's critics have received support from research by Register and Grimes (1991), Argys and Rees (1995), F. H. Nelson and Rosen (1996), and Hoxby (1996).

Zigarelli (1994) also found that unions are positively related to student performance. His model attributes the relationship between unions and student achievement to (1) teacher unions "shocking" school bureaucracies into more efficient practices that generate positive classroom outcomes and (2) union political activities that boost education funding. Zwerling and Thomason (1994), examining the effects of teacher unions on high school dropout rates, found that unions significantly reduce the likelihood of boys dropping out but only slightly decrease the female dropout rate. A reasonable conclusion is that teacher unions do not depress student achievement and, in fact, have a modest positive effect on it (Stone 2000).

In higher education, the most direct measure of faculty productivity is the publication of professional journal articles. Meador and Walters (1994) examined research productivity in 889 Ph.D.-granting departments. Their findings associated faculty unions with both a lower output of published articles and a lower peer assessment of departmental scholarly competence than departments with nonunion faculty. Research has also determined that faculty unions increase the retention rate of more senior faculty (Rees 1999). Because faculty unions tend to favor across-the-board salary increases over merit pay, perhaps productive junior faculty tend to leave, perceiving that their future earnings will be higher at nonunion institutions.

c. Privatization

The transfer of public goods and service provision responsibilities to the private sector has been a worldwide phenomenon since the rise of New Public Management in the 1980s. The movement has several impetuses, including ideological opposition to public sector growth, belief that the private sector can provide goods and services more efficiently (cheaply) than government, and the fiscal squeeze at all levels of government. In the United States, privatization has taken three major forms: construction of a public facility by a private contractor (e.g., prison or highway), government purchases of specialized services (e.g., legal assistance, engineering expertise) on a short-term basis, and contracting out public services to a private or nonprofit organization.

In most jurisdictions, privatization is considered a management right related to the efficient management of the workplace and therefore outside the scope of bargaining. And, in principle, unions do not object to constructing facilities, making specialized purchases, or contracting out professional services that their own members cannot perform, such as architecture, engineering, or creative services. It is when traditional government functions, such as sanitation or fire protection, are given over to the private sector that unions register vociferous opposition. Unions contend that contracting out results in the termination of public employee jobs and the creation of new lower paying jobs in the private sector and tends to displace women and minorities. Therefore, it is a personnel matter that should fall within the scope of bargaining. In state and local government, labor relations boards and the courts, with few exceptions, have supported the union position that the decision to contract out should be a mandatory subject of bargaining and that public employers are obligated to provide notice of the proposed work change to the unions and an opportunity to negotiate the issues.

In the federal sector, agency management clearly controls contracting-out decisions despite union opposition. Fortifying federal management is (1) the Office of Management and Budget's circular A-76, a directive to federal agencies that requires work to be contracted out to a firm if it can conduct the work more economically;

(2) Title VII of the CSRA, which grants management the authority to "make determinations with respect to contracting out"; and (3) actions during the George W. Bush administration that further narrowed the scope of bargaining on contracting activities.

Unions in state and local government tend to discourage employers from contracting out because strident opposition is assured. Any available political strings will be pulled. As suggested above, such opposition is entirely rational, because the record shows that union membership declines where contracting out occurs. Moreover, there can be mutual benefits when unions force a careful, objective pace to privatization that diminishes the possibility of policy mistakes. Increasingly, unions seek to develop competitive bids to retain their public service production responsibilities, thereby eliminating the economic rationale for privatizing. They have done so successfully in several cities, including Phoenix, Philadelphia, and Indianapolis. Nonetheless, privatization has registered substantial gains in such functions as sanitation, street construction, architectural and engineering services, legal counseling, building repair and maintenance, social services, and ambulance services. Chelsea, Massachusetts, even contracted out the entire public school system to Boston University for 10 years. Massachusetts has privatized mental health care, prison health care, and highway maintenance, among many other activities (Wallin 1997). Interestingly, in cities where management–union relations are highly adversarial, the likelihood of privatization is greater than in cities with cooperative relations (Chandler and Feuille 1991). Perhaps management is sorely tempted to try to rid itself of a perceived labor pest in such cities.

Contracting out does not eliminate unionization and the strike threat. To the contrary, private firms can be unionized, too, and often are, and their workers can legally strike. Furthermore, monetary savings may be illusory. Quality and service levels sometimes decline, accountability may suffer, equity in service delivery may be sacrificed, and contracts may be awarded on the basis of political favoritism. Privatization has been particularly controversial in police and fire protection and in education. Still, the outlook is for additional gains ahead, with highways, bridges, mass transit, and water supply showing the strongest potential.

d. Health and Safety

Myriad health- and safety-related issues have found their way to the bargaining table, reflecting new knowledge and information, changing technology, unions' traditional concern for the physical and psychological well-being of workers, and the fact that public employees are not protected by the Occupational Safety and Health Act of 1970 (OSHA). Three particular health issues have received increasing scrutiny from management and unions: smoking in the workplace, HIV-AIDS, and drug testing. Unions want to formally register the perspectives of their membership on these important issues and to defend aggrieved individuals in the bargaining unit.

i. Smoking — The Centers for Disease Control and Prevention have estimated that every pack of cigarettes smoked in the United States results in $7 of costs in medical care and lost productivity. Cigarette smoking is believed to be responsible for more than 400,000 deaths per year from cancer, heart disease, pulmonary disease, and other ailments. Today, only about 21 percent of U.S. adults smoke versus more than 40 percent in 1965 (Centers for Disease Control and Prevention 2008).

Employers are concerned with smoking (and second-hand smoke) because it affects them financially through increased absenteeism, higher insurance and medical care costs, and lost productivity. Moreover, most employers must enforce state and local laws that prohibit or restrict smoking in public places. Although the federal courts have not found a constitutional basis for a smoke-free workplace, some state courts have upheld a common-law right to a safe and healthy workplace, which includes protection from second-hand smoke. An employer that fails to provide a safe and healthy place of work may be held responsible in the courts for negligence.

In response, employers have adopted policies not to hire active smokers and to prohibit employees from smoking on the job altogether. Some have prohibited off-the-job smoking as well, although the legal grounds for such actions are questionable, probably violating the right to privacy and due process (Wilson 1989: 41–42). An additional problem with employer actions against smokers is that it has discriminatory impacts — African Americans and Latinos are more likely to smoke than whites. Finally, employers in most states have a common-law duty to accommodate both smoking and nonsmoking employees, and 16 states prohibit employers from discriminating against smokers (Repa 2005).

Unions, of course, have a legal obligation to represent the interests of all members in the bargaining unit, regardless of smoking preference. Under collective bargaining laws and contracts, management may not alter the terms and conditions of employment unilaterally. Smoking restrictions and rules are terms and conditions of employment unless legislation or a management rights clause clearly places such work rules and conditions within the realm of management authority. Thus, management and unions usually must negotiate or otherwise agree on smoking policy. Even where state or local laws apply, the implementation of statutory restrictions through workplace rules should be negotiated with the unions. The alternative is for management to field any number of formal grievances. Management's right to impose rules concerning smoking may be contested, usually through union representation of a grievant who has been disciplined or dismissed for rule breaking. Furthermore, unions insist on consistent, nonbiased enforcement of smoking policies and sanctions.

ii. Disability — The Rehabilitation Act of 1973 and the Americans with Disabilities Act of 1990 protect persons with disabilities from discrimination in any human resource management process. Disabled workers must be provided with "reasonable accommodation" by employers, subject to "business necessity" limitations. For example, workplaces must be made physically accessible to people in wheelchairs (reasonable accommodation) unless the workplace cannot be modified without extreme cost to the employer (business necessity). The ADA's definition of "disability" is expansive, covering an estimated 58 million Americans, more than one of every six. Within the broad definitional umbrella of the ADA are orthopedic impairments, alcoholism, drug abuse, mental illness, and HIV infection.

For employers, as well as for unions charged with fair representation of all members of the bargaining unit, a fine line must be walked between protecting the rights of the disabled worker and respecting the rights and preferences of their coworkers. For instance, a union must represent both an HIV-infected employee in terms of reasonable accommodation of his or her medical needs and treatments and the concerns of coworkers who (unreasonably) fear becoming infected with the virus. An employer should consult with the union before transferring a disabled worker or making accommodations that affect other employees.

iii. Drug Testing — Alcohol abuse has always been a scourge of the American workplace; it has now been joined by another serious addiction — illegal drugs. These "evil twins" cost the U.S. economy billions of dollars per year and account for a disproportionate percentage of discipline and dismissal cases. Substance abusers are less productive; more prone to turnover, tardiness, property damage, and dismissal; and more likely to get sick or be injured than other employees.

Unions seldom disagree with management rules prohibiting working under the influence, because the safety and productivity of all members are potentially at risk. However, unions do prefer to negotiate specific rules and procedures for addressing the problem. And unions will aggressively defend employees accused of substance abuse. In the case of alcohol abuse, unions frequently argue that discipline is unfair because alcoholism is a disease beyond one's own control. Most government employers accept this view and give alcoholic employees an opportunity for treatment and counseling through an Employee Assistance Program (EAP) or on their own. If the unfortunate worker is unable to conquer the addiction and his or her performance is judged unacceptable, discharge usually follows.

Although both alcoholics and drug addicts have some protection from adverse employment actions by the Rehabilitation Act and Americans with Disabilities Act (they are considered to be disabled), drug abusers are more likely to be treated severely by management. Drug use is, after all, usually illegal, and a greater stigma is attached to it than to drinking. For example, off-duty drug use may directly result in discharge if a court conviction is made, whereas alcohol abuse rarely does, except indirectly through poor attendance and job performance. A worker guilty of using or selling drugs at the place of employment is also asking for discharge. Unions do not raise a significant barrier to such employer actions, as long as members receive due process and any policy alterations are submitted to the union for consideration. The matter of *testing* employees for drug use is more contentious.

Few restraints exist on drug testing in the private or nonprofit sectors, or on testing prospective employees in any setting. In government, constitutional issues are more germane for ongoing employees, including the Fourth Amendment's right to privacy and freedom from unreasonable search and seizure, the equal protection clause of the Fourteenth Amendment, the Fifth Amendment's protection from self-incrimination, and various state constitutional protections. A nonunion jurisdiction may get away with unilaterally imposing a drug-testing policy on current employees, but where unions represent workers, the policy is usually treated as a term or condition of employment — a mandatory bargaining subject.

Under most circumstances, unions are adamantly opposed to drug testing, particularly if it is randomly imposed without a clear purpose. Drug testing is an invasive procedure that requires analysis of urine, blood, hair, saliva, or nail samples. It is not time specific, so it often "reveals more about the employee's off-duty life-style than about his ability to perform on the job" (Denenberg 1987: 305). Laboratory testing procedures are notoriously unreliable.

Courts tend to side with the unions, unless the government employer can demonstrate a legitimate interest in testing (e.g., public safety) and a fair program that adequately guards employee rights. In *Skinner v. Railway Labor Executives' Association* (1989), the U.S. Supreme Court held that urine collection violates the reasonable right to privacy under certain conditions; in *NTEU v. Van Raab* (1989), the Supreme Court restricted the U.S. Customs Service's drug testing program for candidates for promotion to those in "sensitive positions" involved in drug interdiction. Legitimate "reasonable" interest in testing for drug use is easier to prove for employees directly involved in protecting the public health and safety, such as police, firefighters, train and mass transit drivers, air traffic controllers, and any worker who carries a firearm.

Some of the most interesting activity concerning the legality of drug testing has occurred in the federal government. Random drug testing in the military was ordered by President Nixon in 1971, and it continues today. In 1986, President Reagan punctuated his wife Nancy's "Just Say NO!" campaign by directing all executive agencies to randomly test all workers in "sensitive positions." A fury of union litigation ensued, resulting in several court cases, rulings by the Federal Labor Relations Authority, and congressional involvement (Masters 1988). The federal unions claimed that management must prove a link between a positive drug test and an individual's work performance before disciplinary actions can be taken. The federal agencies differed on this issue, asserting that drug testing is a nonnegotiable management right under Section 7106 of the CSRA. Drug-testing programs continue to be challenged in some federal agencies today.

When not fighting over drug testing in the courts, arbitration venues, or across the bargaining table, unions and management can embark on cooperative ventures to address the drug abuse problem. Employee assistance plans provide aid and counseling to drug users that benefit both parties. So do drug prevention programs, sponsored or cosponsored by unions, which can marshal peer pressure against drug abuse and encourage users to seek help.

e. Workers' Compensation

Workers' compensation is a federal–state program that pays benefits to workers injured on the job, regardless of fault. Compulsory in all but three states (New Jersey, South Carolina, and Texas), its annual costs approach $100 billion. A study of workers' compensation claims (Hirsch, McPherson, and Dumond 1997) found that union members were significantly more likely to receive such benefits than were similar nonunion workers. The reasons? Possibly because unions provide their members with more assistance and information about the program and, through the contract and grievance procedures, protect filers from management-imposed penalties for filing claims. Moreover, union workers are more likely to hold dangerous jobs

f. Miscellaneous Terms and Conditions

If a variable in the environment of work can even imaginatively be labeled "working condition," then the odds are that some union, somewhere, has challenged management over it. In many instances, union interest in working conditions has led to improvements, especially within the area of employee safety. Safety, of course, is an important concern to both employees and management. Injuries or deaths at the workplace are anathema to both parties. Their prevention is normally recognized in labor agreements as the joint responsibility of management and labor. Unions, in particular, are vigilant concerning the employer's duty to provide a healthy and safe working environment, including the provision of protective equipment and clothing and expeditiously addressing potential health and safety threats.

For public school teachers, a safety-related issue is the need to protect teachers from violent students. Teachers feel that control over student disciplinary procedures is critical to their physical and emotional well-being. Discipline is an especially salient issue in big city school systems containing many students who are "difficult to teach." Generally, teachers want the right to expel from the classroom students who evidence intractable disciplinary problems, and the right to representation on student disciplinary committees. The courts have affirmed that negotiations over student disciplinary matters are within the scope of bargaining, unless specifically excluded as a management right (*Sutherlin Education Association v. Sutherlin School District No. 130* 1976).

Other work conditions subject to bargaining include meal and rest periods, cleanup time, coffee breaks, locker rooms, clothing allowances, and mileage allowances. One early but exhaustive list of negotiated working conditions was attributed to the Social Service Employees Union in New York City (Stanley 1972: 110–111):

The union's contract contains unusually detailed provisions on working time and free time, including: travel time to get pay checks; grace periods for handicapped employees at the beginning and end of shifts; grace periods for delays due to inadequate elevator service; dismissal at 3 p.m. if the temperature reaches 92 degrees F; dismissal at noon if the temperature falls below 50 degrees outside and 68 degrees inside, or if it falls below those levels after 12 noon, dismissal within an hour ... the contract assures the employee of a place to hang his coat, and — obviously essential in view of the preceding requirements — a thermometer.

You name it — it has been the subject of negotiations somewhere. The Minnesota Supreme Court ruled, on appeal, that facial hair and fingernail length are not mandatory subjects of bargaining for sheriffs' deputies. Ear studs? They are not banned in Boston, but officers are forbidden to wear them in Peotone, California, and Vernon, Connecticut. In Middletown, Connecticut, the town police union filed a grievance against the chief for suspending Chance, a police dog, for eating the dashboard of a police cruiser. Chance apparently became frustrated when his two human cruiser mates got involved in a scuffle with a suspect while the protective canine was locked in the car. In New York, AFSCME negotiated "captivity coverage" for state correctional officers in its contract. Under the coverage, Lloyds of London insures the officers. If they are held captive by inmates, officers are compensated 50 percent of their salary when the traumatic event is over. Death, dismemberment, or disfigurement results in 200 percent compensation.

As mentioned previously, teachers have had more success in broadening the scope of bargaining than any other occupational group, largely because there are significant elements of management and independent decision making in their daily duties. Among the working conditions negotiated in teacher contracts are

Class size provisions
Number and functions of teacher aides
School calendar
Teacher representation on instructional policy committees
Teacher evaluation procedures
Special programs
Curriculum
Grading criteria
Textbook selection
Allocation of federal grant money
Teaching methodologies
Peer evaluation of teachers in lieu of principal's ratings
Provisions for day care centers for teachers' children
Teacher participation in school site selection

The cutting point in the scope of teacher negotiations seems to be how directly an issue affects the well-being of the individual teacher, as opposed to its impact on the operation of the school system as a whole.

IV. Conclusion

As the purse strings of state and local governments have been cinched tight by fiscal constraints, a stingy yet mandate-promiscuous federal government, and a hypercritical citizenry, unions have turned from an almost exclusive concentration on wages and dollar-driven benefits to certain nonmonetary elements of human resource administration. Wages remain a visible and important issue for unions, but future pay gains are likely to be modest.

The clash between bargaining and merit systems is inherently a part of public sector labor relations, as unions seek to extend their sphere of influence and limit management authority. Unions want greater control of the workplace for their members, and they work hard, and often successfully, to get it. Management today, however, is a more forceful and competent adversary in protecting its rights and prerogatives than it once was. In some ways, public management is made more effective and fair by union involvement in workplace decisions. In other respects, the loss of flexibility in a union environment can impede management response and adaptation to social, political, and economic changes.

A precarious balance exists between bureaucracy and democracy in the United States. Unions represent institutionalized bureaucratic power, whereas elected government officials and their appointees defend the principles and processes of representative government. As unions encroach on traditional areas of management rights, they sometimes penetrate the arena of public policy making. This is evident in public education, where teacher unions have fought and won a voice in determining a variety of education policies.

It is difficult to state with any assurance or finality whether union policy involvement is good or bad. In public education it clearly has meant less flexibility for school management and some rigidity in school operations. However, teacher participation in determining how the learning process is structured may produce higher morale and, in the long run, positively affect the quality of program implementation. Perhaps, as a Huntington, New York, teacher contract states, "The members of the teaching profession have a special expertise which entitles them to participate in determining policies and programs designed to improve educational standards." Then again, this claim could be made by almost any occupational group in public employment, from corrections officers to sanitation engineers.

As a practical matter, there is a need for management–labor consultation over the role of public employees in policy determination. Final authority unquestionably should be retained by management, but the union voice is legitimate and can prove invaluable. The wise manager, the democratic manager, should not refuse to discuss policy matters with unions that are of direct concern to them and their members.

Ultimately, the unions get only what management (and arbitrators) gives to them. The protections of collective bargaining statutes, management rights clauses, ordinances, and merit systems shore up the defenses of management. So do political and economic factors in public employment that act as constraints on unions, not the least of which is public opinion. Public management is well served by using available resources and tools in establishing a firm, but not rigid, posture vis-à-vis the unions. Both parties in the relationship should strive to negotiate in an atmosphere of mutual respect and concern for the public interest. As the next chapter points out, however, this is much easier said than done.

Case Study 7.1: A Blooming Labor Dispute

Nine-year-old Katie Corletta, a student at Horton Elementary, was distressed about the condition of a public park across the street from her school. So, she organized a group of fellow third-graders to pick up the trash and plant a flower garden. They did a very nice job, much to the delight of teachers and parents, who were impressed by the community spirit of the children.

Local 1029 of AFSCME was much less pleased. The municipal union, which represents Parks and Recreation Department employees, filed a prohibitive practices complaint, stating that it should have been informed and consulted about the student project because its members maintain the park by picking up broken glass and other trash, mowing the lawn, and repairing playground equipment.

Parents and the PTO were shocked and outraged, and the children were confused: "We didn't think we were taking anything away from the union because they weren't planting flowers," Corletta said in a local newspaper report. "All we were doing is helping pick up trash. We're not mowing the lawn that the union people would do. We're just doing things they don't do."

Kenneth Boulware, president of Local 1029, said that the union had a serious problem with the city's lack of communication. Union members, he asserted, work nearly every day in the park. "Personally, I don't have a problem with third-graders," he said. "My problem is if they abandon the project, I'd have to have our people maintain it as they have in the past. And union workers should perform union work."

Questions

1. Why did the union react as it did when it discovered that the flower garden had been planted by the children? What were the possible justifications for the union action?
2. If bargaining unit members had been laid off recently because of budget cuts, would this be important?
3. What are the implications for union–citizen relationships?
4. How would you have handled the issue if you were the union president?

Case Study 7.2: A Chocolate High?

Jason, an employee of the State Department of Transportation with 18 years' experience, was passing by the coffee service area in the motor pool on a Wednesday when he spied a plate of brownies. Naturally, he ate one. Unfortunately (because he worked in a potentially hazardous environment), it was not an ordinary brownie. Even more unfortunately, he was subject to random drug testing and the next day his number was called.

Jason delivered his urine sample and thought no more of it until Thursday, when he was notified by his supervisor, Javier, that he had tested positive. When questioned about the results by his supervisor, Jason offered no explanation other than that he had been taking an over-the-counter cold medication and a wellness herb. Javier referred Jason to the EAP for counseling. The EAP had no available appointments the next day and neither the EAP nor Jason followed up Monday.

The next Monday morning, Jason was called into the HRM office and discharged for failing the drug test and refusing to seek EAP assistance. Shocked, Jason immediately proceeded to the union steward and filed a grievance seeking reinstatement to his position. In his statement, Jason said that he had not experienced any effects of marijuana and adamantly professed his innocence.

Shortly thereafter, Kenneth, one of Jason's coworkers, came forward to admit that he had baked some marijuana-laced brownies and placed them in the coffee area but that he did not intend them for Jason.

The case moved to a hearing officer. If you were the hearing officer, what would you do after receiving Jason's grievance and Kenneth's admission? Was Jason negligent and culpable for use of illegal drugs?

Chapter 8

Strike!

I. Introduction

As observed in Chapter 1, there is nothing new or entirely surprising about workers withholding their labor. Work stoppages were fairly common in American mines, factories, and transportation industries in the period preceding passage of the National Labor Relations Act (NLRA). Many of these strikes were met with violence. Robert Shogan (2004) relates the story of the country's largest mine strike in *The Battle of Blair Mountain*. In the fall of 1921, more than 10,000 armed members of the United Mine Workers of America's "Red Bandana Army" marched through the mountains and valleys of West Virginia to fight for the freedom of their jailed brothers. Troops from West Virginia and the federal government, along with thugs from the Felt-Dobbs Detective Agency, attacked the miners with clubs and guns in a bloody battle. For the first, and so far only, time, government aircraft dropped bombs on U.S. citizens on domestic soil.

Public strikes have not been so violent, but they have been plentiful. David Ziskind (1940), in *One Thousand Strikes of Government Employees*, chronicled a number of public employee strikes that occurred very early in the history of the Republic, including an 1835 strike of civilian yard workers in the Navy Department and an 1880 walkout by Pennsylvania teachers. Early federal employee work stoppages also occurred in the Government Printing Office (1863) and in federal arsenals (1890s).

However, the first strong wave of government employee strikes did not take place until the early 1900s. The causes of these early work stoppages were as diverse as their participants: Connecticut legislators walked out in 1911, demanding the elimination of "paid agents" who were acting as lobbyists on the floor of the state senate; workers at the Watertown (New York) Arsenal struck during the same year over the introduction of Tayloristic time study techniques; moth workers, whose jobs entailed the extermination of biting moths, struck at least four times in Massachusetts between 1907 and 1917 for higher wages; and gravediggers in Milford, Massachusetts, hung up their shovels over the issue of Sunday work in 1913 (Ziskind 1940: 96). The most controversial strikes during the early 1900s involved firefighters and police. Firefighters, incensed over egregiously poor working conditions (low pay, 24-hour duty with time home only for meals, and 1 day off out of every 8 days) struck in locations all over the country during 1903 to 1921. Police refused the call to duty in a number of large cities, including Cincinnati and Boston (see Case Study 8.1); they, too, demanded improved working conditions, shorter hours, and wage increases.

Today, some of the place names and worker demands have changed, but public employee work stoppages continue to occur. This chapter examines the anatomy of public employee strikes in the United States. First, data on their frequency are presented. Next, arguments for and against the strike are discussed. The relevant legislation on work stoppages in both the public and private sectors is summarized, along with research findings on why public workers go out on strike. Strike tactics and strategies of employers and unions are examined next, including the role of the injunction and penalties for work stoppages. Finally, some speculation is offered on public employee job actions in the future. Throughout the discussion, case studies are used to help capture the flavor of the strike as the ultimate weapon in labor's arsenal.

Case Study 8.1: The Boston Police Strike of 1919

A period of rapid monetary inflation usually characterizes the economy of a nation winding down from a large war effort. This has been the case after all major wars involving the United States. Following World War I, prices of goods and services began climbing rapidly. However, police wages in Boston ranged from only $900 to $1,400 per year, with an average annual salary of $1,000. Out of salary, each officer was required to pay about $200 per year for uniforms and equipment. Inflation hit these and other low-wage public workers very hard indeed.

Compounding the unhappiness of Boston police were exceptionally long working hours: day workers were on duty 73 to 78 hours per week; the night shift 83 to 91 hours; and "wagon men" were required to be on the job up to 98 hours per week. Each officer had to sleep in the station house one night per week, where conditions were filthy and decrepit. The beds were infested with cockroaches and bedbugs. Other, relatively minor job irritants included the necessity to secure special permission to travel out of Boston city limits and the requirement to run personnel errands for superiors. Police spokesmen had taken various grievances to the commissioner on several occasions, but no actions were forthcoming.

In 1919, "Boston's finest" applied for and received a municipal police charter from the American Federation of Labor. The Boston police commissioner declared that union membership was grounds for dismissal from the force, firing several officers as an example to others. In protest, almost the entire force (1,140 out of 1,540) walked off the job. The commissioner responded by firing all striking police officers.

Without adequate police personnel, law and order broke down. Rioting, looting, violence, and general mayhem spread throughout the city, causing the mayor to declare a state of "tumult and riot" and to call in the Massachusetts State Guard. Governor Calvin Coolidge readily complied with the mayor's request, issuing his famous statement that "there is no right to strike against the public safety by anybody, anywhere, any time." Although Coolidge's actual role in ending the strike was limited and the positive publicity he received undeserved (see Spero 1970: 252–281), the episode did help him considerably in his later quest for the presidency of the United States.

The guard established and maintained law and order until new police officers could be recruited. The striking policemen were not rehired, yet they did win something of a pyrrhic victory: new officers were granted virtually all of the demands made by the strikers, including an entrance salary of $1,400, free uniforms, a pension system, and positive changes in working conditions. The strike had the added benefit of encouraging similar improvements in the lot of policemen in numerous other cities around the region.

From the perspective of public sector unionization, however, the strike had to be considered a resounding defeat. Fear resulting from the Boston violence, combined with the more generalized "red scare" of Communists, forced all 37 AFL-chartered police locals and more than 50 IAFF-chartered firefighter locals to relinquish their charters following the strike. Unionization among municipal protective services employees was set back a good 20 years.

Questions

1. Could a strike of this intensity, followed by widespread violence, happen in a major U.S. city today? What circumstances might provoke such an event?
2. What factors would have to be present for a contemporary strike to generate a similar amount of public attention and fear?

II. A Strike by Any Other Name...

The term "strike" is said to be derived from the act of sailors hauling down or "striking" their sails to quit work (Shafritz 1980: 20). Today, however, expressions characterizing a work stoppage are limited in number only by the fertile imaginations of their participants. Across the country, firefighters have called in sick with the "red rash," police with the virulent "blue flu," and teachers with "chalk-dust fever."

In San Diego, on "Human Error Day," members of the county employees' association cut off incoming telephone calls, misfiled and misrouted paperwork, and produced numerous typos and other mistakes to express their opposition to a wage offer by San Diego County. In Knoxville, Tennessee, police officers threatened to engage in a "pray-in" by attending evangelist Billy Graham's Crusade each night until the city council took action on a proposal for 48 hours' pay for a 40-hour work week (Stanley 1972: 182). The president of the local FOP observed, "I cannot advocate work stoppages, strikes, or sick call-ins, but I am a firm believer in prayer." Thousands of state workers in Pennsylvania called in with severe cases of "budgetitis" to protest receiving no paychecks for 4 weeks due to the failure of the state legislature to enact a new budget. For 3 days, Boston City Hospital doctors staged a "heal-in," refusing to release patients from the hospital until exhausting all possible health care options. The physicians were seeking higher pay.

These and other activities, such as mass resignations, continuous "professional meetings," "professional holidays," work slowdowns, "work-to-the-rule," picketing, and protest marches, all come under the rubric of "job actions." Not all job actions, however, are properly labeled "strikes" or "work stoppages." Generally, the courts and other interested parties have interpreted "strike" in accordance with the Taft-Hartley Act (Section 501 Id) definition, which is "any concerted stoppage of work by employees ... and any concerted slow-down or other concerted interruption of operations by employees." Thus, a strike entails the interruption of normal job operations through a walkout, slowdown, sick-out, or any other tactic that disrupts work. Most of the job actions mentioned above probably would be interpreted as work stoppages by the courts (which have been fairly strict in these determinations). Exceptions might include picketing and protest marches by off-duty workers that do not interfere with the job performance of on-duty employees. The NLRA grants all private sector employees the right to withhold their labor through a strike, whether or not they belong to a union. Most public employees do not enjoy a legal right to strike, although several states permit work stoppages for specified groups of workers, subject to certain conditions.

The vast majority of public employee strikes are authorized either formally (through a strike vote) or informally by the employee organization. Those work stoppages that are not formally authorized are referred to as wildcat strikes. A strike that occurs simultaneously among different government services in the same jurisdiction is called a general strike.

Employers can institute a strike of their own, known as a lockout. In a lockout, the employer refuses to permit employees to work, literally or symbolically locking the doors to keep them out. The objective is to apply pressure for a contract settlement to encourage employees to reject, or decertify, the union. Lockouts occasionally occur in the private sector and in professional sports, but they are extremely rare in the public sector.

III. Public Sector Strike Activity

Although comparisons with private sector strike activity vary by year, the evidence is clear that a smaller percentage of public workers go out on strike and that they strike for much shorter periods of time than do workers in the private sector. In 2006, for example, there were 12 major (i.e., 1,000 employees or more) work stoppages in the private sector, versus only 9 in government (USBLS 2008). Government strikes account for a very small proportion of all work stoppages in the United States. That strikes in public employment are briefer (averaging about 12 days compared to 21 days in the private sector) is explained by several factors, including the "essential" nature of some government services, the illegality of some public sector work stoppages, the lack of union "strike funds" to help support strikers, more frequent use of court injunctions to halt stoppages, greater publicity and political pressure for settlement, and the negative political consequences when quick settlements are not attained. In addition, private firms can build up product inventories to help ride out a strike; public employers rarely enjoy that option.

The peak year for public employee turmoil was 1979. Since then, indications point toward a steep drop in work stoppages. However, caution must be used in interpreting federal data. Strike data for 1960 to 1980 include all known work stoppages. In 1981, the Bureau of Labor Statistics stopped collecting information on job actions involving fewer than 1,000 workers. Most strikes in the public sector engage fewer than 1,000 individuals. The other immediate cause of the decline in job actions was the virulent anti-union posture of the Reagan administration, which became painfully palpable during the Professional Air Traffic Controllers strike of 1981 (see Case Study 8.3).

Strikes also declined dramatically in the private sector. During the 1970s nearly 300 major work stoppages occurred per year, compared with fewer than 100 annually during the 1980s and only 33 in the 1990s (U.S. Bureau of Labor Statistics 1999). Here, likely causal factors include weak economic conditions and job displacement in union-intensive manufacturing industries; the willingness of employers to hire permanent replacements for striking workers; the attraction of moving operations to cheaper labor markets in the United States or overseas; and, again, the aggressive actions by the Reagan administration in firing the air traffic controllers.

Hiring nonunion replacement workers has been particularly effective in repressing strikes in business. Historically, even if such workers ("scabs," to the union members) were hired temporarily, they were terminated when the strike ended and union members were reemployed. A 1989 U.S. Supreme Court ruling (*TWA v. Independent Federation of Flight Attendants*) upheld the Mackay Doctrine of 1935, which established the right of private sector employers to hire permanent replacements for strikers and to favor ongoing workers who stay on the job during a job action (*NLRB v. Mackay Radio and Telegraph* 1938).

Permanent replacements were rarely employed until the 1980s. By then, public opinion had slowly turned against the unions on this key issue and competitive pressures increased the inclination of firms to play hardball. A final impetus was President Reagan's firing of striking air traffic controllers in 1981 and replacing them with new employees. By making the strike a double-edged sword that can either win the union concessions from a firm or result in dismissal of strikers and, essentially, the demise of the union, the Mackay Doctrine has seriously undermined the power of the strike and even reformulated it into a management weapon (Victor 1992; Kosterlitz 1997).

The majority of government strikes take place at the local government level, and most have involved teachers, who have accounted for about three out of every four work stoppages since 1982. Five states account for the majority of major work stoppages during the last three decades: California, Michigan, Illinois, Ohio, and Pennsylvania. The data on strike duration vary by issue, function, and region. Work stoppages in the South tend to be larger and more intense, perhaps because of the general absence of legal machinery to guide the parties in resolving disputes and the fierce employer resistance to unions. What may be the longest recorded strike by public workers took place in Maryland, a border state (neither north or south), when Garrett County road workers walked out for 207 days in an effort to gain recognition of their union.

There is a tendency for local government work stoppages to spill over into two or more functions. Police often have been joined on the picket line by firefighters, and vice versa, whereas sanitation, streets and highways, parks, and sewage workers sometimes join ranks. Teachers, hospital employees, and social service workers typically walk out alone.

Something approaching a general strike has occurred in several cities. In Toledo, Ohio, 3,700 city workers went out on strike July 1, 1979, including police, firefighters, and sanitation workers. In nearby Youngstown, city employees walked off the job en masse during May 1980. During a July 1986 strike in Philadelphia, sanitation employees were joined by nearly 10,000 other strikers who shut down libraries, museums, and swimming pools. In April 1991, 5,000 Montana state employees, representing almost every state agency, struck for several days, requiring National Guard troops to staff prisons and the Montana Center for the Aged. And in October 2001, about 28,000 Minnesota state employees left their workplaces for 2 weeks. Among the ranks of striking workers were corrections officers, janitors, computer specialists, highway maintenance workers, zoo employees, and workers in nursing and psychiatric facilities.

Public employee work stoppages have attenuated in general. Nonetheless, arguments for and against the strike continue to be debated among government officials, union leaders, academics, the media, and others. The next section reviews the philosophical and practical points in the debate over the legitimacy of strikes by public servants.

IV. The Right to Strike in Public Employment

The strike issue has been called "the most controversial, urgent, and misunderstood problem of labor relations in public employment" (Spero and Capozzola 1973: 239). The central query to be dealt with here is as follows: Is it equitable and realistic to deny public employees the right to strike while guaranteeing the same right to private workers in vital sectors of the American economy?

A. *The Sovereignty Argument*

Those who would deny the right to strike to all public employees have trotted out the now-stale argument of sovereignty. In his adamant refusal to concede the right of Boston police officers to strike against the city, Massachusetts Governor Calvin Coolidge charged the officers with "desertion of duty." The mayor of Cincinnati called the 1918 strike by that city's police "the most dastardly crime ever committed in the City of Cincinnati" (Ziskind 1940: 3,37). These men, along with other presidents, governors, mayors, and judges, were staunch believers in the notion that a sovereign government has the inherent and unique right to weigh the merits of disputes in which that government is a party, "in order to head off insurrection, rebellion, and eventual anarchy" (Capozzola 1979: 178). Most scholars date the origins of the sovereignty doctrine to Englishman Thomas Hobbes, who laid out the arguments for a sovereign state in Leviathan. Assertions that "the King can do no wrong" were transposed into the American experience through the body of common law planted along with the spring crops by early English settlers.

With respect to public employee strikes, the sovereignty doctrine asserts that because, constitutionally, sovereignty is vested in the people of a democratic nation-state, permitting government workers to strike surrenders, to a special interest, government authority to determine public policy. In theory, a strike constitutes a direct challenge to the people's will; in practice, it creates a climate of disrespect for government and the law. In theory and in principle this is a legitimate concern. However, events have made the practical applicability of the sovereignty argument suspect. The "sovereign" power of the state has long been waived, delegated to, and shared with interest groups, firms, and various other entities (see Lowi 1979). Public employee unions legitimately view the concept as a legal ruse to clothe government with the absolute right to act not only unilaterally and paternalistically but also arbitrarily and capriciously in determining all facets of the employment relationship. Perpetuation of the myth shields inept administrators, blinds the vision of competent ones, and enables irresponsible managers to escape their responsibility by retreating behind a curtain of sovereignty (Capozzola 1979: 179).

Finally, the sovereignty argument has been laid to rest in those states that have in recent years, through democratic processes, permitted strikes by public employees without political, economic, or social collapse. Sovereignty does not, in fact, preclude government from entering into collective bargaining arrangements or legally establishing the right of public employees to strike. That recognition of this fact means that the sovereignty argument is seldom heard in the public employee strike controversy today.

B. Distortion of the Political Process

Early critics Harry H. Wellington and Ralph K. Winter (1971: 25) argued that public employee strikes threaten the survival of the "normal" political process by giving public sector unions political and policy advantages over other interest groups. This excessive power, augmented by union lobbying and voting activities, distorts the political process and diminishes democratic decision making.

Like sovereignty, this is an ill-defined and ambiguous argument. For example, what is the "normal" political process? Where is the evidence of "distortion"? Wellington and Winter's overstatement of the problem is probably a product of the time in which they wrote *The Unions and the Cities* (the late 1960s), a period of strong emergent unionism in governments administered by unprepared and weak public managers.

C. Lack of Market Constraints

In the private sector, high labor costs tend to be held down by competition and consumer product demand. Pay hikes must be accounted for by raising product prices or improving productivity. If labor costs rise excessively, consumers will purchase their goods and services from another producer, substitute for them, or do without. It is argued that in the public sector no such market constraints exist, because public services are monopolies. There is little or no opportunity for comparison shopping by citizens. Thus, unions can make extravagant demands and win them by threatening to strike.

This line of argument has been rebutted on numerous occasions (Burton and Krider 1975; Capozzola 1979; Fowler 1974). Market constraints do operate during public sector strikes. Employees sacrifice wages while tax revenues continue to accrue to the government employer; the workers often come out net financial losers. Although no profit motive can be said to exist in the public sector, there are, frequently, strong political pressures brought to bear on public sector unions to forego the strike or to settle quickly in the event one transpires. Public officials are also under great pressure not to raise taxes or fees, especially to fund employee compensation increases. Pushed too far, city councils and state legislatures may seek to subcontract government services to private and nonprofit providers, thereby creating competition in the market for public goods.

D. Essential Services

According to opponents of the right to strike, public employees are engaged in providing services essential to the community. A strike poses unacceptable threats to the public health, safety, and well-being and prompts public officials to cave in to public pressure to settle with the union. One critic compared a public employee strike to a siege, in which an "indispensable element of the public welfare ... is made hostage by a numerically superior force and held, in effect, for ransom" (Saso 1970: 37).

However, it is clear that not all government services are essential to the public's immediate health, safety, and well-being. Teacher strikes, for example, have lasted for months, disrupting the school year and the lives of pupils and parents. However, it is very unlikely that any long-term damage to the students or the parents has resulted (Thornicroft 1994). Strikes by police, firefighters, and, in some instances, sanitation workers are much more serious and may indeed pose a threat to the well-being of citizens. It must be recognized, however, that state law enforcement personnel have successfully assisted nonstriking police officers in maintaining law and order, that volunteer fire departments effectively protect a much larger geographical area of the United States than municipal firefighters, and that most people are not incapable of delivering their own garbage to landfills or central collection stations. It should further be recognized that many government services are contracted out to private and nonprofit organizations, including private schools, sanitation companies, private security firms, and various health care organizations. Such functions are not so essential that they cannot be handled adequately in the private sector.

It is also important to understand that some services traditionally provided by private and nonprofit concerns are as — if not more — crucial than many public services. This fact has been demonstrated by the serious impact of strikes by railroad workers, coal miners, utility employees, truckers, and nursing home and hospital workers. The Taft-Hartley law recognizes the essential nature of these and other functions in the private sector by providing for presidential and congressional actions to help contain and settle a strike that poses a threat to the well-being of the nation.

Unfortunately, there is no bright line solution to determine which public and private sector services are "essential" and which are not. If there were, then logic would dictate that all strikes by workers in critical functions — regardless of sector of the economy — be prohibited. But it is very difficult to separate essential from nonessential services, especially when matters of strike location and duration are considered along with various extenuating circumstances (such as season of the year during sanitation strikes). There have been some efforts to categorize work stoppages in accordance with their essentiality. For example, Burton and Krider (1975) suggested identifying government services as essential (police and fire protection), intermediate (sanitation, health care, transit, water, sewer), and nonessential (education, streets, parks, recreation, welfare, general administration). Strikes would be prohibited for essential services and permitted for intermediate services unless they presented a threat to citizens' health or safety. Workers in nonessential functions would be granted the right to strike. Some state laws permitting a limited right to strike have taken this approach (e.g., in Alaska).

To many public workers and their unions, the claim that public servants should be saddled with special responsibilities and constraints on their labor activities does not hold water. Since the social turmoil of the 1960s, government workers have increasingly insisted on having the same rights of citizenship as their private sector counterparts, including the right to walk off the job. As Spero and Capozzola (1973: 269–270) put it

> The legalistic public–private dichotomy has little relevance to the municipal employee. He has the same dreams, desires, fears, frustrations, problems and hopes as his counterpart in private industry. Excessive theorizing falls on deaf ears, as the municipal worker pays the same taxes, buys the same food and shelter, and has no more immunity from disease than a private employee.

Should they not enjoy equal protection under the law, as long as a strike does not present a clear and immediate danger to the community?

Strike bans are not particularly effective and are sometimes ignored. Strikes will continue to occur whether or not they are legally forbidden. As a study commission noted in Pennsylvania in recommending the right to strike, "Twenty years of experience [under a no-strike law] has taught us that such a policy is unreasonable and unenforceable, particularly when coupled with ineffective or nonexistent collective bargaining" (see Schneider 1988: 199).

Strikes by federal employees have never been legal, but on March 18, 1970, movement of the U.S. mail slowed to a trickle as postal employees in New York City, then across the nation, walked off their jobs in wildcat strikes over low wage levels, dissatisfaction with their treatment by Congress, and the inability of their unions to "deliver." It was the largest strike of federal employees in American history.

After a back-to-work order was ignored, government and union leaders reached an accord: striking workers would go back to work in return for a formal discussion with administration officials over pay, postal reform, and other issues. However, the union rank and file refused to accept the agreement; the strike continued to spread across the country. By March 20, close to 200,000 workers failed to report to work and much of the nation was without mail service. The strike threatened to disrupt the economy as the flow of financial documents and other important materials was squeezed to a trickle. (One must recognize that UPS, FedEx, and e-mail were not options in 1970.)

President Richard Nixon declared a state of national emergency, ordered federal troops into New York City to move the mail, and called out 15,000 Army reserves and 12,000 members of the National Guard. The president informed the striking postal workers that negotiations would not begin until they returned to work. Through unofficial channels, however, the postal employees were told that if they returned to their jobs Congress would directly address their grievances. By March 25, most of the striking workers were back on the job.

Postal employees soon settled for a retroactive pay increase. Congress approved the pay provisions with great haste and the president signed them into law. Shortly thereafter, with the strong support of the postal unions, the Postal Reorganization Act established the mail service as a government corporation, removing postal workers from labor relations coverage under Executive Order 11491, and granted full private sector collective bargaining privileges (except for the right to strike). Thus, through the strike, postal workers won preferential treatment, including the critical right to negotiate pay and benefits. The financial benefits of the settlement were soon evident. Whereas other federal white-collar workers received a 47 percent salary increase from 1970 through 1977, the postal employees' salaries were hiked by 94 percent.

Moreover, public management has gained experience contending with strikes, and when it receives greater public support than the union, it can win a strike. Striking public workers do not get paid, and public sector unions do not normally maintain strike funds. Yet government revenues continue to come in, improving the employer's financial position (unless the strike does, indeed, ultimately accomplish the financial objectives of the union, including payment of strikers' wages). In addition, a public management skilled in media relations can channel almost unbearable public pressure on a striking union and help force concessions on its leaders and rank and file.

To return to the query that opened this discussion on the right to strike in public employment: Is it equitable and realistic to deny public employees the right to strike while guaranteeing it to private sector workers? As the astute reader has surmised, this author thinks not, as do legislatures or courts in the 14 states that have legalized a limited right to strike for certain categories of state and local employees.

V. Legislation Pertaining to Strikes

In private employment, the rights of workers to strike and employers to lock them out are viewed as essential components of the free process of collective bargaining, as legally embodied in the National Labor Relations Act. In public employment, the right to strike traditionally has been denied by various federal and state laws. Federal employees, in the only section of Taft-Hartley applying to government employment (Section 305), are categorically forbidden to strike and threatened with immediate dismissal and forfeiture of civil service status. In addition, striking federal employees are not eligible for reemployment for 3 years. Federal workers are also forbidden to strike by Public Law 330 (1955) and the 1978 Civil Service Reform Act. Members of the Armed Forces are prohibited from striking by Department of Defense Directive 1354.1.

Following the Boston police strike of 1919, a series of anti-strike ordinances were adopted by numerous cities, including Salt Lake City, Philadelphia, San Antonio, Chicago, and Detroit. The U.S. Congress passed a law outlawing strikes in the

District of Columbia. A second wave of strike prohibitions came just after World War II, when nine states enacted laws banning strikes, with language similar to Taft-Hartley's prohibition against federal employee work stoppages. The constitutionality of these various strike prohibitions has been consistently upheld by the courts. In addition, most state courts (with five exceptions) have held that state employees have no right to engage in work stoppages in the absence of legislative authorization.

Some or all public employee strikes are outlawed in 35 states through statute, court decision, or attorney general opinion. Furthermore, the vast majority of collective bargaining contracts contain no-strike clauses intended to prevent stoppages during the life of the contract. (A typical clause reads, "The union and its employees expressly agree that there will be no strikes, slowdowns, picketing during working hours, work stoppages, mass absenteeism, mass feigned illness, or other forms of interference with the operations of the police department.") Nonetheless, public employees have struck repeatedly. From 1958 to 1968, no state authorized a strike for any of its workers, but the number of public employee strikes increased 17-fold from the previous decade. Penalties were infrequently invoked against striking union members or their organizations.

In recognition of the failure of strike prohibitions to prevent government work stoppages, ten states have now legislatively granted at least some of their employees a limited right to strike. Vermont was the first: Act No. 198 of 1967 provided that local government work stoppages are prohibited only if the strike is found to endanger the public health, safety, or welfare. Pennsylvania followed with permissive legislation of its own in 1970; Hawaii, Alaska, Montana, Oregon, Minnesota, Wisconsin, Ohio, and Illinois complete the list. In addition, state supreme courts in California, Colorado, Idaho, and Louisiana have upheld the right of public employees to strike. Table 8.1 summarizes the policies of those states that have legalized the strike through legislation or court decisions.

Most of these statutes specifically exclude certain essential employees from the strike right, particularly police, firefighters, correctional officers, and hospital workers. Most also require compliance with specific pre-strike provisions, such as mediation, fact finding, and prior notice. All of them have triggers that prohibit strikes in cases involving a threat to the public health and safety.

In Louisiana, Colorado, and Idaho, state supreme courts applied the private sector right-to-strike principle to public employment. But the judicial action with the greatest potential influence in other states occurred in 1985 in California, where the state supreme court ruled that in the absence of express statutory language forbidding the strike, local government employees could legally walk off the job (*County Sanitation District 2 v. Los Angeles County Employees Association, Local 660* 1985). The California Supreme Court has a reputation as a trendsetter among the state high courts, and its opinions are widely disseminated. In this particular case, the court systematically examined, then dismissed, traditional arguments against public sector strikes. It concluded that the conventional common-law prohibition against strikes

Table 8.1 Permissive Strike States, 2008

State	Employees Covered	Policy
Alaska	All public employees	Right to strike for semi-essential and nonessential workers. Police, firefighters, correctional workers, and hospital employees may not strike. Limited strike right for public utilities, sanitation, snow removal, and schools, after exhaustion of mediation. Other workers may strike upon majority vote.
California	Some municipal employees	California Supreme Court held that strikes by nonessential employees were legal except in cases where the strike posed an "imminent threat" to public health and safety.
Colorado	All public employees	Colorado Supreme Court held that public employee strikes are legal.
Hawaii	All public employees	Strike permitted after exhaustion of impasse resolution procedures and 60 days after issue of fact-finding report. Ten-day notice by union is required. Strikes endangering public health and safety are illegal, as are strikes by firefighters and other essential employees.
Illinois	All public employees	Mediation and 5 days' notice required prior to strike. Prohibited if strike constitutes a clear and present danger to public health and safety. Firefighters, law enforcement, and security employees may not strike.
Louisiana	All public employees	Louisiana Supreme Court held that all public employee strikes are legal.
Minnesota	All public employees	Strikes prohibited except where employer refuses request for binding arbitration or refuses to submit to arbitration award. Teachers have right to strike following expiration of contract, 60 days of mediation, and 10 days' notice. Nonteaching local employees and state employees may strike after expiration of contract, 45 days mediation, and 10 days' notice. No strikes by essential employees.

Table 8.1 Permissive Strike States, 2008 (Continued)

State	Employees Covered	Policy
Montana	Public health nurses	Strikes permitted. Nurses must give 30 days' notice; no other nurses' strike may occur within 150 miles.
Ohio	All public employees	Mediation, fact finding, and 10 days' notice required prior to strike. No strikes by public safety personnel.
Oregon	All public employees	Strikes permitted after completion of mediation and fact finding, elapse of 10-day strike notice, and 30-day cooling-off period. No strikes by police, firefighters, or hospital guards.
Pennsylvania	All public employees except prison guards, court employees, police, and fire	Strike permitted after exhaustion of impasse resolution procedures, unless strike presents clear and present danger to public health, safety, or welfare.
Vermont	Municipal employees	Strikes permitted 30 days after fact-finding report where parties have not agreed to arbitration and there is no danger to public health, safety, or welfare. Teacher strike may be prohibited by courts if it endangers a sound program of education. No strikes by state employees.
Wisconsin	Municipal employees, teachers	Strike permitted if both parties withdraw their final offer and 10 days' notice by union. Strike is illegal if it poses imminent threat to public health, safety, or welfare. No strikes by police, firefighters, or state employees.

Source: Cimini (1998: 33–34); updated by the author from various state websites.

was outdated and without merit and that the right to strike was constitutionally protected as a necessary corollary of the right to join a union (Hogler 1986).

The *County Sanitation* decision appeared to infringe on the proper policy domain of the legislature, and it contradicted longstanding precedent that public employees do not possess the right to strike without explicit authorization through statute (Hogler 1986; Baird 1986). A spate of criticism of the court's reasoning ensued, accompanied by concern that the decision would prompt similar findings in other states not expressly prohibiting strikes and a hope that the California legislature would overturn the court ruling through legislation.

So far, no other courts have reached a California-type conclusion. Prospects for emulation by other states appear to be limited by the questionable logic supporting the opinion of the very liberal court of Chief Justice Rose Bird, who, along with two of her colleagues on the court, was defeated at the polls the year following the *County Sanitation* case. (The principal reason for her loss was her unwavering stand against the death penalty.) The most poignant issue, after all, does not concern the strike right, which has been established in a significant number of states. It concerns which political institution has the proper authority and responsibility to decide if strikes by government workers are to be permitted and, if so, under what conditions and restrictions.

VI. Public Policy and the Incidence of Strikes

The relationship between state policies on strikes and the incidence of public employee work stoppages presents an interesting and important question for empirical analysis. Unfortunately, research has been hampered by methodological problems and the lack of comprehensive, reliable comparative data on public employee work stoppages. Since 1981, the federal government has collected and published strike data only on job actions involving 1,000 or more workers. Most government work stoppages involve much smaller numbers. From 1999 to 2007, there were only 48 public sector strikes involving 1,000 or more employees (U.S. Bureau of Labor Statistics 2008).

Further compounding the difficulty of assessing the results of permissive and restrictive strike laws are the effects of various political, economic, and labor force factors on strike incidence. However, published research does permit us to draw several conclusions.

First, a statutory prohibition against strikes may discourage them, but it clearly does not prevent them. This general finding holds both in states that mandate or permit collective bargaining and in those states that do not provide for bargaining. Studies do indicate that the nature of sanctions imposed on striking workers and their unions are related to strike activity. Specifically, consistently enforced penalties tend to reduce the incidence of work stoppages.

Second, compulsory interest arbitration tends to reduce strike activity. Strikes are least likely to occur in states that provide for the finality of compulsory arbitration (Hebdon and Stern 2003; C. A. Olson 1988; Partridge 1996). (Alternatives to strikes are addressed in Chapter 9.)

Third, the effects of permissive strike policies apparently vary from state to state and by employee function. Strike frequency increased markedly in Pennsylvania following enactment of a limited right to strike in 1970. Teachers and other non-uniformed, local government workers so commonly walked off the job in the Keystone State that it impaired the state's ability to attract new business (GERR 1985). Teacher strikes have occurred more frequently in Pennsylvania than in almost any other state.

Other states legally permitting strikes have experienced no greater incidence of work stoppages than those that prohibit it. An examination of strikes 4 years before and 4 years after the adoption of permissive strike laws reveals in most states a brief jump in the number of work stoppages, then a decline to earlier levels (Sterret and Aboud 1982: 41–46). Vermont, the first state to enact a permissive law, did not experience its first strike until 8 years later. Studies of strikes in Ohio, Illinois, and Minnesota, following passage of collective bargaining statutes legalizing work stoppages for certain categories of employees, found a decrease in strike activity in all three states (GERR 1990; Ley and Wines 1993).

The most comprehensive examination of public sector strike bans and consequent strike activity concluded that job actions are more frequent in states with no-strike laws (Hebdon and Stern 2003). The conclusion is that strike bans are ineffective in reducing work stoppages. Clearly, most public employee unions do not look upon permissive strike policies as an open door to walk out. Teacher exceptionalism in Pennsylvania and several other states is more a result of state or school district policies that reschedule missed school days than of strike policies. Jurisdictions mandating a fixed number of workdays during the school year typically reschedule days missed due to teacher strikes by extending the school year or canceling holidays. Thus, the financial costs of striking are low for the teachers, who are paid later for the days they missed while on strike (Olson 1988).

VII. Why Public Employees Strike

With the exception of periodic localized outbursts, public workers until about 1965 generally were perceived to be meek and humble servants of the people. "Public employees were so docile a group that they scarcely seemed part of the American labor movement. Public work was regarded as a short step above the dole, the refuge of lazy, dimwitted people willing to exchange a decent wage and the respect of their fellow men for security and an undemanding job. Public employee uprisings were few, and they met severe censure" (Williams 1977: 16).

Federal employees, in particular, "had been relatively passive for two decades, they were thought to have been professionalized into objective, politically neutral competence, cleansed of radicalism by three decades of loyalty oaths and security investigations, and made both happy and prosperous by very generous salary increases. The outbreak of protest in the federal service obviously jarred these conceptions" (Hershey 1973: xi). Why the sudden militancy of public workers in the 1960s? Why do they continue to engage in disruptive job actions today, albeit at a much slower pace?

Until the early 1980s, the Bureau of Labor Statistics recorded the major reason given for each work stoppage in industry and government. Most private sector strikes were attributed to wage and benefit disputes. The figures were similar for the public sector, with economic disputes also fostering the most strikes. That economic issues have provoked a large percentage of strikes in industry and government reflects the fact that wage and benefit issues usually top a union's list of demands in a new bargaining relationship.

Of course, the official reason given for a work stoppage reveals little about either the broader macro-level factors related to a strike or the more immediate process-related variables that contribute to a complete breakdown in negotiations.

A. Macro-Level Factors

In the private sector, until fairly recently, there was a strong association between unions' propensity to strike and prevailing business conditions (often referred to as the business cycle). Work stoppages had a tendency to increase during periods of rising prices and falling unemployment and decrease during economic recessions. For example, postwar boom periods following World War II and the wars in Korea and Viet Nam saw a substantial rise in the number of work stoppages (Ashenfelter and Johnson 1969). Economic expansion usually means plentiful job opportunities; a striker who is permanently dismissed should be able to find another position. Conversely, during periods of economic decline, unemployment levels rise and jobs are hard to locate. Workers are less likely to risk being fired for a job action. The relationship between strike activity and the business cycle has been similar in public employment (Partridge 1991). What has changed recently is the nature of job opportunities. Private sector manufacturing workers permanently replaced during a strike may find it very difficult to locate a similarly paid job today, regardless of the business cycle, because of the enormous shift in employment to information technology and the service sector.

In the private sector, strikes also are related to the nature of the industry and the work involved. Strikes are most common among homogeneous groups of workers who have little opportunity for economic advancement (e.g., coal miners, dock workers). Physical labor (unskilled or semiskilled), unpleasant or dangerous work surroundings, and seasonal casual jobs have been positively associated with strike behavior as well (see Burton and Krider 1975).

Similar patterns are evident in the public sector. The largest number of strikes has been by homogeneous unions of teachers, transportation workers, health care workers, sanitation workers, and, in the early days, police and firefighters. Working conditions are highly variable in these occupational categories, but dangerous situations are not uncommon in any of them (e.g., teachers in inner-city schools; sanitation workers loading, compacting, and unloading solid waste), and one can imagine few jobs more unpleasant than working all day in an intimate relationship with garbage.

B. Micro-Level Factors

Three types of micro-level variables are related to strike activity: demographic and attitudinal factors, bargaining power and costs of disagreement, and faulty negotiations.

1. Demographic and Attitudinal Factors

Although, for job actions, gender seems to be insignificant, age is more important. Older employees, who have the most to lose and the least to gain from a strike, tend to be more conservative about a job action (Maki and Strand 1984) and younger workers more willing to walk out. Education level may also be related to strike behavior; the higher the level of schooling, the lower the propensity to strike (Maki and Strand 1984; Shutt 1982). Research further suggests that job satisfaction, favorable attitudes toward the employer, worker autonomy in the workplace, and progressive human resource management practices are negatively related to strike activity (Ng 1991; Goddard 1992) and that those most strongly committed to the union are more likely to vote for a strike than less committed members of the bargaining unit (J. E. Martin and Sinclair 2001; Wheeler 1985). Finally, workers consider their potential costs and benefits of going on strike from an individual perspective, including their current level of pay and benefits versus the perceived costs of striking (financial as well as family related), and the availability of job alternatives should the strike fail (J. E. Martin and Sinclair 2001).

2. Bargaining Power and Disagreement Costs

The bargaining power of the respective parties influences strike behavior. Burton and Krider (1975) measure bargaining power as the union's "ability to obtain wages greater than the employer would have voluntarily paid on the basis of market conditions." They assert that strong unions are less likely to strike than weak unions because they tend to accept less than what they could actually get through a full display of power (which would harm the competitive market position of the employer) and because the employer tends to give them "more" to avoid a costly and painful confrontation. Relative bargaining power fluctuates with economic and employment conditions, union membership strength and commitment, the union's ability to control the labor market, effectiveness and leadership skills of management and union negotiators, public opinion, and an almost limitless number of other factors that vary, in government, by service function and employer. Despite impressive attempts, no single, simple equation has been derived to represent all the vicissitudes of public sector bargaining, nor is it likely to be. Furthermore, the relationship of the strike to bargaining power is nebulous: "strikes may be a manifestation of weakness, as well as a demonstration of power" (Spero and Capozzola 1973: 250–251).

Notwithstanding the extreme complexity and turbidity of the bargaining power concept, some useful insights into a bargaining relationship and potential work stoppages can be derived. For instance, the union and management costs of disagreeing may be calculated in the context of the threat of a strike to help discern "true" attitudes and beliefs, or where the parties are "coming from." In *Theory of Wages and Employment*, Alan M. Cartter (1959) was one of the earliest scholars to view strikes from this perspective, as represented by the following equation:

$$\frac{\text{Cost of disagreeing with Y}}{\text{Costs of agreeing on Y's term}} = \text{Bargaining attitude of X}$$

For example, teachers' costs of attempting to settle a bargaining dispute through a walkout are lower in jurisdictions that mandate a fixed number of days in the school year and thus require strikers to make up lost days on holidays or during the early summer. Where strikes result in a reduction in school days, or where school districts fill in for striking teachers with substitutes, the costs of disagreement can be considerably higher, because pay may be deducted. Similarly, as discussed below, the costs of striking are higher in jurisdictions that enforce severe sanctions as a matter of course and lower where strike penalties are rarely applied, often forgiven, or nonexistent.

3. Faulty Negotiations

Strikes may erupt from what Hicks (1932), many years ago, called "faulty negotiations." This ensues when one or both parties err in assessing the other's true bargaining position, willingness to engage in a strike, or understanding of what a "reasonable" settlement would look like.

"Faulty negotiations" may be as elusive an explanation for work stoppages as bargaining power, but there are many instances in which the bargaining process clearly collapses because of inept, or inexperienced, negotiators, personality conflicts, unrealistic demands, communications breakdowns, or the lack of good faith bargaining. An interesting example of faulty negotiations was the 232-day major league baseball strike in 1994–1995. For players and owners, any concept of mutual gains bargaining was as elusive as the triple play. Eight work stoppages were experienced from 1972 to 1995, one for each collective bargaining contract expiration during that period. Players and owners typically distrust and disrespect one another. "Strong-willed and abrasive personalities" on the part of negotiators and hostile negotiating styles have plagued baseball and kept the parties widely apart (Staudohar 1996: 24). Even presidential intervention and appointment of perhaps the nation's most respected and experienced mediator, William J. Usery, Jr., failed in 1995. The strike was finally ended when a U.S. District Court judge issued an injunction against the owners for unilaterally imposing a salary cap (Staudohar 1996).

Faulty negotiations because of severe personality conflicts characterized the Bay Area Rapid Transit strike of 1997. While union and management representatives deadlocked over minor issues and denounced one another in dueling press conferences, the strike of 2,600 SEIU-affiliated workers inconvenienced some 275,000 mass transit riders for several days (Fagan, Cabanatuan, and DelVecchio 1997). In other situations, one party, perceiving a benefit, appears reluctant to negotiate in good faith. The 2004 three-day walkout by New York City day care workers serving poor families followed more than 4 years without a contract and 3½ years without a raise (Kaufman 2004). Another example of faulty negotiations is documented in Case Study 8.2.

In a perfect world, negotiators for both sides would have complete information and full knowledge of all important variables, including the other party's true position. A Pareto-optimal solution would be devised at the bargaining table; both would "win." Unfortunately, this perfect world is ineluctably inhabited by divergent interests and perceptions of reality, schisms within the ranks of both management and labor, unequal bargaining power, the Hydra of public opinion, intense personality conflicts, diabolical political machinations, and uncountable related factors; even the gender of chief negotiators (Montgomery and Benedict 1989).

Faulty negotiations may be minimized by experience and maturity. Over time, bargaining parties develop protocols to reveal indirectly where each truly stands on the issues (Reder and Neumann 1980). As the parties become familiar with one another, the likelihood of a strike occurring because of faulty negotiations is reduced. This view is supported by the higher incidence of strikes in new bargaining relationships and research findings that experienced negotiators make fewer mistakes in assessing their opponents' actual position (Montgomery and Benedict 1989). The greater the bargaining experience, the less the likelihood of a strike. Carried to the extreme, secret agreements between union and management negotiators have been known to make bargaining a charade, with the most important outcomes predetermined.

Case Study 8.2: Faulty Negotiations in Memphis

The Mississippi River City of Memphis, Tennessee, has never had the reputation of being a kind host to labor unions. The political machine of "Boss" E. H. Crump responded harshly to early organizing efforts by firefighters, teachers, police officers, and custodial workers, telling them to quit the union or find another job.

Boss Crump died in 1954, but anti-labor attitudes survived, successfully repressing organizing by public employees until 1964, when sanitation workers chartered local 1733 and affiliated with AFSCME. The garbage workers were driven to the union by extremely poor wages and working conditions. Pay was so low that garbage collectors were reduced to "ragging" household trash for salvageable items. Working conditions were filthy and dangerous, and employees were subject to whimsical dismissal or suspension by supervisors. Only drivers, the majority of whom were white, received paid vacations. All of the trash collectors were African American males.

The sanitation workers attempted to strike in 1963 and again in 1965, but each time failed because of poor organization and a lack of support from the historically submissive black community. By 1968, however, the Civil Rights Movement, rising expectations on the part of blacks, and the election of white conservative Henry Loeb as mayor led to a mood of greater militancy in the black community. On February 12, 1968, the sanitation workers walked out with widespread black community support. The triggering incident came on a rainy day when 35 African American workers were sent home without pay while their white counterparts were allowed to stay on the job for a full day's pay.

Mayor Loeb responded in a fashion consistent with the city's violent labor history. Marchers were maced and clubbed by white police officers, and scab laborers were hired to collect the garbage. Loeb refused to negotiate until the 1,100 strikers returned to work. A relatively minor breakdown in labor relations suddenly took on the dimensions of a major racial confrontation.

Threats of dismissal failed to move the striking sanitation workers. Negotiations were not held at all during the initial 40 days of the strike. When discussion did begin, Loeb's intransigence and the inexperience of negotiators on both sides of the table undermined the chances of a settlement. While Memphis residents carted their own garbage to pickup stations, the strikers held numerous marches and successfully implemented a boycott of white downtown merchants. Assisted by 4,000 Tennessee National Guard troops, Loeb imposed a dawn-to-dusk curfew on the city.

Under pressure from the business community, the city reopened negotiations and attempted to make a settlement. The assassination of Dr. Martin Luther King, Jr., at a Memphis motel on the 4th of April and ensuing negative national publicity exerted tremendous additional pressure for a labor agreement. (King had led a march in sympathy with the strikers.) With the assistance of a federal mediator sent by President Richard Nixon, a memorandum of understanding was signed by both parties, ending the 65-day strike. The city granted most of the union demands, including merit promotion, a grievance procedure, and recognition of Local 1733 through a dues checkoff system. An anonymous benefactor of the city donated $50,000 to make up the wage disparity between the final offers of the city and the union. Satisfied, the sanitation employees returned to their jobs.

Mayor Loeb had remained adamantly opposed to union recognition and the dues checkoff until pressures from the local business community, the governor, and finally the president of the United States moved him into making concessions. The sanitation agreement burst the labor dam in Memphis. Hospital workers were organized by AFSCME in 1973, and firefighters created an IAFF local. An uneasy peace characterized municipal labor relations throughout the early 1970s under the administration of a new mayor. Then, during the hot summer of 1978, "faulty bargaining" resulted in a new episode of labor turmoil.

This round commenced on the first of July with a 3-day strike by firefighters over pay parity with police and the length of the next contract. The walkout was a violent one, with tire slashings and incidents involving arson. It continued with a walkout by 1,100 members of the Memphis Police Association (MPA) on the 10th of August, following the MPA's rejection of the city's wage offer, stalled mediation efforts, and an unsuccessful effort by police, firefighters, and teachers to recall Mayor Wyeth Chandler from office. Chandler, cut from the same labor relations cloth as Loeb, had first alienated Memphis city employees during negotiations the previous year when he convinced police and firefighters to accept a small wage increase because of the city's alleged inability to pay more. Shortly after the agreement was struck, a $1.5 million budget surplus miraculously appeared, leaving union negotiators feeling like utter fools. New — and aggressive — union negotiators were elected to bargain with the city during 1978. The city's bad-faith bargaining had left city employees full of frustration and resentment. These feelings surfaced openly when the police walked out.

Mayor Chandler and his administration were prepared: they quickly implemented a strike plan that included a 6:00 a.m. to 8:00 p.m. curfew and the assumption of law enforcement duties by police supervisory personnel, sheriff's deputies, and the Tennessee Highway Patrol. The National Guard was placed on alert. The next morning, the city obtained a temporary restraining order against the strikers. Police officers ignored the court order; a strike injunction and back-to-work order were secured, but these, too, were rebuked. On the night of August 12, Mayor Chandler, following a script seemingly written in the Bluff City many years before, ordered the dismissal of all police employees not returning to duty within 24 hours.

On August 15, 1,400 firefighters walked off the job in a wildcat strike to express solidarity with the MPA and their own lingering frustrations with the city. Chandler deployed the National Guard, had 50 police arrested for violation of curfew, and threatened to withdraw city recognition of the unions. Then things began to get nasty. Tires on patrol cars were slashed; rocks and bricks were tossed through windows at police headquarters. On August 17 saboteurs caused a 2½-hour power blackout of Memphis and Shelby County. In a reprisal of the 1919 Boston police strike, looting quickly spread throughout the city. Arsonists also had their day: over a single 24-hour period, 166 homes were burned, compared with a norm of six or seven house fires per day.

Once again, outside parties were forced to enter the picture to push an uncompromising mayor who lacked negotiation skills into a compromise. Community leaders joined with AFL-CIO officials and federal mediators to persuade all parties to agree to contracts by August 19 and return to work. The governor did his part to promote settlement by billing the city for the services of the National Guard (more than $1 million) and assessing an additional fee of $65,000 per day until the strike ended.

Negotiations during the labor troubles of 1968 and 1978 were "faulty," to put it mildly. The sanitation workers in 1968 were amateurs in their initial contest with the city; police and firefighters were attempting to negotiate without a great deal of prior experience as well. Perhaps union expectations were too high and union leadership naive. Nonetheless, the city's elected leaders showed an almost complete lack of flexibility, little or no spirit of compromise, and a consummate dearth of negotiating skills. Loeb and Chandler, by making offers and insisting, in the spirit of Boulwarism, that the unions "take it or leave it," left no opportunity for union leaders to claim concessions from city hall. The rank and file could not help but be resentful. Of course, the unions were not without blame themselves. Tire slashings, property damage, arson, and violence pervaded the city during the strikes of 1978 and turned an already anti-labor citizenry vehemently against the unions.

The 1978 round of work stoppages did provide some important "lessons learned" to the citizens of Memphis. During the November municipal elections that same year a charter amendment was approved that prohibited municipal employee strikes, provided strong sanctions against strikers, and established impasse resolution procedures granting the city council the power to make final contract decisions upon a lack of settlement by a specified date. Wyeth Chandler was reelected as mayor in 1979, but when contracts expired the next year negotiations were conducted in a relatively peaceful atmosphere. The MPA signed a 3-year contract in 1980; firefighters ratified a 2-year agreement, as did AFSCME-represented employees. Clearly the unions were willing to give the new labor relations procedures an opportunity to work. Labor–management relations in Memphis during the 1980s remained highly adversarial, but they improved when Mayor Willie Herenton took office for an extended period in 1992 and serious job actions were avoided.

Questions

1. How could the strike situations under the Loeb and Chandler administrations have been avoided?
2. Which side was at fault during the crises — unions or management? Defend your answer.
3. What role did race play in the turmoil?
4. Why hasn't Memphis moved to privatize sanitation services?

VIII. Strike Tactics

A. The Union

Work stoppages usually follow a majority vote of the union membership and rejection of the employer's last offer. Worker solidarity is important. The strike meeting itself is run enthusiastically, with great grandstanding, emotional avowals, and thunderous applause. The union leader's goal is to win a unanimous vote for a walkout.

The union must move quickly to build up maximum pressure on the employer and elected officials. Timing the strike and its announcement to have the fullest impact is important to the union also. For example, maximum media coverage normally is available Monday through Thursday; a strike announcement over the weekend can go relatively unheralded. Similarly, little immediate impact is registered if transit workers walk off the job on a Saturday. When the Bay Area Rapid

Transit (BART) unions struck on a Monday in 1997, service on the 93-mile commuter rail system was curtailed, inconveniencing some 275,000 passengers on their way to work. Pressure tactics are quickly applied: news conferences, mass meetings, media advertisements, lobbying, and picket lines all help apprise the public and elected officials of the union's point of view. Picket lines have high visibility and, if other union members refuse to cross them, they create powerful new pressures on public officials and management. Strikes can even disperse geographically. Striking Houston janitors set up picket lines in Chicago, Washington, D.C., New York City, and other cities in late 2006 to bring national pressure on employers. Sympathizers may also honor picket lines, as the University of Minnesota learned during an AFSCME strike by 3,500 clerical, technical, and health care workers in September 2007. Offices had to be closed or services reduced all across campus for nearly 3 weeks. Elsewhere, picket lines have shut down classrooms, transit systems, and garbage collection.

Ill-timed strikes, however, may produce lingering hard feelings on the part of an inconvenienced or angry public. A 2001 Minnesota state employee strike came on the heels of the September 11 terrorist attacks on New York City and Washington, D.C. Residents of the Gopher State have still not forgiven the strikers. The strategic timing significance of a work stoppage is perhaps no better illustrated than in the 1979 walkout by New Orleans police. The Teamsters-affiliated union announced its strike on the Friday night before Mardi Gras weekend. In more than 120 years, the internationally famed festival had been canceled only seven times — five times during war and twice for epidemics. The walkout, officially over bargaining rights for management-level police officers, fringe benefits, and certain working conditions, also entailed rivalries between two police unions and racial overtones (the mayor was black, the police force largely white). The strike threatened to wreak economic havoc on the city of New Orleans, which expected to realize $250 million from Mardi Gras that year. Before the strike was settled 15 days later, 18 parades were canceled or moved to the suburbs and thousands of tourists left the city early or avoided the festival altogether. The union gained a number of concessions from city officials but lost something perhaps of greater value — its public support. Before the strike ended, anti-union rhetoric had become strident and widespread. Vitriol and "base, vile behavior" on both sides tainted labor–management relations for many years. In retrospect, the union's timing strategy may have been ill advised (see Salerno 1981).

Union leaders do not usually call a strike without carefully considering the possible ramifications and the odds of winning it. A strike committee composed of various stewards and unit representatives is typically formed to analyze the costs and benefits. If a work stoppage is indeed the decision, the strike committee operates out of a control center to direct picketing actions and media relations, handle members' questions, maintain solidarity, and coordinate with other unions (Gagala 1983: 230–241).

Sometimes job actions just short of a work stoppage are employed. By "working to the rule," employees refuse to perform activities not in their job descriptions, turn down overtime work, and otherwise legally interfere with the operations of the employer. For example, Delaware corrections officers refused overtime in 2004 to protest low pay and a record high number of unfilled vacancies (Parra 2004). As another illustration, employees may protest what they consider to be unsafe conditions by assembling en masse in the supervisor's office or filing reams of grievance paperwork. Where strikes are prohibited by law and alternatives such as arbitration are not available, absenteeism, negligence, reduced effort, rudeness in dealing with customers, and even sabotage may occur (Hebdon and Stern 1998).

Events proceed at a rapid pace during most public employee strikes. In private employment, management frequently has accumulated inventories and otherwise prepared itself for a possible work stoppage. Nationally affiliated unions typically maintain strike funds to help out-of-work members get by financially until paychecks begin to flow again. But public sector services are not conducive to inventory accumulation. Public services are provided directly by people; tangible material products seldom exist. There is strong pressure to restore services as soon as possible. For striking public workers, a strike fund exists infrequently (for obvious reasons where work stoppages are illegal), and if it is available it is often depleted within a short period of time. Thus, workers are motivated to seek a speedy settlement — an outcome also appreciated by the inconvenienced general citizenry.

When a quick resolution is not in the cards, a determined union elevates the level of conflict. In his study of social movement unionism, Paul Johnston (1994) suggested that any collective action by public employees is likely to experience greater success if the union is able to (1) frame its demands in terms of the "public interest" and (2) to form coalitions with program clients, other unions and groups of employees, elected officials, agency or departmental management, or other entities. A strike over pay inequities for female employees might be presented as a fight for the interests of all women; a teachers' strike might be articulated as being for the "good of the children"; a walkout by health care workers is framed as being about "patient safety"; and a strike by predominantly African American or Latino workers might be portrayed as a "struggle for civil rights."

B. Management

In some collective bargaining contests, employers must ask themselves how far they will go before taking a strike, how long a strike they can withstand, and what the likely results of it will be. Early in the public sector experience, most employers would go the extra mile to avoid a strike, or, in the event one did occur, settle it as expeditiously as possible with only passing regard for the long-term results.

The tendency of public managers to cave in to avoid the turmoil and confusion of a strike has lessened. Management recognizes that certain factors favor them during work stoppages. As already noted, government tax revenues continue to be collected whereas employee wages stop, unlike in the private sector, where plants may be shut down and sales halted. Without a substantial strike fund, public employees can be seriously inconvenienced both by their loss of wages and benefits and by the curtailment of government services upon which they and their families, like all other citizens, depend. Furthermore, striking public workers face citizen hostility that often tilts public opinion in favor of management. And there is always the disturbing possibility that striking government workers won't be badly missed, thus calling into question the need for the services they have provided in the past or raising the specter of privatization.

Even work stoppages in police and fire services, arguably the most "essential" of all local government functions, do not always have adverse impacts. Although the Boston police strike and the Montreal police strike were accompanied by shocking episodes of crime and general breakdowns in law and order, such was not the outcome in other incidents, including police strikes in New York City, Albuquerque, and San Francisco. In these and many other jurisdictions, public managers utilized long-range planning to cope with strikes by providing for temporary substitute labor. For example, local police supervisors, county law enforcement personnel, and state highway patrol officers can augment nonstriking police personnel, and adjacent districts or volunteer fire departments can assist during firefighter strikes. Through contingency planning, essential services can be maintained during a work stoppage. Planning may have the added benefit of reducing the likelihood of a strike occurring in the first place.

C. Contingency Planning for the Strike

Despite the fact that work stoppages in government are rare today, strike planning is a sound, and necessary, management practice in government if critical services are to be maintained and a strong management bargaining position ensured. Although contingency planning is more common today than in the past, a majority of employers continue to ignore the need for it. For instance, only 38.5 percent of cities surveyed in 1988 reported such plans (International City Management Association 1989: 8).

Comparing municipal strike preparation to disaster and other emergency preparedness requirements is instructive (Levesque 1980). Certain groups of personnel should be identified: (1) a strike task force composed of the city manager, assistant city manager, city attorney, director of public works, chiefs of police and fire, and the HRM director; and (2) strike operations personnel consisting of department heads and other management employees. The principal duties of the task force are to maintain essential services by assessing problems on a day-to-day basis and creating alternative approaches for dealing with them. Strike operations personnel oversee and perform critical services in their functional domains. In the event of a general strike, the task force can implement a strike plan to continue operating designated essential services and as many other services as possible while shutting down government functions not posing a threat to the public health and safety. A strike headquarters may be designated in advance, and, as in any emergency, reliable communications channels must be established to link the task force with the union leaders, strike operations personnel, the media, the legislative body, and the mayor.

The strike contingency plan should identify in detail which personnel can be utilized to maintain essential services. An inventory of supervisory skills and job experiences aids in assigning managers to essential line operations. Private contractors can be enlisted to provide services on a temporary basis. Intergovernmental cooperation through formal, mutual aid pacts also is advised to augment supervisory personnel or to replace them in the unlikely event that they, too, walk out. Possible assistance from other local, state, or federal government units should also be explored. Importantly, the contingency plan should provide for the protection of nonstriking workers through arrangements such as carpools, escorts, and patrolled parking lots.

During the work stoppage, the public employer attempts to garner public support for the management position to apply maximum pressure on wavering union members to return to work. A number of strategies may be used, most of them involving manipulation of the electronic and print media. For example, management might consider publishing salaries of striking workers or showing how increased taxes and/or expenditures will result from bowing to union demands.

Pawtucket, Rhode Island, is a city that once held the dubious honor of experiencing the most teacher strikes in the United States. Its superintendent, Robert J. Gerardi (1986) adds the following suggestions. Be aware of election-year pressures on elected officials for a quick settlement. Designate a single spokesperson to deal with the media, so that conflicting information will be minimal. Be prepared for teacher unions to use pressure tactics on the school board and administrators, such as daily picket lines and unfair labor practice charges. Also, "Stick to your guns ... don't give away the store. The union is counting on your fatigue."

D. The Injunction

An injunction is a request by the public employer (as plaintiff) to a state or local court to halt a strike or other job action. A temporary (or *ex parte*) restraining order, intended to halt a job action until a final determination as to its legality can be made by the court, usually is easily obtained with a *prima facie* showing of jeopardy to the public health or safety, or of the intentional interruption of a legally mandated government function. In practice, the temporary restraining order is often used simply to serve notice on the public employee union of government concern and to set the stage for imposing sanctions such as fines or dismissals. If the work stoppage continues, the court may hold a hearing and issue a preliminary injunction aimed at stopping the job action until a final decision can be reached on whether to issue a permanent injunction. Permanent injunctions normally are not required in public employment because of the short duration of most strikes.

Until passage of the Norris-LaGuardia Act in 1932, the courts tended to be very quick — even to the point of abuse — to issue injunctions against almost any type of job action, from strikes to picketing, thereby immediately placing unions in the unpalatable position of having either to order their members back to work or to keep them off the job in violation of the law. The Norris-LaGuardia Act forbids federal courts from issuing injunctions in labor disputes unless they threaten the public health or safety or are accompanied by fraud or violence. But the act does not cover public employees, who can be enjoined from job actions by state or local courts.

Before 1968, most courts held that injunctions against illegal work stoppages did not require the public employer to demonstrate irreparable harm to the operations of government or to the public health and safety; injunctions were routinely granted upon request. In that year, however, the Supreme Court of Michigan assumed a much stricter approach to issuing injunctions. In *School District for the City of Holland et al. v. Holland Education Association* (1968), the Michigan Supreme Court refused to issue an injunction against teachers who failed to report for work because the school districts did not demonstrate irreparable injury or breach of the peace. The court stated, "We must concede that the mere failure of a public school system to begin its school year on the appointed day cannot be classified as a catastrophic event. We are also aware that there has been no public furor when schools are closed down for inclement weather, or on the day a presidential candidate comes to town, or when the basketball team wins the championship."

The *Holland* case set an important precedent for other states by implying that the employer should approach the court with "clean hands" after having bargained in good faith; the mere injunctive request was not, in and of itself, enough to merit court action. Interestingly, Michigan law expressly forbids public employee strikes.

Today, then, the courts require the public employer to demonstrate that some harm results from a job action before it will enjoin that action. Use of the injunction simply to avoid inconvenience or escape confronting the causes of labor conflict head on has been an increasingly untenable behavior for government employers. Even when injunctions are won, enforcement of contempt of court penalties may be counterproductive, intensifying employer–employee conflict and making martyrs out of jailed leaders. If penalties are not enforced, the credibility of management is damaged. Either way, management may not emerge in a stronger position.

This is not to say that there is no legitimate role for the injunction. To the contrary, serious threats to the health and safety of citizens resulting from a strike are appropriately met with an injunction. A work stoppage in violation of an ongoing contract may properly be enjoined. What is called for is flexibility, with employer and court decision making appropriate to the circumstances surrounding each case.

E. Strike Penalties

If a strike is illegal, or if an injunction and back-to-work order are secured in the court and strikers defy them, should public workers be punished? If so, how severely, and what penalties should be invoked?

Excessively harsh strike penalties imposed by the courts or by the employer may be counterproductive by encouraging strikers to extend their job action with the belief that they have nothing to lose. Alternatively, strikers may take a calculated risk that the employer will not actually follow through with strong sanctions, such as dismissal (Balfour and Holmes 1981).

Illegal walkouts by schoolteachers present a particularly delicate situation because of the special relationship between teachers and their students. Arrests can result in serious and lasting damage to a public school system, including a loss of student respect for a "convicted criminal." When 700 Monmouth, New Jersey, teachers walked out over an increase in their health insurance premiums in 2001, a state judge ordered them back to duty. The teachers defied the order, so the judge, beginning with names starting with the letter A, jailed the teachers (alphabetically) until the union called off the strike 9 days later.

When, however, a walkout extends for an untenable period of time or causes great hardship, the public employer wants to apply new pressures for settlement, and management believes that sanctions must be leveled, a number of options are available. Union members and/or officials may be imprisoned, fined, fired, demoted, or suspended; the union may be decertified; the dues checkoff may be suspended or revoked. Most states provide statutory strike penalties. In Georgia, striking state employees can receive 5 years' probation and no pay increase for 3 years; Nevada law establishes a $50,000 fine per day against a striking union, with a $1,000 daily fine plus imprisonment for the union officials. Michigan levies a fine of 1 day's pay for each day's strike on school employees and daily monetary penalties against the union as well. Striking teachers in Maryland may have their union decertified as exclusive representative in the school district.

New York's Taylor Law sets out substantial penalties for striking workers, including loss of 2 days' pay for each strike day and suspension of the dues checkoff. Generally, the Taylor Law sanctions (as amended in 1968) have been regularly enforced and strike incidence has been minimized, indicating the value of flexibility and consistency in enforcing strike penalties. For instance, New York City transit workers went on strike in December 2005 over pensions, health insurance, and worker safety issues, despite being warned of "dire consequences" by Governor Pataki and Mayor Bloomberg. A state supreme court judge slapped them with one injunction, then a second. The noncomplying Transport Workers Union was held in contempt of court and fined $1 million a day; the union leader, Roger Toussaint, was jailed. When the workers finally returned to their subways, trains, and buses, the fine had run to $2.5 million and Toussaint had sat in jail for 4 days (Greenhouse and Chan 2006; Lueck 2006).

In sum, New York's tough Taylor Law does force striking unions and their members back to the job. In many instances, however, severe punishments, such as dismissals, jail time, and heavy fines, are not carried out or penalties imposed on illegal strikers are forgiven after the strike is settled. Yet mild penalties might be ignored by the union. The middle ground of moderate sanctions consistently enforced may be the best course of action to reduce the probability of strikes, particularly where binding arbitration is available to resolve disputes (Partridge 1996; Currie and McConnell 1994).

Although striking employees are often threatened with dismissal and sometimes fired outright, as in the case of the PATCO strike (see Case Study 8.3), management usually opposes such actions as a practical matter because they do not want to lose good employees for whom they have made an investment in time and training. Often, there is dissension within the ranks of management over such decisions, creating an interesting political rivalry between those who want to dismiss striking workers and those who do not. Elected officials may find themselves deeply divided in such disputes as well.

Case Study 8.3: The PATCO Strike

The Professional Air Traffic Controllers Organization (PATCO) was established in 1968 as a "professional society" of federal air traffic controllers. Relations with the controllers' "employer," the Federal Aviation Administration (FAA), were stormy from the beginning. Within 2 years PATCO had staged a sick-out and the FAA had responded by canceling the organization's dues checkoff system. A report commissioned by the U.S. Department of Transportation (DOT) categorized PATCO–FAA labor–management relations as "the worst in the federal sector."

On March 25, 1970, PATCO called its first nationwide job action — a sick-out that lasted 3 weeks — over FAA transfer of four PATCO members who were engaged in organizing efforts in Baton Rouge, Louisiana. It was a serious mistake, resulting in a union membership decline from more than 7,500 to less than 3,000 and near bankruptcy from a $100 million damage suit brought by the airlines. As part of the settlement, PATCO agreed to a permanent no-strike injunction. PATCO spent the next 3 years seeking reinstatement of hundreds of controllers fired and suspended from duty by the FAA. Meanwhile, the FAA unsuccessfully fought PATCO's petition for certification as exclusive representative of the controllers. In 1973, the first contract negotiations were held. Throughout the remainder of the 1970s PATCO and the FAA negotiated a series of 1-year contracts, almost always in an atmosphere of crisis and work slowdowns.

Accumulating bitterness from hostile contract negotiations and waves of grievances filed under the various written agreements came to a head as the last contract expired in March 1981 and negotiations over a new contract reached an impasse. The dispute involved PATCO's demands concerning salaries, work hours, retirement programs, and other benefits which, to be granted, would require special treatment of the controllers somewhat similar to that accorded postal workers. PATCO President Robert Poli polled his membership on whether to go out on strike. Seventy-five percent voted for a walkout, and when Poli submitted the FAA's last best offer to the rank and file, they rejected the package by a 20-to-1 margin.

After two subsequent months of further negotiation and federal mediation, the two sides were, in mediator Kenneth Moffett's words, "still miles apart." PATCO was asking for $575 million in new salaries and benefits, while the FAA said it would agree to $40 million and no more. On August 3, 1981, 12,000 controllers refused to report to their control towers at airports throughout the United States.

If the controllers thought President Ronald Reagan, a former head of the Screen Actors' Guild (and whom PATCO had endorsed for president), would be sympathetic to their cause, they were sadly and fatally mistaken. Reagan labeled them "lawbreakers," sought the imprisonment of strike leaders, and summarily dismissed from federal service all the strikers who refused to return to work within 48 hours. A federal judge supported the president by imposing accelerating fines on the union that would total $1 million per day within 3 days.

If PATCO leaders were counting on public sympathy for the controllers to help encourage the FAA and the Reagan administration to compromise or back down, they were wrong again. The average citizen — even the typical union member — found it difficult to identify with the relatively well-paid controllers who were demanding a maximum salary of $59,000 (worth perhaps four times as much as today's dollars), almost unexcelled retirement benefits, and a 32-hour work week. Moreover, the strikers were clearly in violation of several federal laws and their oath of office. When Reagan and DOT Secretary Drew Lewis declared the strike over (because all strikers had been fired) and the DOT began hiring new controllers, there was little public outcry. There was, however, concern by air travelers that the nation's air traffic control system would be unable to function safely, amid predictions by the airline industry of massive layoffs and flight cancellations.

Meanwhile, as new recruits began training to become air traffic controllers, some 2,500 supervisors were joined in directing aircraft by about 800 military controllers, the 5,000 civilian controllers who had stayed on the job or returned within the amnesty period, and hundreds of recently retired controllers. Despite PATCO predictions of terrible air disasters and a crippled industry, neither happened. Commercial flights continued, although at reduced levels, and accidents occurred at or below normal levels. The airlines lost a great deal of money, but they never wavered in supporting the president.

Three months later, PATCO was officially decertified as a bargaining representative by the Federal Labor Relations Authority. Subsequent court appeals by the union were fruitless. The once proud and aggressive organization of professional air traffic controllers had been destroyed by its own strategic mistakes and a hostile administration.

In hindsight, the strategic errors of PATCO are obvious. First, the union badly misread public reaction to the strike and to its demands. Little sympathy was offered to the highly paid white-collar workers during a period of citizen resistance to government taxation and spending. Second, the union failed to publicize legitimate grievances, including congested airways, tremendous mental strain on overworked controllers, and the need for improvements in technology. Third, PATCO did not anticipate the strong Reagan administration reaction to the strike and the government's determination to "stick to its guns." Finally, PATCO did not make the time or effort to garner the support of other federal and private sector unions prior to the strike. Although controllers in Canada and Portugal did refuse to route U.S. flights over their air space for several days, the actions were short lived and not very troublesome. Organized labor in the United States abandoned the striking controllers and refused to respect their picket lines. Had domestic union support been stronger, the airline industry could have been brought to the brink of financial disaster, which would have tremendously increased settlement pressure on the administration.

Years later, in 1987, air traffic controllers voted in a new union: the National Air Traffic Controllers Association (NATCA), organized by John Thornton, one of the controllers sacked by Mr. Reagan. The new union adopted a no-strike pledge and disavowed illegal job actions, while renewing many of its earlier complaints concerning heavy workloads and an autocratic FAA. In 1989, NATCA successfully (and peacefully) negotiated its first contract. In 1993, President Clinton lifted the ban on rehiring the controllers fired by Reagan. Sadly, most were past retirement age or had moved on to other careers.

Questions

1. Were "faulty negotiations" in play in the events leading up to the PATCO strike? If so, how?
2. How did public opinion play a role?
3. If he had been able to exercise hindsight, how might Poli have played his cards differently?
4. Why do you think President Reagan reacted so strongly to the air traffic controller strike? How might subsequent presidents (Bill Clinton and George W. Bush) have handled the events differently?

IX. Conclusions and a Look Ahead

Even in the event of initial management determination to dismiss striking workers, it frequently proves difficult to carry out the final action. Firing striking public employees can provoke more problems than officials anticipate, and the real politics of public sector strike policy often diverge substantially from formal provisions in the statutes. Nonetheless, many employee discharges have been announced and permanently carried out. For the public employer, the difficult task is to avoid strikes when possible; always protect the public's health, safety, and well-being; and promote solutions through good-faith bargaining.

Work stoppages and related job actions by public workers have been recorded since the 1830s. The incidence and intensity of government work stoppages increased dramatically from 1965 to the late 1970s, especially at the local level.

Since then, the number of strikes has declined significantly, both in government and in the private sector.

The vast majority of public employee work stoppages have occurred in the face of philosophical and legal prohibitions by governments. The sovereignty doctrine, although essentially irrelevant in those jurisdictions engaging in collective bargaining with their workers, remains pertinent where negotiations are prohibited. Nonetheless, government employee work stoppages have taken place in all states. Early on in the public sector experience, strikes did seem to bias the political process in favor of the unions, but work stoppages today tend to generate strong political and economic counterpressures on the striking employees and their unions. Some government services are not perceived to be quite so "essential" as they once were.

As the "ultimate weapon in labor's arsenal," the public employee work stoppage appears to have lost much of its firepower. Employer recognition of the apparent inevitability of strikes has resulted in a more mature, calculated approach by management. Negotiating skills, training, experience, and planning have improved greatly during the past decade, especially at the local government level. As Tim Bornstein (1980) remarked, "Public management came of age in the 1970s. Public sector negotiators have learned well from the private sector that there are 10,000 ways to say 'no' to a union's demands without bargaining in bad faith. And they have learned the ultimate lesson from private sector management: Never blink an eye at a union's strike threats; talk softly and carry a big strike contingency plan."

Yet several signs would seem to portend heightened public sector strike activity. Government employment has become less desirable because of cost-saving layoffs and hiring freezes, limited wage gains, reductions in pension and health care benefits, outsourcing and contracting out, and bureaucrat bashing by citizens and elected officials. Working conditions have deteriorated for many public workers: classroom teachers face unruly and violence-prone students; police officers endure life-threatening encounters with users, abusers, and purveyors of illegal drugs; social workers must attempt to intervene in the affairs of dysfunctional families. These and many other negative trends and problems are likely to continue.

In view of such factors, the precipitous decline in strike activity seems paradoxical. Closer examination, however, uncovers some powerful deterrents to strikes. Foremost among them is the PATCO debacle, widely seen today as a seminal event in American labor history. That a highly skilled group of professionals could be relatively easily replaced, and their union absolutely crushed, made all organized labor enormously insecure. The PATCO strike marked a major change in political climate, with very negative implications for the unions.

Another factor discouraging government work stoppages is that they are simply not as effective as they once were. Management is more experienced at the bargaining game, and when a strike is called, it is much better prepared to cope effectively. Where strikes continue to be illegal, sanctions, when consistently enforced, can be very painful for the union and for individual members, who face the loss of their livelihood. Concern for job security may override a desire for wage and benefit increases.

Time and political and economic realities are working against the efficacy of strikes. Bargaining relationships have matured and stabilized. Many union leaders have reached a comfortable accommodation with management, and silent understandings and glances have replaced thunderous emotional displays and angry stares.

Finally, and of great importance, alternatives to the strike, as intended, have proven successful in deterring them. Mediation, fact finding, and especially binding interest arbitration provide more peaceful venues for settling contract disputes. They are discussed in Chapter 9.

Chapter 9

Resolving Impasses:
Alternatives to the Strike

I. Introduction

Ultimately, collective bargaining involves people at the table and their constituent advisors, who, together, choose what the nature of the dialogue will be in negotiations and whether settlements will be achieved. Some parties want to walk away or to drag out the talks for reasons that are personal or political. They do not want a deal, or at least they do not want a deal quickly. In other cases, the desired outcome of bargaining — attaining a workable solution that maintains the relationship — gets displaced as the parties get entangled in the processes or become bogged down in personality conflicts. Process issues and party conduct can become so contentious that mediators or other third parties have to remind everyone that the goal is a contract settlement, not landing punches on the other side.

Experienced negotiators know that "all cases settle eventually." But they do not settle in the same ways. No two contract negotiations are the same. Patterns certainly exist, but even subtle differences can matter a great deal in determining bargaining outcomes. As public administrators have learned in many contexts, there is no one best way. Sometimes, despite the best efforts of the parties, a negotiated settlement is not obtained. In the private sector, this usually means a strike. In government, it may produce a strike in some cases, but much more often an impasse is addressed through third-party dispute resolution mechanisms.

Despite the modest trend during recent years for public employers to accept the strike as a legitimate component of labor relations and collective bargaining, the majority of state and local governments continue to prohibit strikes. If strikes are prohibited, labor unions are at a distinct disadvantage in collective negotiations unless alternative impasse resolution procedures are available. In virtually all government jurisdictions in which collective bargaining takes place, some form of impasse device is provided to help balance the power of unions and management. The dispute resolution mechanisms developed in U.S. labor relations are increasingly being adapted to settle conflicts in other venues, from environmental disputes to divorces.

This chapter examines the three principal measures used in public sector impasse resolution: mediation, fact finding, and arbitration (including final offer arbitration). We consider their various permutations, advantages and disadvantages, and relative effectiveness. The chapter concludes with a look at several new techniques that have been suggested or experimented with in various jurisdictions. The focus in this chapter is on disputes over interests, which occur during contract negotiations. In Chapter 10, impasses over rights, or grievances, under the terms of an existing contract are addressed.

II. The Private Sector Experience

The right for unions to strike in the private sector is guaranteed by the National Labor Relations Act (NLRA). It is generally perceived to be a legitimate and fundamental part of private sector labor relations. Third-party procedures for resolving private contract disputes short of the strike are used much less frequently than in public employment, but mediation, fact finding, and arbitration all have a long history in the private sector that predates their utilization in government.

The conventional procedure for private sector parties seeking to avoid a strike is to call in a mediator if no agreement has been attained within 30 to 60 days of contract expiration. Typically, a mediator is assigned by the Federal Mediation and Conciliation Service (FMCS), an independent federal agency established under 1947 amendments to the NLRA. The FMCS is also empowered under the NLRA to offer its services, even if not requested. If the mediator sent by this neutral peacemaker fails to steer the parties into an agreement through the powers of persuasion, fact finding or arbitration may begin.

Fact finding is a quasi-judicial process in which a neutral third party (individual or panel) examines the "facts" of the impasse, hears the arguments of the parties, and issues findings and recommendations. Fact finding's history dates back to 1902, when President Theodore Roosevelt appointed through an executive order the first fact-finding board (the Anthracite Coal Commission). Similar fact-finding entities were established by executive orders of Presidents Woodrow Wilson, Franklin Roosevelt, and Harry Truman. In addition, ad hoc fact-finding boards have been used on many occasions in critical industries such as steel, autos, and railroads.

Binding arbitration by a neutral third party to settle unresolved disputes over the terms and conditions of a new contract, known as interest arbitration, has a long history (it was first recorded in Connecticut copper mines in the 18th century). However, it is seldom used in industry. Generally, the strike is the final impasse resolution procedure in the private sector, although mediation and fact finding are often given an opportunity to work first.

III. Impasse Resolution in Federal Employment

Prior to Executive Order 10988 of 1962, impasses between federal agencies and unions representing their employees were resolved on an agency-by-agency basis without the benefit of legal or statutory guidance. E.O. 10988 only partially filled the legal–structural void, because it provided no binding interest arbitration procedures except for advisory arbitration in cases involving unit determination and representation disputes. The arbitrator's sphere of decision making was highly constrained. This lack of adequate impasse resolution procedures was a major source of criticism of the executive order and a prime reason for issuance of Executive Order 11491 by President Nixon, which authorized the FMCS to aid in resolving federal impasses upon the request of one or both parties. Depending on the situation, the FMCS could recommend mediation, fact finding, or arbitration and assign trained personnel to help settle the dispute.

Under the Civil Service Reform Act of 1978 (CSRA), the FMCS continues to play a leading role in assisting federal agencies to resolve negotiation impasses. FMCS is a major provider of technical assistance in conflict resolution and labor relations across all sectors in the United States and abroad. Under Section 7119 of the CSRA, if FMCS assistance or other voluntary arrangements fail to settle a dispute, either party may request the intervention of the Federal Service Impasses Panel (FSIP) or mutually agree to a binding arbitration procedure, which must win FSIP approval.

The FSIP is composed of a chairperson and six members appointed by the president for overlapping 5-year terms. When asked to intervene in a federal labor dispute, the FSIP can make one of several possible determinations: (1) that it cannot exercise jurisdiction, (2) that negotiations should resume, (3) that negotiations should resume with mediation, (4) that fact finding be implemented, or (5) that other procedures such as arbitration be used. The parties have the option of using FSIP mediators, fact finders, or arbitrators and, with FSIP permission, an outside arbitrator. In cases where voluntary settlement proves elusive, the FSIP is authorized to hold hearings, take sworn testimony or depositions, issue subpoenas, and take "whatever action is necessary" within its authority to resolve the impasse, including final offer arbitration. (Final offer arbitration differs from conventional arbitration in that the arbitrator must accept the "most reasonable" last offer of one party or the other, without modification or "splitting the difference.") FSIP impasse decisions are enforced by the Federal Labor Relations Authority, which can impose unfair labor practice penalties against a noncomplying party (Smith 2006). Issues heard by the FSIP concern disputes over facilities (e.g., parking, office space), hours of work, ground rules for negotiations, and various human resource management issues.

Disputes involving postal workers are covered under the 1970 Postal Reorganization Act. If the parties fail to reach a contract agreement or mutually adopt a binding impasse resolution procedure, the FMCS is authorized to establish a fact-finding panel consisting of three persons (two selected by the parties, a third chosen by the two selectees). The panel must issue a report of its findings within 45 days; settlement recommendations are optional. If an agreement is not forthcoming within 90 days, the FMCS creates a three-member arbitration board through the same procedures. The board holds hearings, takes evidence, and makes a binding decision within 45 days. Costs of the fact-finding panel and arbitration board are shared equally by the two parties.

Postal Service negotiations went to arbitration for the first time in a 1984 dispute involving 500,000 employees, the most ever participating in an arbitration settlement in the United States. The parties were $13 billion apart in their final demands, with the major point of disagreement being how most appropriately to measure wage and job comparability. The arbitration panel found that postal workers were making more money than comparable private sector employees. They issued a salary decision of "moderate restraint," adding about $4 billion to postal costs (Loewenberg 1985). An arbitration panel was recently called upon to impose a settlement after bargaining with the National Rural Letter Carriers Association collapsed in 2007.

IV. State and Local Government Impasse Procedures

At least 38 states have legislation on the books providing for some sort of impasse resolution procedure for one or more categories of employees (see Table 9.1). Mediation is the technique most frequently provided for (36 states), followed closely by fact finding (34 states), then arbitration (30 states). The wide variety of state approaches to resolving contract impasses provides a rich ground for experimentation and research. Not surprisingly, a great deal has been written on the use, and the impacts, of impasse procedures.

Neutral third parties for state and local labor impasses may be obtained from a number of sources, including the state public employee relations board (PERB), state or local impasse agencies, the FMCS, or lists of private third parties provided by organizations such as the American Arbitration Association, the National Academy of Arbitrators, or the National Center for Dispute Settlement. Some states and localities employ part-time, ad hoc neutrals. The FMCS offers its services to help state and local jurisdictions develop their own dispute resolution capabilities. Where such capabilities are not available, the FMCS will assist in resolving disputes

Table 9.1 State Legislation on Dispute Resolution Procedures for State and Local Employees, 2008

State	Mediation	Fact Finding	Arbitration (Conventional)	Arbitration (Final Offer)
Alabama				
Alaska	X		X	
Arizona				
Arkansas				
California	X	X		
Colorado				
Connecticut	X	X		
Delaware	X	X	X	X
Florida	X	X		
Georgia				
Hawaii	X	X	X	X
Idaho	X	X		
Illinois	X	X	X	X
Indiana	X	X	X	X
Iowa	X	X	X	X
Kansas	X	X		
Kentucky	X	X		
Louisiana				
Maine	X	X	X	X
Maryland	X	X		
Massachusetts	X	X	X	X
Michigan	X	X	X	X
Minnesota	X		X	X
Mississippi				
Missouri				
Montana	X	X	X	X

Table 9.1 State Legislation on Dispute Resolution Procedures for State and Local Employees, 2008 (Continued)

State	Mediation	Fact Finding	Arbitration (Conventional)	Arbitration (Final Offer)
Nebraska	X	X		
Nevada	X	X	X	X
New Hampshire	X	X	X	
New Jersey	X	X	X	X
New Mexico	X	X	X	
New York	X	X	X	
North Carolina				
North Dakota	X	X		X
Ohio	X	X	X	X
Oklahoma		X	X	
Oregon	X	X	X	
Pennsylvania	X	X	X	X
Rhode Island	X	X	X	
South Carolina				
South Dakota	X	X		
Tennessee		X	X	
Texas			X	
Utah		X		
Vermont	X	X	X	X
Virginia				
Washington	X	X	X	
West Virginia				
Wisconsin	X	X	X	X
Wyoming			X	

Source: State websites.

when requested to do so by one or both parties. It will also provide technical assistance for training programs.

A. Mediation

An impasse in contract negotiations may be declared when a deadline has been reached, an important bargaining issue appears insurmountable, or the relationship between the parties has degenerated to name calling and accusations. In mediation, an impartial third party helps the others to achieve a voluntary agreement on substantive issues in dispute. He or she also may try to help the parties maintain or improve the quality of their relationship. Mediation may be requested by either or both parties in a state or local dispute. In some states, such as North Dakota, both parties must make the request, whereas in other states, such as New York, the state PERB can intervene at its own initiative. As noted above, the mediator may be provided by the FMCS, state or local agencies, or private sources. The federal service is furnished only where no state or local mediation assistance is available. Where state legislation governs the impasse resolution process, mediators may be selected by the parties from certified lists, or, as in Vermont, the state PERB may assign a neutral party on request. As a general rule, because the success of a mediator is premised upon the degree of confidence and trust with which he or she is held, mediators are sought out who are fully acceptable to both parties.

FMCS-provided mediators generally have achieved an excellent record and reputation. They are experienced, well-trained, full-time professionals (Mareschal 2002; Dilts and Haber 1989). State-assigned and ad hoc mediators vary in skill and experience. The quality of state-appointed neutrals is improving with continued seasoning in public sector impasses. Meanwhile, the parties at impasse usually do well to avoid allowing local community figures or elected officials to serve as mediators. Although the intentions of local notables may be quite honorable, their lack of experience and expertise in resolving labor disputes can lead to unintended and undesirable outcomes.

Mediation is very informal, quite private, and highly individualistic. Records are not kept, so one is forced to rely mostly on anecdotes or personal experience to gain an understanding of what transpires. The process is intriguing. As Zack (1985: 180) observed,

> It brings together two opposing parties, frequently antagonistic and hostile in their relationship; interposes a third party between them, often of their mutual selection; and creates thereby the expectation that the three forces will be able to achieve an agreement when the two parties could not. ... Even the participants in the process often are astonished that it actually works.

The mediator typically begins by calling a joint session to review the most recent proposals on unresolved bargaining issues along with an already agreed upon list of items. At the mediator's discretion, separate meetings may be held. Mediation ground rules must be decided, including no speaking out of turn, no personal attacks, and the need for confidentiality. Formal statements may then be obtained from each party regarding its positions on remaining questions. Next, after considering the respective bargaining postures of the two parties, the mediator is likely to meet with each of them privately in order to gain their confidence and to explore negotiating room on the issues. The mediator strives immediately to gain the confidence of the parties by listening closely to what they have to say and making sure to appear evenhanded in everything that is done. It is important that any contacts with one party be reported to the other and that all relevant information be shared. Through the mediation process all participants are continually made aware of their obligation to reach a settlement. Communication channels must remain open. Indeed, a major function of mediation is to keep the parties at the bargaining table to avoid a lengthy period of stasis or stalemate.

Some mediators believe in doing an extensive analysis of the issues and parties in dispute and designing contingent and noncontingent strategies for dealing with the parties. Other mediators, recognizing that many complications and complexities will work themselves out, focus on the people involved. They know that the parties are more familiar with the jurisdiction and its problems than the mediator can ever be and that they can resolve their difficulties if they can be helped to talk productively and persevere in moving toward settlement.

Two basic strategies are available to mediators. The nondirective, or broad strategy, is aimed at producing a climate conducive to settlement and assisting the parties to become more adept at the bargaining table. The mediator may press the parties to focus first on issues relatively easy to resolve, while suppressing negative or hostile outbursts. Even the nondirective mediator must also "orchestrate" (Kolb 1983) various administrative details (time and place of meetings), structure and order the issues that must be considered, ensure that negotiations move at an orderly pace, and keep the substance of the negotiations private. A major objective of the nondirective mediator is to help the parties to explore potential avenues for accommodation. Trial balloons may be launched by the mediator and pondered without risk to the parties. The mediator can assist the parties in properly presenting offers and proposals at the bargaining table. Seemingly innocuous factors such as the language used or the way an offer is communicated can be a bar to settlement. Often, toning down the language while still preserving the substance of the proposal is effective. Attention by the mediator to such relatively minor problems may mean the difference between settlement and continued impasse.

Directive strategies are intended to help the parties generate options, discern points of compromise, make them face the consequences of their respective situations, offer suggestions for settlement, and, in some cases, apply pressure for settlement. The directive mediator, in other words, attempts to take control of negotiations and bring things to closure. In extreme instances the mediator may even provoke a crisis by, for example, publicly labeling a party as intransigent or obstructive, or by stalking out of a nonproductive caucus in apparent disgust.

The relative usefulness of the strategies depends on the phase of the mediation process. A nondirective posture is good for facilitating an agreement when the parties are comfortable with one another and well intentioned. As negotiations move close to an agreement but remain snagged over one or more issues, the mediator may become more directive in his or her approach. A mismatch between the nature of the dispute and mediation tactics may push the parties into greater intransigence in their positions and doom the process to failure (Posthuma, Dworkin, and Swift 2002). Whatever tactics are brought into play, the successful mediator must maintain the trust of the parties, master the intricacies of the situation, and be persuasive in motivating union and management negotiators to steer towards a conclusion. And he or she must understand that uncontrollable external factors (e.g., economic problems, political variables) may ultimately be more important than the mediator's strategies in determining whether settlement is attained (Kolb and Rubin 1989).

To help the parties work together, the mediator typically calls for joint sessions. In these meetings, he or she employs a variety of techniques. One is "idea charting," which is a form of brainstorming. Here, the mediator goes around the room asking each individual to identify the issues that are most important to resolve. Each issue that is mentioned is written on a flip chart or computer projection screen. The parties discuss and clarify the issues and the underlying interests represented by the issues. Idea charting helps each party focus on the mediator and the written ideas, rather than on their peers and personal notebooks.

For example, suppose a management representative says, "We want to change the way care is provided to certain patients and relocate them to another building." "Why?" someone asks. "Because these patients are dangerous and our visiting psychiatric support people would be better used if we could relocate the patients. We could also use better psychiatric aides, which would benefit our vocational program. And we need to keep costs down, and this might help." The issue here is to move patients into a common facility for the reasons given. The union may agree that this is a legitimate interest of managers and be willing to talk about it. And management's interest may prompt the union to identify its own related issues. The union could observe that "members fear new facilities, current wards are already understaffed, and the proposed changes might put persons in danger by consolidating potentially violent patients. Union members might have to work out of class or have their caseloads increased. Moreover, the building in question is a firetrap." Throughout, the mediator tries to help the parties identify key interests and drop unimportant ones, develop criteria for addressing them, generate alternative proposals, and decide on the most pragmatic path to settlement.

At any time, a team may request a caucus to discuss what concessions or compromises might be offered and under what conditions. Mediators usually attend the caucuses and provide assistance if needed. Mediators can also call a private caucus to remind an obstreperous party about the ground rules, such as no threats and accusations. Eventually, there may come a breakthrough where at least one significant issue is resolved. Once the dam breaks, the chances are improved for more accommodations. However, particularly sticky issues may simply be deal breakers. And the agreement can stand or fall on how the parties treat one another and react when the going gets tough.

The principal goal of mediation is to reach a "good settlement," one that can win widespread acceptance among the constituencies of the parties and can be lived with. For the purposes of the mediator, the public interest or the fairness of the outcome is of secondary importance.

1. Traits of an Effective Mediator

The traits ascribed to effective mediators read like the Scout Code: experienced, skilled, unbiased, open, creative, inventive, patient, persevering. This person should also be intelligent, tenacious, humorous, persuasive, empathetic, and full of stamina. Mediators should have the "patience of Job," "the guile of Machiavelli," and "the wisdom of Solomon" (Simkin 1971: 53). They should evince optimism tempered with realism. They should seek to build trust by being genuine and straightforward. Mediators must accept the need for emotionalism and venting by the parties, but prevent it from shattering the process. Everyone knows that there are games going on at the table, under the table, in the room, and out of the room, and that potential troublemakers hover everywhere. The mediator must try to keep fully abreast of goings on by joining meetings in the halls, parking lot, or local bar. It is often at such "side meetings" that breakthroughs occur. The mediator also needs diplomatic skills in dealing with the media. For instance, there is the classic television shot of a mediator coming out of negotiations to meet the press. "What is going on?" the reporter asks. The response: "They are talking." "How would you characterize the talks?" The mediator observes, "They are frank and candid."

Although these qualities "are not the stuff of which professional curricula are made" (Kressel 1977: 270), formal training in labor relations, labor law, conflict resolution techniques, and facilitation are important for the novice mediator. A task force of the FMCS (1996) identified several competencies that mediators for the agency should achieve, including expertise in collective bargaining and other labor management processes, facilitation, and problem solving skills, knowledge of tools to improve organizational effectiveness, and conflict resolution skills. There remains a certain lack of standards concerning who is qualified to practice mediation (Mareschal 1998; Bellman 1998). Certificate programs abound, but some of them fall well short of being rigorous. Even if a set of universal standards were agreed to and taught, mediation would remain an art, not a science. Effective mediators are adaptive, flexible, and resilient, using their best judgment under the circumstances and making things up when necessary. The road to settlement always has many twists and turns.

2. Advantages and Disadvantages of Mediation as a Technique for Resolving Impasses

Mediation's utility as a dispute settlement technique is evidenced by its frequent application to public sector impasses. A major advantage of mediation over other impasse procedures is its flexibility. It is an inexpensive informal process that permits the parties and the neutral great latitude in devising a settlement, in large part because no written record of the proceedings is required. Thus, alternative settlement packages can be explored through the mediator without placing formal proposals on the table. The informal nature of mediation also helps break down communication barriers that may have developed as negotiations atrophied. Mediation can help "educate" inexperienced negotiators on the vicissitudes of the bargaining process and on the specific viewpoints and positions of the opposing parties. Another advantage is that agreements attained through mediation are reached by the parties voluntarily. Because they are not imposed, terms of the settlement are more likely to be fully accepted by the parties and their constituencies. Finally, mediation moderates labor conflicts by opening points of disagreement to different meanings, interpretations, and possibilities (Kolb and Rubin 1989: 4).

Despite the considerable advantages of mediation as a dispute resolution procedure, there are unfavorable aspects as well. Two major criticisms may be offered. First and foremost, there is no element of finality to mediation. The mediator cannot force a settlement. There is no final report; only a voluntary settlement or a declaration of failure and prompt consideration of other impasse resolution alternatives. Second, good mediators are hard to come by. The special talents and personality traits exhibited by successful mediators are problematic to teach and difficult to emulate.

On balance, mediation is an effective means of resolving an impasse early and relatively amicably. When it succeeds, the impasse is broken, an agreement that both parties can live with is attained, and the future relationship between labor and management is protected.

Mediation is more successful under some conditions than others. The technique appears to be most effective when the mediator is experienced, highly skilled, and tenacious and the parties are less sophisticated and experienced (Karim and Pegnetter 1983; Kochan and Jick 1978). Here, the strategies and personal qualities of the directive neutral have maximum impact (Downie 1992). Experience and tenacity are particularly important traits of the effective mediator. As one commented, "Mediation doesn't start until both of the parties have told the mediator there's no more room for compromise" (Briggs and Koys 1989: 519). In situations in which the two parties have lengthy experience with collective bargaining, the mediator's role may be a less directive one, with attention focused on possible terms of agreement.

Mediation is most effective where (1) overcommitment to a position stifles negotiations, (2) the dispute is of limited difficulty or intensity, open communications and information sharing prevail, and (3) the parties are motivated to attain a settlement. The probability of reaching a settlement increases when mediation is followed by compulsory binding arbitration rather than by fact finding (Payne et al. 2000; Kochan 1979: 179).

Mediation appears to be least fruitful (1) in large jurisdictions, (2) where the parties have a poor relationship, have gone to impasse frequently, and engage in disruptive communication behaviors and dirty tricks, (3) where the basic dispute involves ability of the employer to pay, and (4) where the parties face strong political and/or constituent pressures that encourage them to use the full range of impasse resolution procedures (Payne et al. 2000; Mareschal 2005; Kochan et al. 1979).

B. Fact Finding

As is the case with mediation, fact finding normally may be initiated by either party, although in some states it can be invoked by the PERB. An individual fact finder or a panel (usually composed of three members) is appointed from the same sources used for mediators. Often, the same names appear, because many mediators also act as fact finders. In legal contexts providing for both mediation and fact finding, the latter is usually used only after mediation fails to resolve the dispute. In comparison to mediation, fact finding is a formal proceeding consisting of a quasi-judicial hearing by the neutral of both parties' positions and evidence, a written record of the facts and events, and, in most cases, written recommendations for settlement. The recommendations are not binding.

It has been widely noted in the literature of public sector impasse procedures that "fact finding" is a misnomer. As Simkin (1979: 337) pointed out, "The words fact-finding conjure up notions of preciseness, of objectivity, of virtue. They even have a godlike quality. Who can disagree with facts?" Yet, as McKelvey (1969: 528–529) explained, "Although the 'name of the game' is fact-finding, ... the sport itself has little to do with fact-finding in the literal sense of determining objective facts through the judicial processes of trial and proof to provide evidentiary answers. ..." In other words, rarely is there a single set of "facts" underlying any collective bargaining impasse. On the contrary, there are at least two different "objective" interpretations of the circumstances surrounding all components of any dispute. The principal task of the fact finder is to determine which set or mix of "facts" is most convincing in any given labor relations context.

It should come as no surprise to the student of public administration and politics that two sets of actors portray varying interpretations of reality. If the facts of a situation were apparent to all, the neutral's job would be much simpler. However, public sector employment issues tend to be complex, and "the plethora of facts produced may well overwhelm the fact finders" (Spero and Capozzola 1973: 283). Moreover, each party naturally seeks to put a favorable spin on the facts.

1. The Fact-Finding Process

The formal role of the fact finder is to enter an interest dispute, hear both sides of the story, collect relevant data, and issue recommendations for a settlement. The process is more formal than mediation because it takes place in a quasi-judicial adversarial atmosphere. This does not mean that the two processes are clearly separable. Mediators, too, deal with "facts," and fact finders frequently mediate between the two parties, particularly when fact finding is the last impasse procedure offered before a strike or unilateral imposition of terms by management.

The mediative role of fact finding is evident in a study of the first 7 years of fact finding in Michigan, where it was found that 20 percent of the disputes going to fact finding were settled before a final report and recommendations were issued, even though fact finders in that state are not given formal authority to mediate disputes (Steiber and Wolkinson 1977). Usually, for fact finding to be successful, recommendations must be acceptable to both parties. Thus, the fact finder often probes the range of the parties' expectations through off-the-record meetings and reveals each side's expectations to the other. Sometimes, voluntary agreement results. This practical reality is informally recognized in Iowa, where fact finder reports become de facto arbitration awards (Gallagher and Veglahn 1990), and formally recognized in Ohio, where the collective bargaining law officially encourages fact-finding panels to mediate at any time.

The hearings generally take 1 or 2 days. Transcripts of the proceedings are required in some jurisdictions. After a period of time in which the fact finders examine and analyze the data and testimony presented to them, they normally issue recommendations on all unresolved issues. At this point the formal duties of the fact finder are complete. Informally, the fact finder may act as a mediator by trying to convince the parties to accept the recommendations and settle.

The role of the fact finder varies with the circumstances of the individual dispute. In some cases fact finding is undertaken in a climate of cooperation, as when the parties unite to promote a common goal such as legislative enactment of a statute that would benefit them both. Here the legislative body may be the adversary as the parties look to the fact finder as an important ally in pressing their case. In other situations, fact finding may be used by one or both parties to give credibility to an agreement they would have reached anyway, so that the chances of rank-and-file and/or legislative ratification are heightened. Also, fact finding, if followed by public recommendations, can bring public opinion into play to encourage compromise by an obstreperous party.

In arriving at their conclusions, fact finders often concentrate their investigations on data allowing a comparison of the local circumstances with other, similar jurisdictions. Fact finders are concerned that their recommendations are fair. Thus, wages, benefits, and working conditions in other agencies or jurisdictions are important considerations. Hence, the fact finder can focus on such variables as ability to pay, cost of living, and the nature of the local labor market. In some states, like Florida, fact-finding criteria are delineated in statute. Generally, fact finders strongly desire to convince the parties to accept their recommendations as the best option available for settling the dispute.

The issue of recommendations — whether they should be offered and, if so, to what audience — has been the subject of some controversy. Fact finding without recommendations differs little from mediation, and, as one expert has argued (Simkin 1979: 340), it "is likely to be an exercise in futility." With respect to fact finding *with* recommendations, however, the question arises as to whom they should be issued: to the parties alone, or to the parties and the general public? The recommendations, of course, may be rejected by one or both parties. The potential advantage of public notice of recommendations, as indicated above, is that it can mobilize public pressure for a settlement, especially in the case of an extreme position by one of the parties. Cynics, however, point out the very low level of public interest in most labor disputes and, indeed, politics in general and note the overall lack of citizen understanding of the collective bargaining process. If the local media are also uninformed, indifferent, or otherwise incapable of explaining the complexities of the labor dispute to their reading and viewing audiences, then making public recommendations may seem to be an empty gesture. Furthermore, once recommendations are disclosed, the negotiations process may shut down and the parties become more polarized than ever.

2. Advantages and Disadvantages of Fact Finding

Several benefits are claimed for fact finding as an impasse resolution procedure. It provides an opportunity for the parties to cool off and analyze their positions after temper and patience wears thin. It is a time-consuming process that permits them to collect both their thoughts and data supporting their respective interests. The fact finder's report can lower the expectations of one or both parties (Karper 1994), thereby decreasing the level of uncertainty and the outward ranges for contract settlement (Dickinson and Hunnicutt 2005). It can also serve as a new basis for continued negotiations toward a voluntary settlement, or it can represent a helpful scapegoat to justify a painful settlement (Marmo 1995). Further, fact finding does permit the public to enter the bargaining arena by revealing unresolved issues and how the parties stand on them (Elkouri and Elkouri 2003). In the case of extreme posturing, the taxpaying public has an opportunity to chastise the more immoderate party.

The major criticism of fact finding is that, like mediation, it lacks finality. And even if the parties agree on the basic facts, their interpretations of them may vary wildly. Fact finding is also faulted in many settings for a relatively low rate of success in settling impasses and for drawing out impasses unnecessarily instead of proceeding directly to arbitration or a strike.

Other problems with fact finding have been recognized, some of them of sufficient magnitude to support arguments for elimination of the technique, especially where utilized as an intermediate step between mediation and arbitration. The mere availability of fact finding may lead to excessive use by some parties and thus "chill" the bargaining process. Public opinion appears to exert little influence on the parties' positions. It is further argued that the parties tend to revert to more extreme positions after fact finding fails and that fact finding seldom reduces the number of issues going to arbitration (even though arbitration awards may deviate little from recommendations of the fact finder; in New York, Kochan and his colleagues [1979] determined that they were identical in 70 percent of the cases examined). However, the single most salient criticism of the effectiveness of this method of resolving interest disputes is its lack of finality; either the union or management may reject the fact finder's recommendations

It is difficult to render an accurate assessment of fact finding's effectiveness. Some fact finders act primarily as mediators; others more like a judge and jury. Fact-finding procedures vary from state to state. Generally, only the most difficult disputes — those that cannot be settled with mediation — go to fact finding, which of course depresses the success rate.

Although several collective bargaining states have dropped fact finding, a majority continue to use it as a technique for resolving labor impasses. The process appears to work rather well in Ohio. In 2006 and 2007, for example, the State Employee Relations Board appointed fact finders in 824 disputes. The parties voluntarily settled before the hearing in about 60 percent of the cases, and others were settled before the fact finder's report was issued. The parties accepted the fact finder's recommendations in almost half of the disputes (www.serb.state.oh.us/pdf/Annual__Report_2007.pdf; accessed January 3, 2008).

Florida's experience with fact finding under a "special master" is more ambivalent. A survey of fact-finding participants in 28 cases found that only about 50 percent of labor and management respondents felt fact finding was effective in creating movement toward settlement, exposing the truth, or clarifying issues (Jennings et al. 1988). However, a substantial majority of participants said they would use the process again for a variety of face-saving and political benefits. Another study (Magnusen and Renovitch 1989) was also moderately supportive of the special master procedure, observing that although very few findings are accepted in their entirety, many of the special master's specific recommendations do end up in the labor contract. Florida represents a unique case: if the special master hearing fails to produce an agreement, the dispute is settled directly by the appropriate legislative body (e.g., city council, state legislature, school board).

C. Arbitration

Arbitration, in any of its various permutations, is the most controversial impasse resolution procedure short of the strike. Like fact finding, arbitration involves a formal quasi-judicial setting in which each party presents evidence supporting its position to a single neutral or a multi-member board. The major difference is that the arbitrator's report, in most cases, is final and binding on the parties. Thus, arbitration is intended to serve as a direct alternative to the strike and to unilateral employer decision making. Ideally, it results in a fair settlement for the parties while protecting the public interest. (In this chapter our focus is on interest arbitration, which is concerned with formulating a new contract. In Chapter 10, grievance arbitration is discussed; its purpose is to determine the rights and claims of the respective parties under an existing contract.)

Although the practice of arbitration has ancient historical roots, arbitration in public employment is of fairly recent vintage, having been first established in federal employment with binding arbitration provisions for postal workers under the Postal Reorganization Act of 1970. State governments began enacting public sector arbitration provisions in 1965, starting with Wyoming and Maine.

The arbitrator's decision under some impasse situations is advisory; the parties do not have to accept it as final. This strategy, however, is rare in the public sector and generally out of favor because it is a distinction without a difference from fact finding with recommendations. In the great majority of jurisdictions, arbitration (usually following mediation, fact finding, or both) is binding and final.

Arbitration may be voluntary or compulsory. In the former, the parties jointly agree to settle an impasse through arbitration (often before an impasse even occurs). In the latter, binding arbitration is mandated by statute or by an administrative agency, usually after mediation and/or fact finding have been exhausted. Generally speaking, both management and labor prefer voluntary arbitration, although police and firefighter organizations have been supportive of the compulsory form.

Finally, arbitration may be conventional or final offer. Conventional arbitration is the traditional approach in which the decision-making authority of the neutral is unfettered. He or she may accept one party's last offer or, as is often the case, "split the difference" between the final positions. Final offer requires the arbitrator to select the last best offer of one of the parties as the final terms for settlement; no compromising is permitted. Final offer arbitration may be by package, in which the neutral must select the last best offer of one party or the other in its entirety, or by issue, where the items under impasse are decided on separately by the arbitrator.

At least six states provide for compulsory tripartite arbitration, with each party designating a neutral and the third neutral chosen by the parties' designees or by an administrative agency. Most states, however, make single or tripartite arbitration optional to the parties. In many cases they select a single arbitrator because it is less expensive and time consuming.

The first arbitration statutes were enacted for public safety personnel on the grounds that strikes by police and firefighters could not be tolerated, so some alternative to the strike should be offered. Many states continue to restrict arbitration to public safety services; others have extended the technique to nonprotective service personnel in state and local government.

1. The Arbitration Process

Arbitration involves the following steps: selection of one or more arbitrators, formal hearings with the presentation of evidence (but arbitrators are not bound by the formal rules of evidence that prevail in the courtroom), and a final written decision by the arbitrator.

a. Arbitrator Selection

When a single arbitrator is to rule in a given case, he may be selected by the parties or appointed by a state agency, state court, or independent arbitration agency. (Note that the masculine gender is used here. Arbitration remains a white male–dominated field, although women and minorities are gradually making progress in gaining spots on the rosters.) Careful screening of candidates is necessary to ensure that the selected neutral (1) will evidence no bias towards either party, (2) is cognizant of procedural due process requirements, (3) is experienced, (4) is timely in making decisions, (5) will write clear, unambiguous awards, and (6) will be knowledgeable of any special circumstances surrounding the impasse or its governmental context (Ver Ploeg 1988).

If a tripartite arbitration structure is used, a different situation prevails. Arbitrators selected by the individual parties to take two of the three panel seats typically act as unabashed advocates for their appointing party (Kochan et al. 1979). Therefore, bargaining carries over into tripartite arbitration, with the independent neutral attempting to develop an award acceptable to the other two arbitrators. Evidence of this process is presented by Kochan et al. (1979), who found that about 60 percent of the arbitration awards they examined in New York were unanimous rulings, indicating a compromise settlement was fashioned by the independent neutral.

Labor and management negotiators usually do their homework before arbitrator selection takes place. Names and arbitration history are checked out with colleagues in other jurisdictions. Prior decisions may be read and tallies done on employer–union win/loss records under various arbitrators. Union and industry research departments may be asked for information, Internet searches are run, and law firms may be retained to assess credentials. Some private firms "keep score" and sell their opinions on prospective arbitrators to interested parties. The "overriding goal is (to) select an arbitrator who will maximize [the party's] chance of winning" (Nelson 1986: 703–704).

Interestingly, the disputants do not normally consider fact finders to be acceptable as arbitrators, although arbitrators are usually accepted as fact finders (Dilts 1984; Elsea, Dilts, and Haber 1990). Perhaps this is attributable to the superior training and experience of most arbitrators. Also, some "rights" or grievance arbitrators refuse to work as interest arbitrators. The reasons vary: the pressure cooker and fishbowl environment of interest arbitration; the greater risk to an arbitrator's professional reputation (and monetary income) from a highly visible, interest impasse decision; or a dislike of final offer arbitration (Helburn and Rodgers 1985; Vest, O'Brien, and Vest 1990).

b. Decision-Making Criteria

Most arbitration statutes specify certain criteria that the arbitrators must consider in rendering their decisions. The criteria in some states are rather broad, such as requiring that "equity" and the "public interest" be considered. Other states are more specific. In Massachusetts, for example, the panel must consider ability to pay; comparable wages, hours, and working conditions; cost of living; long- and short-term debt; average property tax burden; and other specific factors (Turpin 1997).

The use of comparative data such as salary and benefit information from similar categories of workers in neighboring jurisdictions or in the private sector plays a very important role in some arbitrators' decision making (Turpin 1998). Inflation and cost-of-living factors are also salient, along with the employer's ability to pay (Bazerman 1985; Bazerman and Farber 1985; Feuille and Schwochau 1988). Typically, however, arbitrators focus narrowly on the immediate bargaining context and "anchor" their judgments to the terms of the previous contract in order to maintain stability in the relationships between the parties. Often this means splitting the difference between final positions, in the case of conventional arbitration, or selecting the most "moderate" last offer when final offer arbitration is used. One specific result is that existing salary structures and relationships are maintained with incremental, percentage-based adjustments (Dell'Omo 1989), yet another illustration of the power of incremental decision making. The predictability of arbitration outcomes led Bloom (1988: 123) to suggest that this process "could probably be accomplished more inexpensively by averaging the parties' final offers and adding on some noise using a computer's random number generator."

But arbitrators vary greatly in the weight they place on various decision criteria (Dell'Omo 1990). Ability to pay offers a good case in point. It is up to the employer to marshal the strongest possible arguments for inability to pay what the union is asking, using revenue and expenditure projections, accounting data, debt levels, and other relevant information, such as a credible listing of potential service and program cutbacks or cancellations. The employer's case may be persuasive to some arbitrators. Others, however, translate inability to pay into unwillingness to pay. If the city or state must hike taxes or fees to comply with the arbitrator's compensation decision, then so be it (Dell'Omo 1989: 11). In all fairness, arbitrator vacillation and uncertainty in applying the ability-to-pay principle is encouraged by ambiguity and the lack of statutory specificity as to which factors should be considered and how they should be weighted. For example, does inability to pay mean that statutory or constitutional spending limitations would have to be breached? That no additional funds could possibly be transferred into salaries? That services could not be maintained at current levels without hiking taxes or fees to meet union demands?

Generally speaking, arbitrators, like fact finders, must be concerned with the fairness of their award and its acceptability to each party. The importance of acceptability is illustrated by the continuation of negotiations and, in some cases, mediation during the arbitration process (see "med-arb," below). For example, Gerhart and Drotning (1980) showed that in Michigan the majority of arbitration cases are settled before the arbitrator issues an award. The neutrals frequently "caucus with the parties privately and give them clues, sometimes subtle and sometimes not so subtle, concerning what the arbitrators are likely to consider the 'more reasonable' position." The arbitrator's concern for fairness means that in states where arbitration is preceded by fact finding, the process often amounts to a "show cause" hearing as to why the fact finder's recommendations should not be imposed by the arbitrator (Holden 1976).

What happens when a final binding award is rendered and one or both parties refuse to accept it? At least ten states provide appellate rights through the courts to ensure due process and a reasonable award. As a general principle, arbitration appeals are strongly discouraged so that they do not become a normal part of impasse resolution; they can be costly, time consuming, and anathema to free collective bargaining (Kochan et al. 1979: 133). Yet, an appellate path must be provided to correct instances of injustice or illegality.

Typically, arbitration decisions may be appealed if obtained by fraud, legal error, or collusion. In New York and Michigan, an appeal may be filed if the decision is not supported by substantial evidence. In Pennsylvania and Ohio, if the decision involves institutional questions or if the arbitrator exceeds his or her authorized powers, the appellate route may be taken. Other states provide for appeals through an administrative body or the legislature.

An unusual statute that served as a compelling example of the need for finality in arbitration was the 1971 Oklahoma Firefighters' and Policemen's Arbitration Act, which provided that rulings by an arbitration panel were binding on the union (if the municipality also accepted the decision), but that the city was not bound to abide by the arbitrators' award. When, in 1975, the Oklahoma City Police Department and Oklahoma City went to arbitration over the size of a wage increase, the city refused to accept the decision of the panel, which had supported the union's position. The police instituted a work slowdown, to no effect, and then marched into the city manager's office en masse to turn in their badges. The strike ended 3 days later when the city made a compromise wage offer (Greer 1978). The law was amended in 2005 to require final offer arbitration. But in another awkard Oklahoma two-step, if a city's offer is not selected by the arbitration board, the city may submit both final offers to the voters in a special election.

Clearly, for arbitration to serve successfully as an alternative to the strike, the arbitrators' decisions must be final and binding on both parties and each must fully accept the process as a legitimate means for resolving interest disputes. For arbitration to function in a meaningful fashion, only the legislative body or, in extraordinary circumstances, the courts or the voters should be able to alter arbitrators' awards. Although arbitration issues are frequently brought into the judicial process, the courts have almost universally adopted the assumption of arbitrability prevalent in the private sector, which recognizes the superiority of the arbitrator's expertise over that of the judge (Jascourt 1979: 159–165).

2. Advantages and Disadvantages of Arbitration

The major advantage of arbitration as compared to mediation and fact finding is that it supplies a balanced measure of finality to impasses. In mediation and fact finding, the employer enjoys more discretion and bargaining power than the union, as long as the strike is illegal or infeasible. With arbitration, the interests of the parties are balanced while an end to the impasse is finalized, avoiding a strike and its accompanying service disruptions. Research indicates that arbitration has, indeed, been more successful in preventing strikes than statutory strike prohibitions alone (Lipsky and Katz 2006; Ichniowski 1982; Gunderson, Hebdon, and Hyatt 1996), although it has not completely eliminated them. Of course, as long as there are public employers and workers, the strike threat can never be totally exterminated no matter what strategy is used. Nonetheless, the tendency of arbitration to settle most public sector impasses short of the strike contributes to rational budget making, the continuous provision of public services, and, in a broader sense, social and political stability.

But to say that the use of arbitration in public sector labor disputes is controversial is to understate the case greatly. The major complaints against arbitration are that (1) it constitutes an illegal delegation of authority to persons not held responsible through democratic processes, (2) it tends to distort settlements and redistribute resources in favor of the unions, and (3) it destroys or chills free collective bargaining. Each criticism is discussed below.

a. Illegal Delegation of Authority

It has been asserted that arbitration constitutes an illegal delegation of authority to persons who, though not responsive or accountable to the electorate, are charged with making decisions on the expenditure of public monies and other important issues related to the provision of public services. Thus, it is claimed that arbitration is inimical to the operation of representative government and democracy because the accountability of elected executive and legislative officials is sacrificed to an arbitration decision on public issues. Clearly, there is no direct link between an arbitrator and the electorate. He or she is at least four levels removed from the electorate if appointed by an administrative agency such as a state PERB. When an arbitrator is provided by a nongovernmental entity, such as the American Arbitration Association, there is scarcely even an indirect link to the citizenry. Such fractures in governmental accountability through the delegation of decision-making authority to private sector entities have been the subject of extensive debate in the literature of political science for many years (see Lowi 1979). In the specific case of public sector arbitration and the delegation of authority, the state courts are the final arbiters on questions of law and arbitrability.

Early judicial decisions were nearly unanimous in declaring arbitration illegal. Arbitration was rejected as early as 1873 by the Illinois Supreme Court and thereafter by attorneys general and courts in Maryland, Ohio, Indiana, Florida, and Minnesota (Spero and Capozzola 1973: 289–290). Along with the allegation of illegal delegation of legislative authority, the principal grounds for court challenge have been that the arbitration statute does not sufficiently limit an arbitrator's discretion, that it unconstitutionally delegates taxation authority, and that the selection of arbitrators violates the principle of "one person, one vote" (Grodin 1979: 242).

Arbitration has been ruled unconstitutional or illegal by courts in five states: South Dakota, Colorado, Utah, Nebraska, and Maryland. The constitutional issue of illegal delegation of authority was the basis for rejection of arbitration in Colorado and Utah. In South Dakota and Maryland, arbitration was prohibited because of the presence of "ripper clauses" in the state constitution that forbid legislative delegation of the municipal fiscal and service provision functions to a private entity (Grodin 1979: 242–243).

These rulings, however, are in the minority; at least 16 state courts have upheld statutes providing for compulsory arbitration. One of the most frequently cited rulings is the Michigan case of *Dearborn Firefighters Local 412 v. City of Dearborn* (1975), in which a divided state supreme court held that a compulsory arbitration statute did not divest home-rule cities of constitutionally granted powers nor, despite the presence of a ripper clause, did it cause an illegal delegation of power to private persons or a surrender of the power of the city to impose taxes. As a general rule, the state courts have upheld compulsory arbitration when they have "found that there is a public interest in preventing strikes, that illegal delegation does not occur when there are statutory provisions of explicit standards and guidelines for arbitrators and procedural safeguards in the form of court review, and that the power to tax has not been transferred in that an arbitration act is regulatory, and does not in itself impose a burden or charge" (Schneider 1988: 206).

Among the actions that legislative bodies can take to make arbitration more amenable in a democracy are to specify in the arbitration statute restrictions on the scope of the arbitrator's authority, limitations on the statute's coverage, and strict decision-making criteria (Feuille 1979: 72). In addition, arbitrators can be compelled to set forth the basis of their findings publicly. And, in the final analysis, the legislature retains the power to override arbitration decisions or to terminate arbitration or any other delegation of legislative power (*Carofano v. City of Bridgeport* 1985). Still, the legal issues surrounding arbitration can be murky. The Ohio Supreme Court struck down the binding arbitration provision in 1988, only to reconsider and uphold it a year later.

b. Arbitration Favors Unions

Ideally, arbitrators should balance the interests of both parties in arriving at the terms of a settlement. Although this certainly is what the arbitrator intends, he or she must contend with competing contradictory values in reaching a decision, particularly the tradeoffs involved with assuring comparable wages, benefits, and working conditions and, on the other hand, protecting the taxpayer from excessive government personnel costs. If such a balance can be attained, then, over time, neither party should benefit from arbitration more than the other.

However, public sector managers widely believe that the interest arbitration deck is stacked against them and in favor of the unions. During state legislative debates in the 1970s and 1980s on proposed arbitration laws, the fervor of union support for the process as a substitute for strikes was exceeded only by that of public managers' opposition. Management resentment and dissatisfaction with arbitration and, in truth, all other third-party procedures except, perhaps, mediation linger. When an unfavorable arbitration award is rendered, employers complain loudly that the decision gives short shrift to the impacts of the decision on taxpayers and the financial health of the jurisdiction.

Has compulsory interest arbitration been a windfall for unions, as management and many public officials believe? The empirical evidence indicates that it has not. Although some studies have found that wage rates are slightly higher in jurisdictions permitting arbitration, the effects are not statistically significant. However, it does appear that the *availability* of arbitration has a significant positive impact on salaries and benefits. This relationship has been associated with police, firefighter, and teacher arbitration (Zigarelli 1996; Feuille and Delaney 1986). Why?

For one thing, the unions have an equal opportunity to submit supporting data to a true neutral whom they have helped select. And from a practical standpoint, the arbitrator must be very careful to render a "fair" compensation decision if he or she wants to work in the same capacity again in another jurisdiction. Word gets around quickly when an arbitration settlement is perceived to be inequitable. Management is aware of these tendencies and consequently may be more likely to settle a contract on terms more favorable to the union than if arbitration were not the next step. The union, of course, will not hesitate to opt for arbitration when management takes a hard position viewed by the union to be against the interests of its membership. Hence, using arbitration is less important to union pay and benefit gains than having the legal authority and potential to use it.

A related impact of arbitration is on the distribution of salaries. Generally, arbitration tends to exert a leveling effect by enhancing the economic status of bargaining units that have lagged in pay gains for their members (Feuille, Delaney, and Hendricks 1985). The availability, and at least occasional use, of compulsory arbitration helps units at the low end of the pay scale catch up with similar units through arbitrators' emphasis on the comparability criterion (Bazerman 1985; Feuille and Schwochau 1988).

It must be noted that arbitration procedures established through state legislation can be amended to tilt the scales in the direction of management. At least three states have restricted terms of settlements and interest arbitration decisions by imposing fiscal considerations, subject to legislative review (Pennsylvania, New Jersey, Wisconsin). Connecticut's arbitration laws for state agencies and municipalities assumed a high profile during the early 1990s, as employers lodged complaints that arbitration rulings were financially crippling them. The state senate responded by rejecting more than 12 contracts that had been decided by arbitrators. The legislature also amended the municipal arbitration law to permit local governments to appeal arbitrator decisions to a second arbitration panel, which may revoke the decision of the first panel (Keating 1994).

c. Arbitration Chills Collective Bargaining

The argument that arbitration destroys free collective bargaining is grounded in certain related assumptions. First, it is claimed that the presence of a credible strike threat forces the parties into a compromise. Where arbitration substitutes for the strike there is less incentive for timely settlement; the bargaining process is chilled. Second, it is said that availability of arbitration leads to its use as a crutch, particularly by the weaker party in a bargaining relationship. Arbitration thus exercises a "narcotic effect": the parties become addicted to its use rather than settling disputes.

The chilling effect argument goes as follows: if one party thinks that it will get a better deal from the arbitrator than from a negotiated agreement, that party thus has an incentive to go to arbitration. Evidence of the chilling effect is found in several studies. In the early Pennsylvania bargaining experience, some 30 percent of police and firefighter disputes went to arbitration, whereas in Wisconsin the incidence of usage was about 15 percent (Rehmus 1975). Other indications of the chilling effect are found in Minnesota from 1973 to 1980. In negotiations involving essential services, which are denied the right to strike, 30 percent of those going to mediation ended in arbitration versus only 9 percent for nonessential services (which are permitted to strike) (Champlin and Bognanno 1985).

The narcotic effect has also been verified by researchers (Bolton and Katok 1998). For example, Kochan et al. (1979) and Lipsky and Drotning (1977) reported evidence of a narcotic effect in New York. Further evidence of the parties becoming habituated to third-party impasse procedures was found for municipal workers in Pennsylvania (Loewenberg and Klinetop 1992) and Ohio (Graham and Perry 1993). Apparently the "new toy" of arbitration is tried out by the parties to see what transpires and, as sometimes happens in the case of hard drugs, the users eventually become addicted.

Stronger indications of the narcotic effect were reported by Kochan and Baderschneider (1978, 1981) for police and firefighters in New York State between 1968 and 1976. During this period, 85 percent of the firefighter bargaining units and more than 90 percent of the police units went to impasse at least once, with the total percentage of units going to impasse increasing steadily from 41 percent in the early part of the period to 65 percent by the latter part. Moreover, 80 percent of those units reaching impasse in the first and second rounds of contract negotiations during this period also went to impasse in the third (Kochan and Baderschneider 1981: 438).

However, different methods of analysis and quantitative techniques have yielded disparate results, indicating that positive narcotic effects characterize the early experience with impasse procedures, followed by stabilization and even negative effects ("rejection") as the parties become dissatisfied with third-party intervention (Lewin 1985; Butler and Ehrenberg 1981; Chelius and Extejt 1985).

Even if, as seems likely, arbitration exerts a modest chilling effect on negotiations, it stretches the point to argue that this constitutes the demise of free collective bargaining. A large majority of settlements continue to be negotiated without arbitration. Even when arbitration is invoked, it frequently serves as a forum for continuing negotiations. And, as discussed below, final offer arbitration reduces the chilling and narcotic effects, helping collective bargaining remain a viable process.

D. Final Offer Arbitration

Final offer arbitration, like conventional arbitration, does not escape the criticism of delegating authority to private individuals who are not responsible to the electorate. However, final offer arbitration is intended to allay concern that arbitration exerts chilling and narcotic effects on free collective bargaining. Presently in use in 15 states and several local governments in some form for one or more employee groups (but most often for police and firefighters), final offer arbitration was first tried by Eugene, Oregon, in 1971. Wisconsin and Michigan adopted it as an impasse strategy in 1972. The final offer may be decided by package, as in Nevada, or by issue, as in Ohio. Among others, New Jersey allows a package final offer for unresolved economic items and issue-by-issue presentation for noneconomic questions.

Regardless of specific form, final offer requires the arbitrator or panel to choose the final proposal of either management or the union. (In some "tri-offer" jurisdictions, the fact finder's conclusions may be substituted for the parties' last offers.) Major objectives of final offer are to increase the risks of not settling and to encourage a narrowing of the differences between the parties. Conventional arbitration has been faulted for chilling the bargaining relationship by tacitly encouraging the parties to assume extreme positions in the hope that the neutral will "split the difference." Under final offer, the most reasonable position normally prevails — no compromise by the arbitrator is permitted.

States that provide package final offer operate under the assumption that the parties will have an incentive to settle out of a fear that even one issue position perceived to be extreme by the arbitrator will result in rejection of the entire last offer and "sudden death." Under final offer by issue, the arbitrator has greater flexibility in settling the impasse. In addition, selection by issue helps preclude a Hobson's choice involving two unreasonable final offer packages.

The two strategies do appear to have divergent effects. Although the evidence is somewhat mixed, there are indications that final offer by package creates a greater level of uncertainty than final offer by issue, thereby providing greater encouragement for the parties to settle (Farber 1980). Using an experimental design under laboratory conditions, Subbarao (1978) found that package selection maximizes pressure on the parties and "generates genuine bargaining," but issue selection "subverts free negotiations" and "may have the same 'narcotic effect' as that of conventional arbitration."

The evidence with regard to the narcotic effect is not entirely clear in comparing final offer arbitration of either the package or issue variety with conventional arbitration. After examining a number of empirical studies, Feuille (1975 p. 302) concluded that "Final-offer arbitration procedures appear to do a somewhat better job of producing negotiated agreements than do conventional arbitration procedures," although in some instances this may be attributable to differences in bargaining climate and bargaining histories in the respective conventional and final offer states rather than to differences in impasse law and procedures (Kochan et al. 1979). Meaningful comparison is further confused because the actual practice of final offer arbitration often diverges from what is stipulated in legislation. For instance, during the final offer hearing, "final" offers may be changed between the hearing's opening and closing by one or both parties; a whole series of "final" offers sometimes are proffered. Such practices are often encouraged by arbitrators who, in effect, are acting as mediators to promote voluntary settlement. In some jurisdictions this process is institutionalized in the form of "med-arb," which is discussed below.

In addition to using final offer by issue, some states distinguish between economic and nonmonetary issues, with final offer on the former and conventional arbitration on the latter. Iowa and Massachusetts permit final offers to be selected from either the last offers of the parties or the fact finder's recommendations.

Finally, several exotic arbitration processes have developed in the private sector that may find use in government. In *high–low arbitration* (aka *bracketed arbitration*) the parties agree in advance to the high and low parameters for the award. If the arbitrator, who is kept in the dark on these parameters or brackets, makes an award in between the high and low figures, that award stands. If the award is lower than the low bracket, the agreed-upon low figure is paid, and vice versa for a high award.

Night baseball arbitration features an exchange of offers by the parties. The arbitrator, operating behind a veil of ignorance concerning the offers, enters the proceedings and makes an award and the parties must accept the last offer closest to the arbitrator's decision. In a variant of the process, final offers are sealed and compared to a nonbinding arbitration decision. The arbitrator then selects the final offer that is closest to his opinion.

E. Other Impasse Resolution Procedures

1. Med-Arb

Med-arb combines the mediation and arbitration functions in a single third party. If mediation fails to produce a settlement, the same neutral has the authority to render a binding decision through arbitration. This technique, "mediation with a club," is intended to provide a strong incentive for voluntary settlement by the parties during the mediation stage by keeping the demands of the parties reasonable. If extreme positions are taken by a party, the med-arbitrator is likely to rule against that party during arbitration. As an alternative to the strike or conventional arbitration, med-arb has the added advantage of the arbitrator's intimate familiarity with the issues gained during the mediation stage. The arbitration award, if it becomes necessary, is likely to be firmly grounded in the facts and circumstances surrounding the dispute and thus acceptable to the parties.

Med-arb has not been widely adopted throughout the United States, which perhaps is explained by the fact that neutrals well trained and experienced in both mediation and arbitration are hard to find. However, the U.S. Postal Service utilized med-arb successfully in resolving an impasse involving 600,000 postal employees in 1978. The procedure was suggested by the FMCS and accepted by both parties in a dispute involving layoffs and the size of future wage increases. The issues finally were resolved through an arbitration award issued by the med-arbitrator.

Other formal experience with med-arb has been in Wisconsin, where the technique has been used for municipal and school district employees, and Ohio and New Jersey, where bargaining laws authorize mediation during arbitration. Under the Wisconsin statute, if a dispute remains unresolved after mediation, the mediator–arbitrator, after an appropriate period of time has expired, must attempt arbitration. The med-arbitrator solicits offers from each party, which may be changed after reading the other party's offer. Offers are exchanged as long as each interaction generates a response from the other party. When progress toward settlement ends, the med-arbitrator assumes the role of final offer arbitrator. The Wisconsin law is intended to seduce the parties into drawing ever closer together until a voluntary compromise has been attained and a mandatory arbitration award avoided.

Results indicate that med-arb has experienced some success in settling impasses prior to arbitration and in discouraging strikes (Lester 1984). If a dispute does move to arbitration, the mediator should have good information on the nature of the dispute and might be able to quickly broker a voluntary agreement. A problem is that the specter of arbitration — and the fear of disclosures — may hinder discussions with the mediator.

2. Arb-Med

Arb-med may be thought of as the reverse of med-arb. The neutral first makes a final arbitration decision on the dispute but does not communicate it to the parties. Mediation then commences with the goal of a voluntary settlement. If one is not produced, then the arbitration decision is announced. The greatest strength of this approach is that it motivates disputants to settle by themselves (Ross 2000). Research indicates that arb-med enjoys a higher success rate than straight mediation, chiefly due to lower expectations that encourage cooperation (Ross and Conlon 2000). Moreover, arb-med tends to move along more expeditiously than med-arb (Conlon, Moon, and Ng 2002).

3. Labor–Management Committees

A labor–management committee is a group of management and labor appointees within an agency or workplace who have agreed to work cooperatively to discuss and resolve workplace issues of concern. They may be authorized by law or collective bargaining contract. The committee may address any matter of mutual concern, but they cannot overturn or contradict any term or provision in the existing contract.

Massachusetts was the first state to experiment with labor–management committees as an impasse resolution strategy in 1978. A breakdown in good faith bargaining in municipal government had occurred, primarily over the issue of how to settle impasses. Former Secretary of Labor John Dunlop, a professor at Harvard University who had experience with establishing labor–management committees in industry, suggested that Massachusetts create its own committee for the resolution of labor disputes (Midwest Center for Public Sector Labor Relations 1979). Shortly thereafter, the Massachusetts Labor–Management Committee for Municipal Police and Fire was incorporated into legislation.

The Massachusetts Joint Committee has statutory authority to invoke jurisdiction over any police or firefighter negotiations either before or during impasse. (If intervention by the committee does not take place, then disputes are settled through final offer arbitration.) The committee enters disputes upon the request of one or both parties. Its job is to confer with the parties and encourage voluntary settlement. If these mediative efforts fail, the committee may invoke binding arbitration in any form it desires. Reports of the Massachusetts experience indicate that it has been a success, with only a small proportion of cases going to arbitration (www.mass.gov/jlmc/arbitration.htm, accessed January 2, 2008).

Alaska, Indiana, Pennsylvania, New York, New Jersey, Oregon and other collective bargaining states have also reported success with labor–management committees, particularly in improving occupational health and safety conditions. Further discussion of labor–management committees is found in Chapter 10.

4. Referenda — Letting the Taxpayers Decide

Strong strains of direct democracy have played on the political heartstrings of many Americans since the earliest European coastal settlements developed independently along the Atlantic. The concept of direct democracy has even been applied to dispute settlement in public employment. When in doubt, some argue, it is best to let the people decide through a vote.

One of the first to interject this line of thought into labor–management conflicts was Sam Zagoria (1973), who suggested granting either party the right to take a contested issue to the public through placing the fact finder's recommendations on a ballot and making the terms of the voters' choice retroactive. Until the people made their decision, issues mutually resolved between the parties could be implemented immediately (Zagoria 1973) or the parties could remain under the terms of the old contract (Foegen 1974). Thus, a strike would be skirted and those who ultimately have to foot the bill for labor settlements, tax-paying citizens, would render a final judgment. Further advantage would accrue, at least in theory, from democratically involving the public in determining what is in its own "interest."

Public referenda have been used to settle limited collective bargaining issues since at least 1947 in Texas, when police and firefighter organizations tried to win increased wages, shorter working hours, pay parity, and changes in civil service laws (Helburn and Matthews 1980). Anti-union charter referenda have been held in a number of California cities. For example, a 1985 San Francisco referendum rescinded comparable worth-based pay increases that had been won in collective bargaining. Oklahoma police and firefighters must take an impasse to randomly selected city council members, who select from the parties' final offers. If one or both parties still refuse to accept the outcome, the dispute goes to the whole council.

Several cities in Colorado are among the few jurisdictions that legislatively provide for impasse resolution through public referendum. An ordinance in Lakewood, for example, requires that interest disputes proceeding without settlement through mediation and fact finding be submitted to the voters if the fact finder's recommendations are rejected by either party. It is the rejecting party's position that is placed in the ballot. In Denver, the positions of both parties may be considered by the voting public if each rejects the fact finder's recommendations. The costs of the election (which are substantial) are paid by the rejecting party or shared by both if neither accepts the recommendations.

On the face of it, resolving bargaining impasses through referendum may sound like an excellent idea. The uncertainty, or outright fear, of public involvement at the ballot box should provide a strong incentive for voluntary settlement. It imposes political accountability on a process often criticized for lacking it. Paying for the referendum represents a measure of economic hardship to the parties, who must also lay out money for campaign expenses (see Hogler and Thompson 1985).

There are some important disadvantages, however. First of all, as any person with survey research experience will attest, it is very difficult to reduce complex issues to simple terms. The problem is patently evident when a referendum is held on any issue. Second, the process assumes that voters will educate themselves on the relevant issues and make an intelligent choice — a risky assumption at best. Third, excessive delays ensue while the election machinery is programmed, ballots prepared, polling places organized, and so on, complicating the budgetary process (although one might point out also the long duration of many other impasse resolution procedures, particularly arbitration). Fourth, excessive politicization of collective bargaining issues can lead to rigid, uncompromising postures by the major parties and harmful outcomes. Fifth, voters are highly unlikely to approve any wage or fringe benefit increase that can lead to higher taxes. This potentially biases the process against the union position. It is little wonder that public employee unions have fought hard to keep off the ballot proposed referenda that could adversely affect them.

5. The Unfair Labor Practice

Another impasse resolution alternative is the unfair labor practice (ULP). The ULP process can be used to resolve issues such as scope of bargaining and complaints concerning the failure to bargain in good faith. In New York State, the PERB rules on ULPs unless it can assist the parties to agree voluntarily. Most of the ULP cases never reach a formal hearing, being resolved successfully beforehand (Riccucci and Ban 1989).

V. The Search for Flexibility

Each interest dispute is different. Given any particular set of circumstances, one or a variety of settlement approaches may be appropriate. As with most everything else, there is no "one best way." When public policy deems the strike unacceptable as a means of settling labor disputes, alternatives to the strike are necessary. Generally, the states have developed approaches that permit more than one impasse resolution procedure. The norm is mediation and/or fact finding followed by compulsory binding arbitration, either conventional or final offer. The exact dispute resolution package varies for different occupational groups, with arbitration often available only to public safety personnel.

One of the most flexible approaches to impasse resolution is found in the Iowa statute. Even before collective bargaining begins, the two parties themselves are required to reach agreement on which dispute resolution procedure will be used in the event of an impasse (a strategy borrowed from the Canadian labor relations experience). If the parties are unable to arrive at a procedural agreement, then statutory impasse procedures will be invoked. Fact finding is required after 10 days of nonproductive mediation (except for teachers, who go directly to arbitration). The fact finder's recommendations are made public if a settlement is not achieved 10 days after the report is first issued. If a settlement continues to prove elusive, the Iowa PERB may impose final offer arbitration by a tripartite or single arbitrator on those issues remaining unsettled. The arbitrator may select from the final offers or the fact finder's report. The timetable for all procedures is coordinated with the jurisdiction's final budget submission date.

Early assessments of the Iowa multi-step procedure were positive (Gallagher and Pegnetter 1979; Gilroy and Lipovac 1977). The parties have made creative use of their right to modify dispute resolution procedures as they wish: time limits have been altered, fact finding has been eliminated as a required step, and the issue-by-issue final offer arbitration stage sometimes has been changed to a package form. Most important, however, is the indication that the Iowa procedures have been successful in holding down the number of disputes going to arbitration or to a strike, thereby encouraging the parties to settle voluntarily.

Other states also have taken a "laundry list" approach to impasse resolution, permitting the parties in dispute to select between final offer arbitration and the strike (Wisconsin) and between assorted arbitration strategies (New Jersey). The police and firefighter statute in New Jersey includes the options of final offer by issue or by package, conventional arbitration, or final offer for some issues and conventional arbitration for others.

Clearly, the state and local governments are serving well in their traditional roles as political laboratories. In developing procedures to resolve interest disputes, the states and localities provide strong evidence of the need to adapt procedures to circumstances. In this sense public sector impasse resolution strategies illustrate the ends (an acceptable bargaining settlement) justifying the means (mediation/fact finding/arbitration, etc.).

No one is more aware of the ends justifying the means than the neutrals themselves. It is not unusual for neutrals to exceed their statutory authority in the quest for a voluntary settlement. As noted above, arbitrators frequently serve a mediative function even in the absence of a med-arb or arb-med provision. In fact, mediation may continue throughout fact finding and arbitration, culminating in a voluntary settlement just before the arbitrator's award. Gradually, distinctions among the various dispute resolution processes have become blurred, as mediation often goes on during, and occasionally even after, fact finding and arbitration.

This supports arguments for combining mediation and fact finding in a single neutral and suggests some potential benefits from conducting fact finding before mediation. If the parties know that fact finding can be followed by mediation through the same person, they should be less apt to hold back information from the neutral; voluntary settlement is encouraged once most of the relevant data have been placed on the table.

Finally, a tripartite arbitration or fact-finding panel composed of a neutral and representatives from each party should be recognized for what it is in reality — mediation at a higher level. In sum, those who argue against permitting mediation during other impasse resolution processes are missing the point: the ultimate goal is a final acceptable settlement that avoids the strike. The means to resolution of the dispute are not as important as the voluntary settlement itself. And flexibility, not ill-founded rigidity, is the key.

VI. Uncertainty: Benefit or Bane?

The conventional wisdom in impasse resolution holds that there is a direct relationship between uncertainty and the likelihood of voluntary settlement. Thus, impasse procedures should create an ocean of insecurity and misgivings so that the parties will be forced to swim to an island of compromise. Arbitration supposedly fulfills this intent, because the parties can never be certain which side will be disadvantaged by the neutral's decision. As noted, however, there is a marked tendency for arbitrators to split the difference between the opposing offers, thus establishing some boundaries within which it normally can be assumed the award will fall. Final offer arbitration, its supporters claim, creates much greater levels of uncertainty through the mandate of an all-or-nothing choice; better for the risk-averse party to compromise than face losing everything.

However, some doubt can be cast upon the conventional assumption regarding uncertainty and propensity to settle (Gerhart and Drotning 1980). Certainly there are some significant costs to both unions and management when an impasse drags on. Union members may sacrifice wages and benefits and the union itself must pay certain monetary costs, including attorney fees and at least part of the fees and expenses for neutrals. Management absorbs costs of attorneys and neutrals also, along with certain political debits as the result of citizen unhappiness if services are disrupted. However, it should not be forgotten that in the event of a work stoppage, management may benefit financially from foregoing wage and benefit payments and politically from "hanging tough" with the union.

Gerhart and Drotning (1980) claimed that when each party feels reasonably certain in its predictions of the costs and benefits of impasse for itself and for the other party, a settlement is highly likely. Uncertainty over the relative costs and benefits of impasse encourages the parties to delay settlement. This hypothesis received support from Farber (1980), whose model of the final offer arbitration process indicates that final offers tend to diverge greatly when uncertainty is high. Knowledge, or at least apparent knowledge, of the respective costs and benefits helps bring the parties to a compromise.

This perspective is intuitive if one considers the nature of the collective bargaining process itself. For example, if both parties are cognizant of the other's bottom line on a disputed issue, then the basis for compromise is readily apparent. To carry the example a step further, a city may truly have an inability to pay a wage increase greater than 6 percent; that is the bottom line. The union's bottom line may be a 4 percent wage increase. Grounds for settlement are readily apparent to both parties if knowledge exists of the respective "unyielding" positions. Of course, the real world of labor relations is not so simple, and knowledge of true bargaining positions is not so easy to gain.

VII. Conclusion: The Benefits of Impasse Procedures

As indicated in the previous chapter, 16 states now permit strikes through statute, state supreme court decision, or de facto procedures for one or more groups of employees. This would not be so if third-party procedures were always success-ful in practice and presented no problems for accountability and representative democracy. A number of troublesome aspects that accompany the use of various impasse procedures have been discussed, including the lack of finality, the chilling and narcotic effects, the delegation of public decision-making authority to parties not accountable to the electorate, and claims by public managers that arbitration awards tend to favor the union's point of view. In addition, third-party procedures can be time consuming and expensive (although a requirement that the parties share expenses or that the losing party pay all costs of the neutral helps overcome this objection).

It is usually in the interests of the parties to settle as soon as possible, so that union members can begin receiving any new pay and benefits and the government employer can finalize the budget and prepare for new compensation arrangements. Time delays as a result of impasse procedures can be enervating. The period from impasse declaration to award may be several months or even a year. In New York, "In many cases, an agreement that the arbitrators were still deciding had (itself) expired, and it was time to renegotiate another contract" (Kochan et al. 1979: 154).

Third-party procedures (particularly arbitration) have clearly been abused in some jurisdictions by the unions. Unions that are small in membership, lacking in political resources, or laboring under other limitations vis-à-vis management may look upon impasse procedures as a means of gaining something not avail-able at the bargaining table. Based on her research in New York City, McCormick (1979) concluded that interest arbitration did not function as a strike substitute for small, less powerful, "nonessential" unions. Rather, arbitration was invoked more than 90 percent of the time by bargaining units that were too weak to mount a meaningful strike. McCormick attributes three different roles to arbitration: (1) providing a forum for less powerful groups to plead for parity arrangements with stronger unions; (2) facilitating intraorganizational bargaining within the union and management ranks, so that a lack of consensus on bargaining positions can be overcome by an arbitrator's ruling (in other words, to promote face saving for top officials in both parties); and (3) helping union leaders "to go all the way" for their membership, thereby asserting a leadership role and strengthening their positions within the organization.

One would assume that the chilling and narcotic effects of third-party proce-dures would lessen in jurisdictions that have bargained collectively for many years and developed negotiating expertise. Arbitration is a "learning experience" for the parties, who adjust their expectations about arbitrators' beliefs in each subsequent contract that goes to arbitration (Olson and Rau 1997). A narrowing gap between the parties' expectations (the settlement zone) should be conducive to a negotiated agreement. Future research should be able to tell us if this is indeed the case.

It must be noted that in the majority of bargaining relationships, third-party procedures work satisfactorily. Mediation continues to be highly valued as a flexible and informal method of resolving disputes, and fact finding has proved useful in many jurisdictions. As a dispute resolution device that includes a distinct measure of finality, arbitration in its various forms has been shown to be a reliable alternative to the strike.

In further defense of the various third-party procedures, it must be recognized [as McCormick (1979) found] that they fulfill important functions not directly related to avoiding the strike. Impasse resolution procedures act as safety valves to help contain labor–management conflict and solve labor-related problems (Babcock and Olson 1992; Lester 1986). For instance, impasse procedures help one or both parties save face when settlements are painful. When a voluntary compromise is unlikely to win acceptance by rank-and-file union members or management, reliance on a third party to dictate the necessary settlement tends to deflect criticism and blame from the negotiating team to the neutral. Thus, union and management leaders can retain their positions of authority by using the neutral as a buffer or scapegoat, and constructive labor–management relations are maintained. These "arbitrated" agreements have been commonplace in many jurisdictions, including New York City, Michigan, New Jersey, and Wisconsin (Lester 1986).

Dispute resolution procedures also act to reduce conflict and build consensus between the two parties on labor relations issues that have been subjects of contention. Actually, the most useful long-term function of impasse procedures, particularly arbitration, "may be the manner in which it quietly absorbs and accommodates conflicting interest group claims over scarce public resources" (Feuille 1979: 75). In this sense, dispute resolution procedures contribute to social and political stability by providing an alternative to overt conflict and the strike.

Are third-party procedures ethically superior to the strike in public employment? In responding to this question, we must defer to John F. Burton, Jr. (1978), who concluded that "the relevant standard is the jurisdiction's law. Public sector strikes that are legal are ethical, and vice versa." Public employee unions are interest groups that have a strong voice in state and local government legislative bodies. Their preferences, as likely as not, are for third-party dispute resolution procedures. Although public employers have demonstrated an increasing propensity to take a strike, they, too, usually prefer settlement through less conflictual means and, like unions, make their desires known to legislators.

Case Study 9.1: Tough Times in Garden Junction

New federal mandates, a failed sewer system, the loss of a major employer, and a national economic recession have slammed the finances of Garden Junction. The city council and City Manager Donald Lilly can't be blamed for worrying about the financial viability of the small (pop. 50,000) town. Few opportunities for growing municipal revenues appear to exist. Hence, the council and Manager Lilly have been engaged in serious discussions about tough long-term changes.

The municipal work force numbers 175 employees. Collective bargaining contracts govern pay, benefits, and working conditions. All six major contracts are presently in negotiations. There has already been a flood of retirements, with the recent retirees joining the ranks of nearly 1,200 earlier pensioners. The retirement plan is defined benefit, with participants enjoying generous payouts that are pegged to cost-of-living increases.

Pension expenses are consuming a growing portion of the operating budget, as the system has been funded from the annual budget. Switching to a defined contribution plan in which the city would dedicate a percentage of employee salary to a fund presents an attractive option. Present contributions would fund future payouts, with participants determining the distribution of their pension investments and the level of their monthly pension check dependent on individual investment choices.

Labor relations in Garden Junction has been fairly constructive, but the shift in retirement plan funding is likely to provoke strident union opposition. Union president Vinny Calabria has already voiced the union's position, and suffice it to say that it is not positive. Calabria asserts that the city pension system is based on past understandings, and benefits cannot be reduced without union agreement. However, a consultants' study has recommended that the city establish a mandatory defined contribution plan for all present and newly hired employees. Significant savings are anticipated once the plan is implemented. The consultant's proposal is brought before council and, following the views of the consultant and the city manager, it is approved. The issue moves to the bargaining table.

Union and management negotiators work out agreements on pay and some minor changes in conditions of work. The pension issue ties them up in a serious impasse. Under state law, the issue moves to conventional, binding arbitration under a single neutral appointed by the state PERB. Each party presents its arguments: the union for continuation of the defined benefit plan, but with a small (2 percent of salary) copayment into the pension fund from the salary of current employees; management for adoption of a defined contribution plan, with the city transferring 6 percent of employee salary matched by 4 percent of city funds into individual retirement accounts.

You are sent by PERB to Garden Junction to settle the impasse:

1. How would you begin carrying out your assignment?
2. What information would you examine in determining the viability of the benefit change and the nature of your decision?
3. Are there reasonable alternatives to a mandatory defined contribution plan for all employees?
4. Explain and defend your decision.

Chapter 10

Living with the Contract

I. Introduction

After the chairs are pushed back from the table, the written agreement signed, hands shaken all around, and photo opportunities provided for the media, the two parties to the agreement must begin the difficult task of applying and interpreting the broad terms of the contract on a day-to-day basis. Although contract negotiations steal the limelight of labor relations, the true test of the soundness and maturity of the relationship between union and management comes with implementation of the agreement. It is through living with the contract that collective bargaining exerts its greatest effects on the behavior and attitudes of individual public workers (Kochan 1980: 384).

A collective bargaining agreement may be effectively administered by each party or it may be poorly administered. The union, like an unruly child, may test management by attempting to tilt interpretation of the contract to its advantage by picketing, walkouts, or job slowdowns. An immature management may ignore the terms of the agreement and attempt to implement terms and conditions of employment unilaterally. Just as in a marriage, conflicts and disputes are inherent in any labor–management relationship. The key to a healthy and stable employment relationship is to manage conflict and controversy over implementation of the contract in a constructive manner, with due consideration of the rights and responsibilities of each party. Both parties must strive to resolve their differences amicably in the short term to maintain a positive long-term relationship.

In this chapter, after a brief examination of collective bargaining agreements and their administration in the public sector, our attention focuses on the primary

291

means for living peacefully with the contract — a responsive and effective grievance procedure culminating in binding grievance arbitration.

II. The Collective Bargaining Agreement

The negotiated contract serves as the legal foundation, or "law of the workplace," replacing the unilateral determination of employment decisions by management with a shared decision-making process between equals.

The collective bargaining agreement is traditionally referred to as a "contract" much in the sense of a commercial contract, and like the commercial contract, the collective bargaining agreement is enforceable in the courts. But a labor agreement is more than a business contract in that it attempts to construct a democratic system for governance of the workplace. Also, when a commercial contract expires, the rights and duties of the parties are terminated. Labor agreements have a life beyond contract expiration, particularly with regard to employer obligations to contribute to health insurance and pension plans and to honor procedures established during the term of the contract.

The basis in the private sector for legal recourse involving contracts is found in Section 301(a) of the Labor–Management Relations Act, which provides that union or management violations of contract terms may be challenged by a lawsuit in federal district court. In the public sector, litigation to enforce contracts is usually taken before a state court or the Federal Labor Relations Authority (FLRA). Other potential remedies are available in both industry and government, including unfair labor practice charges before the National Labor Relations Board (NLRB) or the state labor board or agency. As a general rule, however, contractual disputes are settled within the parameters of the agreement itself, without resort to external appeal.

A. Contents of the Agreement

The typical collective bargaining contract runs anywhere from 10 to 100 pages. The document may be very basic and limited in scope or, especially where bargaining relationships are longstanding, exceedingly detailed and complex. All labor relations contracts, however, are intended to provide rules for governing the parties' relationships on a day-to-day basis and to delineate the duties, rights, and responsibilities of the respective parties.

Generally speaking, contract provisions may be classified as (1) fixed, (2) contingent, or (3) dispute resolution procedures. Fixed provisions usually remain unchanged over the life of the agreement. They typically include the following.

Contract duration (typically 1 to 3 years)
Boundaries of the bargaining unit
Union recognition and rights

Management rights
Wages
Hours of work
Holidays, and vacation and sick leave
Benefits
Union security
Antidiscrimination clauses
Residency requirements
Union political activities
Official time
Reopening clause (may be used to "reopen" another fixed provision, such as
 wage increases in the third year of a contract).

Contingent provisions are intended to govern union or management actions in a changing labor relations environment. They address activities such as:

Discharges
Layoffs
Reductions in force/recall of laid-off workers
Promotions
Work scheduling
Work assignments
Transfers
Discipline
Outsourcing

Dispute resolution procedures are designed to resolve conflicts arising from contract interpretation and application, particularly of the contingent provisions. The vast majority of labor agreements contain a no-strike provision for the life of the contract and a multi-step grievance procedure culminating in binding arbitration of contract disputes. As noted, another common procedure for resolving disputes is to file an unfair labor practice (ULP) complaint with the appropriate state or federal organization.

In living with the contract, dispute resolution provisions are particularly important. Every clause in the contract may be subject to differing interpretations. Like other written instruments, the labor contract simply describes the terms agreed upon by the parties. Like any screed, it may suffer from the vagaries of the written word. The pressure and time constraints of negotiations, along with the fatigue they often precipitate, are not conducive to precise writing. During negotiations, a variety of tones and intonations, facial expressions, body language, and contexts enrich and expand upon formal language. What may appear to be perfectly clear to the negotiating teams may later seem to be riddled with ambiguities to those who have only the written words before them. Furthermore, interpretation of contract provisions can be complicated by deliberately ambiguous language that helps to avoid a negotiations impasse. Poor drafting and "legalese" compound ambiguities.

To minimize contract ambiguity, the drafters of the agreement should (1) use short, declarative sentences; (2) avoid excessive legalisms; (3) be precise with such terms as "agency," "union," and "employee"; (4) carefully outline procedures in a step-by-step format; (5) use examples to clarify abstract clauses; and (6) have a draft of the agreement proofread by individuals who were not present at the bargaining table. The drafters should also strive to avoid polysyllabic words and nebulous terms such as "reasonable," "equitable," and "normally."

Scott and Suchan (1987) assessed the readability of a sample of public sector collective bargaining contracts using three readability formulas, including the Fog Index. They found that virtually all of the contracts were very difficult to read and understand, requiring at a minimum the reading comprehension skills of a college graduate. Obviously, many stewards, front-line supervisors, and union rank and file may be expected to have difficulty applying the provisions of such contracts. Scott and Suchan (1987) recommend that technical writers be used to draft contracts in plain, lucid language. Nonetheless, as long as humans are fallible, vagueness and contradictions will be found in their written agreements.

B. Disseminating the Agreement

Just as management is the initiator of most personnel-related actions, management also has the primary responsibility for implementing the collective bargaining contract. As the action agent, management initiates policy under the agreement and the union reacts, either through compliance or challenge. It is commonly observed that "management administers the contract and the union enforces it." But management may also be accused of errors of omission or inaction (Meyer 2002).

Assuming legislative ratification of a negotiated collective bargaining agreement, management's first task is to disseminate the contract throughout the organization and to educate the respective constituencies on specific provisions and grievance procedures. The contract may be reproduced in its entirety and, as is often the case with lengthy or complex documents, its important provisions summarized and explained. A fundamental principle of contract administration is that all managers and members of the bargaining unit should receive a copy of the contract as soon as possible. Supervisors should be allocated a sufficient number of copies to distribute to each of their subordinates, including those who are not members of the union (they are parties to the contract nonetheless). Usually the public employer assumes responsibility for the costs of printing and distributing the agreement and collateral materials.

The key individuals in contract dissemination are management supervisors and union stewards. If these persons become intimately familiar with the contract terms early in the life of the agreement, there should be fewer misunderstandings and, as a consequence, fewer unnecessary grievances. In fact, it is not a bad idea for supervisors to begin familiarizing themselves with a new contract while it is still being negotiated. Such early involvement enhances understanding of contract provisions as they are finalized, enables supervisors to serve as valuable channels of communication between employees and management during negotiations, and provides an early assessment of the potential impact of various union and management proposals. Once a new contract is signed, supervisors should quickly be given a written analysis of each provision, and special training sessions should be held to explain the management perspective on each clause and its intent.

The union should also train its stewards in the provisions of the new contract. The bargaining agreement is "the most tangible product the union has to sell," and it can be used to elevate member commitment to the union (P. F. Clark and D. G. Gallagher 1988:16). New members may be familiarized with contract provisions during both union- and management-sponsored orientation programs. Benefits could accrue to both labor and management from joint training and orientation sessions, but such programs are relatively uncommon.

C. Administering the Agreement

Management organization for administering the contract varies with the size of the employer. In smaller school districts or municipalities, communication usually flows freely within the ranks of management, and authoritative interpretation of contract clauses is readily forthcoming. In governmental units of greater size, multiple levels of supervision can hinder prompt and effective contract administration. Informal communication channels that function very well in smaller jurisdictions tend to be supplanted by formal integrative structures, such as a central labor relations office, which coordinates labor relations policies between agencies or departments. Interorganizational politics frequently makes the job of the central office difficult at best. For example, a district director of a state social service agency who is well connected with the agency head or influential political figures may decide to run personnel operations in her own way, ignoring the contract.

For successful administration of the bargaining agreement, two important objectives must be met. First, the contract must be implemented in a uniform and consistent manner by both parties. Management should almost compulsively enforce all contract provisions in order to avoid undermining the agreement. The supervisor who, in an effort to be a "nice guy," violates the contract by, for example, permitting employees to leave work a couple of hours before quitting time to get an early start on vacation or holiday leave, is inadvertently sacrificing a management right and setting the table for future grievances. The same is true of the supervisor who overlooks an employee violation of agency rules to "give him(her) a break." In sum, administrators must be very cautious in making ad hoc exceptions and modifications to contractual procedures. The union steward, for his or her part, should police the agreement vigorously and represent all members of the bargaining unit, whether union member or not, in an impartial manner. Although stringent adherence to the formal contract by the parties may seem to be impersonal, inflexible, and overly rigid at times, labor relations experts insist that a commitment to make no exception to the rules is much preferred to inconsistent contract administration and the inevitable perceptions of unfairness that result.

The second essential objective for successful contract administration is to maintain open communication channels between union and management representatives. The adversarial approach that typically characterizes the contract negotiations process should be replaced by a more cooperative relationship once the agreement is signed. It has been estimated that managers spend up to 50 percent of their time resolving conflicts.

Conflict between the parties is certain to continue during contract implementation. But conflict is not necessarily an undesirable thing. Constructive confrontation can be carried out in a healthy and positive atmosphere through negotiated grievance procedures. Careful monitoring of the labor–management relationship through, for example, grievance analysis can provide appropriate feedback for identifying problems at an early stage. Effective grievance procedures are a necessary prerequisite of successful contract administration and, indeed, an important extension of the collective bargaining process. Grievances effectively addressed today help prevent new grievances tomorrow. The union benefits both tangibly and intangibly from representing members of the bargaining unit, and management gains from improved work force morale and early problem identification. Conflict within the contract permits members of the organization to confront important issues constructively and cooperatively while advancing the organization's mission (Rahim 1992).

III. Grievance Procedures

A grievance is an employee or union complaint (or, albeit infrequently, a management complaint) arising out of dissatisfaction with some aspect of the contract or the work environment. The primary purpose of a grievance is to overturn a management action. Usually the grievance involves an alleged violation of a clause in the negotiated contract. The nature of a grievance is limited only by circumstance. The most common grievance subjects are disciplinary actions, such as reprimands, suspensions, or discharges; absenteeism; health and safety issues; vacation assignments; job assignments; promotions; discrimination; overtime; layoffs; and reductions in force.

Employee grievances over the terms, conditions, or continuation of employment may be resolved in several ways in the public sector, including unilateral determination by management, civil service procedures, ULPs, and contractual grievance procedures. The primary objective of a grievance procedure is to provide a means for a worker to register a formal complaint about working conditions, arbitrary management actions, or other matters and receive a fair hearing. In the absence of unions and contractual grievance procedures, employees usually must either represent themselves or privately secure the services of an attorney. It is not uncommon in nonunion jurisdictions for official grievance processes to seriously disadvantage the employee and favor management. Where unions are present, negotiated grievance procedures and union representation level the playing field or even tilt it in favor of the employee.

Although nearly all negotiated agreements contain grievance procedures (the estimate is 95 percent), their scope varies. Some contracts stipulate grievance procedures but never directly address the issue of what constitutes a grievance. Most contracts, however, either define grievances very broadly, as any disagreement or dispute between management and the employee or union, or define them narrowly by specifying the types of grievances that may be raised under the terms of the agreement. Some contracts specifically exclude certain matters from the negotiated grievance procedure, such as designated management rights (e.g., selection, promotion, performance appraisal).

Even for noncontract-related grievances, however, some means of resolution should be provided, because if a grievance is raised, a problem exists whether or not it is grievable under the contract. By addressing noncontract grievances through, for example, alternative dispute resolution procedures, management gains an opportunity to resolve potential problems in an early stage of development, before the acorn of a problem grows into a hulking oak.

Negotiated grievance procedures have supplanted traditional civil service appeals systems in virtually all jurisdictions in which unions engage in collective bargaining. There are important distinctions between the two legal settings. Civil service grievance procedures are established in statute or by the employer, whereas negotiated procedures are established bilaterally through union and management negotiations and embodied in the contract. A grieving worker under a civil service system is essentially appealing a management decision to higher authority; a negotiated grievance procedure represents a continuation of the collective bargaining process through which the parties' rights and responsibilities are clarified continually. Final decision-making authority in a civil service system typically resides in a commission of elected or appointed officials who must attempt to balance dual, and sometimes conflicting, responsibilities as both the executive personnel arm of management and the protector of classified employees and the merit system; negotiated grievance procedures normally provide for final decision making by a "disinterested" third-party arbitrator. Finally, the scope of civil service grievance procedures is typically restricted by state law, municipal ordinance, or commission rules and regulations; negotiated procedures are usually much less limited in scope.

The functions of negotiated grievance procedures go beyond merely furnishing a basic forum for employee complaints. Grievance procedures also help resolve differences in interpreting the written agreement, protect the rights of the union, avoid strikes over contract application, identify new issues for negotiations, and, in general, promote labor–management harmony in living together with the contract. Other important functions of the negotiated grievance procedure include detecting underlying problems in the agreement and in the basic functions of human resource management. In all the foregoing respects, the grievance procedure represents an extension of the bargaining process.

Although negotiated and civil service grievance procedures differ conceptually, in practice they sometimes overlap, providing multiple points of access to the grievant. For example, an adverse action such as dismissal may be appealed to a civil service commission or taken to arbitration through the negotiated contract in some jurisdictions. Additional appellate venues exist if the dismissal results in charges of sexual, racial, or other forms of discrimination.

Federal sector grievance procedures represent the best (or worst) example of multiple dispute resolution venues. A single dispute between a union-represented grievant and an agency "may be litigated before four separate agencies and with as many as ten different procedures" (Feder 1989: 269). At any given time a grievance may be pending before the FLRA (contract dispute), MSPB (disciplinary action), the Office of Special Counsel (whistleblower reprimand), and the EEOC (discrimination complaint). Within the FLRA alone, there are several alternative dispute resolution paths. Not surprisingly, confusion and lengthy delays plague the process. "Mixed cases" involving allegations of discrimination and one or more related matters often take 4 years or longer for settlement, especially if findings of the various grievance-deciding bodies diverge. Clearly, such costly, convoluted, and bewildering procedures negatively affect the quality of federal labor–management relations. This has led to suggestions to replace this multiplicity of grievance-hearing bodies with a single federal dispute resolution board (Feder 1989).

Similar levels of redundancy and complexity are also found in some states. Others (e.g., New Jersey, Maine, New York) have attempted to end the confusion by amending their collective bargaining laws so that the negotiated contractual procedure takes precedence over all other channels of appeal. Florida requires the grievant to choose either the negotiated procedure or a civil service procedure.

A. Causes of Grievances

As noted above, grievances spring from diverse sources in the workplace. The three major causes of grievances are misunderstandings, intentional violations, and symptomatic grievances.

Misunderstandings, which probably represent the most frequent source of grievances in most employment relationships, can result from deliberate or unintentional ambiguities in a negotiated contract, misinterpretation or misunderstanding of contract language by one or both parties, or ignorance or ineptitude in contract administration on the part of the union steward or the supervisor. For example, a manager who demonstrates incompetence in applying the terms of the contract is likely to find his or her decisions increasingly challenged by a leery steward. As a result, the number of grievances will rise.

Intentional violations typically involve management's circumvention of a contract provision because of "special circumstances" that have developed. For example, management may change the hours of work to meet client demands or reduce working hours because of a budget shortfall. To foreclose a waiver of future contract rights, the union grieves.

Symptomatic grievances are indicative of some underlying problem in the workplace that is causing employee frustration. For example, an under- or overqualified worker may file a petty grievance out of personal frustration; stewards may raise grievances to harass management just before or during contract negotiations; or a "hard ass" supervisor may arbitrarily crack down on coffee breaks and casual conversation. Conflictual relations during contract negotiations often carry over into the administration of the agreement, and any particularly contentious issues remaining unresolved in the contract are apt to generate grievances.

Environmental factors that induce complaints may be included within the category of symptomatic grievances. These factors, which characterize the broad organizational context of union–management relationships, are found in the work environment, task organization and technology, and socioeconomic conditions. In an early study of the U.S. steel industry, Peach and Livernash (1974) found that grievance rates were higher in work units with low-skilled employees, repetitious work, jobs requiring constant attention, and other unfavorable working conditions. In a study testing the applicability to two large state agencies in Iowa, Muchinsky and Maasarani (1980) had findings similar to those of Peach and Livernash. In Iowa, the work environments at the Department of Social Services (DSS) and the Department of Transportation (DOT) were closely related to the frequency and subject matter of grievances. For instance, state hospital and prison employees in DSS filed a great many grievances over matters of discipline, health, safety, and transfers, which the authors suspected were related to the stress-ridden nature of their work. At DOT, the majority of grievances were concerned with hours of work, wages, and benefits.

Grievances have also been associated with characteristics of the individual worker. Grievants tend to be younger, have more formal education, exhibit greater absenteeism, earn lower wages, be more active in their union than non-grievants, and have a weak commitment to the job (especially students or part-time workers) and to their supervisors. Some studies have found that minorities are more likely to file grievances than whites (Labig and Greer 1988).

An organization characterized by a comparatively high number of grievances is not necessarily an "unhealthy organization," although grievances are costly in terms of their demands on management time, energy, and resources. The emergence of many grievances may simply reflect the lack of an effective union screening process to shut off frivolous complaints or combative union stewards (Bemmels 1994). A relatively small number of grievances may signal trouble in terms of a lack of employee faith in the grievance procedure or their union, or, as is sometimes the case, the availability of a more frequently used alternative such as a civil service system appellate route. Alternate grievance procedures, in conjunction with a narrower scope of bargaining, have been cited as major reasons for the lower incidence of grievances in government as compared to industry (Stewart and Davy 1992: 323).

There is probably some "ideal" range of grievances per employee in a healthy organization, but no mathematical equation or metric has been derived that accurately reflects the total ambience of the workplace. It is important, however, that grievance channels be kept open and functional to serve as a safety valve, clear up ambiguous contract language, and otherwise ensure an adequate flow of employee feedback.

B. The Grievance Process

Although there is a great deal of variance in written, negotiated grievance procedures among public employers, almost every plan consists of step-by-step techniques for grievance resolution, with nearly all culminating in binding arbitration. Two overriding concerns for any grievance procedure, whatever the specific steps, are that they (1) encourage the rapid and fair settlement of complaints, and (2) promote resolution of the grievance at the lowest possible level. The number of steps in the procedure usually corresponds with clear lines of management authority.

Most grievance plans include three basic steps, followed by arbitration (see Figure 10.1). First, the complaint is raised and responded to at the supervisory level. During this initial phase a strong effort should be made to settle the grievance informally. Often the grievance is handled orally, which permits more flexibility than can exist once the complaint is reduced to a written form. The duty of the supervisor during this phase is to get the full story from the grieving employee, consult with the union steward if necessary, investigate the complaint through collecting data and/or interviewing other workers to determine if there are adequate factual grounds for the complaint, and render a decision one way or the other. The supervisor should record the basis of his or her decision and document any corroborating information in anticipation of an employee appeal.

The usual second step in the grievance procedure involves union intervention and marks the commencement of a "formal" grievance. If the union grievance committee determines that further action should be taken on appeal, the complaint is summarized in writing, signed by the grievant, and forwarded to the next management level (see Figure 10.1). At this point both parties are well served by carefully collecting and retaining complete and accurate records of the case. The responsibility of management at this juncture is to review the complaint in view of relevant contract language and other significant information and try to find a means for resolving the dispute. Fairness and promptness should be of major concern to both union and management to demonstrate to all interested parties, especially the rank and file, that the grievance system works as intended.

If the complaint remains unresolved, higher levels of management become involved. In municipalities the department head may make the final pre-arbitration determination or, especially in middle-sized and smaller localities, the mayor

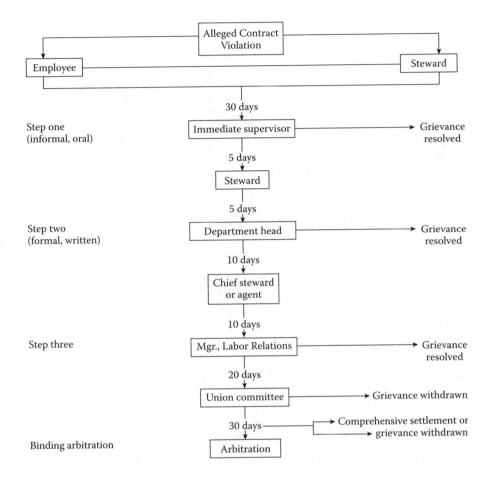

Source: Adapted from McPherson (1983).

Figure 10.1   Grievance process.

or city manager may function as penultimate arbiter of the grievance. In school districts the local school board or superintendent often makes the final management decision prior to third-party intervention. Policy in state governments varies, with state grievance committees, agency and department heads, or labor relations divisions making final pre-arbitration judgment. Even when grievances are settled during the early procedural stages, top management often plays an important role by consulting informally with supervisors.

The final venue in more than 90 percent of negotiated public sector grievance procedures is binding grievance arbitration by a neutral third party. In contracts

GRIEVANCE FORM

NAME _____ DEPARTMENT/BUREAU _____

POSITION TITLE _____ WORK PHONE _____

INSTRUCTIONS: The Grievance procedure has three steps. The first is informal resolution, the second is a formal written grievance, and the third a review by the agency head or hearing. This form may be used by an employee to initiate a formal grievance at Step 2.

If you are considering initiating a grievance, you should review the complete Grievance policy, number 3-0125, effective 6/2/97. The policy is found in the Montana Operations Manual, volume III, or is available from the agency personnel office.

STEP 1 INFORMAL RESOLUTION

Step 1 of the grievance process is the informal resolution. You and your supervisor are encouraged to resolve your grievance at this step.

STEP 2 FORMAL GRIEVANCE

From the date of the grievable event, you have 15 working days to file a formal, written grievance. The written grievance is considered filed when it is submitted to your immediate supervisor or the next level above your immediate supervisor.

You must provide the following information:

1. The date of the grievable event. _____

2. A specific statement of the written law, rule, policy and/or procedure violated. What action or conduct constituted the violation and what happened?

_____

_____

_____ Total number of pages attached _____

3. The resolution or remedy you want.

_____

_____

_____ Total number of pages attached _____

4. Employee signature and date filed by supervisor.

Figure 10.2   Grievance form.

not calling for third-party intervention, management makes the final determination unilaterally or some other alternative such as grievance mediation is employed.

To encourage prompt processing of unresolved grievances through the system, most contracts specify time limits. Normally a grievance must be initiated within a certain period of time or it will not be permitted to go forward through the appellate route. Such time constraints benefit labor by precluding management delaying tactics and they help alleviate employee frustration over untreated complaints. They

Employee's Signature	Date

Supervisor's Signature	Date received from employee

STEP 3 FORMAL GRIEVANCE

If yo do not resolve your grievance at Step 2, you may advance the grievance to Step 3 by notifying the management representative in your agency who is designated to receive grievances at this step. Contact your agency personnel officer for the name of the designated representative. The notification must be in writing and must be received within 10 working days of receipt of management's response at Step 2.

Source: State of Montana

Figure 10.2   Grievance form (continued).

also help management avoid work disruptions and retroactive pay awards. Both parties gain from the timely use of evidence concerning the grievance. Although the exact time limits vary among contracts, a common requirement is that management representatives at each step render a decision and forward it to the grievant within 5 or 10 working days of receiving the complaint. The employee, if still dissatisfied, has the same period of time to take the case to the next level of appeal.

The time required for grievance resolution is "largely a function of the complexity of the issue and its importance to [the] basic interests" of the parties involved (McPherson 1983: 31). If the parties mutually seek to resolve the dispute quickly and satisfactorily, that is likely what will happen. If one or both parties choose to "stand on principle" or fight it out to the end, binding arbitration is the result.

Occasionally, management's interests may be served by foot dragging. For example, where management intentionally violates a work rule in the legitimate interests of efficiency or serving the public, there is little incentive to handle the resulting grievance in a timely fashion. This is because the conventional rule is for employees to "follow the order then grieve" to avoid insubordination charges. Thus, management can get away with a contract violation or unfair labor practice while the grievance is pending, although time limits place a ceiling on such delaying tactics.

C. Representation of the Grievant

1. The Steward

An employee registering a grievance under the contract is entitled to representation by the union steward and, in a growing number of instances, a union or personal attorney. The employee also has the right in most public jurisdictions to have union representation during disciplinary hearings, investigations of alleged employee misconduct, and arbitration proceedings. The steward plays a key part in representing the employee and, in general, ensuring that management implements the provisions of the contract evenhandedly.

The steward fills an elected or appointed position within the union for a term that runs 1 year or more. The steward typically is obliged to deal with employee problems during working hours. Management recognizes the importance of the steward function by releasing the steward for union work with pay at the regularly assigned rate. "Superseniority" generally is granted to protect the steward from layoffs or other management actions that could adversely affect the performance of his or her duties. Another major function of the steward is to enlist new union members. A bargaining unit may have several stewards consistent with different levels of management authority. If so, a chief steward exercises some authority over the various shop stewards.

The steward's role can be quite complicated when supervisors belong to the bargaining unit. A steward can find himself representing his own supervisor before higher management, or a steward who also happens to be a supervisor may have to represent a subordinate. Even more confounding, the steward's supervisor may have taken the action that gave rise to the grievance. Thus the steward can represent a grievant who has a grievance against the steward's immediate supervisor, who is also in the bargaining unit and presumably has the right to union representation. Such role confusion stands as compelling testimony for the need to exclude supervisors from rank-and-file bargaining units.

Grievance handling can be a sensitive area for the steward and the union, and it is clearly of fundamental importance to both the union and the overall quality of labor–management relations. The steward is in a key role to influence the behavior and attitudes of bargaining unit members. Effective stewards can nurture strong commitment to the union and maximize dues-paying membership (Clark 1989a; Clark and Gallagher 1988). The quality of labor–management relations is enhanced by stewards who can work effectively with supervisors while fully discharging their representation duties. Stewards rarely receive extra monetary compensation for their efforts to carry out union–management relations within a high-pressure, stressful environment. In many ways, it is a labor of the heart.

2. Union Duty of Fair Representation

The union's duty of fair representation results from its designation as exclusive bargaining agent for all employees in the bargaining unit. In exchange for this designation the union agrees to represent fairly, honestly, and in good faith all employees even if they are not members of the union. The union's legal duty to represent all members of the bargaining unit is provided for in the contract or in state labor legislation. The standards for determining fair representation were developed in the federal courts for the private sector and applied to public employment, with little consideration given to public/private sector differences. Several key court cases delineate the duty of fair representation.

The most frequently cited case is *Vaca v. Sipes* (1967), in which the Supreme Court held that the only instance in which a union violates its duty of fair representation in deciding not to arbitrate a grievance is when it acts in an arbitrary or discriminatory fashion or in bad faith. The burden of proof, therefore, would rest with the grievant. However, a later decision, *Hines v. Anchor Motor Freight* (1976), held that the "perfunctory" processing of a grievance may also violate the duty of fair representation, particularly where the union does not investigate the potential merits of a grievance before dropping it. Because unions have limited funds for grievance processing, they cannot take every complaint all the way to arbitration. Under most public sector contracts and statutes, the union — not the grievant — decides which cases it will take to arbitration, eschewing those that have questionable merit or reflect narrow interests or settling before arbitration.

Although "mere negligence" in grievance handling does not necessarily breach the duty of fair representation, the union does have the legal responsibility to exercise a minimum level of care in meeting time limits and pursuing the evidence submitted by the grievant. The best route for the union is usually to file the grievance, then conduct as thorough an investigation as feasible, dropping the grievance only if it clearly has no merit. Otherwise, the union may be subjected to an unfair labor practice charge or a civil suit for breach of contract.

The union that neglects the duty of fair representation may be courting financial catastrophe. In *Bowen v. U.S. Postal Service* (1983), the U.S. Supreme Court ruled that a union failing to properly represent an employee fired illegally from the job is liable for a portion of the employee's lost wages. Charles V. Bowen, a member of the American Postal Workers' Union, was dismissed by the Postal Service because of an alleged altercation with a fellow worker. He requested the union to initiate arbitration proceedings, but the APWU refused. Bowen sued the Postal Service for illegally firing him and sued the union for failing to discharge its duty of fair representation under Section 301(a) of the Labor–Management Relations Act of 1947. A 5:4 majority held that Bowen was entitled to recover financial damages from both the employer and the union, apportioned according to degree of fault. The Court reasoned that the union's liability begins at the time when final resolution of the dispute would have been obtained through the grievance procedure, had the union fully represented the employee. Thus, the employer's liability is limited, but the union could be held responsible for back wages for years, as a case slowly makes its way through the courts. One outcome could be union bankruptcy. Another result of *Bowen* is that unions, to the consternation of management, now tend to err on the side of caution by carrying even meritless grievances all the way to arbitration, with some inevitable congestion and delay in the grievance process.

Bowen sounded a warning bell for unions at all levels of government, but it applied specifically only to postal workers covered by the Labor–Management Relations Act. A 1989 U.S. Supreme Court decision held that other federal employees cannot sue their union for breach of the duty of fair representation, because an administrative remedy (the Federal Labor Relations Authority) is provided for by the CSRA of 1978 (*Karahalios v. NFFE* 1989). At the state and local levels, state courts and public employee relations boards make determinations concerning the duty of fair representation.

IV. Grievance Arbitration

Any grievance procedure is intended to provide strong incentives for the parties to settle quickly. Both generally want to avoid the trouble and expense of a prolonged grievance and to maintain a healthy, cooperative labor relations environment. Inevitably, however, some grievances are not easily resolved. For these troublesome cases grievance arbitration (also known as rights arbitration) is used as the final step in meeting the complaint. An outside neutral is brought in by the parties to review the facts and hear the evidence and testimony favoring each position and then to render a final binding judgment based on presentations of the evidence and the language of the contract. The union attempts to show that the contract, language, precedent, or past practice covers the facts of the grievance and that the action taken by management was inappropriate in light of these considerations.

Grievance arbitration was first used in the United States in 1871 in the coal industry. It gained widespread acceptance throughout the private sector during World War II as a technique strongly advocated by the War Labor Board to avoid the time and monetary costs of taking contract disputes to the courts. Grievance arbitration was granted formal legal status in Section 203(d) of Taft-Hartley and received further protection through a series of Supreme Court cases known as the Steelworkers trilogy (see below), which set down the doctrine that arbitration awards are not subject to review in the courts unless due process has been denied or the arbitrator has exceeded his or her authority. Today, grievance arbitration has achieved almost universal acceptance in unionized settings in the private sector and is used in many government settings as well. Arbitration of grievances is required in the federal sector as a final step in the negotiated grievance procedure.

Although widely used, grievance arbitration, like interest arbitration, has been condemned by critics as an illegal delegation of government authority to an outside party who is not responsible to the citizenry or to elected officials. There are alternative public sector forums for the binding settlement of grievances, including civil service commissions, state or local government grievance committees, state labor agencies, federal or state equal employment opportunity commissions, and the courts. Although the practical effects of such arguments have been few, the courts generally have held that public sector grievance arbitration is not legal unless specifically provided for in appropriate enabling legislation (Bowers 1976: 35). Where enabling legislation exists and the parties consent to the binding arbitration of grievances, as long as the arbitrator does not exceed his or her legal authority in making the decision, the courts have generally held that grievance arbitration is legal and desirable.

A. Arbitrability

Before a grievance can be taken to binding arbitration and the merits of the case considered, the dispute must be found to be arbitrable. In other words, the disputants must have agreed to place the case before the arbitrator and the arbitrator must have the requisite authority to rule. Claims of nonarbitrability are most often made by management, whose previous decision or action is upheld when arbitration is denied. Claims of nonarbitrability may be raised on procedural or substantive grounds. A determination of procedural arbitrability depends on the extent to which there has been compliance with the requirements set forth in the contract for filing and processing grievances. Substantive arbitrability refers to whether the agreement and the law include or specifically exclude the issue(s) in question from arbitration (Bowers 1976: 65).

Examples of procedural arguments against arbitrability include failure to sign the grievance or submit it in a timely manner, failure to cite the provision of the contract purportedly violated, or other such irregularities. The claim that a dispute should not be arbitrated because the contract has expired has not been supported by the courts as long as it can be demonstrated that the grievance definitely occurred during the life of the contract. Even when grievances are filed after contract expiration, grievance arbitration is usually extended as part of the continuing duty to bargain (Decker 1994: 160–162).

Substantive grounds for challenging arbitrability include the scope of the definition of "grievance" in the contract, management rights, and conflicts with state or administrative rules. For example, management may claim that an employee's copayment of a physician's bills is to be settled by the employer and the insurance company, not by an arbitrator. Most questions of arbitrability are decided by the arbitrator, although the courts sometimes must make the determination (Decker 1994: 151). Often, an arbitrator will take arbitrability arguments under advisement and hear the merits of the case the same day so that if he decides the case is arbitrable he can then render a judgment. This increases the risk for both parties and may encourage them to settle voluntarily.

B. Court Review of Arbitrators' Decisions

The presumption of the federal courts in private sector cases has been that issues taken to arbitration should be settled by the arbitrator — not by the courts — based on the terms of the contract. Judges should not substitute their opinions for those of the arbitrator unless the arbitrator is guilty of fraud, misconduct, or gross unfairness, or the award violates established public policy. This basic principle was established in the "Steelworkers trilogy," three Supreme Court cases in 1960 involving the United Steelworkers of America. The Court's decisions established arbitration as final and binding and essentially exempt from court review (see H. T. Edwards, Clark, and Graver 1979: 73–77; Coleman and Vasquez 1997).

However, deference to the Steelworkers trilogy was relaxed somewhat in *Alexander v. Gardner-Denver* (1975), where the U.S. Supreme Court ruled that, contrary to the trilogy, an "arbitrator's decision is not final and binding" if a violation of Title VII of the Civil Rights Act of 1964 has occurred. Thus, a grievant can pursue a Title VII case through grievance arbitration under the contract or independently in the courts. In other words, statutory rights may outweigh contractual rights. This principle was applied in *Barrentine v. Arkansas Best Freight Systems* (1981), in which the Supreme Court ruled that a grievant's claim arising from statutory rights (the Fair Labor Standards Act, in this case) may be subject to judicial review, even if submitted to arbitration earlier.

Some state courts (e.g., Wisconsin and Minnesota) have adopted the trilogy standards wholesale, deciding that arbitrators, not judges, should resolve labor disputes. Other state courts, however, have ignored or given short shrift to the trilogy principles. Some courts have substituted a scope of bargaining test to determine the breadth of the arbitrator's authority, juxtaposing the legal scope of bargaining and the subject of the grievance to decide whether the grievance should have been submitted to arbitration. In other states, courts have overturned arbitrators' rulings because they violated public policy as embodied in statutes, previous court decisions, or common practice (Nicolau 1997: 261; Bodah 1999). Other grounds for setting aside an arbitrator's decision are fraud or misconduct by the arbitrator. Errors of fact, law, or interpretation by the arbitrator are not sufficient to invalidate an award (Decker 1994: 152).

Thus, public sector grievance arbitration may lack a strong presumption of finality depending on the government jurisdiction. The use of grievance arbitration could be significantly altered through court actions involving federal and state regulations, such as EEO, disability, and occupational health and safety standards, if the courts determine that certain individual rights go beyond contract stipulations (M. J. Levine 1985). In public employment the problem is accentuated by various federal, state, and local laws that precede collective bargaining and provide employees with rights and remedies beyond those established in the bargaining contract.

Perhaps nowhere is this problem better illustrated than in equal employment opportunity issues, where multiple forums exist. As noted earlier, a discrimination complaint may be taken to grievance arbitration, the FLRA, the EEOC or a state or local counterpart, the federal district court, a state court, or other venues. A grievance arbitration decision is not final and binding in discrimination cases, which may be carried from forum to forum with *de novo* consideration in a continuing search for a finding that satisfies the grievant.

C. Selection of the Arbitrator

Like interest arbitration, grievance arbitration may be conducted by a single neutral or by a tribunal. Three- or five-member arbitration panels usually are composed of each party's appointees and one or more mutually agreed-upon third-party neutrals. Tribunals offer the opportunity for a full accounting of relevant information and arguments by the parties. The advocate-members can clarify their parties' positions, identify possible problems with a proposed award, and even negotiate a settlement. The single arbitrator is less expensive and more expeditious in issuing a decision — an important advantage that helps account for its substantially greater use (see Veglahn 1987).

Grievance arbitrators, like interest arbitrators, are usually selected from rosters provided by the American Arbitration Association (AAA), the National Academy of Arbitrators, the Federal Mediation and Conciliation Service (FMCS), the relevant state agency, or a local bar association. The organizations furnish management and the union with biographical information on prospective arbitrators. AAA biographical sketches include such pertinent background information as experience, qualifications, and fees. FMCS's ARBIT (Arbitration Information Tracking) system provides a computerized biographical data retrieval system, updated after each case decided by an arbitrator, and rotates FMCS arbitrator designees for panel referrals to encourage balanced use of qualified neutrals. These services are provided free by FMCS. Generally, whereas both the union and management are very interested in the arbitrator's track record, years of experience, and demographic traits, such data are of limited utility in predicting an arbitrator's decision (Kauffman, Vanlwaarden, and Floyd 1994). Ordinarily, if the parties are unable to agree on a selection, they will strike names from the FMCS or AAA list until only one remains. Lists typically contain five to seven names.

All arbitrators, regardless of the list on which their name is found, must be paid for their time. Compensation usually varies from $1,000 to $3,000 per day, depending on the reputation, experience, and demand for individual arbitrators and the nature of the case. Additional costs of arbitration include the filing fee; arbitrator's meals, lodging, and travel; and payment for researching and writing the opinion.

Arbitrators vary in their academic training, but most hold graduate or professional degrees and are associated with universities in some manner. Many are based in law schools. The heavy involvement of law school faculty and attorneys has been vigorously criticized by those who claim that lawyer-arbitrators tend to be too technical in procedure, overly aggressive with witnesses and the opposing counsel, overly reliant on precedent, and excessively concerned with winning instead of problem solving. Pro-legalists, who favor lawyers' skills in analyzing and interpreting facts and information and presenting them in an orderly fashion in the courtroom, defend them. Still, it is generally recognized that one does not require legal training to perform well as an arbitrator.

Excellent qualifications and pedigrees notwithstanding, new rights arbitrators have a difficult time gaining acceptance. The number of cases going to arbitration has increased steadily, much faster than the number of arbitrators deemed widely acceptable by labor and management representatives. The qualified but inexperienced arbitrator faces a Catch-22 situation familiar to many university graduates: one needs experience to be hired, but one cannot obtain experience without a job. Arbitrator selection consistently favors a relatively small pool of experienced neutrals. These arbitrators have large caseloads and, as a consequence, are slower in deciding awards.

D. Problems in Grievance Arbitration

Two major grievance arbitration problems already have been alluded to: monetary costs and lengthy delays. Given a reasonably healthy labor–management relationship, perhaps the price of arbitration is not completely undesirable; it may inspire the parties to settle at an early stage in the process. Further economic incentive to settle a grievance prior to arbitration can be achieved through "loser-pays arbitration," in which the party with the weakest case must pay the arbitrator's fees and expenses in their entirety.

When the union and its members, out of frustration or for other reasons, constantly file grievances, petty or otherwise, the work environment is poisoned and the union can quickly deplete its financial reserves. Sometimes, good faith and common sense are more important to the long-term relationship between the union and management than is resolute attention to contract details. For example, municipal unions in Hartford, Connecticut, spawned widespread criticism by filing grievances over work done by volunteers. When students from local colleges painted some rooms in a public school, the janitors' union forced the city to pay the janitors hundreds of dollars on the grounds that the union should have done the painting. Similarly, the AFSCME local filed a grievance over volunteers painting and repairing park benches. Also, after the city hired a private contractor to clean up elephant dung tracked into the civic center by workers during a circus (city equipment could not remove the smell), the union filed a grievance. Of course, the shoe can fit the other foot as well: a recalcitrant management may constantly violate the contract, forcing the frustrated union to go broke from the expense of appeals or to go on strike in violation of the agreement.

Excessive time delay is the most maligned aspect of grievance arbitration. It may take months from the day a grievance is filed before it reaches arbitration, and then a year or more before a final judgment is rendered by the arbitrators. Such delays, sometimes exceeding a total of 2 or 3 years, can lower employee morale and destroy faith in the collective bargaining agreement. As Coulson (1980: 496) explained: "Union members expect arbitration to be a swift and rational avenue of justice. Members become frustrated, alienated, and bitter when they are faced with unexplained delays, when legal mumbo jumbo keeps them from telling their story, and when the resolution of their case becomes lost behind the opaque innuendoes of the lawyers."

The grievance arbitration process, like any legal or quasi-legal proceeding, is fraught with opportunity for delay and procrastination. Quoting Coulson (1980: 496) again, there are "tedious multiple steps in the grievance procedure; delays; unnecessary formality; briefs and transcripts; ... long-winded arguments by lawyers about arbitrability; attempts to keep out evidence; and adjournment, delays, and postponements, for reasons that often relate more to the convenience of attorneys or union officials than to the merits of the case."

The "tedious multiple steps" Coulson refers to are similar to those in a civil or criminal court case, including the following:

1. Preparation for the arbitration hearing (assembling facts and records, obtaining depositions, scheduling witnesses and testimony, and other preliminary matters)
2. Setting the hearing date and format
3. Opening statements to the arbitrator
4. Presentation of the case by the initiating party (documentary evidence, witness testimony, cross-examination, etc.; transcripts may be made)
5. Presentation of the case by the responding party
6. Closing arguments
7. Preparation of the post-hearing briefs (written arguments) and transmittal to the arbitrator
8. Making the award (may consist of single statement of findings or summary of hearing and arbitrator's reasoning in making the award)

Monetary costs and delays in grievance arbitration are considered to be more serious problems by unions than by management. Management has deeper pockets to pay arbitration costs, and, as observed above, delays often result in management getting its way at least until the arbitration award is rendered. Management's principal concern, according to a survey of users of FMCS arbitration services, is the poor quality of arbitrators' decisions (Berkeley 1989).

Another problem with grievance arbitration has to do with what happens to the grievant and his or her supervisor once voluntary or arbitrated settlement occurs. A disturbing analysis of outcomes of grievance activity in four unionized organizations over 2- and 3-year periods indicates that grievants and their supervisors suffer retribution from their employers. Lewin and Peterson (1999) examined grievance activity and post-settlement outcomes in a steel manufacturing firm, a retail department store, a nonprofit hospital, and a local public school district. Results indicated that grievants' performance ratings, work attendance rates, and promotion rates declined whereas turnover rates increased in comparison to non-grievants. Similarly, supervisors of grievance filers received lower performance ratings and promotion rates and "were significantly more likely to be terminated from their jobs than supervisors of non-filers" (Lewin and Peterson, 1999: 572).

These chilling findings were not attributable to grievance filers and their supervisors being less competent performers than non-grievants and their supervisors, because no significant differences were detectable in job performance evaluations between the two groups in years prior to and during the filing and settling of grievances. The conclusion, then, is that personnel involved in grievances tend to be punished, much like whistle-blowers experience retribution after they expose their employer's wrongdoing. The unfortunate implication for employees who feel unfairly treated on the job is that they should suffer silently or face retribution

(Boroff and Lewin 1997). The message to supervisors is to overlook minor offenses by subordinates.

E. Standards for Arbitrator Decision Making

The degree of arbitrator emphasis on legal principles and procedures is a reflection of the approach taken to grievance arbitration. Those assuming a strict constructionist posture believe the contract should be the primary instrument governing the relationship between the parties and the decision of the arbitrator. Such an approach is likely to require procedural rules as extensive as those used in the courtroom and to mandate written transcripts, court reporters, and post-hearing briefs. "Problem-solving" arbitrators, on the other hand, view the contract as a document providing general guidelines for the parties and the arbitrator, with the arbitrator's function being primarily mediative in promoting mutual accommodation between the parties. Problem-solving neutrals tend to take a more expansive and innovative approach than strict constructionists with their narrow judicial perspective.

Of course, any arbitrator's principal interpretive duty is to make an award in accordance with the express terms and conditions of the contract and the key testimony, evidence, and other elements of the case at hand. The legal doctrine of *stare decisis* used to establish case precedent in the courtroom does not usually apply to grievance arbitration. Rather, each decision is arrived at *de novo*, with the existing agreement serving as the primary benchmark for the arbitration award. Among the specific case-related factors arbitrators take into account in arriving at a decision are management's conduct and consistency in applying the language of the contract; the grievant's work history, job performance, and seniority; procedural errors by either party; and various mitigating circumstances (Bohlander 1994; Simpson and Martocchio 1997; Haber and Karim 1995).

In attempting to interpret the contract, arbitrators sometimes find that the language is unclear or ambiguous. For example, a contract may state that leave time around Christmas should be applied for "as soon as possible." As a commentator observed long ago, "Given the obvious pressures of labor–management relations and the steady deterioration of English prose usage, it is no wonder that collective bargaining agreements are generally clumsy, inarticulate, and replete with provisions that are mutually contradictory" (Rubenstein 1966: 704–705). In such cases, certain "rules of contract construction" are adopted by arbitrators, including the following:

1. The common or popular meaning of language takes precedence over a special meaning.
2. Technical words are ascribed technical meaning unless local usage clearly indicates a different intention by the parties.
3. Conflicts between general provisions and specific provisions are settled in favor of the latter.

4. The express inclusion of certain items or guarantees in the contract means that those not listed were intentionally excluded.
5. The intent of the parties when the language was written is considered. Witnesses, notes, rough drafts, and other sources may be examined to help determine what the parties intended by certain words.

When the language of the agreement is exceedingly ambiguous or incomplete with regard to the grievance, the arbitrator must step beyond the contract to determine the parties' intent. Several standards may be used to discern the intent of the parties when they signed the agreement.

1. Past Practice

Past practice is the standard most frequently used to clear up hazy language or to guide the arbitrator when the contract is silent. A widely accepted definition of past practice is "a reasonably uniform response to a recurring situation over a substantial period of time which has been recognized by the parties implicitly or explicitly as the proper response" (R. L. Miller 1979: 203). As "the objective manifestation of the meanings the parties assumed at the time the agreement was signed" (Ferris 1975: 226), past practices carry great weight in contract interpretation. For example, if municipal trash collectors have been provided with cleanup time at the end of their shift for several years and the Director of Sanitation suddenly revokes this practice even though job conditions have not changed, an arbitrator (barring contract language to the contrary) would have strong reason for siding with the grieving sanitation workers.

2. Prior Bargaining Record

The second standard used by arbitrators to clarify contract language is the prior bargaining record of the parties, particularly when new language is confusing. Here the neutral may examine minutes or other records of bargaining sessions, contract supplements, or, on occasion, oral testimony. A common practice is for the arbitrator to find against the party who drafted new contract language when an ambiguity forces the loss of a benefit by the other party, the logic being that the drafting party had the opportunity to avoid any potential doubt of the intended meaning of the language. Only when the drafting party can show that the other party had not been confused or misled as to the intent of the language is the drafting party freed of this responsibility.

3. Previous Arbitration Awards

As noted earlier, *stare decisis* does not formally have standing in grievance arbitration awards. Each case is treated as unique. Nonetheless, prior decisions can and do exert an impact on subsequent rulings when circumstances are similar. Many awards are published and read by other arbitrators. Although not legally binding, such decisions are likely at least to have an indirect instructive influence on some neutrals.

4. Other Considerations

After listening to the arguments and examining the evidence and elements of the grievance case, the arbitrator must determine which party should prevail. In most grievance arbitration hearings, the burden of proof rests with the party that brings the action. Management has the burden of proof in disciplinary and discharge cases, whereas the union normally shoulders the burden in contract interpretation issues. Studies have shown that the party bearing the burden of proof loses more often than it wins, no doubt because "it is more difficult to prove a claim than to refute it" (Dilts and Leonard 1989: 340). Interestingly, public sector grievants tend to fare better than private sector grievants in winning cases (Mesch 1995).

Like decision makers in all settings, arbitrators often unconsciously filter case information through their sets of personal values. If they permit their personal values to influence their decisions, arbitrators can be guilty of bias. For example, alcohol abusers are often treated more sympathetically in substance abuse discharge cases than are abusers of illegal drugs. The alcoholic tends to be viewed as a person suffering from an illness, but the illegal drug user is held personally responsible for misbehavior. Yet, most contracts do not distinguish between the use of alcohol or other "intoxicants" on the job (Thornicroft 1989).

Does the grievant's gender matter? The evidence is inconclusive. Early studies found that women were more likely than men to win their grievances (Bemmels 1988). The implication was that arbitrators, who are predominantly male, tend to give women preferential treatment (as do judges in criminal cases). More recent research either finds no gender-associated differences in arbitration outcomes (Steen, Perrewe, and Hochwater 1994) or at least in one study, that women lose more cases than men do (Mesch 1995). If male arbitrators once acted paternalistically toward female grievants, perhaps they are now sensitized to avoid gender bias. In general, the arbitrator's gender, experience, training, and occupation are not important determinants of case outcomes (Zirkel and Breslin 1995).

V. Grievance Procedures in Federal Employment

No uniform system for handling federal employee grievances was established until President Kennedy issued Executive Order 10988 in 1962, directing all federal agencies to develop grievance and appellate procedures, including, if desired, advisory arbitration as a final step. Final decision-making authority on grievance systems continued to reside with agency heads, as they were free to reject the advisory opinion of an arbitrator. Meanwhile, grievants could process their complaints through regular, preexisting agency procedures if they so desired. This bifurcated system was roundly criticized by both unions and management, and the absence of a final and binding step short of unilateral management action was a source of particular discontent for the unions.

The inadequacies of the federal grievance procedures were addressed in President Richard Nixon's Executive Order 11491 of 1969, which permitted negotiated procedures, including binding arbitration, to serve as the exclusive method for resolving grievances over the life of the contract. A subsequent amendment to E.O. 11491 (Executive Order 11616) mandated negotiated grievance procedures in all federal labor–management contracts. Under these executive orders, federal agencies and their unions established step-by-step procedures similar to those in the private sector and state and local government, with many of them culminating in binding arbitration.

Federal grievance procedures today are provided for in Title VII of the Civil Service Reform Act of 1978, which incorporated many of the executive order provisions. Under the CSRA, federal employees and their unions are guaranteed the right to present and process grievances under either the negotiated system or regular agency statutory procedures, but not both, for cases involving demotions, dismissals, and other adverse actions.

The negotiated grievance procedure is the only channel available to employees in the bargaining unit for matters covered solely by the contract. Complaints involving discrimination, occupational health and safety, and other matters addressed in federal laws may be processed through the contractual procedure without prejudice to subsequent review of the case by the EEOC, the MSPB, or the federal courts. A federal arbitration award may be appealed by either party to the FLRA on grounds that the terms of the award conflict with existing statutes or agency regulations, the arbitrator exceeded his or her authority, the award was not taken from the written contract, the arbitrator was biased or refused to hear pertinent information, or the award was based on incomplete information (Edwards et al. 1979). The award must be appealed within 30 days or it becomes final. All federal labor agreements today must provide for some form of final binding arbitration. A majority stipulate that a single arbitrator is to be chosen from lists provided by the AAA or FMCS and that arbitration costs be shared by the parties.

Although the grounds for contesting arbitration awards are fairly narrow, and appeals pertaining to adverse actions by management may be taken directly to the federal courts, a relatively high percentage of federal awards are appealed to the FLRA (Frazier 1986), causing case backlogs. The FLRA usually upholds the arbitrator's decision.

Generally, the federal grievance process has not received great acclaim. Frivolous and frequent complaints clog up a system that becomes plagued by high costs and cumbersome lengthy procedures; options for informal resolution of problems at an early stage are scarce (Sulzner 1997; Roberts 1994).

VI. New Directions in Grievance Handling

Criticisms leveled at conventional grievance procedures have led to a search for reforms and alternatives that would be faster, simpler, and less expensive. One reform, known as expedited arbitration, essentially speeds up existing arbitration processes. Other new directions in handling grievances are characterized by the term "alternative dispute resolution."

A. Expedited Arbitration

Expedited grievance arbitration (also known as "instant arbitration") is designed to reduce the time and monetary costs of resolving grievances. It was first used in the private sector in a 1971 contract between ten steel producers and the United Steelworkers of America to reduce a large backlog of unsettled grievance cases. In public employment, expedited arbitration was initiated in a 1973 contract between postal workers and the U.S. Postal Service (USPS).

Expedited arbitration systems vary from place to place, but most are characterized by the following:

1. Cases are screened to identify routine, non-precedent-setting grievances and send them to expedited arbitration.
2. An informal atmosphere is maintained, with no transcripts or written briefs.
3. The arbitrator must issue the award within a very short period of time (often following a brief recess or 24 hours).
4. The award is written in one page or less.
5. The arbitrator may hear more than one case in a single day.
6. Costs are low and are shared by the parties.

Expedited arbitration differs from conventional grievance arbitration in its informal, nonjudicial atmosphere and the more timely nature of the proceedings. Expedited arbitration is not intended to replace regular arbitration, but rather to be used in conjunction with it for quickly resolving less important or minor grievances.

A large accumulation of minor disciplinary cases persuaded the USPS and four major unions to implement expedited arbitration on an experimental basis in 1973. Within 2 years the backlog had been reduced substantially (Frost 1978: 468). Today, expedited arbitration in the Postal Service begins with a national screening committee that assigns grievances to expedited or regular arbitration. Cases to be expedited are listed with the FMCS or AAA for assignment by those organizations to individual arbitrators. Decisions may be issued either orally or in a one-page written form required within 48 hours of the completion of the hearing. Awards may not be used as precedent for subsequent cases.

Although expedited arbitration in the Postal Service has recorded time and cost savings, some difficulties have arisen. Initially there was a high rate of resignations by arbitrators who felt overburdened by the pressure of hearing up to three cases per day, although the dropout rate decreased considerably as arbitrators became more accustomed to the procedure. In addition, like other grievance procedures, expedited arbitration suffers from a shortage of trained personnel. However, the Postal Service instituted a training program in conjunction with the AAA that has helped alleviate this problem.

Although critics have charged that expedited arbitration discourages joint problem solving between the parties, and that the lack of precedent and written decisions discourages uniformity in arbitration awards, the process offers important advantages. When routine, relatively uncomplicated complaints are processed, there should be little or no loss of decision quality. Grievances concerning job reinstatement or back pay are especially suited for expedited arbitration because the rapid decision diminishes the financial liability of the employer while ensuring that a wronged employee receives what is coming forthwith. Expedited arbitration does cut costs and reduce delays in settling grievances. A popular adage holds that "justice delayed is justice denied." As long as its limitations and proper applications are understood, expedited arbitration can help public employees receive a fair and timely hearing of their grievances.

B. Alternative Dispute Resolution

Labor–management conflict tends to escalate. Conflict may grow directly, such as through increasingly vitriolic confrontations, or indirectly, through ignoring the conflict until the problem inflates into significant proportions. As noted above, the conventional grievance processes, court actions, and regulatory procedures are likely to be time consuming, expensive, and frustrating. In these adversarial processes, for every winner there is a loser. The basic premise of alternative dispute resolution (ADR) is that labor and management representatives can constructively confront issues and mutually explore their fair resolution. Conflict is viewed not as warfare, but as an opportunity to develop positive outcomes that reasonably satisfy both parties (Faerman 1996).

ADR includes a variety of processes and mechanisms that involve joint decision making in which the parties, with the assistance of a facilitator or mediator, work through their problems until they find a settlement with which they can live. Hence, grievances are resolved before they move to arbitration. The relationship between the parties does not suffer from adversarial engagement; ideally, it even improves.

C. Grievance Mediation

Grievance mediation involves intervention by a neutral mediator into a potential or actual impasse over the application or interpretation of contract terms. The goal of grievance mediation, like mediation of interest disputes, is for the neutral to help the parties resolve their differences voluntarily. The mediators act much as they would in an interest dispute, meeting individually and jointly with the parties to try to devise a mutually acceptable settlement. Grievance mediators may use their knowledge of the facts to convince the party with the weaker position to settle instead of going to arbitration (Caraway 1989: 496).

Grievance mediation offers cost savings because it avoids arbitrator fees, attorneys' fees, travel, and related legal costs. Cost advantages also accrue because grievance mediation is a much faster process than arbitration. The mediator operates in a relatively informal and highly flexible atmosphere free from the procedural constraints placed on an arbitrator. The mediator's proposed solution, for instance, normally does not have to be reduced to writing, and case preparation is much less thorough. Monetary savings are particularly significant for federal sector grievance mediation, where the FMCS will furnish a mediator to the parties without charge, and in state and local jurisdictions that avail themselves of FMCS services or free mediation aid from the state labor relations agency. Even when mediators must be paid, savings over arbitration may easily run into thousands of dollars.

An additional advantage of grievance mediation is that it sets no precedents for future contract interpretation. If, for example, a grievance arises over an issue that has not fully ripened, such as discrimination against a domestic partner, it may be more advisable to mediate a settlement than arbitrate it because the binding feature of arbitration may cause future problems. Thus, grievance mediation allows a new issue or problem to develop more fully before a precedent-setting ruling addresses it.

Users of grievance mediation (both grievants and management) report greater satisfaction with the final resolution of the dispute than do those who go to arbitration. The process is much less adversarial and combative than arbitration. It relies on joint problem solving by the parties, who may explore a variety of options without risking anything even if arbitration must ultimately be employed. The mediator helps the parties sort out the key issues from the less important ones and to discover where their true interests reside. Then, the mediator helps develop a solution that satisfies the interests of both parties (Kriesky 1994: 243). Favorable results have been reported from California (Caraway 1989), Massachusetts (Bonner 1992), Michigan (Gregory and Rooney 1980), Ohio (Nelson and Uddin 1995: 208), Washington (Skratek 1987), the USPS, and several federal agencies.

The USPS has been a leader in grievance mediation, implementing a number of pilot projects during the 1990s. For example, under the REDRESS program (Resolve Employment Disputes Reach Equitable Solutions Swiftly), members of bargaining units are offered an alternative to the conventional EEO complaint process (USOPM, 2008). Within 2 weeks of receiving a request, the USPS schedules mediation. The Justice Center of Atlanta selects and sends an experienced neutral to the USPS facility. The employee may choose to be represented by a private attorney, a union representative, or a coworker. The mediator applies interest-based techniques to help resolve the dispute. If mediation fails, the employee may return to the conventional EEO process. A 71 percent settlement rate was recorded (Bingham 1997). REDRESS users report satisfaction with outcomes, as well as with their ability "to control the process, present one's views and participate in the process, and receive respect and fair treatment from the mediator" (Bingham 1997: 29).

Reports on grievance mediation experiences in state and local government also indicate substantial savings in time and money, remarkably high rates of settlement, and overall satisfaction with the process on the part of both unions and management (Kriesky 1994: 244–245).

Are the much-touted benefits of grievance mediation as great as reported? Feuille (1992) has raised questions about the accuracy of reported time and monetary savings. He suggested that a large proportion of the grievances sent to mediation would not have been arbitrated anyway because of being dropped or settled before arbitration. Moreover, he has proposed that the existence of mediation might keep grievances "alive" longer and thereby increase total costs. Thus, the purported benefits of grievance mediation could be illusory (Feuille 1992: 137–139).

There are other disadvantages to grievance mediation. There is the predictable shortage of trained neutrals. Arbitrators appear to be unsuitable for grievance mediation chores because of a basic professional conflict of interest: if grievances can be settled at a low cost through mediation, fewer cases will pass on to arbitration and as a consequence the income of arbitrators will atrophy. Also, the lack of a written record and formal procedures makes grievance mediation inappropriate for seminal, precedent-setting cases or complex EEO-type cases that can be litigated beyond the contractual procedures.

Other ADR methods include the ombudsman and peer review. The ombudsman is a neutral third party designated by an organization to assist a grievant in resolving a conflict. The ombudsman may provide counseling, help develop factual information, and attempt to reconcile the disputing parties through his or her powers of persuasion. Usually, the ombudsman is hired by the organization to work full time at resolving conflicts.

In peer review, a panel of employees (or employees and managers) listens to the parties' arguments and reviews evidence to decide an issue in dispute. The decision of panel members, who receive training in handling sensitive issues, may or may not be binding on the parties (U.S. General Accounting Office 1997).

VII. Conclusion

Labor and management alike share important responsibilities to ensure that they and their constituencies live with the contract in a reasonably efficacious fashion. In a healthy cooperative relationship, they eschew "brinkmanship," constantly pushing grievance procedures to the final step in an effort to make the other side blink. Both parties strive to ensure that their representatives in labor–management relations, especially supervisors and union stewards, are well trained in grievance handling and intimately familiar with the terms and conditions of the agreement. Both explicitly seek to keep communication channels open and clear and resolve grievances at the lowest level possible. Finally, both strive to keep time and monetary costs low.

Each party has its own special responsibilities in effectively administering the agreement and handling grievances. For its part, management should monitor the behavior of supervisors in administering the contract to ensure negotiated grievance procedures are functioning properly and grievants receive a fair hearing. Management also should be willing to admit when it is wrong.

Union representatives should carefully screen employee complaints and drop those that are petty, and at the same time take great care to ensure that valid grievances receive a fair hearing. The union must also take caution to represent each member of the bargaining unit with the same energy and dedication, whether a member of the union or not. Conflict on the terms and conditions of the contract is both inevitable and healthy. The goal is to manage that conflict productively and avoid damaging the long-term relationship between the parties.

Case Study 10.1: Chain of Custody

On March 1, the city of Garden Way hired Thelma Woodall, age 23, as an administrative assistant in the office of the mayor. Thelma was the top candidate among those interviewed for the job, and she appeared to be a bright, energetic, and personable employee.

Garden Way had recently begun a mandatory drug-testing program in which all essential and confidential employees are randomly screened for illegal drug use. Thelma was tested on May 3, and her urine sample was positive for marijuana. At first Thelma denied using marijuana, but finally she admitted taking two puffs on a reefer at a party on February 10. She said it was the only occasion she had ever used any prohibited substance.

Thelma was discharged both for the positive drug test results and for initially lying about her drug use. She appealed through the grievance procedure and was represented by her local AFSCME unit. In arbitration, management introduced as evidence the two reasons for Thelma's discharge along with the fact that she was still a probationary employee. The union introduced evidence that a significant chain-of-custody problem existed with the urine sample and asserted that the sample could not be traced conclusively to Thelma. Additionally, the union stated that Thelma's drug use occurred before she was hired, that it took place off the job, and that her performance on the job to date had been excellent.

Questions

1. If you were the arbitrator hearing this case, explain what your ruling would be and the reasons you would give for your decision.

2. Explain what additional evidence, facts, or testimony you would seek.
3. Is it fair and reasonable to discharge Thelma, given the circumstances of the case?

Case Study 10.2: The Arbitration Case of Keyshaun King

Keyshaun King, a motor pool mechanic, had been a good employee for more than 7 years. But he was fed up with Billy Barnhill, another mechanic. Barnhill was a bumbler, always dropping tools, nicking hoses, and banging bumpers. However, he tended to do okay when closely supervised. He had occasionally made comments to King and other African American workers that could be interpreted as racist, but they tried to overlook his insensitivity in the interest of positive workplace relations.

King had tried his best to be tolerant but on August 2, when Barnhill's wrench slipped from an alternator and smacked into King's cheek, leaving a 2-inch gash and a certain bruise, King's patience evaporated. In pain, King grabbed the wrench from Barnhill and pushed him away. Two other employees heard King yell in pain and saw him grab the wrench and shove Barnhill.

Barnhill took exception to King's reaction, muttered "You people are all alike!" and marched into the shift supervisor's office to report the incident, asserting that King had attacked, assaulted, and threatened him. The supervisor, Jimmy Jackson, dismissed Barnhill and called King into his office. "What happened, Keyshaun?," he asked. King admitted seizing the wrench with one hand and bracing against Barnhill's shoulder with the other. He also related what he heard Barnhill say. Jackson sent both employees home for the day.

Jackson was aware that Barnhill was borderline incompetent, but he had had no cause to take disciplinary action against him until now. He liked Barnhill's loyalty and dependability along with his willingness to pitch in and work overtime when needed, but this incident troubled him. Was there just cause to fire one or both of them? Or would a lesser disciplinary action be more appropriate?

Jackson went to the employee manual, where he read the following passage:

> Just cause shall serve as the basis for disciplinary action and includes, but is not limited to: dishonesty, inefficiency, unprofessional conduct, falsification of records, fighting, racial or sexual taunting, violation of city policy, destruction of property, or possession or being under the influence of alcohol or narcotics.

He would have to take the issue to higher management authority, the chief motor pool supervisor.

The chief supervisor, Hank Hawkings, was known as a hard ass. He had recently dealt with another physical altercation on a different shift, for which he fired both combatants without a hearing. This case did not appear to be terribly distinct; so, in the interest of consistency, Hawkings called each worker into his office the next morning when they reported to work and sacked them both.

King and Barnhill both appealed the action. You are the grievance arbitrator.

Questions

1. Which arguments should be given greatest weight: those based on the employee manual, the collective bargaining agreement, or mitigating factors given by the grievant and his witnesses? Explain.
2. How might "unprofessional conduct," "taunting," and "fighting" be defined? Explain.
3. How would you rule in this case? Explain the reasons for your decision.

Chapter 11

Public Employee Unions in the Future

I. Introduction

Unions in the United States seem to be perpetually "at a crossroads." Private sector labor organizations have been buffeted by many forces during the past half century and, as noted in Chapter 1, if there is to be a "final" crossroads, they may be poised at that very intersection today. Public employee unions are not immune to the dilemmas of their private sector counterparts, and they face special challenges of their own. Following a brief discussion of the steady decline of private sector unions and hints of a resurgence, this concluding chapter examines the challenges and opportunities for unions in government.

II. The Decline of Private Sector Unions

For some 45 years labor union membership in the private sector workplace has been falling. At the apex of union density, one third of the nation's nonagricultural workers were members of unions. The proportion had fallen to about 12 percent by 1990 and hovered around 8 percent in 2008. Despite occasional excitement in the labor community, the promises of more vigorous national leadership, and the optimistic writings of labor scholars, the labor movement continues to struggle.

As we observed in Chapter 1, the fading fortunes of private sector unions have brought forth an abundance of discussion, debate, and scholarly research. Membership decline is attributed to far-reaching economic changes in the United States and abroad that have both shifted jobs from high-wage, union-friendly locations to low-wage, union-hostile areas of the country and altered the composition of the labor force and the very nature of work itself. Union leaders and sympathizers lay the blame on an unfavorable legal environment that constrains organizing and encourages bias against unions, the anti-union posture of corporate media (C. R. Martin 2003), and aggressive management opposition and corporate "union busting." It is also suggested that old-style, self-serving union leaders have failed to steer their organizations successfully in the new economic climate, have faltered badly at organizing new members, and, at times, have been their own worst enemies when it comes to cultivating public support for organized labor.

If one thinks of organizations as living organisms struggling for growth and survival, they must maintain or even grow their resources and strategically adapt to the inevitable and unceasing changes and turbulence in their environment (Kearney 2003). Those that do adapt successfully will grow and prosper. Those that fail to do so will follow the dinosaurs into eventual extinction. The forces aligned against effective adaptation tend to produce organizations that are "prisoners of inertia" (Raskin 1986: 4). There are internal constraints against upsetting prevailing economic and political relationships. There are exchange relationships that benefit organizational leaders and internal groups, but which can contribute to the displacement of primary organizational goals. And there are external forces that influence an organization towards inertia and staleness, such as public policy barriers, economic limitations, and constraints of legitimacy (Hannan and Freeman 1977).

All of these and more have combined to hamper private sector unions. Structural shifts in the nature, location, and technology of employment have an impact on a union's ability to recruit new members and maintain membership strength. Today, a growing number of jobs are not linked to the traditional workplace, but rather to information technology and the "virtual office." The world today, in the memorable phrase of Tom Friedman (2007), is "flat." Anything can be made anywhere and sold everywhere, and information flows freely through the Web. Changes in social and political values have elevated individualism and the pursuit of wealth over the values of social equity and collective action that have nurtured unionization. Public policy under the National Labor Relations Act (NLRA) is less than conducive to unionization and collective bargaining in the corporate sector (Forbath 1991; Dunlop Commission 1994). Under Bush administration appointees (2000–2008), the NLRA was consistently hostile toward unions and collective bargaining. For example, its rulings extending collective bargaining exemptions by expanding the definition of "supervisor" cost large numbers of union members their bargaining rights. Yet the likelihood of congressional action to "level the playing field" for unions is slim. Unions are hanging their hopes on the proposed Employee Free Choice Act, which would establish the right of employees to win union representation through majority signup rather than by secret ballot elections. Unions allege that elections permit employers to routinely bully workers with threats of losing pay, benefits, or even their jobs. With the possible election of a Democratic, pro-labor president and Democratic majorities in Congress in 2008, Free Choice could reach fruition.

The revitalization of the AFL-CIO under the leadership of John Sweeney raised hopes of boosting the fortunes of unions, but they were soon dashed against the rocks of intense internal crisis in the AFL-CIO that resulted in several large unions bolting from the federation. As noted in Chapter 1 these rebel organizations, including SEIU, UNITE-HERE, and the Teamsters, established their own umbrella organization called Change to Win. The new organization differs fundamentally with the AFL-CIO over how to strengthen the labor movement. In addition to bestowing friendly candidates with campaign donations, Change to Win believes that a priority should be to strengthen and grow union membership through aggressive organizing. The key targets have been child care and health workers. This sets the table for an interesting test of competing hypotheses: Does organizational strength flow from large size or from specialization? Is bigger and denser better? Or specialization and competition?

Organizing successes have been recorded in the health care and textile sectors, among others, and the profile of private sector unions has been elevated through the national political arena. Still, the political strength of Republicans and conservative Democrats in Congress has mitigated the possibility of significant union breakthroughs in public policy.

Ultimately, the bulk of the responsibility for the failure of private sector unions to adapt to their changing environment must be laid at the feet of unimaginative, reactive, and in some situations, self-interested and corrupt union leadership. Labor, "neck deep in its own failures and betrayals, corruptions, and bad faith" (Fraser 1998), has poisoned its own well, as illustrated by the frequent involvement of the International Brotherhood of Teamsters, the International Longshoremen's Union, and others in sordid scandals and entanglements with organized crime.

Unions have broken free of more severe constraints in the past than those they confront today, such as the repression of unionization under the criminal conspiracy doctrine in the early 1800s and the violent suppression of strikers by company-hired goon squads during the 1870s. If private sector unions can truly pull themselves out of the doldrums and shake off the bureaucratic and other rigidities that constrict them, and demonstrate their continuing relevance to the new labor force, membership and resource growth will follow (Shostak 1991). More broadly, labor must redefine its mission as one that moves beyond "more" and toward equating the goals and purposes of the union with those of a broader, more mobile, and "sector-shifting" aggregation of prospective members. Organized labor must, in short, offer a coherent appeal to the nonunion workplace to bring its members into the ranks of organized labor.

III. Challenges for Public Employee Unions

Like their counterparts in the world of business, unions in government are also poised at something of a crossroads. Although they have not yet experienced the downward spiral suffered by private sector organizations, public employee unions reached a growth plateau during the early 1980s. They have also been weathering an uncomfortably high level of public and legislative attacks through calls for outsourcing and privatization of public services, citizen resistance to paying taxes and fees, negative public opinion, and legislative rollbacks of longstanding collective bargaining arrangements. For purposes of discussion, the principal challenges confronting public employee unions today may be categorized as fiscal, structural, public policy, and strategic.

A. The Continuing Fiscal Squeeze

Following decades of steadily rising revenues, spending, and employment, governments at all levels have experienced lengthy periods of retrenchment. Even during periods of strong national economic prosperity, government growth has been moderate. The federal budget was finally balanced in 1998–1999, only to soar to record deficits in 2006. Powerful pressures for tax cuts, the financial weakness of Social Security, and the persistent policy problems of illegal drugs, public education, environmental protection, criminal justice, Medicaid and Medicare, and many others continued to constrain the amount of federal dollars passed through to the states and localities. Raising new state and local revenues to fund programs to relieve these policy problems has been extremely difficult within the context of taxation and expenditure limitations and fervent anti-tax sentiment. The taxpayer revolt that commenced in California in 1978 with Proposition 13 kicked off a national movement to slash taxing and spending, as well as the size of government, that still resonates today in city halls and state capitals and depresses public employment and compensation.

The implications for public employee unions are not positive. Compensation gains have been modest even during recent years of strong economic growth. State and local employment has been rising only marginally — if at all — even in growing jurisdictions, limiting opportunities for union membership gains. Contracting out government services to private and nonprofit providers has displaced some public employees' jobs. New Public Management (NPM) reforms have victimized public employees in the federal government, which downsized by more than a quarter-million jobs in the 1990s. As unwilling pawns in political conflicts between elected officials, top administrators, and angry taxpayers, public workers have learned the hard way that the job security that once characterized public employment is little more than a fond memory today. Downsizing, decentralization, privatization, and performance improvement demands brought forward under the NPM banner have damaged morale in many settings and placed public employees in difficult and uncertain situations (Kearney and Hays 1998).

For the unions, these trends have important implications. First, membership rolls have stabilized or declined in most jurisdictions, with a corresponding weakening or stagnation in union financial resources and bargaining power. Second, fiscal constraints mean that unions are able to do less for the members of their bargaining units in terms of wages and benefits, no matter how fiercely they engage in collective bargaining. Ironically, public employees may perceive the need for collective representation most strongly during times of government fiscal stress, but they may also see unions as less able to deliver the goods for them.

B. Structural Challenges

Like the business sector, the U.S. public sector is experiencing new global economic, political, and social forces. Among the most critical of these forces for public employees and their unions are technological change, the attractions of a market economy that has produced a resource shift from government to the private sector, and the new demographics of the work force.

Public employee unions enjoyed some of their greatest early success in organizing blue-collar and clerical workers who discharged job tasks that essentially replicated those in the private sector. Gradually, however, technological innovations have made it increasingly feasible to replace such employees with machines or software. The character of much government work (e.g., police and fire protection, classroom teaching, social service casework) makes technological substitution for labor very difficult. Nevertheless, new technology has supplanted some public employees, such as the personal computer for typists and clerical workers, the scanner for data entry personnel, and the single operator sanitation truck for the three-member crew. More recently, government data entry, call centers, and other mundane activities have been outsourced to India and other countries. There are many other examples of technologically driven attrition, and additional ones will emerge. For unions to maintain their present levels of membership and financial resources, every member displaced by technology must in turn be replaced by signing up new members or establishing new bargaining units for previously nonrepresented workers.

A second structural threat to unions is a shift in resources from government to the private economy. A multiplicity of forces and agents, including tax resistance, negative public opinion toward government, public affection for the private marketplace, and the NPM movement, are conspiring to transfer government functions and activities to the private and nonprofit sectors. These powerful forces, augmented by the common perspective that, at least in theory, nearly all of the work of government could be accomplished by private and nonprofit service providers, represent a serious threat to public employee unions.

The effects of privatization and outsourcing are both subtle and overt. The subtle effects include privatization's generally depressing influence on public employment, pay, and benefits. Most of the jobs being outsourced are those of direct service providers such as counselors, caseworkers, and laborers. One result is that the relative proportion of predominantly nonunion professional and administrative positions is growing. Privatization's effects are registered with every public job lost to a private or nonprofit provider. Privatization's frightful reputation may exceed the empirical reality of jobs lost, but that could change relatively quickly. For example, several states have turned over various components of welfare program administration to private contractors, placing "at risk" an estimated quarter of a million government social service jobs (Kosterlitz 1997). In the embattled public education community, hundreds of thousands of teaching jobs could be lost to private schools if voucher plans were implemented nationwide.

The third structural problem is a human capital challenge. It is common knowledge that the U.S. labor force is becoming increasingly female, older, Latino, African American, Asian, and foreign-born, and these trends are projected to extend into the foreseeable future. Some of these new workers require special accommodations by employers and unions. The culture of work is undergoing dramatic change, with important implications for interpersonal, interorganizational, and supervisor–subordinate relations.

Unions are struggling to clearly define their role in attracting and representing this socially diverse work force. Their organizational health and well-being depend greatly on how effectively they respond to the new employment issues associated with demographic and sociocultural changes in the labor force. To remain viable organizations, unions must convince the new work force that it can effectively represent their interests and concerns and serve their job-related needs.

As demonstrated by largely unsuccessful efforts to organize Southern workers and recruit new members from the expanding information technology sector, the unions' record is mixed. In general, out of necessity, public sector unions have chalked up a much better record of incorporating women and minorities into union affairs and leadership positions than private sector unions. AFSCME, NEA, AFT, and SEIU report substantial numbers of women in their ranks. AFSCME has aggressively pursued discrimination complaints and filed lawsuits to force employers to adopt comparable worth policies. Public employee unions have also promoted and bargained for more flexible and family-friendly benefits.

Research indicates that nonunion workers in government tend to exhibit a strong affinity for unions, and most would join one if they could. Pro-union sentiment is most pronounced among African American and Latino workers; women's desire for unionization is approximately equal to that of men (Leigh and Hills 1987). It would seem, then, that in those unorganized public jurisdictions in which the legal environment permits union recognition and collective bargaining, women and minorities are waiting for unions to provide them with tangible and compelling reasons to join. Among the possible avenues for unions to demonstrate their relevance to these workers is through negotiated benefits such as health care and wellness programs, family-friendly benefits, specialized training and education opportunities, mortgage assistance programs, purchase discounts, and even favorable rates on union-sponsored credit cards.

As if these other structural challenges were not daunting enough, the baby-boom retirement bulge presents another. With estimates that up to 60 percent of today's federal, state, and local workers will be eligible for retirement in the next few years, unions are staring in the teeth of a significant loss of union advocates and leaders. The need to turn their unwavering attention to new labor force entrants is patently obvious.

C. Public Policy Challenges

Whether one subscribes to the theory that comprehensive bargaining laws generate high levels of union membership or to the competing theory that high levels of unionization impel such laws, there is a strong positive relationship between the two variables. Public employees in comprehensive bargaining states are in a highly favorable policy environment, as reflected by strong membership figures. As is true of distributive and redistributive policies everywhere, what is once granted is difficult to take away. Public managers and most elected officials have little incentive to take on public employee unions in jurisdictions in which bargaining rights are strong and widely applied. Managers do not want to sacrifice valuable time and human resources to a losing assault on unions. For their part, politicians must take into account public employee votes and union campaign contributions. It is very rare indeed for a comprehensive bargaining law to be revoked by a state legislative body. (New Mexico was an exception to the rule, but has since reinstated collective bargaining for state employees.) Attacks on the political use of union dues are another matter. State crackdowns on the political use of union dues have become more frequent, as demonstrated in early 2000s in Utah, Idaho, and Ohio.

The legal status quo, however, is very difficult to modify when it comes to expanding bargaining rights as well. Any new upsurge in public employee unionization will require (1) an amendment of federal law to expand the scope of bargaining for federal employees to union security and compensation issues; and (2) federal legislation compelling collective bargaining for certain categories of state and local employees; and (3) a parade of new bargaining laws in the noncomprehensive bargaining states. The first — facilitative federal legislation for federal, state and local workers — has been raised regularly in Congress since the 1980s, but to no effect because of conservative opposition. As noted earlier, in 2007 the U.S. House of Representatives passed by a large margin a bill granting collective bargaining rights to all public safety personnel in state and local governments, including those in nonbargaining states. Although the Senate has taken no action, this represented a tantalizing new possibility for a strong congressional Democratic majority and a Democratic president to push forward in 2009. New state legislative actions may occur, as well as expansion of bargaining rights through executive orders or court decisions, which would produce incremental increases in membership levels and new collective bargaining relationships.

Without membership expansion, unions in government risk the same stagnation, followed perhaps by the absolute membership losses that have afflicted their counterparts in the corporate world. If public sector unions cannot at least maintain the existing level of their most critical asset (members) they may step on the same slippery slope of decline that private sector unions have experienced. Even if unions succeed in meeting their public policy challenges, privatization looms large. Whether under the guise of NPM, reengineering, right sizing, or whatever the next management fad is called, privatization has the countenance of a long-lived phenomenon that could significantly deplete union membership and resources and keep public sector unions in a reactive and defensive posture. Federal employee unions have experienced the brunt of privatization so far, losing at least 165,000 members to the National Performance Review reforms ("Downsizing Hits Unions" 1997) and countless others from Bush administration actions. The body count for state and local unions could rise as well because of persistent pressures to contain labor costs and the size of government.

D. Strategic Challenges

The strategic choices to be made by public employee unions are equally daunting. Like their private sector counterparts, they are caught in a web of global and domestic forces that threaten to deplete their political and economic resources and reduce membership levels. The redistribution of service-provision activities and jobs to the private and nonprofit sectors represents a prodigious challenge for public sector unions, as does the weak support for public service on the part of citizens and elected officials. However, in comparison to private sector unions, those representing government employees generally function in a much less hostile political environment. And, in general, their strategic choices and actions have been more astute and their national leadership more adept at coping with emerging challenges and issues than has been the case with unions in the private sector.

Their political proclivities mean that public employee unions are pulled toward the Democratic party. However, especially at the local level, union leaders have learned how to work all sides of the table. Symbiotic relationships between unions and elected and appointed officials of all political persuasions are common. The mutuality of interests ranges from fighting for better health care to seeking jurisdiction-wide improvements in pay and benefits for all public servants. The opportunity for multilateral bargaining with elected officials provides public employee unions with multiple paths to political influence during contract negotiations.

Despite these positive relationships, low public esteem for government, public employees, and unions has pushed management into a more aggressive posture with respect to organized employees. Teacher unions, for example, have received more than their fair share of blame for the perceived shortcomings of public educa-tion. Potentially threatening education reform proposals such as abolishing teacher tenure or establishing voucher plans encounter union opposition. In such cases, teacher organizations have come to be perceived as a major obstacle to change.

One of the first notable elected officials to take on the teacher unions was Michigan Governor John Engler, who demonstrated in the early 1990s that instead of being an act of unthinking political suicide, attacking teacher unions as defend-ers of the increasingly unacceptable education status quo could actually be politi-cally advantageous (Mahtesian 1995: 36). Teacher unions were soon under assault by elected officials in a growing number of states. Yet, from a practical perspective, management has only one possible nonlegislative means of ridding itself of unions — privatization. Decertification of an existing union or dissolution of a bargain-ing unit is extremely problematic, and unlike a firm, the public jurisdiction cannot move its operations to South Carolina or Virginia to escape organized labor.

Nonetheless, unions are concerned about the relatively low esteem in which they are held by the general public. Approval of unions has waxed and waned since the public was first queried on the topic in the mid-1930s. Approval ratings peaked in 1957 in the Gallup Poll at 72 percent and then declined significantly to an all-time low of 55 percent in 1979. Data over the past decade indicate a low level of confi-dence in labor unions: about one third of respondents to various polls report having very little or no confidence in them, and some 15 percent report having a great deal or quite a lot of confidence in them. (Interestingly, these are about the same levels as for big business; http://www.pollingreport.com/institut.htm; accessed march 4, 2008.) Similarly, by large majorities, poll respondents indicate very little confidence in the people running labor organizations.

Thus, a majority of the U.S. public appears to approve of labor unions in principle, and unions are valued by the public in terms of what they do for their members, but only a relatively small proportion of citizens have much confidence in them or their leaders. Undoubtedly, the scandals, corruption, and felonious behavior associated with several high-profile private sector unions have contributed to this low esteem. Unfortunately, the surveys do not isolate public opinion toward public employee unions specifically. By inference and anecdotal information, however, one must assume that public sector unions are not unscathed by public opprobrium of all labor organizations, particularly when considered in the context of taxpayer displeasure with government.

Within a difficult and ever-changing economic and political environment, pub-lic sector unions have generally demonstrated a remarkable degree of adaptability. They have achieved much better results from their organizing activities than private sector unions. Since the beginning of the modern era of public sector collective bargaining, nearly all unions in government have, perhaps as much out of necessity as by choice, made special efforts to organize women and minorities and to elevate them into leadership positions. (Exceptions are police and firefighter organizations, which, until recently, resisted members who were not white males.) Successful unions have sought out dissatisfied workers of all demographic characteristics in any setting. SEIU and AFSCME, in particular, have demonstrated that they have learned this key principle about leveraging public employee work dissatisfaction into membership gains. Pay inequity is an example of an issue causing dissatisfaction among female workers that unions have successfully exploited. Another is poor treatment of immigrant workers. Low pay, minimal benefits, and poor working conditions for custodial, nursing home, and health care workers present organizing opportunities as well.

In more instances than the unions would care to admit, their locals have acted selfishly, irresponsibly, and stupidly in assiduously protecting their perceived rights and contract provisions. Featherbedding, working to the rule, insisting that volunteers be forbidden to perform needed union-related work, calling ill-advised work stoppages, and aggressively defending felonious or incompetent members are some examples. On the whole, however, public employee union leadership at the national level has been far superior to and much more statesmanlike than that of private sector organizations. Union presidents have helped their respective organizations strategically adapt and respond to enormous changes in their environments, finding ways to float with the social, economic, and political currents rather than trying to swim upstream. Such adaptive behavior will continue to be critical to public employee unions as they marshal their resources to confront the challenges ahead.

Astute national leadership is critically important to the future success of unions in the public sector, but so, too, is the quality of leadership in the thousands of locals throughout the federal, state, and local governments. Strategic errors and public relations miscues at the lowest levels can rebound into issues of national media visibility, confirming the beliefs of those who dislike unions and causing a negative bias in the opinions of previously neutral observers. It is impossible to know with any degree of empirical precision just how adept local leadership is, but it is known that a large proportion of local union presidents are part-time representatives who have risen through the ranks with little or no specialized training or preparation other than on-the-job experience (Sulzner 1997: 168–169). The potential benefits of training and education for these individuals should be obvious to national organizations.

IV. Opportunities

The profound structural, technological, economic, and related changes that are affecting public employee unions pose various known and unknown dangers, but they also present opportunities. To survive, let alone prosper, public employee organizations must adapt to these critical changes in their environment through innovative strategies and actions.

Although there is very little if anything that unions can do about the fiscal squeeze that throttles units of government and constrains public employee pay and benefits, they can help management search for productivity and efficiency improvements that enhance organizational performance. Recognizing — if not fully accepting — that employee financial gains are seldom going to exceed the annual rise in the cost-of-living index, many unions are focusing their attention at the bargaining table on working conditions, nonmonetary benefits, and various human resource policies. Many potential bargaining issues do not have significant financial impacts. Examples include flexible working hours, telecommuting, and flexible benefits packages.

The structural changes confronting unions also present opportunities. NPM poses a number of challenges to unions, but it is simply not going to succeed in organized jurisdictions without union cooperation. Management recognizes that employee organizations must be closely involved in reengineering, job redesign, privatization, and other initiatives if they are to get off the ground, let alone succeed. Rather than the typical knee-jerk opposition to contracting out work, for example, public officials can provide unions with opportunities to demonstrate how they can help cut costs and enhance efficiencies through participation and collaboration in work design (Gerhart 1994: 125–129). Unions in Cleveland, Indianapolis, Phoenix, and other cities have insisted on submitting their own bids to win back contracted work, and in many instances they have been successful. When public officials are determined to fully shift a service to a private or nonprofit provider, unions can turn their effort to ensuring that no current union members will lose their jobs. They can also commit resources to organize those nongovernment workers who are performing the contract work.

The rapidly expanding ranks of public employee telecommuters and contract workers offer an interesting but still relatively untested opportunity to unions. Telecommunications and computer technology have moved the "virtual office" from concept to reality. A growing number of jobs can be performed almost anywhere and do not require fixed office space and standard work hours. Federal and state government employees are increasingly telecommuting part time or full time from home or suburban satellite work centers. Some "road warriors" operate from a portable office as they travel from location to location.

Telecommuting is recognized as being good for the environment (fewer cars on the road), good for employees' stress levels (no long morning and afternoon commutes), and good for the organizational budget (reduced need for physical office space). But is telecommuting good for unions? The virtual office removes employees from much daily interaction with their coworkers and effectively makes them free agents, working on their own with minimal daily supervision. The tendency is toward worker autonomy, not collective action through an employee organization. On the other hand, even the stay-at-home employee may perceive a need for representation on such issues as the type of equipment needed and who should provide and service it, ergonomic and health and safety considerations, and the need for an organization to look out for employee interests when they cannot be on the job (physically) every day.

Information technology itself presents opportunities and challenges to unions. Cyber-organizing is a useful tool for enhancing member services through website applications, rallying union support, and countering management opposition (Shostak 2002; Lucore 2002). On the other hand, it poses a threat to unions as organizations and as representatives by transforming work from a communal enterprise to an autonomous individual activity. Further, it gives workers a new type of voice through blogs, wikis, and other avenues; a voice that can substitute for that traditionally offered by the union (Chaison 2002).

Despite the stagnation in public employee union membership percentages for the past two decades or so, several potentially rich organizing opportunities are available. One of them is rather conventional in that it involves low-wage workers in tough working environments, the traditional mother lode for union organizing in private employment. Sometimes neglected in the scholarly and media attention paid to globalization, information technology, government reinvention, outsourcing, and other trends, is the lot of the low-paid but very important public and nonprofit workers who clean office buildings, empty bed pans, and attend to young children and senior adults who cannot help themselves.

Paul Johnston (1994) has described the organizing possibilities presented by "social movement unionism," in which the interests of custodial workers, nurses, and others converge with social causes involving women, minority, and immigrant workers in low-wage public jobs. According to Johnston, when unions frame their demands for these workers in such as manner as to make them congruent with public policy in the public interest, they have the potential for success. Examples include framing improved pay and benefits and favorable work rule changes in the context of union demands for racial, social, gender, and economic justice.

An early success was the Justice for Janitors movement, which tied together demands for improving the compensation and working conditions of custodial workers with a call for an end to economic and social bias against predominantly black and Latino workers. SEIU 1199 in Florida represents low-wage workers in nursing homes and other facilities. Florida 1199 has partnered with local chapters of the NAACP, Haitian organizations, immigrant rights organizations, and others to create progressive alliances in advocating for workers' rights (Nissen, 2003: 141–143). An important target today is the burgeoning health care industry, which lies at the nexus of the public, nonprofit, and private sectors in hospitals, clinics, nursing homes, and related entities. When SEIU and other health care unions link increased pay and benefits for health care employees with broader public interest issues such as the quality and availability of health care, they stand to benefit in any number of ways. As a general principle, then, "Unions need to demonstrate that they do not exist solely to enhance the private interests of their members" (Sulzner 1997: 166).

The Change to Win unions have focused significant attention on the nonprofit sector, especially hospitals, home health care organizations, nonprofits that transport patients, and charitable organizations. This often poses a conflict of interest. Unions and nonprofits are often aligned on issues of economic justice, such as immigration, the living wage, and health care, but today, unions are organizing these nonprofits' employees. Nonprofit boards and managers typically have pro-union sympathies, but when their own workers organize, managers may be conflicted in their feelings. In large nonprofits, however, it is natural for there to be a growing division between management and workers that spawns a perceived need for a greater employee voice. Employees may become dissatisfied with a nonprofit's bottom line posture, particularly when there is a perception that clients, such as patients, are put at risk (Clark and Clark 2006). As observed in Chapter 3, new structural arrangements may be needed to organize some nonprofit workers such as those who work in the client's home, with the operative question being, "Who is the employer?" (Mareschal 2006; Delp and Quan 2002).

Public employee unions have ramped up their electoral activities in efforts to influence the views of candidates and the outcomes of elections. Union members are more likely to vote than nonmembers and they are most likely to vote for candidates endorsed by unions. During the last several general elections, unions have shown increased sophistication in mobilizing their members and their families. As the 2008 elections approached, with significant implications for the presidency, Congress, and redistricting of congressional and state election districts, national labor organizations were committing substantial human and financial resources to campaign-related activities.

Clearly, unions need to do a better job of promoting more positive public opinion. AFSCME, NEA, AFT, SEIU, and other public employee unions periodically run local, regional, and national publicity campaigns to influence opinion on specific issues (e.g., environmental protection, public education) as well as to engender warmer feelings towards the organization and its membership. This is a long-range strategy that may have payoffs, though any positive outcomes are difficult to measure.

More immediately effective are prompt, adept union responses to local or state situations that threaten to smudge the union's reputation in the eyes of the public. Often, when a union, one of its representatives, or members of the bargaining unit have done wrong in a legal or moral sense, it is best simply to admit the error and get on with more productive activities. For instance, national leaders of AFT and NEA publicly admitted that blocking education innovations and adamantly protecting failed teachers is wrong (Chase 1997–1998). Following the self-critical analytical tradition of the late president Al Shanker, the AFT reexamined many of its former positions and sought to take a leadership role in such critical areas as reducing violence in the schools and helping develop national education standards. The NEA has focused its attention on improving teachers' performance, enhancing teacher professionalism, and "reconnecting with parents." The NEA even broke with tradition and came out in support of charter schools, national standardized student testing, and peer review of classroom teachers (Stanfield 1997).

V. Labor–Management Cooperation and Participative Decision Making

The movement from an adversarial to an interest-based approach to collective bargaining was discussed at length in Chapter 5. This and other forms of labor–management cooperation represent a potentially profound transformation in how decisions are made and conflicts resolved in a union setting.

Various mechanisms exist for labor–management cooperation, including "quality improvement" approaches, labor–management committees, and employee involvement programs. Each involves regularly scheduled meetings of labor and management representatives to discuss, analyze, and resolve problems either arising under the interpretation and application of the contract or appearing in the workplace but outside the purview of the contract. Ideally, the core feature of each of them is participative decision making (PDM), defined as a formal operative vehicle for exercising employee voices in organizational decision making in which employee views and decisions are given serious consideration by management representatives (Kearney and Hays 1994). The model envisions bottom-up authority structures and meaningful employee participation in organizational decisions. Today, PDM programs are widespread in the private sector, with an estimated 50 percent of large firms having adopted them in one form or another (Delaney 1996: 47).

A. Advantages of Cooperation

An extensive literature on private sector PDM indicates positive impacts on individual worker productivity, job satisfaction, personal growth and development, and willingness to change (Kearney and Hays 1994). PDM's benefits to the individual employee are believed to contribute directly and indirectly to desired organizational outcomes. For example, when participation increases worker satisfaction with, and commitment to, the job, it may also produce less turnover, fewer absences and sick days, lower accident rates (Schwochau et al. 1997: 381), stronger commitment to the organization (Verma and McKersie 1987), and improvements in communication patterns (Ospina and Yaroni 2003). PDM's organizational benefits include improving employees' ability to perform technical tasks (Mohrman and Lawler 1988: 47), to respond effectively to a rapidly changing work environment, and to accommodate changes in the nature of work. There may also be fewer grievances, unfair labor practices, and other conflictual activities. Research findings are less conclusive concerning the effects of PDM on organizational efficiency and productivity (Wagner 1994), but there is evidence that organizational performance is enhanced through the early identification of work problems and related benefits (Levine 1995). From a broader perspective, participation has civic and social value as well. It "can stimulate the development of civil society because it encourages individuals to develop and practice habits that are critical to self-sufficiency, self-rule, and ... individual responsibility" (Delaney 1996: 46). In other words, PDM helps encourage responsible self-government and adds value to employees, the workplace, and the employing organization (see Nissen 2003: 134–138).

Despite the many advantages associated with PDM, its application to private employment is restricted by language of the National Labor Relations Act. Prior to legalization of full collective bargaining rights for private sector unions by the

NLRA of 1935, it was not uncommon for employers to resist unions through "representation plans" that established committees of workers and managers that were supposed to meet on workplace concerns. But these plans were forced on workers by management, which strictly reserved its power to make all important decisions. Unions viewed such plans as subterfuges for corporate opposition to unions and collective bargaining (Kelly 1998). A related tactic was the "company union," created and essentially directed by the employer under the pretense of being a legitimate labor organization.

To preclude such evasions by businesses, the NLRA (labor friendly in those days) provided that it is an unfair labor practice for an employer to "dominate or interfere with the formation or administration of any labor organization or contribute financial or other support to it ..." [NLRA, Section 8(a)(2)]. Federal case law and National Labor Relations Board hearings determined that labor–management committees and similar mechanisms are illegal under the NLRA if they are created and dominated by the employer. To be legal, employee participation programs in the private sector must be established and operated with a substantial degree of employee independence from management. The implication is that the only legal PDM program is either one with strong employee decision-making authority or one created and implemented with union participation (Delaney 1996). Not surprisingly, unionized workers in the private sector are much more likely to be involved in PDM programs than are nonunion employees (Baton and Voos 1992).

In the public sector, little systematic empirical research has been published on the PDM experience. Yet, government will probably be the playing field where most of the future PDM action will transpire. This is not to say that the path to PDM is all downhill; a strong adversarial spirit still prevails in most unionized jurisdictions. Moreover, NLRA language, principles, and procedures are embedded in many state bargaining statutes, and in federal employment, the narrow scope of bargaining restrictions constrains opportunities for meaningful participation.

Yet experimental participative approaches such as the labor–management committee (LMC) date back to the early 1920s in government and they are gradually garnering support at all levels of government. LMCs have been used to develop day care and employee assistance programs in New York State, with outcomes of lower health care costs and higher employee morale and attendance rates. In Massachusetts, LMCs were established throughout state government to address health and safety, career ladders, child care, performance appraisal, and other issues. In Ohio, LMCs have dealt with staffing patterns, employee security, and dress codes.

In federal employment, "partnering" initiatives between unions and management to solve workplace problems were required of all federal agencies by President Clinton's Executive Order 12871. By 1996, it was reported that almost 90 percent of federal agencies were actively partnering (Lane 1996: 41). Many of these partnerships reported significant improvements in various federal organizational maladies, including communications and collaborative decision making (Masters and Albright 2005: 358). The changes registered were not earth shattering, but most participants reported improvements in overall labor–management relationships (Masters and Albright 2005; Tobias 2004). When, upon assuming office and with the stroke of a pen, President Bush revoked President Clinton's executive order and soon, thereafter, peppered agency leadership with anti-union appointees, the partnerships rapidly deteriorated (Masters and Albright 2005).

A different administration could allow for a future rebirth of such partnerships at all levels of government. Public and nonprofit managers are generally receptive to labor–management cooperation. Labor relations in some jurisdictions may be replete with ugly adversarial encounters, but, in general, relationships between the parties are much more pacific than those in the private sector. The fierce battles that characterized many public jurisdictions during the early years of unionization and bargaining gradually moderated in most cases, as union and management roles and expectations stabilized and matured. With the almost shocking exception of President Reagan's mass sacking of 12,000 striking air traffic controllers in 1981, very few government workers have lost their jobs during the past three decades because of union organizing or work stoppages. And, of course, public managers and those who work for them share important characteristics and interests. Most of them consider themselves to be public service professionals who work for the public interest in critical fields such as health care, education, and law enforcement. They do not pursue profits or the short-term interests of owners or shareholders. Program success and gains in productivity can produce compensation gains for all public employees and special recognition for managers. Labor and management also share key enemies: namely, bureaucrat bashers, hostile politicians, and negative public opinion. This assortment of characteristics and interests shared by public managers and workers makes cooperation and PDM more feasible than in most private sector settings.

B. Conditions Necessary for Successful Labor–Management Cooperation

To succeed, PDM and other cooperative approaches and techniques cannot simply be imposed by a reform-minded elected official or agency head. Certain facilitative conditions are necessary to create a receptive environment. The most critical facilitative conditions are a foundation of trust and mutual respect among managers and workers, a strong level of commitment by all key parties to make the program work over the long haul, win–win expectations, and an appropriate technique for bringing PDM to fruition.

Constructing a foundation of trust and mutual respect requires overcoming suspicions of union leaders that PDM is a new way to manipulate employees and their unions and that it is likely to weaken collective bargaining, grievance systems, and employee commitment to the union. Suspicions and doubt may also infect the ranks of mid-level managers, who feel threatened by a potential loss of authority, or even their jobs, when PDM programs are implemented (Lawler and Mohrman 1985).

In negative adversarial settings, trust and respect must be constructed from the ground up. This is a tough task, and failures have been recorded. The U.S. Postal Service's history of confrontational labor relations within a context of an autocratic management style, rigid work rules, and difficult working conditions has created a setting predisposed against meaningful PDM (U.S. General Accounting Office 1994). Labor–management partnerships in Miami, Florida, have struggled in the face of high levels of workplace conflict, low employee morale, and a chaotic labor relations climate that includes serious internal divisions in the ranks of both labor and city management (Bryson et al. 1999).

However, other jurisdictions have reported success in converting hostile relationships into a productive cooperative situation. For example, the San Francisco Bay Area Union Sanitation District, long burdened by adversarial relations and low levels of trust and morale, engaged in a far-reaching change strategy that opened direct communication lines between management and union representatives, promoted less contentious contract negotiations, and attained impressive improvements in operations (Berazon, Drake, and Hayashi 1999).

The second precondition for successful PDM is a strong level of commitment by top officials, managers, and employees. Significant levels of time, attention, and resources must be invested in the program if it is to work over the long haul. The heaviest burden rests with mid-level managers and union leaders, but virtually all employees must shoulder some responsibility by committing themselves to work cooperatively with former adversaries. Top officials must exercise leadership and make available sufficient financial and personnel resources for training, oversight, and related activities. Sincere sustained commitment from top-level officials is especially important. This is difficult to secure when newly elected officials or their appointees fail to continue the collaborative policies adopted by their predecessors, or when financial problems lead to work force cutbacks or reorganizations.

The third condition for successful PDM is that the parties must be committed to discovering interest-based, win–win solutions to organizational problems and conflicts. Examples of successful win–win expectations and outcomes may be found at all levels of government. Under the National Performance Council, federal agencies developed partnerships premised on interest-based processes that effectively addressed contract and workplace disputes and myriad other problems. Federal partnerships have dealt with EEO concerns, grievance prevention and resolution, unfair labor practices, incentive pay systems, and a gainsharing program (Ferris and Cooper 1994). Numerous examples of interest-based programs have been reported in state and local jurisdictions, including Wisconsin state government; Ramsey County, Missouri (Brainerd 1998); and Portland, Maine (Peightal et al. 1998). Successful collaborative programs have been operational in school districts as well. For example, site-based management, in which administrators and teachers jointly determine rules, procedures, and policy for a school through PDM, has been adopted in school systems (B. N. Rubin and Rubin 1997).

Finally, PDM requires an appropriate technique for effective implementation. Many different but related tools are available to structure participative interactions, from health and safety committees and quality of work life programs to Quality Circles (small groups of workers that meet regularly to develop suggestions for improving work procedures, product or service quality, or other concerns) and Total Quality Management (TQM; a participative strategy that concentrates on continuously improving products and services, preventing errors, and satisfying customers). Through such techniques, employees are involved and empowered to engage as partners in decision making. When present, unions are formally involved in TQM (Verma and Cutcher-Gershenfeld 1996: 223–227). By 2000, TQM, like Quality Circles, had morphed into new techniques, such as gainsharing, which distributes to bargaining unit members a portion of dollars saved from making work rule changes, process improvements, and other efficiencies. Gainsharing is typically negotiated as part of the collective bargaining contract. The most widely adopted participation strategy today is the labor–management committee, discussed above. Operating to resolve issues outside the formal contract, LMCs are found at all levels of government. LMCs apply win–win principles and push decision making to as low a level of the organization as possible.

In sum, numerous techniques are available for structuring and implementing meaningful employee participation in making organizational decisions. The specific technique is not nearly as critical to program success as are the needs for mutual trust and respect, strong commitment, and win–win expectations.

C. The Future of Labor–Management Cooperation

Significant obstacles litter the path to labor–management cooperation. The NLRA's outdated premise of adversarialism as the answer to all labor–management conflicts remains firmly embedded in the legal framework and mentality of most unionized jurisdictions. The lengthy and emotional history of early organizing campaigns and bargaining encounters is tough to overcome. Mutual distrust and suspicion prevail among union and management representatives in most bargaining settings. Management's innate discomfort with unions is amplified by a nagging fear of losing authority and control over employees in the bargaining unit. Union leaders, many of whom made their reputations by aggressively fighting management, are fearful that consultative and participative management proposals are Trojan horses that will unleash demands to eliminate jobs, dilute union power, impose givebacks and concessions, and ultimately displace the union as the collective voice of workers. Finally, the sustained commitment of resources needed for successful PDM is always problematic in a political system characterized by frequent turnover of elected and appointed officials and personal and special interest groups' political agendas.

A comfortable and functional relationship between collective bargaining and PDM is the key to expansion. Collective bargaining continues to serve a compelling purpose by jointly setting wages, benefits, and terms and conditions of employment. Union representation in grievance procedures remains important as well. But PDM opens a new window of joint problem-solving possibilities. Which problems and issues should be addressed through conventional or interest-based collective bargaining and grievance procedures, and which should fall within the purview of new participative arrangements? Clearly, a rational and logical means of separating issues into their proper spheres should be developed (Reeves 1997). Role conflicts are endemic, as management and union representatives must make the transition back and forth from adversarial to cooperative interactions. Perhaps unions should designate "partnership stewards" for PDM activities and "grievance stewards" for more traditional encounters with management.

As an alternative form of representation, PDM is not a quick cure for all that ails labor–management relations. But clearly, changes in work practices are rapidly eroding the boundaries between supervisors and subordinates, reducing the number of supervisory levels, and promoting more group-oriented work. Whether embodied in statute or common practice, the conventional distinction between supervisors and workers is blurring in practice, with significant implications for unions and collective bargaining. In this context, participative decision-making approaches appear to be an appropriate path for unions moving forward.

VI. Public Employee Unions in the 2000s: Conclusion

Despite some recent signs of rejuvenation, unions in the private sector of the United States have been resolutely marching toward oblivion for about 45 years. Only about 8 percent of private sector workers belong to unions today. This appears to be a global phenomenon; unions are in decline in virtually all economically advanced nations. Numerous factors have contributed to union decline, the most important of which are probably the shift from manufacturing to service and knowledge-based economies and the globalization of labor and production. However, the extent of union decline is much greater in the United States. For instance, organized labor claims more than 40 percent of the German, Canadian, and United Kingdom work forces, and unions remain powerful political and economic forces in Western Europe.

In the U.S. public sector, union membership has leveled off since the late 1970s. The likelihood of dramatic membership drops in government is quite slim, as long as legal protections remain in place. Nonetheless, public employee unions face their own challenges, including privatization, government financial stress, citizen hostility, negative actions by state legislatures, and the Reinventing Government movement. But a resurgence of public employee unionism is not entirely out of the question. Additional states could enact comprehensive bargaining laws; new governors could issue executive orders. Congress could expand the scope of bargaining in federal labor relations, which would induce membership gains. The burgeoning health care sector, which straddles public, private, and nonprofit employment, presents a potentially rich source of new members, including medical interns and physicians.

All things considered, however, the political and economic tea leaves do not portend a rosy scenario for public employee unions in the 2000s. The unions need to engage in continuous soul searching and reinvention if they are to move beyond rhetoric on key issues and maintain relevance for the increasingly diverse public and nonprofit work force. Traditional adversarial bargaining will hold its place at most bargaining tables and in most grievance proceedings, but there is growing acceptance that zero-sum relationships are becoming antiquated and dysfunctional for both unions and management. To do well what they do best — collectively express the voices of those whom they represent (Freeman and Medoff 1984) — unions must improve their ability to identify workers' needs. If the best way to meet those needs is through cooperation with management through PDM or related approaches, then unions owe it to their present and future members to take that path. Management, for its part, should respect the right of unions to participate in a serious and meaningful way in all matters affecting or potentially affecting members of the bargaining unit.

The winds of change in public sector management and labor relations have gusted strongly during the past several years. Coping effectively with the characteristics of the dramatically changing workplace of the future is a responsibility that must be widely shared. Effective organizations of the future will be those that have the capability to respond and adapt to a rapidly shifting environment. The traditional union determination to limit management discretion and authority through restrictive contract language and grievance procedures appears to be increasingly out of step with the needs of competent, and particularly high-performance, organizations. Public employee unions and management have made commendable progress in recent years, especially in the states and localities that serve so well as laboratories of innovation and democracy. In many ways, they are more important today than ever with respect to the objective and subjective well-being of workers (Radcliff 2005). Further innovation and experimentation in labor relations structures and processes hold the promise of gaining improvements in the efficiency and effectiveness of service delivery, while at the same time enhancing the dignity, morale, and quality of work life for public employees.

References

Abood v. Detroit Board of Education. (1977). 430 U.S. 209, 975 Ct. 1782.

AFSCME Local 201 v. City of Muskegon. (1963). 369 Mich. 384, 120 N.W. 2d. 197.

AFSCME v. State of Washington. (1983). 578 F. Supp.

Alexander v. Gardner-Denver. (1975). 415 U.S. S. Ct. 36, 7 EPD.

Allshouse, D. H. (1985). The role of the appropriations process in public sector bargaining. *Urban Lawyer* 17, 165–198.

Argys, L. M., and Rees, D. I. (1995). Unionization and school productivity: A reexamination. *Research in Labor Economics* 14, 49–68.

Aronowitz, S. (1998). Are unions good for professors? *ACADEME* (Nov.–Dec.), 12–17.

Ashenfelter, O. C. (1971). The effect of unionization on wages in the public sector: The case of fire fighters. *Industrial and Labor Relations Review* 24 (Jan.), 191–202.

Ashenfelter, O. C., and Johnson, G. E. (1969). Bargaining theory, trade unions, and industrial strike activity. *American Economic Review* (March), 35–49.

Asher, H. B., Heberlig, E. S., Ripley, R. B., and Snyder, K. (2001). *American Labor Unions in the Electoral Arena.* Lanham, MD: Rowman & Littlefield.

Ashraf, J. (1997). The effects of unions on professors' salaries: The evidence over twenty years. *Journal of Labor Research* XXIII (Summer), 339–449.

Ashraf, J. (1998). Collective bargaining and compensation at public junior colleges. *Journal of Collective Negotiations* 27(4), 393–399.

Atkins v. City of Charlotte. (1969). U.S. Dist. Ct. 296, F. Supp.

Babcock, L. C., and Olson, C. A. (1992). The causes of impasses in labor disputes. *Industrial Relations* 31(2).

Baird, C. W. (1986). Strikes against government: The California State Supreme Court decision. *Government Union Review* 7 (Winter), 1–29.

Baker v. Carr. (1962). 369 U.S. 186.

Balfour, A., and Holmes, A. B. (1981). The effectiveness of no-strike laws for public school teachers. *Journal of Collective Negotiations* 10, 133–144.

Ban, C. (1995). Unions, management and the NPR. In D. F. Kettl and J. J. DiIulio, Jr. (Eds.), *Inside the Reinvention Machine: Appraising Governmental Reform,* 131–151. Washington, DC: Brookings Institution.

Barbezat, D. A. (1989). The effects of collective bargaining on salaries in higher education. *Industrial and Labor Relations Review* 42 (April), 443–455.

Barrentine v. Arkansas Best Freight Systems. (1981). 450 U.S. 728, 90 LC.

Barrett, J. T. (1995). *P.A.S.T. Is the Future* (4th ed.). Falls Church, VA: Barrett and Sons.

Barrett, T. (1973). Prospects for growth and bargaining in the public sector. *GERR* 534, F1–F4.

Baton, A. E., and Voos, P. B. (1992). Unions and contemporary innovations in work organization: Compensation and employee compensation. In Lawrence, Mishel, and P. B. Voos, Eds. *Unions and Economic Competitiveness,* 173–215. New York: M. E. Sharpe.

Battaglio, R. P., and Condrey, S. E. (2006). Civil service reform: Examining state and local government cases. *Journal of Public Personnel Administration* 26 (June), 118–138.

Bazerman, M. H. (1985). Norms of distributive justice in interest arbitration. *Industrial and Labor Relations Review* 38 (July), 558–570.

Bazerman, M. H., and Farber, H. (1985). Arbitrator decision making: When are final offers important? *Industrial and Labor Relations Review* 39 (Oct.), 76–89.

Befort, S. F. (1985). Public sector bargaining: Fiscal crisis and unilateral change. *Minnesota Law Review* 69, 1221–1275.

Behr, J. G. (2000). Black and female municipal employment: A substantive benefit of minority political incorporation? *Journal of Urban Affairs* 22(3), 243–264.

Bellman, H. S. (1998). Some reflections on the practice of mediation. *Negotiation Journal* 14, 205–210.

Belman, D., and Heywood, J. S. (1991). Direct and indirect effects of unionization and government employment on fringe benefit provision. *Journal of Labor Research* XII (Spring), 111–122.

Belman, D., and Heywood, J. S. (1995). State and local government wage differentials: An intrastate analysis. *Journal of Labor Research* XVI (Spring), 187–201.

Belman, D., and Heywood, J. (2004). The structure of compensation in the public sector. *Public Finance Review,* 32(6), 568–587.

Belman, D., Heywood, J. S., and Lund, J. (1997). Public sector earnings and the extent of unionization. *Industrial and Labor Relations Review* 50 (July), 610.

Bemmels, B. (1988). The effect of grievants' gender on arbitrators' decisions. *Industrial and Labor Relations Review* 41 (Jan.), 251–262.

Bemmels, B. (1994). The determinants of grievance initiation. *Industrial and Labor Relations Review* 47 (Jan.), 285–301.

Benecki, S. (1978). Municipal expenditure levels and collective bargaining. *Industrial Relations* 17 (May), 216–230.

Berazon, J. R., Drake, D., and Hayashi, S. T. (1999). Reinventing Local Government Together. The National Academy of Public Administration, http://www.alliance.napawash.org.

Berkeley, A. E. (1989). The most serious faults in labor-management arbitration today and what can be done to remedy them. *Labor Law Journal* (Nov.), 728–733.

Bernstein, J. (1985). The evolution of the use of management consultants in labor relations: A labor perspective. *Labor Law Journal* (May), 292–299.

Bingham, L. B. (1997). Mediating employment disputes: Perceptions of REDRESS at the United States Postal Service. *Review of Public Personnel Administration* 17(2), 20–30.

Blanchflower, D.G., and Bryson, A. (2004). What effect do unions have on wages now and would Freeman and Medoff be surprised? *Journal of Labor Research* 25 (Summer), 1–31.

Bloom, D. E. (1988). Arbitrator behavior in public sector wage disputes. In R. B. Freeman and C. Ichniowski (Eds.), *When Public Sector Workers Unionize,* 107–128. Chicago: University of Chicago Press.

Blum, A. A., and Helburn, I. B. (1997). Federal labor management relations: The beginning. *Journal of Collective Negotiations* 26, 256–277.

Bodah, M. (1999). Rethinking the Rhode Island trilogy: An erosion of the judiciary support for arbitration. *Journal of Collective Negotiations* 20(1), 53–67.

Bohlander, G. W. (1994). Why arbitrators overturn managers in employee suspension and discharge cases. *Journal of Collective Negotiations* 23(1), 73–89.

Bonner, R. (1992). Grievance mediation in state and local government. *State and Local Government Labor Management Committee.* Washington, DC.

Bornstein, T. (1980). Legacies of local government collective bargaining in the 1970s. Address to 1980 annual LMRS-AAA Conference. Reprinted in *GERR* 1/21/80, 33–37.

Boroff, K., and Lewin, D. (1997). Loyalty, voice and intent to exit a union firm: A conceptual and empirical analysis. *Industrial Labor Relations Review* 51 (Oct.), 50–63.

Bowen v. U.S. Postal Service. (1983). 103 S. Ct. 588.

Bowers, M. H. (1976). *Contract Administration in the Public Sector.* PERL No. 53. Chicago: IPMA.

Brainerd, R. (1998). Interest based bargaining: Labor and management working together in Ramsey County, Minnesota. *Public Personnel Management* 27 (Spring), 51–68.

Briggs, S., and Koys, D. J. (1989). What makes labor mediators effective? *Labor Law Journal* (Aug.), 517–520.

Brook, D. A., and King, C. L. (2007). Civil service reform as national security: The Homeland Security Act of 2002. *Public Administration Review* (May/June), 399–407.

Brotherhood of Railway Clerks v. Allen. (1963). 83 S. Ct. 1158.

Brown, R. G., and Rhodes, T. L. (1991). Public employee bargaining under prohibitive legislation: Some unanticipated consequences. *Journal of Collective Negotiations* 20(1), 23–30.

Bryson, W., et al. (1999). The Miami Story: The Pros and Cons of the Comparative Process. National Academy of Public Administration, www.alliance.napawash.org.

Buhle, P., and Buhle, N. (2005). *Wobblies! A Graphic History of the Industrial Workers of the World.* London: Verso.

Burton, J. F. (1972). Local government bargaining and management structure. *Industrial Relations* 11 (May), 123–140.

Burton, J. F., Jr. (1978). *Public Sector Strikes: Legal, Ethical, and Practical Considerations.* New York: Cornell University, New York State School of Industrial and Labor Relations. Reprint Series No. 448.

Burton, J. F., and Krider, C. E. (1975). The incidence of strikes in public employment. In D. Hammermesh (Ed.), *Labor in the Public and Nonprofit Sectors,* 135–177. Princeton, NJ: Princeton University Press.

Butler, R. J., and Ehrenberg, R. G. (1981). Estimating the narcotic effect of public sector impasse procedures. *Industrial and Labor Relations Review* 35 (Oct.), 3–20.

Capozzola, J. M. (1979). Public employee strikes: Myths and realities. *National Civil Review* 68 (April), 178–188.

Caraway, J. M. (1989). Grievance mediation: Is it worth using? *Journal of Law and Education* 18 (Fall), 495–502.

Card, D. (2001). The effect of unions on wage inequality in the U.S. labor market. *Industrial and Labor Relations Review* 54(2), 296–315.

Carofano v. City of Bridgeport. (1985). 196 Conn. 623, 495 A.2d 1016.

Carrter, A. M. (1959). *Theory of Wages and Employment.* Homewood, IL: Irwin.

Cassidy, G. W. (1979). An analysis of pressure group activities in the context of open meeting and public employee relations laws. *Journal of Collective Negotiations* 9(1), 3–17.

Centers for Disease Control and Prevention. (2008). http://www.cdc.gov/tobacco/basic_information/fastfacts.htm#facts. Accessed Jan. 30, 2008.

Chaison, G. (2002). Information technology: The threat to unions. *Journal of Labor Research* 23(2), 249–259.

Chaison, G. (2004). Union mergers in the U.S. and abroad. *Journal of Labor Research* 25(1), 97–116.

Chamberlain, N. W., and Kuhn, J. W. (1965). *Collective Bargaining* (2nd ed.). New York: McGraw-Hill.

Champlin, F. C., and Bognanno, M. F. (1985). "Chilling" under arbitration and mixed strike-arbitration regimes. *Journal of Labor Research* VI (Fall), 375–387.

Chandler, T. D. (1995). Sanitation privatization and sanitation employees wages. *Journal of Labor Research* (Fall), 137–153.

Chandler, T., and Feuille, P. (1991). Municipal unions and privatization. *Public Administration Review* 51 (Jan./Feb.), 15–22.

Chandler, T., and Gely, R. (1995). Protective service unions, political activities and bargaining outcomes. *Journal of Public Administration Research and Theory* 5(3), 295–318.

Chandler, T. D., and Judge T. (1993). Collective bargaining with police unions: Characteristics of negotiators and bargaining strategies. *The Municipal Year Book* 1993. International City Management Association.

Chase, B. (1997–1998). The new NEA: Reinventing teacher unions for a new era. *The American Educator* (Winter), 12–15.

Chelius, J. R., and Extejt, M. M. (1985). The narcotic effect of impasse resolution procedures. *Industrial and Labor Relations Review* 38 (July), 629–637.

Chicago Teachers Union v. Hudson. (1986). 475 U.S. 292.

Child, J., Loveridge, R., and Warner, M. (1973). Towards an organizational study of trade unions. *Sociology* 7 (Jan.), 71–91.

Choudhury, S. (1994). New evidence on public sector wage differentials. *Applied Economics* (March), 259.

Clark, P. F. (1989a). Determinants of the quality of union-management relations: An exploratory study of union member perceptions. *Journal of Collective Negotiations* 18(2), 103–115.

Clark, P. F. (1989b). Union image-building at the local level. *Labor Studies Journal* 14 (Fall), 48–68.

Clark, P. F., and Clark, D. A. (2006). Union strategies for improving patient care: The key to nurse unionism. *Labor Studies Journal* 31(1), 51–70.

Clark, P. F., and Gallagher, D. G. (1988). The role of the steward in shaping member attitudes toward the grievance procedure. *Labor Studies Journal* 13 (Fall), 3–17.

Clark, T., Jr., and Powers, J. J. (2003). Constitutional and practical pitfalls of a federally-mandated public sector collective bargaining system. *Journal of Labor Research* 24(4), 621–641.

Clark, T. N., and Ferguson, L. C. (1983). *City Money.* New York: Columbia University Press.

Cleveland Board of Education v. Loudermill. (1985). 470 U.S. 532, 118.

Coleman, C., and Vasquez, J. (1997). Mandatory arbitration of statutory issues under collective bargaining: Austin and its progeny. *Labor Law Journal* 48(12), 703–726.

Commons, J. R. (1980). American shoemakers, 1648–1895. In R. L. Rowan (Ed.), *Readings in Labor Economics and Labor Relations* (4th ed.), 57–69. Homewood, IL: Irwin.

Commons, J. R., and Associates (1936). *History of Labor in the United States.* New York: Macmillan.

Commonwealth v. Hunt (1842). 45 Mass. Ill, 38 Am. Dec. 346.

Communications Workers of America v. the City of New York. (1972). OCB Decision No. B-7-72.

Condon, T. (1998). Public job too often a safe bet. *Hartford Courant,* April 26, p. Bl.

Cooper, B. S. (1988). National union competition and the school reform movement: Will the NEA and AFT merge? In *41st Proceedings of the IRRA.* New York: IRRA.

Cooper, R. and Ferris, F. Two views at One Agency: The IRS and NTEU.

Coulson, R. (1980). New views of arbitration: Satisfying the demands of the employee. In *Proceedings of the 1980 Spring Meeting,* 495–497. New York: IRRA.

Coursey, D., and Rainey, H. G. (1990). Perceptions of personnel system constraints in public, private, and hybrid organizations. *Review of Public Personnel Administration* 10 (Spring), 54–7 1.

Cox, W., and Brunelli, S. A. (1992). America's protected class: Why excess public employee compensation is bankrupting the state. *The State Facts* (Feb.), 1–32.

Craft, J. A., Abboushi, S., and Labovitz, T. (1985). Concession bargaining and unions: Impacts and implications. *Journal of Labor Research* VI (Spring), 167–180.

Crouch, W. W. (1978). *Organized Civil Servants: Public Employer–Employee Relations in California.* Berkeley: University of California Press.

Currie, J., and McConnell, S. (1994). Collective bargaining in the public sector: The effect of legal structures on dispute costs and wages. *The American Economic Review* 81 (Sept.), 693–718.

Dade County Classroom Teachers Association v. Ryan. (1968). 225 So. 2d 903.

Dahl, R. (1957). The concept of power. *Behavioral Science* 2 (July), 201–205.

Daley, D. M. (1998). An overview of benefits for the public sector. *Review of Public Personnel Management* (Summer), 5–22.

Dark, T. E. (1999). *The Unions and the Democrats: An Enduring Alliance.* Ithaca, NY: Cornell University Press.

Darko, R. J., and Knapp, J. C. (1985). A guide to the changing court rulings in union security in the public sector: A union perspective. *Journal of Law and Education* 14(1), 57–69.

Dearborn Firefighters Local 412 v. City of Dearborn. (1975). 394 Mich. 229, 231 N.W. 2d. 226.

Decker, K. H. (1994). Public sector grievance arbitration procedures. In Jack Rabin et al. (Eds.), *Handbook of Public Sector Labor Relations,* 135–182. New York: Dekker.

DeFreitas, G. (1993). Unionization among ethnic and racial minorities. *Industrial and Labor Relations Review* 46(2), 284–301.

Delaney, J. T. (1988). Teachers' collective bargaining outcomes and tradeoffs. *Journal of Labor Research* IX (Fall), 363–377.

Delaney, J. T. (1996). Workplace cooperation: Current problems, new techniques. *Journal of Labor Research* XVII (Winter), 45–61.

Delaney, J. T., Fiorito, J., and Jarley, P. (1999). Evolutionary politics? Union difference and political activities in the 1990s. *Journal of Labor Research* XX (Summer), 277–295.

Dell'Omo, G. G. (1989). Wage disputes in interest arbitration: Arbitrators weigh the criteria. *Arbitration Journal* 44 (June), 4–13.

Dell'Omo, G. G. (1990). Capturing arbitrator decision policies under a public sector interest arbitration statute. *Review of Public Personnel Administration* 10 (Spring), 19–38.

Delp, L., and Quan, K. (2002). Homecare worker organizing in California: An analysis of a successful strategy. *Labor Studies Journal* 27(1), 1–23.

Denenberg, T. S. (1987). Substance abuse: The challenge to industrial relations. In *40th Annual Proceedings of the Industrial Relations Research Association.* Washington, DC: IRRA.

Dickinson, D. L., and Hunnicutt, L. (2005). Does Fact-Finding Promote Settlement? Theory and a Test. *Economic Inquiry* 43(2), 401–416.

Dilts, D. A. (1984). An examination of fact finding as a method of dispute settlement and training grounds for arbitrators. *Journal of Collective Negotiations* 13(1), 251–258.

Dilts, D. A., and Haber, L. J. (1989). The mediation of contract disputes in the Iowa public sector. *Journal of Collective Negotiations* 18(2), 145–151.

Dilts, D. A., Boyda, S. W., and Sherr, M. A. (1993). Collective bargaining in the absence of protective legislation: The case of Louisiana. *Journal of Collective Negotiations* 22(3), 259–265.

Doeringer, P. B., et al. (1996). Beyond the merit model: New directions at the federal workplace? In D. Belman, M. Gunderson, and D. Hyatt (Eds.), *Public Sector Employment in a Time of Transition*, 163–200. Madison, WI: IRRA.

Doherty, R., and Lipsky, D. B. (1988). The education reform movement and the realities of collective bargaining. In B. D. Dennis (Ed.), *Proceedings of the 41st Annual Meeting of the IRRA*, 51–59. New York: IRRA.

Douglas, J. M. (1992). State civil service and collective bargaining: Systems in conflict. *Public Administration Review* 52 (Jan./Feb.), 162–171.

Downie, B. M. (1992). *Strikes, Disputes and Policy Making: Resolving Disputes in Ontario Education*, 233–249. Kingston, Ontario: IRC Press.

Downsizing hits unions. (1997). *Government Executive* (Aug.), 19.

Dunlop Commission. (1994). *Report and Recommendation of the Commission on the Future of Worker Management Relations.* Washington, DC: U.S. Department of Labor.

Eberts, R. W., and Stone, J. A. (1987). Teacher unions and the productivity of public schools. *Industrial and Labor Relations Review* 40 (April), 354–363.

Edwards, H. T., Clark, R. T., Jr., and Graver, C. B. (1979). *Labor Relations Law in the Public Sector* (2nd ed.). Indianapolis, IN: Bobbs-Merrill.

Edwards, L. N., and Edwards, F. R. (1982). Wellington-Winter revisited: The case of municipal sanitation workers. *Industrial and Labor Relations Review* 35 (April), 307–318.

Ehrenberg, R. G. (1972). *The Demand for State and Local Government Employees: An Economic Assessment.* Lexington, MA: Heath.

Ehrenberg, R. G., and Goldstein, G. S. (1975). A model of public sector wage determination. *Journal of Urban Economics* (July), 223–245.

Elazar, D. J. (1966). *American Federalism: A View from the States.* New York: Crowell.

Elkouri, F. and Elkouri, E. A. (2003). *How Arbitration Works* (6th ed.). Washington, D.C., Bureau of National Affairs Books, 1266.

Ellis v. Railway Clerks. (1984). 466 U.S. 435.

Elsea, S. W., Dilts, D. A., and Haber, L. J. (1990). Factfinders and arbitrators in Iowa: Are they the same neutrals? *Journal of Collective Negotiations* 19(1), 61–67.

Faerman, S. R. (1996). Managing conflicts creatively. In James L. Perry (Ed.), *Handbook of Public Administration*, 632–646. San Francisco: Jossey-Bass.

Fagan, K., Cabanatuan, M., and DelVecchio, R. (1997). Acrimonious BART talks go nowhere. *San Francisco Chronicle*, Sept. 13.

Farber, H. S. (1980). An analysis of final-offer arbitration. *Journal of Conflict Resolution* 24 (Dec.), 683–705.

Farber, H. S. (1987). The recent decline of unionization in the United States. *Science* 238 (Nov. 13), 915–920.

Farber, H. S., and Western, B. (2001) Accounting for the decline of unions in the private sector: 1973–1998. *Journal of Labor Research* 22(3), 459–485.

Feder, D. L. (1989). Pick a forum — any forum: A proposal for a federal dispute resolution board. *Labor Law Journal* 40 (May), 268–280.

Feldman, R. (1982). The union impact on hospital wages and fringe benefits. *Industrial and Labor Relations Review* 35 (Jan.), 196–206.

Ferris, F. D. (1975). Contract interpretation — a bread-and-butter talent. *Public Personnel Management* 4 (July–Aug.), 223–230.

National Treasury Employees Union. *The Public Manager* 23(2), 27–31.

Feuille, P. (1975). Final-offer arbitration and the chilling effect. *Industrial Relations* 14(3), 302–310.

Feuille, P. (1979). Selected benefits and costs of compulsory arbitration. *Industrial and Labor Relations Review* 33(1), 64–76.

Feuille, P. (1992). Why does grievance mediation resolve grievances? *Negotiation Journal* 8(2), 131–145.

Feuille, P., and Delaney, J. T. (1986). Collective bargaining, interest arbitration, and police salaries. *Industrial and Labor Relations Reviews* 39 (Jan.), 228–240.

Feuille, P., and Schwochau, S. (1988). The decision of interest arbitrators. *Arbitration Journal* 43 (March), 28–35.

Feuille, P., Delaney, J. T., and Hendricks, W. (1985a). The impact of interest arbitration on police contracts. *Industrial Relations* 24 (Spring), 161–181.

Feuille, P., Delaney, J. T., and Hendricks, W. (1985b). Police bargaining, arbitration, and fringe benefits. *Journal of Labor Research* VI (Winter), 1–20.

Field, C., and Keller, R. L. (1976). How salaries of large cities compare with industry and federal pay. *Monthly Labor Review* 99 (Nov.), 23–28.

Figart, D. M. (1989). Collective bargaining and career development for women in the public sector. *Journal of Collective Negotiations* 18(4), 301–313.

Fiorito, J., Gallagher, D. G., and Fukami, C. V. (1988). Satisfaction with union representation. *Industrial and Labor Relations Review* 41 (Jan.), 294–307.

Fisher, R., and Ury, W. (1981). *Getting to Yes.* New York: Penguin.

Flaherty, S., and Caniglia, A. (1992). Relative effects of unionism on the earnings distribution of women and men. *Industrial Relations* 31(2), 382–400.

Flammang, J. A. (1986). Effective implementation: The case of comparable worth in San Jose. *Policy Studies Review* 5 (May), 815–837.

Foegen, J. H. (1974). Public sector strike prevention: Let the taxpayer decide. *Journal of Collective Negotiations* 3(3), 221–225.

Forbath, W. E. (1991). *Law and the Shaping of the American Labor Movement.* Cambridge, MA: Harvard University Press.

Fowler, R. B. (1974). Normative aspects of public employee strikes. *Public Personnel Management* (March/April), 129–137.

Fox, M. J., Jr., and Shelton, H. E., Jr. (1972). The impact of executive order 11491 on the federal labor management relations program. *Journal of Collective Negotiations* (May), 113–124.

Fraser, S. (1998). Is democracy good for unions? *Dissent* 45 (Summer), 33–39.

Frazier, H. B., III. (1986). Arbitration in the federal sector. *The Arbitration Journal* 41 (March), 70–76.

Freeman, R. B. (1978). Should we organize? The effects of faculty unions on academic compensation. Working Paper No. 301. National Bureau of Economic Research, Washington, D.C.

Freeman, R. B. (1996). Through public sector eyes: Employee attitudes toward public sector labor relations in the United States. In D. Belman, M. Gunderson, and D. Hyatt (Eds.), *Public Sector Employment in a Time of Transition,* 59–84. Madison, WI: IRRA.

Freeman, R. B., and Icniowski, C., Eds. Washington, DC: BNA 81–95.

Freeman, R. B., and Kleiner, M. M. (1990). Employee behavior in the face of union organizing drives. *Industrial and Labor Relations Review* 43 (April), 351–365.

Freeman, R. B., and Medoff, J. L. (1984). *What Do Unions Do?* New York: Basic.

Freeman, R. B., and Valletta, R. G. (1988). The effects of public sector labor laws on labor market institutions and outcomes. In R. B. *When Public Sector Workers Unionize,*

Freund, J. L. (1974). Market and union influences on municipal employee wages. *Industrial and Labor Relations Review* 27 (April), 391–404.

Friedman, B. A., Abraham, S. E., and Thomas, R. K. (2006). Factors related to employees' desire to join and leave unions. *Industrial Relations* 45(1), 102–110.

Frost, F. W. (1978). New developments in labor arbitration: Expedited arbitration experience in the U.S. Postal Service. *Labor Law Journal* (Aug.), 465–469.

Fuller, H. L., Mitchell, G. A., and Hartmann, M. E. (2000). Collective bargaining in Milwaukee public schools. In T. Loveless (Ed.), *Conflicting Missions? Teachers Unions and Educational Reform,* 110–149. Washington, DC: Brookings Institution Press.

Gagala, K. (1983). *Union Organizing and Staying Organized.* Reston, VA: Reston Publishing.

Galenson, W. (1980). Why the American labor movement is not socialist. In R. L. Rowan (Ed.), *Readings in Labor Economics and Labor Relations* (4th ed.), 70–80. Homewood, IL: Irwin.

Gallagher, D. G., and Clark, P. F. (1989). Research on union commitment: Implications for labor. *Labor Studies Journal* 14 (Spring), 52–71.

Gallagher, D. G., and Pegnetter, R. (1979). Impass resolution under the Iowa multistep procedure. *Industrial and Labor Relations Review* 32(3), 327–338.

Gallagher, D. G., and Veglahn, P. A. (1990). Changes in bargaining behavior as a result of experience under a statutory impasse scheme: Theory and evidence. *Journal of Collective Negotiations* 19(3), 175–188.

Garcia v. San Antonio Metropolitan Transit Authority. (1985). 105 S. Ct. 1005.

Gardner, S. E., and Daniel, C. (1998). Implementing comparable worth/pay equity: Experiences of cutting edge states. *Public Personnel Management* 27 (Winter), 475–483.

Gely, R., and Chandler, T. D. (1993). Determinants of management's organizational structure in the public sector. *Journal of Labor Research* XIV(4), 381–397.

Gely, R., and Chandler, T. D. (1995). Protective service unions' political activities and departmental expenditures. *Journal of Labor Research* XIV(2), 171–186.

Gerardi, R. J. (1986). Recommendations for handling a strike. *Journal of Collective Negotiations* 15(4), 367–372.

Gerhart, P. F. (1973). *Political Activity by Public Employee Organizations at the Local Level: Threat or Promise* (PERL No. 44). Chicago: IPMA.

Gerhart, P. F. (1976). Determinants of bargaining outcomes in local government labor relations. *Industrial and Labor Relations Review* 29 (April), 331–350.

Gerhart, P. F. (1994). Maintenance of the union-management relationship. In J. Rabin et al. (Eds.), *Handbook of Public Sector Labor Relations,* 97–132. New York: Dekker.

Gerhart, P. F., and Drotning, J. E. (1980). Do uncertain cost/benefit estimates prolong public-sector disputes? *Monthly Labor Review* 103(9), 26–30.

GERR. (1985). Aug. 26, 1216.

GERR. (1990). Aug. 6, 991–992.

Gilroy, T. P., and Lipovac, J. A. (1977). Impasse procedure utilization: Year one under the Iowa statute. *Journal of Collective Negotiations* 6(3), 181–191.

Goddard, J. (1992). Strikes as collective voice: A behavioral analysis of strike activity. *Industrial Labor Relations Review* 46 (Oct.), 161 –175.

Goldfield, M. (1987). *The Decline of Organized Labor in the United States.* Chicago: University of Chicago Press.

Goldschmidt, S. M., and Stuart, L. E. (1986). The extent and impact of educational policy bargaining. *Industrial and Labor Relations Review* 39 (April), 350–360.

Gomez-Mejia, L. R., and Balkin, D. B. (1984). Union impacts on secretarial earnings: A public sector case. *Industrial Relations* 23 (Winter), 95–102.

Goode, S. J., and Baldwin, N. J. (2005). Predictions of African American representation in municipal government. *Review of Public Personnel Administration* 25(29), 29–55.

Gordon, M. E., and Denisi, A. S. (1995). A re-examination of the relationship between union membership and job satisfaction. *Industrial and Labor Relations Review* 48(2), 222–236.

Gordon, M. E., Philpot, J. W., Bun, R. E., Thompson, C. A., and Spiller, W. E. (1980). Commitment to the union: Development of a measure and examination of its correlates. *Journal of Applied Psychology* 65(4), 479–499.

Gotbaum, V. (1972). Collective bargaining and the union leader. In S. Zagoria, (Ed.), *Public Workers and Public Unions,* 77–88. Englewood Cliffs, NJ: Prentice-Hall.

Graham, H., and Perry, J. (1993). Interest arbitration in Ohio: The narcotic effect revisited. *Journal of Collective* 22(4), 323–366.

Green, J. (2006). *Death in the Haymarket: A Story of Chicago, the First Labor Movement and the Bombing that Divided Guilded Age America.* New York: Pantheon Books.

Greenhouse, S. (2004). Deep distrust slows contract talks with teachers. *The New York Times,* Dec. 15.

Greenhouse, S., and Chan, S. (2006). In transit dispute, navigating without a map. *The New York Times,* Jan. 22. Accessed Jan. 23, 2006.

Greer, C. R. (1978). Public sector bargaining legislation and strike: A case study. *Labor Law Journal* (April), 241–247.

Gregory, G. A., and Rooney, R. E., Jr. (1980). Grievance mediation: A trend in the cost-conscious eighties. *Labor Law Journal* (Aug.), 502–508.

Gross, J. A. (1995). *Broken Promise: The Subversion of U.S. Labor Policy 1947–1994.* Philadelphia: Temple University Press.

Guiler, J. K., and Shafritz, J.M. (2004). Dual Personnel Systems — Organized Labor and Civil Service: Side by Side in the Public Sector. *Journal of Labor Relations* 25(2), 199–209.

Gunderson, M., Hebdon, R., and Hyatt, D. (1996). Collective bargaining in the public sector: A comment. *American Economic Review* 86(3), 315–326.

Guthrie-Morse, B., Leslie, L. L., and Hu, T.-W. (1981). Assessing the impact of faculty unions. *Journal of Higher Education* 52(3), 237–255.

Haber, L. J., and Karim, A. R. (1995). Arbitral standards in public sector and private sector substance abuse discharge cases: A comparison. *Journal of Collective Negotiations* 24(1), 55–61.

Hall, W. C., and Vanderporten, D. (1977). Unionization, monopsony power, and police salaries. *Industrial Relations* 16 (Feb.), 94–100.

Hammer, T. H., and Wazeter, D. L. (1993). Dimensions of local union effectiveness. *Industrial and Labor Relations Review* 46(2), 302–3 19.

Hannan, M. T., and Freeman, J. (1977). The population ecology of organizations. *American Journal of Sociology* 82(5), 929–964.

Hartford Courant. (1992). May 11, p. C10.

Hays, S. W. (1995). Employee discipline and removal: Coping with job security. In S. B. Hays and R. C. Kearney (Eds.), *Public Personnel Administration: Problems and Prospects,* 145–161. Englewood Cliffs, NJ: Prentice-Hall.

Hebdon, R. P., and Stern, R. N. (1998). Tradeoffs among expressions of industrial conflict: Public sector strike bans and grievance arbitration. *Industrial and Labor Relations Review* 51 (Jan.), 204–221.

Hebdon, R., and Stern, R. (2003). Do public-sector strike bans really prevent conflict? *Industrial Relations* 42(3), 493–512.

Helburn, I. B., and Matthews, J. L. (1980). The referendum as an alternative to bargaining. *Journal of Collective Negotiations* 9(2), 93–105.

Helburn, I. B., and Rodgers, R. C. (1985). Hesitancy of arbitrators to accept interest arbitration cases: A test of conventional wisdom. *Public Administration Review* 45 (May/June), 398–402.

Helsby, R. D., and Tener, J. B. (1979). Structure and administration of public employment relations agencies. In M. K. Gibbons, R. D. Helsby, J. Lefkowitz, and B. Z. Teher (Eds.), *Portrait of a Process — Collective Negotiations in Public Employment,* 31–54. Fort Washington, PA: Labor Relations Press.

Hershey, C. (1973). *Protest in the Public Service.* Lexington, MA: Lexington Books.

Hicks, J. R. (1932). *The Theory of Wages.* London: Macmillan.

Hill, M., Jr., and Dawson, D. (1985). Discharge for off-duty misconduct in the private and public sectors. *The Arbitration Journal* 40 (June), 24–37.

Hills, S. M. (1985). The attitudes of union and nonunion male workers toward union representation. *Industrial and Labor Relations Review* 38 (Jan.), 179–194.

Hines v. Anchor Motor Freight. (1976). 424 U.S. 554, 96 S. Ct. 1048.

Hirsch, B. T. (2004). Reconsidering union wage effects: Surveying new evidence on an old topic. *Journal of Labor Research* 25(2), 233–266.

Hirsch, B. T., McPherson, D. A., and Dumond, M. A. (1997). Recipiency in union and nonunion workplaces. *Industrial and Labor Relations Review* 50(2), 213–236.

Hirsch, B. T., and Schumacher, E. J. (2001). Private sector union density and the wage premium: Past, present, and future. *Journal of Labor Research,* 22(3), 487–518.

Hirschman, A. (1970). *Exit, Voice, and Loyalty.* Cambridge, MA: Harvard University Press.

Hoell, R. C. (2004). The effect of interpersonal trust and participativeness on union member commitment. *Journal of Business and Psychology* 19(2), 161–177.

Hogler, R. L. (1986). The common law of public employee strikes: A new rule in California. *Labor Law Journal* 37 (Feb.), 94–103.

Hogler, R. L., and Thompson, M. J. (1985). Collective negotiations in education and the public interest: A proposed method of impasse resolution. *Journal of Law and Education* 14 (July), 443–469.

Holden, L. T., Jr. (1976). Final-offer arbitration in Massachusetts: One year later. *Arbitration Journal* (March), 26–35.

Holzer, M. (1988). Productivity in, garbage out: Sanitation gains in New York. *Public Productivity Review* XI (Spring), 37–50.

Holzer, H., and Neumark, D. (2000). Assessing Affirmative Action. *Journal of Economic Literature* 38 (Sept.), 485–568.

Hoover, G. A., and Peoples, J. (2003). Privatization of refuse removal and labor costs. *Journal of Labor Research* XXIV(2), 293–305.

Horton, R. D. (1973). *Municipal Labor Relations in New York City.* New York: Praeger.

Hoxby, C. M. (1996). How teachers' unions affect education production. *Quarterly Journal of Economics* 111(3), 671–718.

Hoxie, R. F. (1928). *Trade Unionism in the United States.* New York: Appleton.

Hoyman, M. M., and Stallworth, L. (1987). Participation in local unions: A comparison of black and white members. *Industrial and Labor Relations Review* 40 (April), 323–335.

Hu, T.-W., and Leslie, L. (1982). The effects of collective bargaining on college faculty salaries and compensation. *Applied Economics* 14 (June), 269–277.

Hundley, G. (1988). Who joins unions in the public sector? The effects of individual characteristics and the law. *Journal of Labor Research* 9 (Fall), 301–323.

Hunter, W. J., and Rankin, C. H. (1988). The composition of public sector compensation: The effect of unionization and bureaucratic size. *Journal of Labor Relations* IX, 29–42.

Ichniowski, C. (1982). Arbitration and police bargaining: Prescription for the blue flu. *Industrial Relations* 21(2), 149–166.

Ichniowski, C., Freeman, R. B., and Laver, H. (1989). Collective bargaining laws, threat effects, and the determination of police compensation. *Journal of Labor Economics* 7(2), 191–209.

Indianapolis Education Association v. Lewallen. (1969). 72 L.R. Rm. 2071 (7th Cir.).

Ingraham, P. (1996). Evolving public service systems. In J. L. Perry (Ed.), *Handbook of Public Administration* (2nd ed.) 375–391, San Francisco: Jossey-Bass.

International Association of Machinists v. Street. (1961). 367 U.S. 740.

International City Management Association. (1989). Labor-management relations in local government. *The Municipal Year Book.* Washington, DC: ICMA.

Jascourt, H. D. (1979). Recent trends and developments. In H. D. Jascourt (Ed.), *Government Labor Relations: Trends and Information for the Future,* 3–31. Oak Park, IL: Moore.

Johnson, S. M., and Kardos, S. M. (2000). Reform bargaining and its promise for school improvement. In T. Loveless (Ed.), *Conflicting Missions? Teachers Unions and Educational Reform,* 7–46. Washington, DC: Brookings Institution Press.

Johnston, P. (1994). *Success While Others Fail: Social Movement Unionism and the Public Workplace.* Ithaca, NY: Cornell University Press.

Juravich, T., and Shergold, P. R. (1988). The impact of unions on the voting behavior of their members. *Industrial and Labor Relations Review* 41 (April), 374–385.

Juris, H., and Feuille, P. (1973). *Police Unionism.* Lexington, MA: Heath.

Karahalios v. NFFE. (1989). 57 *Law Week* 43 11.

Karim, A., and Pegnetter, R. (1983). Mediator strategies and qualities and mediation effectiveness. *Industrial Relations* 22 (Winter), 105–114.

Karper, M. D. (1994). Fact finding in public employment: Promise or illusion revisited. *Journal of Collective Negotiations in the Public Sector* 23(4), 287–297.

Karper, M. D., and Meckstroth, D. J. (1976). The impact of unionism on public wage rates. *Public Personnel Management* 5 (Oct.), 343–346.

Kauffman, N., Vanlwaarden, D., and Floyd, C. (1994). Values and arbitrator selection. *Labor Law Journal* 45(1), 49–54.

Kaufman, L. (2004). *New York Times.* Dec. 18.

Kearney, R. C. (1979). The impact of police unionization on municipal budgetary outcomes. *International Journal of Public Administration* 1(4), 361–379.

Kearney, R.C. (2003). Patterns of union decline and growth: An organizational ecology perspective. *Journal of Labor Research* 24(4), 561–578.

Kearney, R. C., and Berman, E. M. (1999). *Public Sector Performance: Management, Motivation and Measurement.* Boulder, CO: Westview.

Kearney, R. C., and Hays, S. (1994). Labor management relations and participative decision making toward a new paradigm. *Public Administration Review* 54(1), 44–51.

Kearney, R. C., and Hays, S. (1998). Reinventing government: The new public management and civil service systems in international perspective. *Review of Public Personnel Administration* 18 (Fall), 38–54.

Kearney, R. C., and Morgan, D. R. (1980a). The impact of unionization on the compensation of municipal police. *Journal of Collective Negotiations* 9 (Spring), 361–379.

Kearney, R. C., and Morgan, D. R. (1980b). Unions and state employee compensation. *State and Local Government Review* 12 (May), 115–119.

Keating, C. (1994). Arbitrator withdraws teachers' raises. *Hartford Courant,* Feb. 17, pp. A1, B9.

Kellough, J. E. (1990). Integration in the public workplace: Determinants of minority and female employment in federal agencies. *Public Administration Review* 50 (Sept./Oct.), 557–566.

Kelly, E. P. (1998). Historical perspectives on ideological and legal challenges to labor management participation efforts. *International Journal of Organizational Theory and Behavior* 4, 459–479.

Kemp, D. R. (1987). *Supplemental Compensation and Collective Bargaining.* Alexandria, VA: International Personnel Management Association.

Kesselring, R. G. (1991). The economic effects of faculty unions. *Journal of Labor Research* XII (Winter), 61–72.

Keyeshian v. Board of Regents. (1967). 385 U.S. 589.

Kleiner, M. M. (2001). Intensity of management resistance: Understanding the decline of unionization in the private sector. *Journal of Labor Research* 22(3) (Summer), 528–532.

Klingner, D. E., and Smith, D. B. (1981). What happens when a state's collective bargaining law is declared unconstitutional? The case of Indiana. *Journal of Collective Negotiations* 10(1), 85–94.

Kochan, T. A. (1973). *Resolving Internal Management Conflicts for Labor Negotiations* (PERL #41). Chicago: International City Management Association.

Kochan, T. A. (1975). City government: A path analysis. *Industrial Relations* 14 (Feb.), 90–101.

Kochan, T. A. (1979). Dynamics of dispute resolution in the public sector. In B. Aaron, J. R. Grodin, and J. L. Stern (Eds.), *Public-Sector Bargaining,* 150–190. Washington, DC: Bureau of National Affairs (IRRA Series).

Kochan, T. A. (1980). *Collective Bargaining and Industrial Relations.* Homewood, IL: Irwin.

Kochan, T. A., and Baderschneider, J. (1978). Dependence on impasse procedures: Police and firefighters in New York State. *Industrial and Labor Relations Review* 31 (July), 431–449.

Kochan, T. A., and Baderschneider, J. (1981). Estimating the narcotic effect: Choosing techniques that fit the problem. *Industrial and Labor Relations Review* 35 3–20 (Oct.), (1).

Kochan, T. A., and Jick, T. (1978). The public sector mediation process. *Journal of Conflict Resolution* 22 (June), 209–238.

Kochan T. A., Mironi, M., Ehrenberg, R. G., Baderschneider, J., and Jick, T. (1979). *Dispute Resolution Under Fact-Finding and Arbitration: An Empirical Evaluation.* New York: American Arbitration Association.

Kolb, D. M. (1983). *The Mediators.* Cambridge, MA: MIT Press.

Kolb, D. M., and Rubin, J. Z. (1989). *Research into Mediation.* Washington, DC: Dispute Resolution Forum, National Institute for Dispute Resolution.

Kosterlitz, J. (1997). Busted unions. *National Journal* 29 (Dec. 20), 2522–2555.

Kramer, L. (1962). *Labor's Paradox.* New York: Wiley.

Kressel, K. (1977). Labor mediation: An exploratory survey. In D. Lewin, P. Feuille, and T. A. Kochan (Eds.), *Public Sector Labor Relations: Analysis and Readings,* 252–272. Glen Ridge, NJ: Horton.

Kriesky, J. (1994). Workers rights and contract grievance dispute resolution. In J. Robin et al. (Eds.), *Handbook of Public Sector Labor Relations,* 233–252. New York: Dekker.

Kurth, M. M. (1987). Teachers' unions and excellence in education: An analysis of the decline in SAT scores. *Journal of Labor Research* VII (Fall), 351–367.

Labig, C. E., Jr., and Greer, C. R. (1988). Grievance initiation: A literature survey and suggestions for future research. *Journal of Labor Research* IX (Winter), 1–27.

Labor–Management Services Administration. (1972). *Collective Bargaining in Public Employment and the Merit System.* Washington, DC: Government Printing Office.

Ladd, E. C., Jr., and Lipset, S. M. (1973). *Professors, Unions, and American Higher Education.* Washington, DC: American Enterprise Institute for Public Policy Research.

Lane, C. M. (1996). Bittersweet partnerships. *Government Executive* (Feb.), 41–44.

Lawler, E. E., III, and Mohrman, S. A. (1985). Quality circles after the Fed. *Harvard Business Review* 85 (Jan.–Feb.), 65–71.

Leach, W. D., and Sabatier, P. A. (2005). To trust an adversary: Integrating rational and psychological models of collaborative policymaking. *American Political Science Review* 99(4), 491–503.

Legler, J. I. (1985). City, county and state government liability for sex-based wage discrimination after *County of Washington v. Gunther* and *AFSCME v. Washington. The Urban Lawyer* 17 (Spring), 229–275.

Lehnert v. Ferris Faculty Association. (1991). 89 U.S. S. Ct. 1217.

Leibig, M. T., and Kahn, W. L. (1987). *Public Employee Organizing and the Law.* Washington, DC: Bureau of National Affairs.

Leigh, D. E., and Hills, S. M. (1987). Male-female differences in the potential for union growth outside traditionally unionized industries. *Journal of Labor Research* 8 (Spring), 131–142.

Leighley, J. E., and Nagler, J. (2007). Unions, voter turnout, and class bias in the U.S. electorate, 1964–2004. *The Journal of Politics* 69(2), 430–441.

Lester, R. A. (1984). *Labor Arbitration in State and Local Government: An Examination of Experience in Eight States and New York City.* Princeton, NJ: Princeton University Industrial Relations Section.

Lester, R. A. (1986). Lessons from experience with interest arbitration in nine jurisdictions. *Arbitration Journal* 41 (June), 34–37.

Letter Carriers v. Blount. (1969). 305 F. Supp. 546 (D.D.C.).

Leventoglu, B., and Tarar, A. (2005). Prenegotiation public commitment in domestic and international bargaining. *American Political Science Review* 99(3), 419–433.

Levesque, J. D. (1980). Municipal strike planning: The logistics of allocating resources. *Public Personnel Management* 9 (March–April), 61–67.

Levine, D. I. (1995). *Reinventing the Workplace: How Businesses and Employees Can Both Win.* Washington, DC: Brookings Institution.

Levine, M. J. (1985). Judicial review of arbitration awards: Criticisms and remedies. *Employee Relations Law Journal* 10 (Spring), 669–683.

Lewin, D. (1985). The effects of regulation on public sector labor relations: Theory and evidence. *Journal of Labor Research* VI (Winter), 77–95.

Lewin, D. (1986). Public employee unionism and labor relations in the 1990s: An analysis of transformation. In S. M. Lipset (Ed.), *Unions in Transition,* 241–264. San Francisco: Institute for Contemporary Studies.

Lewin, D., and Peterson, R. (1999). Behavioral outcomes of grievancy activity. *Journal of Industrial Relations* 38(4), 554–575.

Lewis, C. (1994). Budgetary balance: The norm, concept and practice in large U.S. cities. *Public Administration Review* 54 (Nov./Dec.), 515–524.

Lewis, G., and Stein, L. (1989). Unions and municipal decline. *American Politics Quarterly* 17 (April), 208–222.

Lewis, H. G. (1986). *Union Relative Wage Effects: A Survey.* Chicago: University of Chicago Press.

Ley, R. D., and Wines, W. A. (1993). Teacher bargaining in Minnesota: Retrospect on the 1980's and prospect of fewer bargaining units. *Journal of Collective Negotiations* 22(3), 233–244.

Lieb, D. A. (2007, May 30). Mo.: Bargaining Rights for Public Employees. http://www. Forbes.com. Accessed June 14, 2007.

Lincoln, M.G. (2000). Negotiation: The Opposing Sides of Verbal and Nonverbal Communication. *Journal of Collective Negotiations* 29(4), 297–306.

Linneman, P. D., and Wachter, M. L. (1990). The economics of federal compensation. *Industrial Relations* 29 (Winter), 58–76.

Lipsky, D. B., and Drotning, J. E. (1977). The relation between teacher salaries and the use of impasse procedures under New York's Taylor Law: 1968–1972. *Journal of Collective Negotiations* 6(3), 229–244.

Lipsky, D. B., and Katz, H. C. (2006). Alternative approaches to interest arbitration: Lessons from New York City. *Public Personnel Management* 35. (December) 265–282.

Local 189, United Papermakers and Crown-Zellerback Corp. v. United States. (1969). 416 F. 2d. 980.

Loewenberg, J. J. (1985). What's $13 billion among friends? The 1984 postal arbitration. In *38th Annual Proceedings of the IRRA.* Washington, DC: IRRA.

Loewenberg, J. J., and Klinetop, W. A. (1992). The second decade of interest arbitration in Pennsylvania. *Journal of Collective Negotiations* 21(4), 353–367.

Lowi, T. (1979). *The End of Liberalism* (2nd ed.). New York: LRP.

Lueck, T. J. (2006). Transit union is fined $2.5 million over December strike. *The New York Times,* April 18.

Luger, M. I., and Goldstein, H. A. (1989). Federal labor protections and the privatization of public transit. *Journal of Policy Analysis and Management* 8(2), 229–250.

Lund, J., and Maranto, C. L. (1996). Public sector laws: An update. In D. Belman, M. Gunderson, and D. Hyatt (Eds.), *Public Sector Employment in a Time of Transition,* 21–58. Madison, WI: IRRA.

Magnusen, K. O., and Renovitch, P. A. (1989). Dispute resolution in Florida's public sector: Insight into impasse. *Journal of Collective Negotiations* 18(3), 241–252.

Mahtesian, C. (1995). The chastening of the teachers. *Governing* 8 (Dec.), 34–37.

Maier, M. H. (1987). *City Unions: Managing Discontent in New York City.* New Brunswick, NJ: Rutgers University Press.

Maki, D., and Strand, K. (1984). The determinants of strike activity. *Relations Industrielles* 39 (Winter), 77–91.

Malek Manual. (1980). In F. J. Thompson (Ed.), *Classics of Public Personnel Policy* (2nd ed.), 58–81. Pacific Grove, CA: Brooks/Cole.

Mareschal, P. M. (1998). Providing high quality mediation. *Review of Public Personnel Administration* (Fall), 55–67.

Mareschal, P. M. (2002). Mastering the art of dispute resolution: Best practices from the FMCS. *International Journal of Public Administration* 25(11), 1351–1377.

Mareschal, P. M. (2005). What makes mediation work? Mediators' perspectives on resolving disputes. *Industrial Relations* 44(3), 509–517.

Mareschal, P. M. (2006). Innovation and adaptation: Contrasting efforts to organize home care workers in four states. *Labor Studies Journal* 31(1), 25–49.

Marmo, M. (1995). The role of fact finding and interest arbitration in selling a settlement. *Journal of Collective Negotiations* 24(1), 77–96.

Marshall, J. (1979). The effect of collective bargaining on faculty salaries in higher education. *Journal of Higher Education* (May–June), 310–322.

Martin, C. R. (2003). Framed! Labor and the corporate media. *Labor Studies Journal* 30(3), 102–104.

Martin, J. E., and Sinclair, R. R. (2001). A multiple motive perspective on strike propensities. *Journal of Organizational Behavior* 22, 387–407.

Masters, M. F. (1988). The negotiability of drug testing in the federal sector: A political perspective. *Journal of Collective Negotiations* 17(4), 309–325.

Masters, M. F., and Delaney, J. T. (1987). Union political activities: A review of the empirical literature. *Industrial and Labor Relations Review* 40 (April), 336–353.

Matzer, J., Jr. (1988). A practical approach to productivity bargaining. In J. Matzer, Jr. (Ed.), *Pay and Benefits: New Ideas for Local Government.* Washington, DC: International City Management Association.

McAuliffe v. City of New Bedford. (1892). 155 Mass. 216, 29 N.E. 517.

McCormick, M. (1979). A functional analysis of interest arbitration in New York City municipal government, 1968–1975. In M. J. Levine and E. C. Hagburg, (Eds.), *Labor Relations in the Public Sector.* Salt Lake City: Brighton.

McDonnell, L. M., and Pascal, A. H. (1979). National trends in teacher collective bargaining. *Education and Urban Society* 11 (Feb.), 129–151.

McKelvey, J. T. (1969). Fact-finding in public employment disputes: Promise or illusion? *Industrial and Labor Relations Review* 22(4), 528–543.

McLaughlin v. Tilendis. (1967). 398 F. 2d. 287.

McPherson, D. S. (1983). *Resolving Grievances: A Practical Approach.* Reston, VA: Reston Publishing.

Meador, M., and Walters, S. J. K. (1994). Unions and productivity: Lessons from academe. *Journal of Labor Research* XV (Fall), 373–386.

Memphis Firefighters Local Union No. 1784 *v. Stotts.* (1984). 34 EPD 34, 415, 467 U.S. 561 S. Ct.

Merrifield, J. (1999). Monopsony power in the market for teachers: Why teachers should support market-based education reform. *Journal of Labor Research* XX (3), 377–391.

Mesch, D. (1995). Arbitration and gender: Analysis of cases taken to arbitration in the public sector. *Journal of Collective Negotiations* 24(3), 207–218.

Metchick, R. H., and Singh, P. (2004). Yeshiva and faculty unionization in higher education. *Labor Studies Journal* 28(4), 45–65.

Meyer, D. (2002). Problem creation and resolution in unionized workplaces: A review of the grievance procedure. *Labor Studies Journal* 27(3), 81–99.

Michels, R. (1949). *Political Parties.* Glencoe, IL: Free Press.

Midwest Center for Public Sector Labor Relations. (1979). *Labor Legislation in the Public Sector.* Bloomington, IN: Indiana University School of Public and Environmental Affairs.

Miller, B., and Canak, W. (1991). From "porkchoppers" to "lambchoppers": The passage of Florida's Public Employee Relations Act. *Industrial and Labor Relations Review* 44 (Jan.), 349–366.

Miller, M. L. (1996). The public/private pay debate: What do the data show? *Monthly Labor Review* (May), 18–29.

Miller, R. L. (1979). An arbitrator looks at contract interpretation. *Journal of Collective Negotiations* 8(3), 197–208.

Miranda v. Arizona. (1966). 384 U.S. 436.

Mitchell, M. S. (1978). Public sector union security: The impact of *Abood. Labor Law Journal* (Nov.), 697–711.

Mladenka, K. R. (1991). Public employee unions, reformism, and black employment in 1200 American cities. *Urban Affairs Quarterly* 26 (June), 532–548.

Mohnnan, S. A., and Lawler, E. E. (1988). Participative management behavior and organizational change. *Journal of Organizational Change Management* (I), 45–59.

Montgomery, E., and Benedict, M. E. (1989). The impact of bargainer experience on teacher strikes. *Industrial and Labor Relations Review* 42 (April), 380–392.

Moore W. J. (1998). The detriments and effects of right to work laws: A review of the recent literature. *Journal of Labor Research* XIX (3), 445–469.

Moore, W. J., and Raisian, J. (1987). Union-nonunion wage differentials in the public administration, educational, and private sectors: 1970–1983. *The Review of Economics and Statistics* 69, 608–616.

Morgan, D. R., and Kearney, R. C. (1977). Collective bargaining and faculty compensation: A comparative analysis. *Sociology of Education* 50, 28–39.

Moskow, M. H., Loewenberg, J. J., and Koziara, E. C. (1970). *Collective Bargaining in Public Employment.* New York: Random House.

Muchinsky, P. M., and Maasarani, M. A. (1980). Work environment effects on public sector grievances. *Personnel Psychology* 33, 403–414.

Muhl, C. J. (2001). The Employment-at-Will Doctrine: Three major exceptions. *Monthly Labor Review* 124(1).

National Labor Relations Board v. Yeshiva University. (1980). 444 U.S. 672.

Nelson, F. H., and Rosen, M. (1996). Are teachers' unions hurting American education? A state-by-state analysis of the impact of collective bargaining among teachers on student performance. In T. Loveless (Ed.) (2000), *Conflicting Missions? Teachers Unions and Educational Reform,* 47–68. Washington, DC: Brookings Institution Press.

Nelson, N. E. (1986). The selection of arbitrators. *Labor Law Journal* (Oct.), 703–711.

Nelson, N. E., and Uddin, M. (1995). Arbitrators as mediators. *Labor Law Journal* (April), 205–213.

Nesbitt, M. B. (1976). *Labor Relations in the Federal Government Service.* Washington, DC: The Bureau of National Affairs.

Newland, C. A. (1972). Personnel concerns in government productivity improvement. *Public Administration Review* 32 (Nov./Dec.), 807–815.

Newland, C. A. (1984). Crucial issues for public personnel professionals. *Public Personnel Management* 13 (Spring), 15–46.

Newland, C. A. (1 987). Public executives: Imperium, sacerdatrum, collegium? *Public Administration Review* 47 (Jan./Feb.), 45–56.

Ng, I. (1991). Predictors of strike voting behavior: The case of university faculty. *Journal of Labor Research* XII (Spring), 123–134.

Nicolau, C. (1997). Whatever happened to arbitral finality? Is it their fault or ours? *Labor Law Journal* 40(5), 151–160.

Nigro, F. A. (1976). A possible federal mandate: The present picture. *State Government* 49 (Autumn), 202–206.

Nissen, B. (2003). Alternative strategic directions for the U.S. labor movement: Recent scholarship. *Labor Studies Journal.* 28(1), 133–155.

NLRB v. Health Care and Retirement Corporation of America. (1994). 511 U.S. 571.

NLRB v. Mackay Radio and Telegraph. (1935). 304 U.S. 333 585 Ct. 904.

NLRB v. Yeshiva. (1980). 444 U.S. 672, 103 LRRM 2526.

NTEU v. Van Raab. (1989). 109 S. Ct. 1384.

O'Brien, K. M. (1994). The impact of union political activities on public-sector pay, employment and budget. *Industrial Relations* 33(3), 265–278.

O'Brien, K. M. (1996). The effect of political activity by police unions on nonwage bargaining outcomes. *Journal of Collective Negotiations* 25(2), 99–116.

Oestreich, H. H., and Whaley, G. L. (2001). *Transit Labor Relations Guide.* Mineta Transportation Institute, San Jose, CA.

Olson, C. A. (1988). Dispute resolution in the public sector. In B. Aaron, J. M. Najita, and J. L. Stern (Eds.), *Public-Sector Bargaining* (2nd ed.). Washington, DC: Bureau of National Affairs 160–188.

Olson, C. A., and Rau, B. L. (1997). Learning from interest arbitration: The next round. *Industrial and Labor Relations Review* 50(2), 237–251.

Olson, M. (1965). *The Logic of Collective Action.* Cambridge, MA: Harvard University Press.

Orr, D. (1976). Public employee compensation levels. In *Public Employee Unions,* 131–144. San Francisco: Institute for Contemporary Studies 131–144.

Osborne, D., and Gaebler, T. (1992). *Reinventing Government: How the Entrepreneurial Spirit Is Transforming the Public Sector.* Reading, MA: Addison-Wesley.

Ospina, S., and Yaroni, A. (2003). Understanding cooperative behavior in labor management cooperation: A theory-building exercise. *Public Administration Review* 63 (July/Aug.), 455–471.

Parra, E. (2004). Support grows for prison OT protest. *Delewareonline.com.*

Partridge, D. M. (1991). A time series analysis of public sector strike activity. *Journal of Collective Negotiations* 20(1), 3–21.

Partridge, D. M. (1996). Teacher strikes and public policy — Does the law matter? *Journal of Collective Negotiations* 25(1), 3–21.

Patent answers. (1999). *Government Executive* (Feb.), 81–84.

Payne, K., Kohler, P., Cangemi, J. P., and Fuqua H., Jr. (2000). Communication and strategies in the mediation of disputes. *Journal of Collective Negotiations* 29(1), 29–47.

Peach, D., and Livemash, R. (1974). *Grievance Initiation and Resolution.* Cambridge, MA: Harvard University Press.

Peightal, P., et al. (1998). Labor management cooperation: City of Portland, Maine. *Public Personnel Management* 27 (Spring), 85–92.

Peng, J. (2004). Public pension funds and operating budgets: A tale of three states. *Public Budgeting and Finance,* 24(2), 59.

Perlman, S. (1928). *Theory of the Labor Movement.* New York: Macmillan.

Perloff, J. M., and Wachter, M. L. (1984). Wage comparability in the U.S. Postal Service. *Industrial and Labor Relations Review* 38 (Oct.), 26–35.

Perry, J. L., and Angle, H. L. (1981). Bargaining unit structure and organizational outcomes. *Industrial Relations* 20 (Winter), 47–59.

Phelan, C. (2000). *Grand Master Workman: Terence Powderly and the Knights of Labor.* Westport, CT: Greenwood Press.

Pickering v. Board of Education. (1968). 391 U.S. 563, 88 S. Ct. 1751.

Pierce, N. R. (1980). Auto-based recession clouds rebirth. *Public Administration Times* (July IS), 2.

Piskulich, J. P. (1995). Collective bargaining among local government executives: The stand-off in Michigan. *Labor Law Journal* 46, 479–485.

Posthuma, R. A., Dworkin, J. B., and Swift, M. S. (2002). Mediator tactics and sources of conflict: Facilitating and inhibiting effects. *Industrial Relations* 41(1), 94–109.

Premack, S. L., and Hunter J. E. (1988). Individual unionization decisions. *Psychological Bulletin* 103(2), 223–234.

President's Pay Agent. (1990). *Annual Report.* Washington, DC: President's Pay Agent.

Rabin, R. J. (1979). The protection of individuals and their rights. In M. K. Gibbons, R. D. Helsby, J. Lefkowitz, and B. Z. Teher (Eds.), Lessons from America: Changes in the US Trade Union Movement. *Portrait of a Process — Collective Negotiations in Public Employment,* 291–310. Fort Washington, PA: Labor Relations Press.

Rachlett, P. (1999). Learning from the past to build for the future, 87–96. In R. M. Tillman and M. S. Cummings (Eds.). Boulder, CO: Lynne Rienner.

Radcliff, B. (2005). Class organization and subjective well-being: A cross-national analysis. *Social Forces* 84(1), 513–530.

Rahim, M. A. (1992). *Managing Conflict in Organizations* (2nd ed.). New York: Praeger.

Railway Employee Department, IAM v. Hanson. (1956). 351 U.S. 255.

Raskin, A. H. (1972). Politics up-ends the bargaining table. In S. Zagoria (Ed.), *Public Workers and Public Unions,* 122–146. Englewood Cliffs, NJ: Prentice-Hall.

Raskin, A. H. (1986). Labor: A movement in search of a mission. In S. Martin (Ed.), *Unions in Transition,* 3–38. San Francisco: Institute for Contemporary Studies.

Reder, M. W. (1975). The theory of employment and wages in the public sector. In D. S. Hammermesh (Ed.), *Labor in the Public and Non-Profit Sector,* 1–18. Princeton, NJ: Princeton University Press.

Reder, M. W. (1988). The rise and fall of unions: The public sector and the private. *Journal of Economic Perspectives* 2 (Spring), 89–110.

Reder, M., and Neumann, G. (1980). Conflict and contract: The case of strikes. *Journal of Political Economy* 88(5), 867–886.

Reed, W. R. (2003). How right-to-work laws affect wages. *Journal of Labor Relations* 24(4), 713–730.

Reeves, T. Z. (1997). Labor management partnership in the public sector. In C. Ban and N. Riccucci (Eds.), *Public Personnel Management: Current Concern, Future Challenges*, 173–186. New York: Longman Press.

Register, C. A., and Grimes, P. W. (1991). Collective bargaining, teachers, and student achievement. *Journal of Labor Research* XII (Spring), 99–109.

Rehmus, C. M. (1975). Binding arbitration in the public sector. *In Proceedings of the Twenty-Seventh Annual Winter Meeting*, 307–314. Ann Arbor, MI: The University of Michigan, IRRA Series.

Repa, B. K. (2005). *Your Rights in the Workplace*. Berkeley, CA: Nolo.

Reynolds v. Simms. (1964). 84 S. Ct. 1362.

Rhodes, T. L., and Brown, R. G. (1992). Divided we fall — Employee perceptions of a legal prohibition on collective bargaining: A closer look. *Journal of Collective Negotiations* 21(1), 1–14.

Riccucci, N. M. (1990). *Women, Minorities, and Unions in the Public Sector*. New York: Greenwood.

Riccucci, N., and Ban, C. (1989). The unfair labor practice process as a dispute-resolution technique in the public sector: The case of New York State. *Review of Public Personnel Administration* 9 (Spring), 51–67.

Roberts, H. C., Jr. (1994). Contemporary perspectives and the future of American unions. In J. Rabin (Ed.), *Handbook of Public Sector Labor Relations*, 393–417. New York: Marcel Dekker.

Rosemont, F. (2002). *Joe Hill, the IWW and the Making of a Revolutionary Workingclass Counterculture*. Chicago, IL: Charles H. Kerr Publishing Company.

Rosenbloom, D. H. (1989). The federal labor relations authority. *Policy Studies Journal* 17 (Winter), 695–697.

Ross, W. H. (2006). Should "night baseball" arbitration be used in lieu of public sector strikes: Psychological considerations and suggestions for research. *Journal of Collective Negotiations* 31(1), 45–70.

Ross, W. H., and Conlon, D.E. (2000). Hybrid forms of third-party dispute resolution: Theoretical implications of combining mediation and arbitration. *The Academy of Management Review* 25(2), 416–427.

Rubenstein, J. S. (1966). Some thoughts on labor arbitration. *Marquette Law Review* 49, 704–714.

Rubin, B. N., and Rubin, R. S. (1997). A heuristic model of collaboration within labor management relations. *Journal of Collective Negotiations* 26(3), 185–202.

Rubin, J. Z., Pruitt, D. G., and Kim, S. H. (1993). *Social Conflict: Escalation, Stalemate and Settlement* (2nd ed.). New York: McGraw-Hill.

Rubin, R. S. (1979). Procedures in unit determination. In M. K. Gibbons, R. D. Helsby, J. Lefkowitz, and B. Z. Teher (Eds.), *Portrait of a Process — Collective Negotiations in Public Employment*, 122–134. Fort Washington, PA: Labor Relations Press.

Salerno, C. A. (1981). *Police at the Bargaining Table*. Springfield, IL: Charles C Thomas.

Saltzman, G. B. (1985). Bargaining law as a cause and consequence of the growth of teacher unions. *Industrial and Labor Relations Review* 38 (April), 335–351.

Saso, C. D. (1970). *Coping with Public Employee Strikes*. Chicago: Public Personnel Association.

Sass, D. R., and Troyer, J. L. (1999). Affirmative action, political representation, unions and female public employment. *Journal of Labor Research* 20 (Fall), 571–587.

Savas, E. S., and Ginsburg, S. G. (1973). The civil service: A meritless system? *The Public Interest* 32 (Summer), 70–85.

Schneider, B. V. H. (1988). Public sector labor legislation — An evolutionary analysis. In B. J. Aaron, J. R. Grodin, and J. L. Stern (Eds.), *Public Sector Bargaining*, 191–223. Washington, DC: Bureau of National Affairs.

School District for the City of Holland et al. v. Holland Education Association. (1968). 380 Mich. 312, 157 NW 2d. 206.

Schwochau, S., et al. (1997). Employee participation and assessment of support for organizational policy change. *Journal of Labor Research* XVIII (Summer), 379–401.

Scott, C., and Suchan, J. (1987). Public sector collective bargaining agreements: How readable are they? *Public Personnel Management* 16 (Spring), 15–22.

Seaver, D. F. (1984–85). The *Stotts* decision: Is it the death knell for seniority systems? *Employee Relations Law Journal* 3 (Winter), 497–504.

Shafritz, J. M. (1980). *Dictionary of Personnel Management and Labor Relations.* Oak Park, IL: Moore.

Shapiro, D. (1978). Relative wage effects of unions in the public and private sectors. *Industrial and Labor Relations Review* 31 (Jan.), 193–204.

Shaw, L. C., and Clark, T., Jr. (1972). Collective bargaining and politics in public employment. *UCLA Law Review* 19 (Aug.), 887–1051.

Sherer, P. D. (1987). The workplace dissatisfaction model of unionism: What are its implications for organizing blacks and women? In *IRRA 40th Annual Proceedings*, 135–141.

Sherman, J. J. (1979). The role of the public in the bargaining process. In M. K. Gibbons, R. D. Helsby, J. Lefkowitz, and B. Z. Teher (Eds.), *Portrait of a Process — Collective Negotiations in Public Employment*, 269–277. Fort Washington, PA: Labor Relations Press.

Shostak, A. B. (1991). *Robust Unionism — Innovations in the Labor Movement.* Ithaca, NY: ILR Press.

Shostak, A. B. (Ed.). (2002a). *The Cyber Union Handbook: Transforming Labor Through Computer Technology.* Armonk, NY: M.E. Sharpe.

Shostak, A. B. (2002b). Today's unions as tomorrow's cyberunions: Labor's new hope. *Journal of Labor Research* 23(2), 237–248.

Shutt, R. K. (1982). Models of militancy: Support for strikes and work actions among public employees. *Industrial and Labor Relations Review* 35 (April), 406–422.

Shutt, R. K. (1986). *Organizations in a Changing Environment.* Albany: State University of New York Press.

Simkin, W. E. (1971). *Mediation and the Dynamics of Collective Bargaining.* Washington, DC: BNA.

Simkin, W. E. (1979). Fact-finding: Its values and limitations. In M. J. Levine and E. C. Hagburg (Eds.), *Labor Relations in the Public Sector: Readings, Cases, and Experiential Exercises.* Salt Lake City: Brighton.

Simpson, P. A., and Martocchio, J. J. (1997). Factors on arbitration outcomes. *Industrial and Labor Relations Review* 50(2), 252–267.

Singh, P., Zinni, D.M., and MacLennan, A.F. (2006). Graduate student unions in the United States. *Journal of Labor Research* 27(7), 55–73.

Skinner v. Railway Labor Executives' Association. (1989). 109 S. Ct. 1402.

Skratek, S. P. (1987). Grievance mediation of contractual disputes in Washington State public education. *Labor Law Journal* 38 (June), 370–376.

Slater, J. E. (2004). *Public Workers: Government Employees Unions. The Law, and the State, 1900–1962.* Ithaca: Cornell University Press.

Sloane, A. A., and Witney, F. (1981). *Labor Relations* (4th ed.). Englewood Cliffs, NJ: Prentice-Hall.

Smith v. Arkansas State Highway Commission Employees Local 1315. (1979). 441 U.S. 463, 101 L.R.R.M. 2091.

Smith, C. G. (2006). Interest arbitration in the federal service. *International Journal of Public Administration* 29(9), 639–660.

Smith, R. L., and Lyons, W. (1980). The impact of fire fighter unionization on wages and working hours in American cities. *Public Administration Review* 40 (Nov./Dec.), 568–574.

Smith, R. M. (2003). *From Blackjacks to Briefcases: A History of Commercialized Strikebreaking and Unionbusting in the United States.* Athens: Ohio University Press.

Smith, S. P. (1976). Pay differences between federal government and private sector workers. *Industrial and Labor Relations Review 29* (Jan.), 14–15.

Sniffen, M. J. (2007). Air traffic controllers exit in droves. *The News and Observer,* p. 3A.

Spero, S. D. (1970). *Government as Employer.* Carbondale: Southern Illinois University Press.

Spero, S. D., and Capozzola, J. M. (1973). *The Urban Community and its Unionized Bureaucracies.* New York: Dunellen.

Stahl, O. G. (1990). A retrospective and prospective: The moral dimension. In S. W. Hays and R. C. Kearney (Eds.), *Public Personnel Administration: Problems and Prospects,* 308–321. Englewood Cliffs, NJ: Prentice-Hall.

Stanfield, R. L. (1997). Remedial lessons. *National Journal* 29 (Nov. 8), 2244–2247.

Stanley, D. T. (1972). *Managing Local Government Under Union Pressure.* Washington, DC: Brookings.

State of Montana v. Public Employees Craft Council. (1974). 87 LRRM 2101.

Staudohar, P. D. (1973). The emergence of Hawaii's public employment law. *Industrial Relations* 12 (Oct.), 338–351.

Staudohar, P. D. (1996). The baseball strike of 1994–95. *Monthly Labor Review* (March), 21–27.

Steen, J., Perrewe, P., and Hochwater, W. (1994). A reexamination of gender bias in arbitration decisions. *Labor Law Journal* 45(5), 298–305.

Stein, L. (1986). Representative local government: Minorities in the municipal workforce. *Journal of Politics* 48 (May), 694–713.

Stein, R. M. (1990). The budgetary effects of municipal service contracting: A principal agent explanation. *American Journal of Political Science* 34 (May), 471–502.

Steinhauer, J. (2004). Labor demands cast a rich mayor in a miserly light. *The New York Times,* www.nytimes.com. Accessed June 11, 2004.

Stenger, W. (1990). *Joe Hill: A Biographical Novel.* New York: Penguin.

Sterret, G., and Aboud, A. (1982). *The Right to Strike in Public Employment.* Ithaca, NY: ILR.

Stewart, G., and Davy, J. (1992). An empirical examination of grievance resolution and filing rates in the public and private sectors. *Journal of Collective Negotiations* 21(4), 323–335.

Stieber, J. (1973). *Public Employee Unionism.* Washington, DC: The Brookings Institution.

Stieber, J., and Wolkinson, B. W. (1977). Fact-finding views by fact-finders: The Michigan experience. *Labor Law Journal* 28 (Feb.), 89–101.

Stone, J. A., (2000). Collective bargaining in public schools. In T. Loveless (Ed.), *Conflicting Missions? Teachers Unions and Educational Reform,* 47–68. Washington, DC: Brookings Institution Press.

Subbarao, A. V. (1978). The impact of binding interest arbitration on negotiation and process outcome. *Journal of Conflict Resolution* 22 (March), 79–103.

Sulzner, G. T. (1997). New roles, new strategies: Reinventing the public union. In C. Ban and N. M. Riccuci (Eds.), *Public Personnel Management: Current Concerns, Future Challenges* (2nd ed.), 157–172. New York: Longman.

Sutherlin Education Association v. Sutherlin School District No. 130. (1976). 548 P. 2d. 208.

Swope, C. (1998). The living wage wars. *Governing* (Dec.), 8.

Tannenbaum, F. (1921). *The Labor Movement, Its Conservative Functions and Social Consequences.* New York: Putnam.

Thompson, J. R. (2007). Federal labor-management relations reforms under Bush: Enlightened management or quest for control? *Review of Public Personnel Administration* 27(2), 105–124.

Thornicroft, K. W. (1989). Arbitrators, social values, and the burden of proof in substance abuse discharge cases. *Labor Law Journal* (Sept.), 582–593.

Thornicroft, K. W. (1994). Teacher strikes and student achievement: Evidence from Ohio. *Journal of Collective Negotiations* 23(1), 27–39.

Tillman, R. M., and Cummings, M. S. (1999). *The Transformation of U.S. Unions: Voices, Visions and Strategies from the Grassroots.* Boulder, CO: Lynne Rienner.

Tobias, R. (1998). Federal employee unions and the human resource management functions. In S. E. Condrey (Ed.), *Handbook of Human Resources Management in Government*, 258–274. San Francisco: Jossey-Bass.

Tobias, R. (2004). The future of federal government labor relations and the mutual interests of Congress, the administration, and unions. In *Journal of Labor Research XXV* (1) (Winter), 19–41.

Toulmin, L. M. (1988). The treasure hunt: Budget search behavior by public employee unions. *Public Administration Review* 48 (March/April), 620–680.

Trejo, S. J. (1991). Public sector unions and municipal employment. *Industrial Labor Relations Review* 45, 166–180.

Turnley, W. H., Bolino, M. C., Lester, S. W., and Bloodgood, J. M. (2004). The effects of psychological contract breach on union commitment. *Journal of Occupational & Organizational Psychology* 77(3), 421–428.

Turpin, R. (1997). Factors considered by public sector interest arbitrators in assessing ability to pay. *Journal of Collective Negotiations* 26(1), 1–7.

Turpin, R. (1998). An analysis of public sector interest: Arbitrators assessment of wage comparability. *Journal of Collective Negotiations* 27(1), 45–51.

U.S. Airways v. Barnett. (2002). 535 U.S. 391.

U.S. Bureau of Labor Statistics. (1999). *The Employment Situation.* October, 1–25, Washington, DC.

U.S. Bureau of Labor Statistics. (2005). *National Compensation Survey: Employee benefits in the private industry in the United States.* www.bls.Gov/ncs/ebs/sp/ebsm002.pdf. Retrieved May 23, 2005.

U.S. Census Bureau. (2007). www.census.gov.

U.S. General Accounting Office. (1994). *U.S. Postal Service: Labor Management Problems Persist on the Workroom Floor.* Washington, DC: Government Printing Office, GAOIGGO 94-201 A.

U.S. General Accounting Office. (1997). *Alternate Dispute Resolution. Employers Experience with ADR in the Workplace.* Washington, DC.

U.S. National Partnership Council. (1994). *A New Vision for Labor Management Relations.* Washington, DC: Government Printing Office.

Vaca v. Sipes. (1967). 386 U.S. 171, 87 S. Ct. 903.

Valletta, R. G. (1989). The impact of unionism on municipal expenditures and revenues. *Industrial and Labor Relations Review* 42 (April), 430–442.

Veglahn, P. A. (1987). Grievance arbitration by arbitration boards: A survey of the parties. *The Arbitration Journal* 42 (June), 47–54.

Verma, A., and Cutcher-Gershenfeld, J. (1996). Workplace innovations and systems of change. In D. Belman, M. Gunderson, and D. Hyatt (Eds.), *Public Sector Employment in a Time of Transition,* 201–242. Madison, WI: IRRA.

Verma, A., and McKersie, R. B. (1987). Employee involvement: The implication of noninvolvement by unions. *Industrial and Labor Relations Review* 40 (July), 556–568.

Ver Ploeg, C. D. (1988). Labor arbitration: The participants' perspectives. *Arbitration Journal* 43 (March), 36–43.

Vest, M. J., O'Brien, F. P., and Vest, J. M. (1990). Explaining rights arbitrator willingness to accept public sector interest arbitration cases. *Public Personnel Management* 19 (Fall), 331–343.

Victor, K. (1992, June 6). Labor's sawed-off stick. *National Journal*, pp. 1353–1356.

Virginia v. Arlington County Board of Education. (1977). 232 S.E. 2d. 30, 94 L.R.R.M. 229 1.

Volz, W. H., and Costa, D. (1989). A public employee's "fair share" union dues. *Labor Law Journal* (March), 131–137.

Wagner, J. (1994). Participation effects on performance and satisfaction: A reconsideration of research evidence. *Academy of Management Review* 19 (April), 312–330.

Wallin, B. A. (1997). The need for a privatization process: Lessons from development and implementation. *Public Administration Review* 57(4), 11–20.

Walsh, M. W. (2007). $58 Billion shortfall for New Jersey retiree care. *The New York Times.* www.nytimes.com. Accessed July 25, 2007.

Walters, J. (1999). The power of pay. *Government Executive* (Jan.), 32–35.

Walton, R. E., and McKersie, R. B. (1965). *A Behavioral Theory of Labor Negotiations.* New York: McGraw-Hill.

Wanamaker, D. K. (1977). Kentucky: From organizing the street sweepers to bargaining in the sunshine. *Southern Review* of *Public Administration* (Sept.), 175–191.

Waters v. Wisconsin Steelworks. (1974). 502 F. 2d. 1309 CA-7.

Waters, M. S., Hill, R. C., Moore, W. J., and Newman, R. J. (1994). A simultaneous-equations relationship between public sector bargaining legislation and unionization. *Journal of Labor Research* XV(4), 355–372.

Watkins v. Steelworkers Local 2369. (1975). 516 F. 2d. 41 CA-5.

Webb, S., and Webb, B. (1897). *Industrial Democracy.* London: Longmans.

Wellington, H. H., and Winter, R. K., Jr. (1971). *The Unions and the Cities.* Washington, DC: Brookings.

West, J. P., and Feiock, R. C. (1989). Support for sunshine bargaining in Florida: A decade later. *Review of Public Personnel Administration* 9 (Spring), 28–50.

Williams, R. M. (1977, March 5). The clamor over municipal unions. *Saturday Review,* pp. 5–7.

Wilson, T. M. (1989). Smoking in the workplace: Dimensions of policy. *Review of Public Personnel* 9 (Summer), 32–45.

Woodbury, S. A. (1985). The scope of bargaining and bargaining outcomes in the public schools. *Industrial and Labor Relations Review* 38 (Jan.), 195–209.

Wurf, J. (1974). Merit: A union view. *Public Administration Review* 34 (Sept./Oct.), 431–434.

www.cpsInfo.bls.gov (accessed Jan25) (1999).

Wygant v. Jackson Board of Education. (1986). 476 U.S. 267.

Zack, A. M. (1985). *Public Sector Mediation.* Washington, DC: Bureau of National Affairs.

Zagoria, S. (1973). Resolving impasses by public referendum. *Monthly Labor Review* (May), 36–38.

Zax, J. S. (1988). Wages, nonwage compensation, and municipal unions. *Industrial Relations* 27 (Fall), 301–317.

Zax, J. S. (1989). Employment and local public sector unions. *Industrial Relations* 28 (Winter), 21–31.

Zigarelli, M. A. (1994). The linkages between teacher unions and student achievement. *Journal of Collective Negotiations.* 23(4), 299–319.

Zigarelli, M. A. (1996). Dispute resolution mechanisms and teacher bargaining outcomes. *Journal of Labor Research* XVII (Winter), 135–148.

Zirkel, P. A., and Breslin, P. H. (1995). Correlates of grievance arbitration awards. *Journal of Collective Negotiations* 24(1), 45–54.

Ziskind, D. (1940). *One Thousand Strikes of Government Employees.* New York: Columbia University Press.

Zwerling, H. L., and Thomason, T. (1994). The effects of teacher unions on the probability of dropping out of high school. *Journal of Collective Negotiations* 23(3), 239–250.

Index